T0347307

John Milton

Twentieth-Century Perspectives

General Editor

J. Martin Evans
Stanford University

Contents of the Collection

John Milton

Twentieth-Century Perspectives

Volume 2
The Early Poems

Edited with introductions by

J. Martin Evans
Stanford University

Routledge
Taylor & Francis Group
NEW YORK AND LONDON

First published 2003 by Routledge
605 Third Avenue, New York, NY 10017
2 Park Square, Milton Park, Abingdon, Oxon OX14 4RN

Routledge is an imprint of the Taylor & Francis Group, an informa business

Library of Congress Cataloging-in-Publication Data

John Milton : twentieth century perspectives / edited with introductions by J.
Martin Evans.
    v. cm.
    Includes bibliographical references.
    Contents: v. 1. The man and the author — v. 2. The early poems — v. 3. Prose
— v. 4. Paradise lost — v. 5. Paradise regained and Samson Agonistes.
ISBN 0-415-94046-X (set: alk paper)—ISBN 0-415-94047-8 (vol. 1: alk. paper)
— ISBN 0-415-94048-6 (vol. 2: alk. paper) — ISBN 0-415-94049-4 (vol. 3: alk.
paper) — ISBN 0-415-94050-8 (vol. 4: alk. paper) — ISBN 0-415-94051-6 (vol.
5: alk. paper)
    1. Milton, John, 1608–1674—Criticism and interpretation. I. Evans, J. Martin
(John Martin).
PR3588 .J66 2002
821'.4—dc21   2002006044

ISBN 13: 978-0-415-88519-5 (POD set)
ISBN 13: 978-0-415-94046-7 (set)
ISBN 13: 978-0-415-94047-4 (v. 1)
ISBN 13: 978-0-415-94048-1 (v. 2)
ISBN 13: 978-0-415-94049-8 (v. 3)
ISBN 13: 978-0-415-94050-4 (v. 4)
ISBN 13: 978-0-415-94051-1 (v. 5)

ISBN 13: 978-0-415-94048-1 (hbk)

Acknowledgments

I would like to express my gratitude to the Department of English and the Office of the Dean of Humanities and Sciences of Stanford University for making available the resources that permitted me to bring this project to a timely conclusion.

These volumes are dedicated to the more than five hundred students who have studied Milton with me over the past forty years, either as undergraduate and graduate students at Stanford University, or as students in Stanford's Master of Liberal Arts program, or as participants in my Milton seminars for teachers sponsored by the National Endowment for the Humanities.

Contents

Volume Introduction

For a writer with such a notoriously strong personality, Milton was surprisingly reticent about taking public credit for his poems. His first published work, "On Shakespeare," was printed anonymously in the second Folio (1632); his second, "A Mask Presented at Ludlow Castle" (1637), was "not openly acknowledged by the Author," as Henry Lawes put it in the dedication; and his third, "Lycidas" (1638), had affixed to it only his initials, J.M. Not until the collected edition of 1645 was "Mr. John Milton" openly acknowledged as the author of any of his published poems, and even there his identity was immediately problematized by the Greek epigram that was printed under what purports to be his portrait:

> That an unskilful hand had carved this print
> You'd say at once, seeing the living face;
> But, finding here no jot of me, my friends,
> Laugh at the botching artist's misattempt.

No sooner does Milton appear in person, as it were, than we are told that it really isn't him at all. Now you see him, now you don't.

It is hardly surprising, therefore, that a good deal of critical energy has been devoted to the task of defining the nature of the authorial persona projected by *The Poems of Mr John Milton . . . 1645*. In the first of the essays reprinted here, Louis Martz argues that the dominant theme of the volume as a whole is Milton's "growth toward maturity," his gradual development from a youthful poet "free from adult cares, sometimes wandering alone, amusing himself, sometimes making music for his friends or acquaintances, sometimes writing in his native vein, sometimes evoking a strain from idealized antiquity," to the inspired seer who would one day write *Paradise Lost*. The poems are arranged, Martz suggests, to convey to Milton's readers an irresistible sense of "the predestined bard's rising powers." In a somewhat similar vein, Leah Marcus calls attention to Milton's self-conscious construction of his own poetic identity not only in the poems themselves but in the authorial interventions on the title page and in the brief notes that preface many of the poems and that in one case ("The Passion") serves as a retrospective judgement. The result, she claims, is a portrait of the artist as a young man that inaugurated an entirely "new view of literary subjecthood." In a trenchant critique of this widely accepted theory of Milton's self-presentation, Randall Ingram suggests, rather, that the basic pattern of the 1645 volume consists of "claiming the authority associated with printed books for the *Poems* and then disavowing it." In poem after poem, he argues, the author's repeated failures to escape from the materiality of writing call into question the capacity of the printed word to express the spiritual essence of sacred song.

The main focus of the following section, devoted to Milton's Odes, is inevitably on the so-called *Nativity Ode*, which occupies the place of honor at the very beginning of the 1645 collection. In an influential essay on the poem's pattern, Arthur Barker reads it as an essentially autobiographical account of the author's conversion, a moving testimony of Milton's own religious experience. My brief rejoinder suggests, on the contrary, that the *Nativity Ode* is the most rigorously depersonalized of all Milton's nondramatic works. Indeed, compared with other celebrations of Christ's birth written in the sixteenth or seventeenth centuries, it is notable for the poet's refusal to permit any human presence to intervene between the reader and the babe in the manger. We are forced to respond to the scene not vicariously through the experience of the shepherds, the wise men, or even the poet, but directly.

In the third and most recent of the articles on the *Nativity Ode,* David Quint claims that "Milton's first great poem succeeds by staging the failure of its fondest dreams." Basing his argument on the parallels between Milton's ode and a choral ode in Euripides' *Iphigenia in Tauris*, the *Homeric Hymn to Apollo*, and Julian the Apostate's prose hymn to King Helios, Quint reveals a recurrent pattern of disappointed expectation that reflects the poet's vision of his own career while at the same time providing "a pledge of greater things to come." Some of those "greater things" form the subject of the last article in this section, in which John K. Hale examines the way in which the Milton experimented with the genre of the Pindaric ode not only in the *Nativity Ode, The Passion, Upon the Circumcision, On Time*, and *At a Solemn Music*, but also within the formal structure of such works as *Lycidas, Paradise Lost,* and the choral odes in *Samson Agonistes*.

Following (with a few omissions) the order of the poems in the 1645 volume, the next two articles analyze the companion poems, *L'Allegro* and *Il Penseroso*. In the first one, David Miller argues against the long-standing tradition that sees the two poems as reciprocal and mutually negating rhetorical exercises modelled, as Tillyard suggested, on the university declamation. According to Miller, their trajectory is linear rather than circular, tracing out the Christian ascent to divinity, with the result that the second poem contains and transcends its predecessor. For Thomas M. Greene, on the other hand, the substantive and stylistic differences between the two poems are blurred by the mysterious figure who intrudes at the end of each poem to issue a challenge to its presiding deity. The near identity of the two challenges suggests, according to Greene, that they are made by the same individual, in which case "we seem to be left with a pair of essays in temperament, playful experimentation with two invented sensibilities by an invisible third presence who is tempted by each but committed to neither."

The problem of unity is no less acute in the case of the sonnets, the first ten of which were printed in the 1645 volume. In an overview of all of Milton's sonnets, including those that were written after the publication of *The Poems of Mr John Milton*, William McCarthy makes the case for regarding them as a coherent sequence that traces out the principal outlines of Milton's literary career from amatory exercises (numbers 1–6) through political engagement (numbers 8–18) to private contemplation in retirement (numbers 20–23), with numbers 7 and 19 marking the crucial turning points in that developmental pattern. Annabel Patterson, however, lays more emphasis on the relationship between Milton's self-presentation and the historical circumstances in which he wrote. In constructing his sonnet sequence, she believes, Milton gave expression to a theory that literature can only be understood "in the perspective of history, which in turn cannot be understood *except* by finessing the subjective/objective dilemma."

In addition to the ode and the sonnet, the other genre that dominates the 1645 collection is, of course, the elegy, of which the volume contains numerous examples both in English (*An Epitaph on the Marchioness of Winchester, On Shakespeare, On the University Carrier*) and in Latin (*Elegia II, Elegia III, In Obitum Praesulis Eliensis, Epitaphium Damonis*). *Lycidas* is the last and greatest of Milton's English experiments in this form, though its origins, as James Holly Hanford demonstrated in a classic study of the pastoral elegy, go all the way back to Theocritus' first *Idyl* and Virgil's tenth *Eclogue*. In my essay on "Lycidas, Daphnis, and Gallus," I trace the reception history of these two interrelated texts with special attention to their translation and interpretation in the sixteenth and seventeeth centuries. Seen in this context, as I believe it should be, *Lycidas* turns out to be a deeply troubled meditation on the validity of the kind of life Milton himself had been leading since his graduation from Cambridge in 1632.

Taking his cue from John Crowe Ransom's famous essay "A Poem Nearly Anonymous," Stanley Fish challenges the common view that the poem is "the expression of a unified consciousness." Rather than presenting us with "an integrated and consistent first person voice," the elegy records the speaker's gradual loss of control until, in the final eight lines, he is silenced and replaced by "an entirely new voice" that is utterly impersonal and conventional. If *Lycidas* records "a struggle of personality against anonymity," Fish asserts, "it is a struggle the first person speaker loses." Lawrence Lipking's essay is more concerned with the political implications of Milton's tribute to Edward King. The dominant theme of the first part of the poem, he suggests, is "frustrated protection. Neither pagan nor Christian watchmen have kept harm away." The apotheosis of Edward King at the end of the elegy, however, provides a guardian spirit who will protect all who travel on "that perilous flood" to complete the task of converting the Irish. Like Adamastor in Camoes' *The Lusiads*, Lycidas "functions as a defense mechanism that shields the poet and his audience from having to face the brutal truth that storms and death and oppression happen . . . and that neither the gods nor nature cares."

The section on *Comus* begins with A. S. P. Woodhouse's seminal analysis of the way in which "the order of nature" and the "order of grace" function in Milton's masque. Within this "intellectual frame of reference," the distinction among temperance, which "operates on the natural level," chastity, "which moves in an area common to nature and grace," and virginity, which "belongs exclusively to grace," is the key both to the Lady's temptation and to the masque as a whole. For Robert Adams, such elaborate interpretations amount to a "major overreading" of a text that was written for public performance in a specific social and political situation. The composition of the original audience, he points out, would have served to restrict the range of possible meanings in a variety of ways. One does not, for instance, tell an earl that his daughter "is chaste only by the grace of God," nor does one "offhandedly tell the members of a Christian commonwealth that grace is unknown to them, that they trample it underfoot." Rather than succumbing to the Byzantine ingenuities of critics like Woodhouse, we should rest content with "the simple beauties of obvious commonplaces set in musical language."

In the next two essays, George Sensabaugh and Leah Marcus call attention to two of the most significant historical contexts that bear on the interpretation of *Comus*—the cult of platonic love being practiced at the court of King Charles I and Queen Henrietta Maria, and the legal cases involving the earl of Bridgewater (notably the Castlehaven scandal and the case of Margery Evans) in the years leading up to the masque's production at Ludlow Castle. Finally, Jeanne Martin examines the generic transformations that Milton has introduced into the masque form itself, showing how *Comus* explores subjects traditionally associated with such works as Ben Jonson's *Pleasure Reconciled to Virtue* while at the same time formulating a position with respect to those subjects that "consciously diverges from that generally taken by his predecessors." Because of the way Milton uses the conventions of the masque form, she concludes, he denies his audience the kind of direct participation in an ideal world they had enjoyed in Jonson's work and leaves them instead with "a world which is formidable indeed and far from ideal."

This volume concludes with two essays on the Latin "poemata," which constituted the second part of Milton's "twin volume." In the first, Ralph Condee provides a comprehensive survey of all of Milton's Latin poetry, which, he reminds us, comprised an important part of Milton's early literary career and which, in Condee's judgement, contains some of the finest verse Milton ever wrote. In the second, Thomas Corns analyzes the ideological contradictions between such texts as the *Elegia III* (containing a respectful panegyric to Bishop Lancelot Andrewes) and *In Quintum Novembris* (in which King James I is praised as a peacemaker), on the one hand, and Milton's antiepiscopal and antimonarchical views in 1645 on the other. Like the rest of the volume, Corns concludes, the "poemata" document the transformation of Milton's poetic and political sensibility over the preceding twenty years or so.

CHAPTER 2

The
Rising
Poet

It is hard to maintain a clear view of Milton's volume of 1645, since the editions that we are most likely to be using have broken up Milton's groupings and have rearranged the poems in chronological order, interspersed with other poems that Milton did not choose to publish here. I do not mean to quarrel with these rearrangements, which have the advantage of allowing one to trace the development of Milton's early poetical career. And indeed Milton himself has taken the lead in making such a view of his career possible, since his volume of 1645 takes care to date many of the poems and arranges them in rough chronological order, within various groups.[1] At the same time Milton's original arrangement creates the growing awareness of a guiding, central purpose that in turn gives the volume an impressive and peculiar sense of wholeness. In order to regain the significant integrity of the volume one must, now and then, go back to the original.

Perhaps the best way into the volume is to follow Milton's own description of it, in the Latin ode that he sent in January, 1646–47, to John Rouse, Bodley's librarian, with a copy of the book. This is a mock-heroic poem of remarkably high spirits, written in an unprecedented form that MacKellar calls a "metrical experiment or jest."[2] The manner is one of learned wit that makes translation almost impossible; I give here a composite version of the first strophe, with intermittent comments:[3]

> Gemelle cultu simplici gaudens liber,
> Fronde licet geminâ,
> Munditiéque nitens non operosâ,
> Quam manus attulit
> Juvenilis olim,
> Sedula tamen haud nimii Poetae;
> Dum vagus Ausonias nunc per umbras
> Nunc Britannica per vireta lusit
> Insons populi, barbitóque devius
> Indulsit patrio, mox itidem pectine Daunio
> Longinquum intonuit melos
> Vicinis, & humum vix tetigit pede . . .

"Book in twin parts, rejoicing in a single cover, yet with a double leaf" [these are "Poems of Mr. John Milton, both English and Latin," with a separate title page for the Latin poems and separate pagination for the English and the Latin parts; the "double leaf," however, may allude not only to the two title pages, or the two parts, but at the same time may suggest the double wreath of laurel that the poet has won for his performance in two languages], "and shining with unlabored elegance which a hand once young imparted—a careful hand, but hardly that of one who was too much a poet—" [that is, not yet a master-poet] "while he played, wandering, now in the forest-shades of Ausonia and now on the lawns of England" [*Ausonias umbras:* the phrase may be taken to include a reference to his own Italian journey, to the poems in the Italian language, to the Latin poems, and to the pervasive atmosphere of Greek and Roman pastoral that plays throughout the volume: Ausonia includes Magna Graecia]; "aloof from the people, and forsaking the common paths, he indulged his native lute, and presently in like fashion with Daunian quill called forth for his neighbors a melody from far away, his foot scarcely touching the ground" [*pectine Daunio:* the song and instrument of ancient Italy].

Here is the picture of a youthful poet, free from adult cares, sometimes wandering alone, amusing himself, sometimes making music for his friends or acquaintances, sometimes writing in his

native vein, sometimes evoking a strain from idealized antiquity—but with a light and dancing posture that we do not
usually associate with John Milton: *et humum vix tetigit pede.* It is
clear, from many indications, that Milton has designed his book
with great care to create this impression.

The entire volume strives to create a tribute to a youthful era
now past—not only the poet's own youth, but a state of mind, a
point of view, ways of writing, ways of living, an old culture and
outlook now shattered by the pressures of maturity and by the
actions of political man. Even the frontispiece, by William Marshall, attempts to set this theme. The aim of the engraving is
clearly to present the youthful poet surrounded by the Muses,
with a curtain in the background lifted to reveal a pastoral landscape of meadow and trees, where a shepherd is piping in the
shade, while a shepherd and a shepherdess are dancing on the
lawn. The legend around the portrait identifies it as a picture of
the poet in his twenty-first year—but in fact the portrait presents
the harsh and crabbed image of a man who might be forty or fifty!
Marshall could do better than this, as his engraving of the youthful Donne testifies; one almost suspects deliberate sabotage here.[4]
If so, Milton performed slyly an appropriate revenge. For under
the portrait, neatly engraved in Greek—engraved no doubt by
Marshall himself—we have the following comment by Milton:

> That an unskilful hand had carved this print
> You'd say at once, seeing the living face;
> But, finding here no jot of me, my friends,
> Laugh at the botching artist's mis-attempt.

With this learned practical joke, the volume begins in high spirits;
how can we doubt, after this, that Milton had a considerable sense
of humor?

Meanwhile, the facing title page prepares us for a volume that
will contain songs of unlabored elegance, in the recent courtly
style: "The Songs were set in Musick by Mr. Henry Lawes Gentleman of the Kings Chappel, and one of His Maiesties Private
Musick"—a notice quite in line with Moseley's preface, which associates Milton's volume with the poems of Waller that Moseley
had published a year before. Waller, as everyone knew, had been

exiled for his plot against the Parliament on the King's behalf; nevertheless Moseley insists on saying: "that incouragement I have already received from the most ingenious men in their clear and courteous entertainment of Mr. *Wallers* late choice Peeces, hath once more made me adventure into the World, presenting it with these ever-green, and not to be blasted Laurels." This bland ignoring, or bold confronting, of the political situation, with its emphasis upon the transcendent values of art, is maintained by reprinting here, from the 1637 edition, Henry Lawes's eloquent dedication of Milton's *Maske* to a young nobleman with strong royalist associations; by the Latin poems in memory of the bishops of Winchester and Ely; by the complimentary writings prefixed to the Latin poems, showing the high regard that Milton had won in Catholic Italy; and by the sonnet beginning: "Captain or Colonel, or Knight in Arms, / Whose chance on these defenceless dores may sease."

> Lift not thy spear against the Muses Bowre,
>   The great *Emathian* Conqueror bid spare
>   The house of *Pindarus,* when Temple and Towre
> Went to the ground: And the repeated air
>   Of sad *Electra's* Poet had the power
>   To save th' *Athenian* Walls from ruine bare.

But will the King's Captain do the same for one who is not yet "too much a poet"? There is room for doubt, and hence the plea, with its undertone of self-irony;[5] but there is no doubt at all about the power of poetry and this poet's hopes to achieve the immortality of Fame. He has told us this through the motto on the title page, there identified as coming from Vergil's seventh eclogue:

> ————Baccare frontem
> Cingite, ne vati noceat mala lingua futuro.

The whole context is essential: the lines are spoken by Thyrsis as he opens his answer in the singing match with Corydon, *Arcades ambo:*

> Pastores, hedera crescentem[6] ornate poetam,
> Arcades, invidia rumpantur ut ilia Codro;
> aut, si ultra placitum laudarit, baccare frontem
> cingite, ne vati noceat mala lingua futuro.

POEMS

OF

Mr. *John Milton*,

BOTH

ENGLISH and LATIN,

Compos'd at several times.

Printed by his true Copies.

The S o n g s were set in Musick by Mr. H e n r y L a w e s Gentleman of the K i n g s Chappel, and one of His M a i e s t i e s Private Musick.

——*Baccare frontem*
Cingite, ne vati noceat mala lingua futuro,
Virgil, Eclog. 7.

Printed and publish'd according to ORDER.

LONDON,
Printed by *Ruth Raworth* for *Humphrey Moseley,*
and are to be sold at the signe of the Princes
Arms in S. *Pauls* Church-yard. 1645.

Bring ivy-leaves to decorate your rising poet, shepherds of Arcady,
and so make Codrus burst his sides with envy. Or, if he tries to
harm me with excessive praise, twine foxglove round my brows, to
stop his evil tongue from hurting your predestined bard.
[7.25–29, trans. Rieu][7]

Thyrsis loses the match, but other contests no doubt lie ahead; he
ends by sending his love to his friend Lycidas.

That epigraph, summoning up the world of Vergil's *Eclogues*,
prepares the way for the many Vergilian characters and scenes to
be encountered in the English poems here: Corydon and Thyrsis,
Phillis and Thestylis, in *L'Allegro;* Thyrsis and Meliboeus in the
Maske; Lycidas, with Amaryllis, and Damoetas, and the setting of
Vergil's seventh eclogue, "where the Mincius embroiders his
banks with a green fringe of bending rushes";[8] and the shepherds
of *Arcades*—the entertainment at Harefield. The epigraph prepares us too for the echoes of Vergil's Messianic eclogue that
occur in the volume's opening poem, the Nativity Ode; and, above
all, it prepares us to watch, as we read the Latin poems, the poet's
growth away from the light elegy toward the Vergilian mode in
which Milton wrote the most mature and the finest of all the Latin
verses in this volume: *Ad Patrem, Mansus,* and *Epitaphium Damonis,*
all three of which confirm the "rising poet's" place as a "predestined bard."

The *Epitaphium Damonis,* spoken by Thyrsis, becomes appropriately the final poem of the entire volume, for with all its echoes
of Greek pastoral it is the most deliberately Vergilian poem in the
book. Here, clustered together, are those pastoral names that
Vergil drew together in his *Eclogues:* Thyrsis and Damon,
Daphnis, Tityrus, Alphesiboeus, Aegon, Amyntas, Mopsus,
Aegle, and Menalcas; the use of the refrain recalls Vergil's eighth
eclogue, the singing match between Damon and Alphesiboeus,
while the words of Milton's refrain are modeled upon a line from
the seventh eclogue (7.44) and also upon the final line of the last
eclogue; the account of the two cups which Manso gave the poet is
bound to recall the pairs of cups carved by Alcimedon, as described in Vergil's third eclogue; and verbal echoes of Vergil are
so frequent that the poem seems to grow within a Vergilian ma-
trix.[9]

The unity of Milton's volume, from title page to final poem, is further suggested by the fact that the *Epitaphium Damonis* laments the death of the very friend to whom the first Latin poem in the book had been written—*Elegia prima,* that playful and thoroughly Ovidian elegy composed by the arrogantly clever and quite unrepentant sophomore during his rustication. At the same time, the reader is bound to recall that *Elegia sexta* and the fourth sonnet have also been explicitly addressed to this same friend, Charles Diodati. The final poem, then, in paying tribute to a friend of youth, becomes a farewell to the pleasures and attitudes of youth, including the pleasures of pastoral poetry and the imitative pleasures of writing such Latin verse—a farewell that Milton appropriately gives with unmistakable echoes of Vergil's *Eclogues:*

> Ipse etiam, nam nescio quid mihi grande sonabat
> Fistula, ab undecimâ jam lux est altera nocte,
> Et tum forte novis admôram labra cicutis,
> Dissiluere tamen rupta compage, nec ultra
> Ferre graves potuere sonos, dubito quoque ne sim
> Turgidulus, tamen & referam, vos cedite silvae.

And I—for I know not what my pipe was grandly sounding—it is now eleven nights and a day—and then perhaps I had put my lips to new pipes, but they burst asunder, broken at the fastening, and could no more bear the deep tones—I hesitate too lest I seem puffed up, yet I will tell the tale—give place then, O forests.

[155–60, trans. MacKellar]

Milton's *vos cedite silvae* is a clear echo of the *concedite silvae* with which Gallus bids farewell to Arcadian pleasures in Vergil's last eclogue (10.63); while Milton's following farewell to Latin poetry and Latin themes is based explicitly on the wording of Vergil's seventh eclogue:

> aut, si non possumus omnes,
> hic arguta sacra pendebit fistula pinu.   [7.23–24]

Thus, after the famous passage in which Milton tells of his resolve to write an epic on British themes, he cries:

> O mihi tum si vita supersit,
> Tu procul annosa pendebis fistula pinu
> Multum oblita mihi, aut patriis mutata camoenis

Brittonicum strides, quid enim? omnia non licet uni
Non sperâsse uni licet omnia . . .

Ah! then if life remain, you, my pipe, shall hang on some aged pine
far off and forgotten, unless forsaking your native songs you shrilly
sound a British theme. Why not a British theme? One man cannot
do all things, cannot hope to do all things.

[168–72, trans. MacKellar]

MacKellar's version of these lines helps to bring out the complexity of the state of mind here expressed. The poet is resolved to leave behind the *fistula,* the reed pipe of his pastoral muse, and he will turn instead to write of those deeper themes which have already on one occasion proved to be stronger than that youthful pipe could bear. At the same time the *fistula* may represent Latin poetry, and the words *patriis camoenis* may thus suggest the Latin language itself.[10] That is to say, the poet is contemplating deeper themes, British themes, and themes composed in English. The power of poetry represented by these early compositions on the *fistula* will not be developed unless the poet can commit himself to English. Perhaps he has already tried those deeper themes in Latin, but without success: the rising poet knows, as Vergil says in the eighth eclogue, *non omnia possumus omnes* (63); and he foresees that his future fame must be entrusted to his native tongue.

His maturing prowess in that tongue has already been demonstrated in the other pastoral monody that, with beautiful symmetry, closes the series of his shorter English poems in the first part of his double book. *Lycidas,* like the *Epitaphium Damonis,* represents the climax of its part; each monody is the culmination of the many strands of experimentation that have been growing throughout each part. The Ludlow *Maske* is printed after *Lycidas,* as a work distinctly separate from the preceding groups; it is provided with elaborate introductory matter and a separate half-title—almost a full title-page, for it bears the imprint "Anno Dom. 1645." The pagination, however, is continuous throughout the English part. The whole book, then, displays particular care for balance and harmony in all its proportions, while the poems themselves have been arranged to convey a sense of the predestined bard's rising powers.

8

II

The theme of poetical development is particularly clear in the Latin poems, most of which, as the Latin title page points out, were written *intra Annum aetatis Vigesimum:* that is, before his twentieth year had ended. In keeping with this emphasis, Milton has taken unusual care in dating his Latin poems, so as to make clear their youthfulness and the rising poet's precociousness. This atmosphere is borne out, in the elegies, by their heading *Liber primus*—a first book, a primer, for which no second book follows; and also by the retractation which ends the sequence of the seven numbered elegies. There is no need to suspect a misprint in the dating of the seventh, which comes out of chronological order,[11] for the placing of this elegy seems to be dictated by the presence of the retractation, evidently written for the seventh elegy alone, and not for this whole set of elegies; yet placed here as it is, the retractation covers any similar materials in the preceding poems and puts last the latest piece of composition, the retractation itself. This palinode creates the impression of having been composed for some special occasion (such as, perhaps, a recitation of the seventh elegy before one of those "privat Academies in *Italy*," where Milton tells us that he presented "some trifles . . . compos'd at under twenty or thereabout"),[12] when it was appropriate for the poet to speak of this youthful love poem with a tone of humorous exaggeration and a touch of mock-heroic banter:

> Haec ego mente olim laevâ, studioque supino
>   Nequitiae posui vana trophaea meae.
> Scilicet abreptum sic me malus impulit error,
>   Indocilisque aetas prava magistra fuit.
> Donec Socraticos umbrosa Academia rivos
>   Praebuit, admissum dedocuitque jugum.
> Protinus extinctis ex illo tempore flammis,
>   Cincta rigent multo pectora nostra gelu.
> Unde suis frigus metuit puer ipse Sagittis,
>   Et Diomedéam vim timet ipse Venus.

These are the monuments to my wantonness that with a perverse spirit and a trifling purpose I once erected. Obviously, mischievous error led me astray and my undisciplined youth was a vicious teacher until the shady Academy offered its Socratic streams and taught me how to escape from the yoke to which I had submitted. From that hour those flames were extinct and thenceforward my breast has been rigid under a thick case of ice, of which the boy himself fears the frost for his arrows, and Venus herself is afraid of my Diomedean strength.   [trans. Hughes]

After this coda to the formal elegies Milton adds his epigrams written in the same verse form: first, a group of five pieces related to the Gunpowder Plot, which we assume must be early, because of their relation to *In quintum Novembris, Anno aetatis 17;* and lastly, three epigrams that we know to be late, since they deal with the singer Leonora Baroni, whom Milton heard during his visits to Rome in 1638–39.[13] By this method of grouping Milton has managed to end his section devoted to elegiac verse with poems that give exalted praise to the Orphic powers of voice and verse, married in song:

> Altera Torquatum cepit Leonora Poëtam,
>   Cujus ab insano cessit amore furens.
> Ah miser ille tuo quantò feliciùs aevo
>   Perditus, & propter te Leonora foret!
> Et te Pieriâ sensisset voce canentem
>   Aurea maternae fila movere lyrae,
> Quamvis Dircaeo torsisset lumina Pentheo
>   Saevior, aut totus desipuisset iners,
> Tu tamen errantes caecâ vertigine sensus
>   Voce eadem poteras composuisse tuâ;
> Et poteras aegro spirans sub corde quietem
>   Flexamino cantu restituisse sibi.

Another Leonora captivated the poet Torquato, who for frenzied love of her went mad. Ah, poor unfortunate! How much more happily had he been lost in your times and for love of you, Leonora! He would have heard you singing with Pierian voice as the golden strings of your mother's lyre moved in harmony. Though he had rolled his eyes more fiercely than Dircean Pentheus, or all insensible had raved, yet you by your voice could have composed his senses wandering in their blind whirl; and, inspiring his distempered heart with peace, you could have restored him to himself with your soul-moving song.   [trans. MacKellar]

The same Orphic theme dominates the conclusion to the second, much longer grouping here, the *Sylvarum Liber,* poems in various meters, where the growth toward maturity of poetic power is marked by the poet's growing appreciation of the philosophic and religious meaning of music's power in the universe. The first poem in this section is headed *Anno aetatis 16. In obitum Procancellarii medici,* with the date given special prominence by thus forming part of the title; and the same is true of the two following poems dated *Anno aetatis 17.* Thereafter the poems are not dated, but the first three headings have served to suggest a chronological movement while implicitly apologizing for the immaturity (and by the way implying perhaps the precocity?) of these opening pieces. After the two academic exercises that follow, the remaining poems are drawn together by interlocking themes, above all by the theme of poetical dedication set forth in *Ad Patrem*—still, as he says, one of his youthful works (*iuvenilia carmina*)—but nevertheless a poem that by its fervor and wit and firm command of hexameter marks the beginning of this poet's mature strength:

> Nec tu vatis opus divinum despice carmen,
> Quo nihil aethereos ortus, & semina caeli,
> Nil magis humanam commendat origine mentem,
> Sancta Promethéae retinens vestigia flammae.
> Carmen amant superi, tremebundaque Tartara carmen
> Ima ciere valet, divosque ligare profundos,
> Et triplici duros Manes adamante coercet.

> Scorn not the poet's song, a work divine, which more than aught else reveals our ethereal origin and heavenly race. Nothing so much as its origin does grace to the human mind, possessing yet some sacred traces of Promethean fire. The gods love song, song that has power to move the trembling depths of Tartarus, to bind the nether gods, and restrain the cruel shades with triple adamant.
> [17–23, trans. MacKellar]

The implicit allusion to Orpheus is made explicit a few lines later, after Milton has imagined "the bard, seated at the festal board," singing of "the feats of heroes" and of "chaos and the broadly-laid foundations of the world."

> Denique quid vocis modulamen inane juvabit,
> Verborum sensusque vacans, numerique loquacis?
> Silvestres decet iste choros, non Orphea cantus,
> Qui tenuit fluvios & quercubus addidit aures
> Carmine, non citharâ, simulachraque functa canendo
> Compulit in lacrymas; habet has à carmine laudes.

And finally, what will the empty modulation of the voice avail, void
of words and sense, and of eloquent numbers? That song will do for
the sylvan choirs, but not for Orpheus, who with song and not with
lute held back the rivers, and gave ears to the oaks, and moved the
shades of the dead to tears; these praises he has from song.

[50–55, trans. MacKellar]

This passage prepares the way for the Orphic allusion at the close
of the poem written to the Roman poet Salzilli, where Milton
hopes that this poet's illness may be cured so that he may resume
his writing, with the result that "Swollen Tiber himself, charmed
by the song, will favor the annual hope of the husbandmen" (36–
37, trans. MacKellar).

But what shall we make of the two poems in Greek that lie
between *Ad Patrem* and *Ad Salsillum*? The first of these, the Greek
version of Psalm 114, can be securely dated in November 1634, as
we know from Milton's letter to Alexander Gill, in which he describes how he was inspired to adapt this work of the "truly divine
poet . . . to the rules of Greek Heroic song."[14] The poem thus
follows chronologically after *Ad Patrem,* if we believe, as I do, that
Ad Patrem dates from 1631–32, or, as Parker has argued, from the
earlier part of 1634.[15] But more important, the Greek version of
the psalm follows naturally after the gratitude that the poet has
just expressed to his father for encouraging him to learn, not only
Latin, but also Greek, French, Italian, and Hebrew. By his skill
in adapting and expanding the Hebrew original into Greek
hexameters we may see how far this poet has travelled intellectu-
ally since that time when, "at fifteen yeers old,"[16] he had made an
English paraphrase of the same psalm in the style of Sylvester's
Dubartas, using the current English versions as his guides. The
brief Greek epigram that follows is easily brought in here
(whenever it was written) as further evidence of linguistic command.

Then the whole volume closes with the two latest and most
complex of his Latin poems, *Mansus* and the *Epitaphium Damonis,*
bound together by Milton's elaborate description in the *Epitaphium* (181–97) of the two "cups" (*pocula*) that Manso gave to
Milton—gifts that Milton had hoped to show to Diodati—books,
perhaps, that they might have discussed together, as in their

younger days.[17] But above all, these two closing poems are linked
by their revelation of this poet's hopes to write a British epic:

> O mihi si mea sors talem concedat amicum
> Phoebaeos decorâsse viros qui tam bene norit,
> Si quando indigenas revocabo in carmina reges,
> Arturumque etiam sub terris bella moventem;
> Aut dicam invictae sociali foedere mensae,
> Magnanimos Heroas, & (O modo spiritus ad sit)
> Frangam Saxonicas Britonum sub Marte phalanges.

O, if my lot might but bestow such a friend upon me, a friend who
understands how to honor the devotees of Phoebus—if ever I shall
summon back our native kings into our songs, and Arthur, waging
his wars beneath the earth, or if ever I shall proclaim the magnanimous heroes of the table which their mutual fidelity made invincible, and (if only the spirit be with me) shall shatter the Saxon
phalanxes under the British Mars!

> [*Mansus*, 78–84, trans. Hughes]

> Ipse ego Dardanias Rutupina per aequora puppes
> Dicam, & Pandrasidos regnum vetus Inogeniae,
> Brennúmque Arviragúmque duces, priscúmque Belinum,
> Et tandem Armoricos Britonum sub lege colonos;
> Tum gravidam Arturo fatali fraude Jögernen
> Mendaces vultus, assumptáque Gorlöis arma,
> Merlini dolus.

I would tell of Dardanian ships along the Rutupian Sea, and of the
ancient realm of Imogen, Pandrasus' daughter, of the leaders
Brennus and Arviragus, and old Belinus, and of colonists in Ar-
morica under British laws; then I would tell of Igraine pregnant
with Arthur by a fatal fraud, of the seeming face and counterfeit
arms of Gorlois, Merlin's artifice.

> [*Epitaphium*, 162–68, trans. MacKellar]

"Quid enim?" Milton asks—"Why not a British theme?"

III

The dating of the English poems is less explicit in most cases,
but the mode of arrangement is clear. As with the Latin poems,
the over-arching structure runs from poems of early youth to
poems that enact a movement toward the broader visions of
maturity. Within this larger movement the poems are then sorted

into subordinate groupings: devotional poems, secular poems in the Jonsonian mode, sonnets, and pastoral poems; and within each of these a rough chronological arrangement can be discerned.[18]

The group headed "Sonnets," for example, opens with the English love sonnet that echoes Italian addresses to the Nightingale, but basically follows the medieval and pseudo–Chaucerian tradition of the Cuckoo and the Nightingale. Then follow the five sonnets in Italian, with their *Canzone,* paying tribute to the Petrarchans by using, as Milton says, "the language of which Love makes his boast" ("Questa e lingua di cui si vanta Amore").[19] These are all poems written in the atmosphere of the "young, unassuming and artless lover" suggested by the opening line of Sonnet 6 ("Giovane piano, e semplicetto amante"), and dramatized in the *Canzone,* where the poet shows himself surrounded by "Amorous young men and maidens . . . jesting."[20] After these playful exercises in a fading, once-popular mode, the stern lines of Sonnet 7, on the flight of his three-and-twentieth year, come with the shock of a sudden recognition, setting a severe Calvinist view of life against these early trifles:

> All is, if I have grace to use it so,
> As ever in my great task Masters eye.

The meaning of these lines, I think, is clarified if we take the word "grace" in a strict Calvinist sense: the speaker's future lies completely in the hands of God.[21] Though Time has stolen away his youth, all his hopes remain as valid as they ever were; nothing has really changed, for the use of his life depends upon the timeless will and eye and grace of God. Nothing could form a sharper contrast with the preceding sonnets; and yet the sternness of the doctrine itself may suggest a veering from one youthful extreme to another—especially since the movement of the sonnet still maintains a conventional, end-stopped, balanced manner. The succeeding sonnet on the military threat to London shows (as the earlier discussion has implied) a greater maturity, reflected in its ironic posture and in the graceful sentence that winds its sinewy length over the last five lines.

Then the group closes with two more sonnets addressed to

women, both sonnets forming a tacit contrast with the Petrarchan
mode, in theme and in technique. Recalling the "Donna" of Milton's Italian sonnets, we are alert to appreciate the growth and
change represented in the suspended opening of Sonnet 9:

> Lady that in the prime of earliest youth,
>   Wisely hast shun'd the broad way and the green,
>   And with those few art eminently seen,
>   That labour up the Hill of heav'nly Truth,
> The better part with *Mary,* and [with] *Ruth,*
>   Chosen thou hast . . .

Lastly, Sonnet 10, with an even greater suspension and involu-
tion,[22] addresses a married lady who in herself maintains the virtues that once ruled in England, before the turmoil of the present
age began:

> Daughter to that good Earl, once President
>   Of *Englands* Counsel, and her Treasury,
>   Who liv'd in both, unstain'd with gold or fee,
>   And left them both, more in himself content,
> Till the sad breaking of that Parlament
>   Broke him, as that dishonest victory
>   At *Chaeronéa,* fatal to liberty
>   Kil'd with report that Old man eloquent,
> Though later born, then to have known the dayes
>   Wherin your Father flourisht, yet by you
>   Madam, me thinks I see him living yet;
> So well your words his noble vertues praise,
>   That all both judge you to relate them true,
>   And to possess them, Honour'd *Margaret.*

Thus the syntax involves the troubled, more inclusive vision of
maturity, while the *disio amoroso* of the Italian sonnets lies far in
the past.

   Similarly, it is helpful to read *L'Allegro* and *Il Penseroso* in the
context of Milton's chosen arrangement; for these two poems
come at the end of a group that might best be described as Jonsonian: poems in the mode of the "terse" couplet characteristic of
Jonson and his Sons. First, the "witty" *Epitaph on the Marchioness of
Winchester;* next, that perfect distillation of the Elizabethan madri-
gal, the *Song On May morning;* then the rather labored epigram on
Shakespeare, dated 1630, and marked as early by the archaic

"Star-ypointing"; and then the two jocular epitaphs for the University Carrier. Out of these experiments arise the two great companion poems, or twin poems, or the double poem, as we have come to call them. Reading these two poems in their original context may guide us toward a slight modification or qualification of these descriptive phrases. They are companion poems, certainly, but they are not of equal strength and stature.[23] Their relation is rather that of Younger Brother to Elder Brother. The parallels between them, so familiar to everyone, should not lead us to read the poems in parallel, as though they were two sides of a coin, or two sides of an academic debate. For the poems develop a linear, sequential effect, moving from youthful hedonism toward the philosophic, contemplative mind.[24]

It has often been noted that *L'Allegro* is looser in its handling of versification and syntax than *Il Penseroso*. According to Sprott, for example, the basic iambic tetrameter is varied with trochaic lines thirty-two percent of the time in *L'Allegro*, but only sixteen percent of the time in *Il Penseroso*.[25] Hence the subtle effect of "uncertainty" that Weismiller finds in reading the rhythms is much greater in *L'Allegro* than in *Il Penseroso*.[26] As for syntax, its occasional looseness in *L'Allegro* may be indicated by the sharp debate[27] that has arisen over these lines:

> To hear the Lark begin his flight,
> And singing startle the dull night,
> From his watch-towre in the skies,
> Till the dappled dawn doth rise;
> Then to com in spight of sorrow,
> And at my window bid good morrow,
> Through the Sweet-Briar, or the Vine,
> Or the twisted Eglantine.   [41–48]

Is it the lark or is it L'Allegro who comes to the window to greet the speaker in his bed? At first "to com" may seem to be in parallel with "to hear". Yet consideration of the context indicates that this cannot be so, for the lines immediately following, and all the rest of the poem, present L'Allegro as the receiver of impressions from without—"list'ning," "walking," measuring the landscape with his eye, hearing tales about the "lubbar Fend," and so on. No, "to com" is rather in rough parallel with "begin." It is the lark who greets L'Allegro with his song, just as in the next lines "the Cock with lively din, / Scatters the rear of darknes thin."

A greater freedom of syntax occurs in the speaker's memory of the tales about the goblin:

> She was pincht, and pull'd she sed,
> And he by Friars Lanthorn led
> Tells how the drudging *Goblin* swet,
> To ern his Cream-bowle duly set . . .   [103–06]

In the edition of 1673 the second line is altered to read "And by the Friars Lanthorn led"—but this change does not affect the colloquial looseness of the phrasing.

Such syntactical looseness is hardly a defect in the poem, any more than the striking variations in meter: these are all part of a poem designed with "wanton heed, and giddy cunning," the poem of "fancies child," warbling "his native Wood-notes wilde," a poem that moves with "light fantastick toe" to celebrate "The Mountain Nymph, sweet Liberty." Freedom of movement, without concentration of mind, is implicit in those floating participles: "list'ning" (53) and "walking" (57), which relate to the wish of the "I" and "me" (34–35) some twenty lines before. Indeed the pronouns "I" and "me" occur only four times in *L'Allegro*, as compared with eleven times in *Il Penseroso*. Instead it is "mine eye"— an "it"—that measures the lawn and sees the towers; and when the "upland Hamlets . . . invite," they invite no particular person, but everyman; and later on "Towred Cities please *us*." In every possible way a generalized receiver of shifting impressions is created, so that at the close even Orpheus becomes, not a singer, but a listener! For the speaker wishes

> That *Orpheus* self may heave his head
> From golden slumber on a bed
> Of heapt *Elysian* flowres, and hear
> Such streins as would have won the ear
> Of *Pluto,* to have quite set free
> His half-regain'd *Eurydice*.   [145–50]

All this presents a sharp contrast with the poem of "the fixed mind" whose presiding goddess, "Sober, stedfast, and demure," is urged to keep her "wonted state, / With eev'n step, and musing gate." The "Cherub Contemplation" here works within a personal

presence whose mind not only receives impressions from without, but also actively addresses and "woos" their action:

> Sweet Bird that shunn'st the noise of folly,
> Most musicall, most melancholy!
> Thee Chauntress oft the Woods among,
> I woo to hear thy eevn-Song . . .   [61–64]

This speaker does not float with loose participles; his stance is
precise, active, personal: "I walk," "I hear". He hopes to set his
lamp in the lonely tower in order to spend the night in deep study
of Hermes, Plato, and the great tragedians, while his mind longs
to behold Orpheus in vital action:

> But, O sad Virgin, that thy power
> Might raise *Musaeus* from his bower,
> Or bid the soul of *Orpheus* sing
> Such notes as warbled to the string,
> Drew Iron tears down *Pluto's* cheek,
> And made Hell grant what Love did seek.   [103–08]

And after his dreams, set in an harmonious Theocritean landscape, he hopes to hear the music represented in *Arcades* and the
Ludlow *Maske:*

> And as I wake, sweet musick breath
> Above, about, or underneath,
> Sent by som spirit to mortals good,
> Or th'unseen Genius of the Wood.   [151–54]

But even such listening is too passive for this speaker: he soon
directs himself "To walk the studious Cloysters pale," and to
"love" the beauties of Gothic architecture, while "the pealing Organ" and "the full voic'd Quire" will, he hopes, inspire the contemplative mind to its highest reaches, and

> through mine ear
> Dissolve me into extasies,
> And bring all Heav'n before mine eyes.   [164–66]

Looking back now, we can see that the first poem has summed
up a youthful world of Elizabethan poetry now past; the tone has
been set in the opening archaism, "In Heav'n ycleap'd *Eu-
phrosyne.*" It is full of all the maying and the pastoral joys cele-

brated in hundreds of Elizabethan airs and madrigals, including the famous "Come live with me," strongly echoed near the beginning (39) and at the very end; and it remembers too those popular legends about Mab and the drudging goblin, celebrated by Shakespeare and Drayton. Then there are the allusions to the "high triumphs" of archaic chivalry, to the courtly "Ladies, whose bright eies / Rain influence" in Petrarchan fashion, to "mask, and antique Pageantry," to Jonson's comedies, and to Shakespeare in his comic and pastoral vein.[28] It is a joyous celebration and re-creation of an era, a state of mind, now past; but we note that it ends with hints that suggest this is not the highest mode of harmony. As every Platonist knew, Plato had condemned the "soft *Lydian* Aires," and Milton subtly recalls the condemnation, while seeming to ignore it:

> With wanton heed, and giddy cunning,
> The melting voice through mazes running . . .   [141–42]

But the words "wanton," "giddy," and "melting" recall the implications of the *Republic:*

> Again, drunkenness, effeminacy, and inactivity are most un-suitable in Guardians. Which are the modes expressing softness and the ones used at drinking-parties?
> There are the Ionian and certain Lydian modes which are called "slack."
> You will not use them in the training of your warriors?
> Certainly not.   [III.398c–400c, trans. Cornford][29]

The final picture of Orpheus heaving up his head "From golden slumber on a bed / Of heapt *Elysian* flowres" carries on, however beautifully, the "softness" of the Lydian mode, in contrast to the potent, active Orpheus of *Il Penseroso.* Furthermore, this second reference to Orpheus is subsumed within the middle of *Il Penseroso,* where he is only one of many great poets and thinkers. The spirit of Plato's "shady Academy"[30] (derived traditionally from Orpheus and Pythagoras) dominates *Il Penseroso,* from the opening salutation of the Goddess "sage and holy" to the grand musical close which extends this poem two dozen lines beyond the length of *L'Allegro.* All is, however, subtly qualified at the very end, as the poem presents a picture that is too obviously archaic and senti-

mental to be taken solemnly: its excess tells us that Melancholy too
needs tempering:

> And may at last my weary age
> Find out the peacefull hermitage,
> The Hairy Gown and Mossy Cell,
> Where I may sit and rightly spell,
> Of every Star that Heav'n doth shew,
> And every Herb that sips the dew;
> Till old experience do attain
> To somthing like Prophetic strain.
> These pleasures *Melancholy* give,
> And I with thee will choose to live.

That echo of "Come live with me" is phrased more positively than
the closing couplet of *L'Allegro:*

> These delights, if thou canst give,
> Mirth with thee, I mean to live.

Yet the echo reminds us that either choice involves a limitation.

Thus the two poems move from youth to age—the word
"youthfull" is invoked twice in *L'Allegro,* and not at all in *Il
Penseroso*—while in their movement these two unequal but compatible companions suggest the growth toward maturity that constitutes this volume's dominant theme.

IV

Turning now, finally, to the devotional group that begins Milton's book, we note that he has carefully stressed the youthfulness
of the four opening poems. First, out of strict chronological order,
we have the poem headed: *On the morning of Christs Nativity. Compos'd 1629.*—with the date thus given prominence as part of the
title.[31] Then come the two psalms, "don by the Author at fifteen
yeers old," as the headnote tells us. Then the unfinished poem on
the Passion, with the famous note at the end: "This Subject the
Author finding to be above the yeers he had, when he wrote it,
and nothing satisfi'd with what was begun, left it unfinisht." One may
wonder why Milton bothered to include this acknowledged failure
and fragment, when he did not include the more interesting and
at least completed English poems that he added in 1673: the poem

On the Death of a fair Infant, and the lines from the *Vacation Exercise.* But the inclusion of the fragment has a clear function: to stress the immaturity of these opening pieces, to suggest the ambitious young man outreaching his powers, and achieving poetical success only when he can subject his muse to some deliberate limitation. What he can accomplish is then demonstrated in the three short pieces that follow: *On Time, Upon the Circumcision,* and *At a solemn Musick;* these are undated, and thus, we assume, not quite so youthful. *Upon the Circumcision,* in particular, suggests a new beginning, in a less venturous mode, after the false start of *The Passion;* here the poet, by skillfully imitating the stanza-form of Petrarch's canzone to the Virgin, creates a carefully controlled meditation on the love of the suffering Infant.[32] The other two lyrics are experiments in the handling of the canzone, anticipating the flexible verse-form of *Lycidas. At a solemn Musick* bears a special significance as the final poem in this group, for its transcendent praise of the wedded powers of voice and verse links with the view of music's power to be found in *Arcades,* the Ludlow *Maske,* the epigrams to Leonora, *Ad Patrem,* and *Mansus.* It is thus a poem that helps to tie the entire volume together, as well as this small opening group, where the final lyric recalls the heavenly music heard by the shepherds in the long youthful poem on the Nativity that Milton has wisely chosen to open his book, as prologue to the rising poet's achievement.

The dating, "Compos'd 1629," accords with the Nativity poem's relation to an age and mode of English poetry now outgrown, both by the nation and by the poet. In understanding this poetical mode, one may gain important clues from Milton's description of the Nativity Ode in his sixth Latin elegy—especially when we read this elegy in Milton's chosen context, between the Ovidian celebration of Spring in *Elegia quinta* and the mildly Ovidian eroticism of *Elegia septima.* Read thus, *Elegia sexta* does not lend itself easily to the widely held view that the Ode "teaches us to read the contrast of the elegiac and the heroic vein as a repudiation of the former, to transliterate the description of the heroic poet into Christian terms as the account of a dedicated spirit divinely inspired."[33] This elegy begins with a broad joke about Diodati's feasting at the Christmas season:

21

> Mitto tibi sanam non pleno ventre salutem,
>   Quâ tu distento forte carere potes.

With a stomach anything but full, I send you a prayer for sound health, of which, perhaps, you, with your stomach stretched to its uttermost, may be in sore need.   [trans. Knapp][34]

Then follows lively praise of festive poetry and the "light elegy," in a passage twice as long as the subsequent praise of epic: wine, feasting, maidens, and dancing inspire, says Milton, an excellent kind of poetry, blessed by many gods. Of course, he adds, if a poet wants to write on grand epic themes, then he must live quite differently; and Milton proceeds to write a hyperbolical account of the ascetic life required for such a bard:

> Ille quidem parcè Samii pro more magistri
>   Vivat, & innocuos praebeat herba cibos;
> Stet prope fagineo pellucida lympha catillo,
>   Sobriaque è puro pocula fonte bibat.

let him live sparingly, like the Samian teacher [Pythagoras] and let herbs furnish his innocent diet. Let the purest water stand beside him in a bowl of beech and let him drink sober draughts from the pure spring.   [59–62, trans. Hughes]

He goes on to express his belief in the exalted power of this kind of bard, but he does not wholly lay aside the tone of "Ovidian banter" that Rand has found in the earlier part.[35] Milton no doubt hopes to reach that higher vein himself; but he does not appear to be saying so here. When he turns to discuss himself at the end of the poem, he makes a clean break with the previous discussion of elegy and epic; both are excellent in their kinds, the poet implies, but he is not writing in either vein at the moment:

> At tu siquid agam, scitabere (si modò saltem
>   Esse putas tanti noscere siquid agam)
> Paciferum canimus caelesti semine regem,
>   Faustaque sacratis saecula pacta libris,
> Vagitumque Dei, & stabulantem paupere tecto
>   Qui suprema suo cum patre regna colit.
> Stelliparumque polum, modulantesque aethere turmas,
>   Et subitò elisos ad sua fana Deos.
> Dona quidem dedimus Christi natalibus illa,
>   Illa sub auroram lux mihi prima tulit.   [79–88]

One must stress the *At tu siquid agam, scitabere:* "But if you will know what I am doing (if only you think it of any importance to know whether I am doing anything)"—note how he maintains the familiar tone with which the poem has opened—"I am singing the heaven-descended King, the bringer of peace, and the blessed times promised in the sacred books—the infant cries of our God" [which in fact are not mentioned in the Nativity poem as we have it; but Milton is emphasizing the poem's allegiance to the naïve tradition of the Christmas carol, as his next words further indicate] "and his stabling under a mean roof who, with his Father, governs the realms above. I am singing the starry sky and the hosts that sang high in air, and the gods that were suddenly destroyed in their own shrines. These are my gifts for the birthday of Christ—gifts which the first light of its dawn brought to me" (trans. Hughes). In that last clause Milton seems to be saying only that the writing of the poem began at dawn; there seems to be no indication of a special experience of religious dedication.

In this elegy's final couplet the opening *Te quoque* has allowed various interpretations:[36]

> Te quoque pressa manent patriis meditata cicutis,
> Tu mihi, cui recitem, judicis instar eris.

In some versions it appears that Milton is referring to certain *other* English poems that he has also written; but the *quoque* modifies *te;* or, rather, it is pleonastic and is best omitted, as in the revised translation of Hughes, which makes it plain that the passage is still alluding to the Nativity poem: "For you these simple strains that have been meditated on my native pipes are waiting; and you, when I recite them to you, shall be my judge." *Patriis meditata cicutis:* meditated on the native hemlock pipes of the humble shepherd. Milton has suggested here the Nativity poem's basic decorum.

It is, first of all, a poem that declares, in many ways, this poet's indebtedness to his predecessors in the line of English poetry. The four prefatory stanzas, written in a variation of rhyme royal, suggest the use of this ancient stanza-form by Chaucer and the Chaucerians, by Spenser, in *The Ruines of Time* and the *Fowre Hymnes,* and by Shakespeare, in *Lucrece;* while the modification

into hexameter in the final line declares a further allegiance to
Spenser and the Spenserians. The stanza of the Hymn proper is
even more significant, for its first six lines suggest the movement
of a popular song or carol:

> It was the Winter wilde,
> While the Heav'n-born-childe,
> 　　All meanly wrapt in the rude manger lies;
> Nature in aw to him
> Had dofft her gawdy trim,
> 　　With her great Master so to sympathize.

The use of three-foot and five-foot lines, in various combinations,
is found in many Elizabethan songs: thus among Thomas Mor-
ley's canzonets we find this stanza running 335335335, though the
rhyme differs from Milton's:[37]

> 　I follow, lo, the footing
> 　Still of my lovely cruel,
> Proud of herself that she is beauty's jewel.
> 　And fast away she flieth,
> 　Love's sweet delight deriding,
> In woods and groves sweet Nature's treasure hiding.
> 　Yet cease I not pursuing,
> 　But since I thus have sought her,
> Will run me out of breath till I have caught her.

But the first six lines of Milton's stanza also suggest another pattern: the combination of two- and three-foot lines, with Milton's
rhyme scheme, found in some of the ancient Christmas carols:

> The God Almyght
> And Kyng of Lyght,
> 　Whose powr is ouer all,
> Gyue vs of grace
> For to purchas
> 　Hys realme celestyall.
>
> Wher hys aungels
> And archangels
> 　Do syng incessantly,
> Hys princypates
> And potestates
> 　Maketh gret armony.
>
> The cherubyns

And seraphyns
> With ther tvnykes mery,
The trones al,
Most musycall,
> Syng the heuenly Kery.[38]

Then, by allowing his last line to swell out into a Spenserian
alexandrine, Milton draws his poem out of the realm of the popular song into the larger area of this poet's predestined goals. In
stanza after stanza we may feel this change from the simple language and steady beat of the ballad into the realms of a more
ambitious art:

But wisest Fate sayes no,
This must not yet be so,
> The Babe lies yet in smiling Infancy,
That on the bitter cross
Must redeem our loss;
> So both himself and us to glorifie:
Yet first to those ychain'd in sleep,
The wakefull trump of doom must thunder through the deep.
[149–56]

With all the poem's lofty expansions in rhythm, in language,
and in rich allusion, the poet's chosen method of control never
falters: he clings to the central mode of the ancient naïve, the
mode of the Nativity ballad, the mode that Milton points to in his
prologue when he calls his poem a "humble ode" that he seeks to
lay "lowly at his blessed feet." The touches of archaic, Spenserian
language sprinkled throughout, very lightly, are all adjusted to
maintain this effect, as in the "ychain'd" of the stanza just quoted,
the "lusty Paramour" of the Hymn's opening stanza, the "silly
thoughts" of the shepherds, or the "dusky eyn" of the doomed
god Osiris. At the same time touches of old-fashioned heavy allit-
eration recall the style, not only of Spenser, but of all those lesser
writers whom Sidney mocked for their "rimes, running in ratling
rowes."

This decorum of an ancient and traditional simplicity pervades
every aspect of the poem, versification, language, scene painting,
imagery, and theme.[39] The scenes and images are given in broad
and simplified terms, as in some old tapestry or pageant. The

original line (143) in which Truth and Justice wear "Th'enameld
Arras of the Rainbow" is more closely in accord with the poem
than Milton's more sophisticated revision: "Orb'd in a Rain-bow."
Thus Nature seeks to hide her "guilty front" with "The Saintly
Vail of Maiden white"; and "the meek-eyd Peace . . . crown'd
with Olive green, came softly sliding / Down through the turning
sphear" (39,42,46–48). "The Shepherds on the Lawn . . . Sate
simply chatting in a rustick row"; then

> At last surrounds their sight
> A Globe of circular light,
>   That with long beams the shame-fac't night array'd,
> The helmed Cherubim
> And sworded Seraphim,
>   Are seen in glittering ranks with wings displaid.
>   [85,87,109–14]

One should note, too, in these quotations, the curious mixture
of past and present tense, which Lowry Nelson has ably interpreted to indicate the poem's sense of a timeless world;[40] this is so,
yet Milton's manner of thus mixing past and present also adds to
the effect of the naïve, as though the poet were artlessly following
the instinct of a momentary mood or were using past and present
tense as the needs of rhythm and rhyme might, for a moment,
require.

Then, in the latter half of the poem, this effect is strongly
heightened by Milton's treatment of the various characters that
here are shown in action. The Dragon of Revelation is presented
in the guise of a dragon out of folklore:

> And wrath to see his Kingdom fail,
> Swindges the scaly Horrour of his foulded tail.   [171–72]

And his antagonist, the blessed Babe, is likewise shown in the
manner of some ancient folk-hero, some infant Hercules:

> Our Babe to shew his Godhead true,
> Can in his swadling bands controul the damned crew.   [227–29]

Meanwhile, in the superb rendition of the fall of the pagan deities,
it is helpful, while we recognize the foreshadowing of *Paradise
Lost,* to notice also how utterly lacking in sophistication this ac-

count is, when compared with Milton's later roll call of the fallen
angels. In *Paradise Lost* it is made plain that these are devils adored
as deities, and the horror of the deception is brought home by
showing in detail the effect of these devils upon mankind:

> First *Moloch,* horrid King besmear'd with blood
> Of human sacrifice, and parents tears,
> Though for the noyse of Drums and Timbrels loud
> Their childrens cries unheard, that past through fire
> To his grim Idol. Him the *Ammonite*
> Worshipt in *Rabba* and her watry Plain . . .   [1.392–97]

and so on for eight more lines of particular detail, showing the
ravages wrought by Moloch on the earth.

But here in the Nativity poem Moloch is simply mentioned as a
totally defeated character, while the scene of his idolatry is represented in elementary colors and sounds:

> And sullen *Moloch* fled,
> Hath left in shadows dred,
>   His burning Idol all of blackest hue,
> In vain with Cymbals ring,
> They call the grisly king,
>   In dismall dance about the furnace blue.   [205–10]

These vanquished gods are not devils in disguise; they are the
supernatural beings of antique folklore, who exist in their own
right as a part of nature, a part of man's primitive consciousness
of forces that lie beyond his control:

> The lonely mountains o're,
> And the resounding shore,
>   A voice of weeping heard, and loud lament;
> From haunted spring, and dale
> Edg'd with poplar pale,
>   The parting Genius is with sighing sent,
> With flowre-inwov'n tresses torn
> The Nimphs in twilight shade of tangled thickets mourn.
>   [181–88]

Finally, bringing to a brilliant close this basic effect of the simple
and naïve, Milton ends with two stanzas that sum up the basic
techniques and attitudes of the poem. First we have the poem's
most extravagantly naïve image—one that would have offended at

the outset—but, now, with our minds attuned to the poem's peculiar decorum, we can perhaps accept it as a youthful excess:

> So when the Sun in bed,
> Curtain'd with cloudy red,
>   Pillows his chin upon an Orient wave . . .   [229–31]

Then come the ghosts and fairies of folklore, treated with sympathy and even affection:

> The flocking shadows pale,
> Troop to th'infernall jail,
>   Each fetter'd Ghost slips to his severall grave,
> And the yellow-skirted *Fayes,*
> Fly after the Night-steeds, leaving their Moon-lov'd maze.
>   [232–36]

And lastly, we return to the traditional scene, ten thousand times
represented in ancient poetry and painting: the manger scene
upon which this technique of the naïve has been based:

> But see the Virgin blest,
> Hath laid her Babe to rest.
>   Time is our tedious Song should here have ending.

Here, still, is the simple, humble singer, who is well aware of his
defects, but nevertheless has been led by gratitude to sing this
song of praise:

> Heav'ns youngest teemed Star,
> Hath fixt her polisht Car,
>   Her sleeping Lord with Handmaid Lamp attending:

All Heaven, whether physical or spiritual, stands fixed in a service
of unlabored elegance:

> And all about the Courtly Stable,
> Bright-harnest Angels sit in order serviceable.

The last rhyme seems to call attention to the way in which
Milton has contrived, within his chosen mode, to make even the
poem's defects appear as virtues, contributing to the total effect of
the youthful singer writing as well as he can in an ancient, traditional manner of tribute. The poem is a total success because
Milton has chosen and maintained a mode of writing that does not
tempt him beyond the range of his precocious powers.

That is not to say that the poem is simple-minded in the range of its implications, but that the chosen mode of simplicity creates a world in which theological problems are pushed beyond the fringe of our vision; there is no sense of struggling with theological issues, no sense that we need to consult the church fathers, no sense of attempting to enforce anything but the most easily grasped and broadly acceptable truths. This, says the poet, is the happy morn when, as everyone knows,

> the Son of Heav'ns eternal King,
> Of wedded Maid, and Virgin Mother born,
> Our great redemption from above did bring.   [2–4]

Everyone shares the story, how the Son laid aside the majesty that was his due as part of Trinal Unity,

> and here with us to be,
> Forsook the Courts of everlasting Day,
> And chose with us a darksom House of mortal Clay.   [12–14]

How can we express our gratitude for this gift of the Almighty? By a song of praise for the peace and harmony that the divine child has brought to earth, not only on the day of his birth, and in the long-range future, but, in some measure, now: it "now begins," as this poet can best testify by writing a song that in itself represents a simple and unworried harmony.

But—"Compos'd 1629." More difficult and much more complex harmonies lie ahead for the rising poet, the predestined bard.

marks. "Shakespeare" in quote marks is Shakespeare called into question, made to denote a set of shifting cultural functions rather than a known literary figure with an established historical identity. It is curious how little of this vast interplay of poststructuralist energies has been brought to bear on the equally interesting subject of Milton. There have been exceptions, of course, but to a significant degree, Milton in 1990 remains Milton without the deauthorizing bracket of quotation marks, an identifiable historical figure seen against a landscape of significant historical developments in England, but never allowed to "die" in proper poststructuralist fashion, never allowed to meld into his or our own climate of ideas to the point that he loses his identity and becomes a set of cultural operations in the manner of "Shakespeare."

To say that Milton, in late twentieth-century critical discourse, has not been turned into a set of cultural functions is not to suggest that "Milton"—and here you must imagine that I have given him the dreaded quotation marks—fails to perform an important set of functions. Rather, I would like to argue, in the critical community today the name of Milton works to guarantee the continuation of a certain pervasive style of literary subjecthood that he himself may be credited with having invented and that we as Miltonists are reluctant to move out of. If Milton refuses to disappear under the rubric of history, or of deconstruction, or of the postmodernist "death of the author," that is because "Milton"_to_us means—quite precisely—resistance to all such decentering impulses. He, as much as any other single historical figure of the English Renaissance, may be credited with having inaugurated a new way of situating the author within literary history, or rather, of asserting the author's resistance to or transcendence of historical contingency by incorporating history within his conception of individual authorship.

In suggesting that Milton was at the defining forefront of new notions of literary authorship and literary history I am, of course, doing something that Miltonists love to do and that we seem to find reassuring on some very basic level. We

Milton as Historical Subject
Milton Banquet Address
Chicago, 1990

Leah Marcus

During the last ten years, Shakespeare has become the interpretive center for a vast interplay of poststructuralist methodologies. He has been deconstructed, decentered, unauthored, deauthorized, new-historicized, culturally materialized, his very name as often as not put in quotation love to think of Milton as a great originator, and he seems to have liked to imagine himself that way. We love to think of Milton also as a great repository, encompassing all the knowledge of his day. The first time I taught Milton at the graduate level, I confidently assured my students that Milton could read Sanskrit. How could Milton not read Sanskrit? He could read just about every other known language. The next class period, I had to go back in chagrin and tell my students that the first Sanskrit scholars in England appeared only in the eighteenth century and that no, Milton could not read Sanskrit. But, we are likely to assert by way of damage control, he would have learned it with alacrity had the texts been made available to him, just as (I am convinced) he may well have learned Anglo Saxon in order to read Junius's *Genesis B.*

If we are to locate a specific point at which Milton may be said to have inaugurated the new view of literary subjecthood for which I am giving him credit, that point is his 1645 *Poems of Mr. John Milton, Both English and Latin, Compos'd at several times* and printed, the title page tells us, *"by his true Copies."* As Louis Martz has argued in his essay "The Rising Poet," Milton's volume of poems, with its many Virgilian echoes and its scrupulous attention to genre, asks us to view his achievement in terms of the development of his powers as a poet: "Milton's original arrangement creates the growing awareness of a guiding, central purpose that in turn gives the volume an impressive and peculiar sense of wholeness" (31). One of the things the volume does that I, at least, have not seen in earlier volumes of poetry in England, is to identify many of the poems in terms of the author's personal artistic development. The title page itself suggests attention to the "several times" at which the poems were "compos'd." For many of them, Milton supplies his age at the time of composition (though he appears to have erred on the side of precocity in some of his datings). The poems are ordered for the most part chronologically, so that we can follow his development as a poet. Milton asserts on the title page of the Latin poems that they were written *"Annum aetatis Vigesimum,"* before the

end of his twentieth year. He even includes botched attempts, as a way of calling attention to the growth of his poetic powers. "On the Passion," as we all know, is printed in the 1645 volume (and in modern editions) incomplete, with the author's explanation, *"This Subject the Author finding to be above the yeers he had, when he wrote it, and nothing satisfi'd with what was begun, left it unfinisht."* To us, with our post-Romantic inheritance of critical attention to the "growth of the poet's mind," Milton's authorial interventions in the 1645 volume may appear rather unremarkable: one of the achievements of the nineteenth century was to look at literary authorship in developmental terms, to chart the biographical emergence and transformations of genius for all canonical writers, not only for Milton. I suspect, however, that Milton's tactic looked much newer, perhaps even strange, to his contemporaries. His authorial interventions are quite unprecedented in an English volume of poems; at least I have never seen anything earlier approximating Milton's, although Janell Mueller has suggested to me that George Gascoigne can be considered a partial precursor. Earlier authors had arranged their work in a way that marked a pattern of poetic development in general rather than individual terms, according to the Virgilian *rotula,* for example, but none had so overtly inserted his own voice in the text as a commentary on what he had achieved (and even the age at which he had achieved it). By comparison with Milton, the *Workes* of Ben Jonson is quite reticent—Jonson offered dates for some of his works and placed them in an order that might suggest poetic development and generic significance—his "Epigrams" suggest a biographical trajectory, but one offered only silently through the poems themselves. Other near-contemporary volumes, like Milton's, celebrate the poetic precocity of the author. Thomas Randolph's poems were published after his untimely death in 1630 at the age of twenty-nine or thirty. The title-page portrait to the second edition shows him as a mere youth—much younger than his age at the time of his death, given as twenty-seven on the title page. One of the dedicatory epistles asserts,

He lisp'd Wit worthy th'Presse, as if that he
Had us'd his Cradle as a Librarie.
Some of these Fruits had birth, when other
Boyes
(His elders) play'd with Nuts; Books were his
Toyes.

(sig. B3ʳ)

But Randolph's poems are not otherwise dated
or arranged in any discernible order of personal
and poetic development: the whole point of the
commemorative volume is the author's *absence*
through death. Abraham Cowley was another
poetic boy wonder; his works were published a
little after Milton's by the same Humphrey Moseley who published Milton. Cowley's volume also
lacks the interweaving of biographical and poetic
development that is such a striking feature of
Milton's 1645 *Poems*.

But, a proper poststructuralist or even a careful student of seventeenth-century print culture
might want to ask, what gives us the right to say
that it is *Milton* talking through the volume's many
references to the poet's age and capacities? Such
information, even though it presumably derived
from Milton's own data, could have been affixed
by the publisher Humphrey Moseley, whose ad-
miring preface "to the Reader" asserts that he
himself had solicited Milton's poems for publication and that he regarded Milton to be "*as true a
Birth as the Muses have brought forth since our famous* Spencer *wrote.*" Or—a much less likely but not
inconceivable possibility—it could have been added by the printer Ruth Raworth, who was, interestingly enough, a woman. But the main reason
we identify the biographical commentary so readily with the voice of the author is, I would suggest, that the voice has been firmly established by
the frontispiece, with its puzzling portrait of the
author, its depiction of distant shepherds, and its
sardonic Greek inscription.

The frontispiece to Milton's 1645 *Poems* has
long intrigued readers because of its contradictory messages. The oval frame around the central
portrait asserts Milton's age in the "effigy" to be
twenty-one or in the twenty-first year. Yet the effigy itself depicts a man who looks much older—

perhaps forty or fifty. The figure in the oval is
slightly turned toward the window, as though he
has been observing the shepherds sporting without. They too are within the oval: might it be
they, not the larger and more aged figure, who
depict the author aged twenty-one? As more than
one reader has noted, the frontispiece can be
glossed by reference to the final lines of Milton's
Lycidas, which is printed next to last in the English half of the volume. In the final verse paragraph of the poem, the "uncouth" shepherd who
has been singing up to that point is suddenly
viewed from a distance, his voice replaced by a
seemingly older and wiser voice who narrates the
youth's departure as something that has already
happened:

Thus sang the uncouth Swain to th'Oaks
and rills,
While the still morn went out with Sandals
gray;
He touch't the tender stops of various Quills,
With eager thought warbling his *Doric* lay:
And now the Sun had stretch't out all the hills,
And now was dropt into the Western bay;
At last he rose, and twitch't his Mantle blue:
Tomorrow to fresh Woods, and Pastures new.
(*Complete Poems* 186–93)

In the same way, the central figure in the frontispiece seems to gesture toward the distant shepherds as toward an earlier, and now superseded,
version of himself—a self, perhaps, that had parti-
cipated in a prewar "Politics of Mirth" with
which seventeenth-century pastoral was closely associated, but which an older and wiser poet now
found himself obliged to repudiate (Marcus,
Politics 169–212).

But that reading of the frontispiece is still too
simple. Lest we be tempted to identify the more
elderly figure with Milton in the present (1645)
as opposed to a pastoral "Swain" from the past,
the Greek verses beneath assure us that the portrait is no such thing:

That an unskilful hand had carved this print
You'd say at once, seeing the living face;
But, finding here no jot of me, my friends,

Laugh at the botching artist's mis-attempt.
(Masson trans. 3:459)

Traditionally, these lines have been interpreted as a malicious jibe at William Marshall, who meticulously carved out the Greek letters with (we are asked to suppose) not the least knowledge of Greek or curiosity about what the lines might mean. We are invited to recognize the "real" Milton here, in these verses, through language rather than picture. By these lines, Milton is establishing a "fit audience though few"—those readers learned_enough to comprehend the Greek are treated. with intimate familiarity. They are "my friends," *filoi*; they are invited, implicitly, to form a kind of learned coterie in recognition of Milton—to compare the engraved face with his real, living face, and to laugh along with Milton at the engraver's incompetence.

English engravers were indeed, by and large, less than skillful, at least if one compares them, as Milton surely did, with their more expert counterparts on the Continent. I wonder, though, whether William Marshall was either so incompetent or so ignorant a gull as Milton's verses imply. Other portrait frontispieces by him (like that of Donne in the 1635 *Poems* or Robert Herrick in his *Hesperides*) display considerable skill. Readings of the frontispiece to Milton's 1645 *Poems* assume that Milton's joke was on Marshall: the engraver was doomed, not knowing it, to carve out his own condemnation by fashioning the inscription. I would suggest, instead, that Marshall may well have been in on the joke, and that Milton's frontispiece needs to be read in terms of a long line of earlier English examples that all assert, through one device or another, the inadequacy of the visual by comparison with the verbal as a means for communicating the author's mind and being. The title page and frontispiece to the Shakespeare First Folio provide an excellent example which I have analyzed at some length in *Puzzling Shakespeare*: the strikingly large picture of Shakespeare seems to intimate the author's presence; the verses opposite assert otherwise. A "true" portrait of Shakespeare and his "wit" is to be found in his writing, not his

effigy: "Reader, looke, / Not on his Picture, but his Book." There are many other examples. Du Bartas's *Devine Weekes and Workes*, as Georgianna Zeigler has been kind enough to point out to me, similarly offers a portrait, but cautions the reader that Du Bartas has "limned" himself much more successfully with the pen through his writings within. Similarly, an engraving of Jonson from the 1620s declares, "O could there be an art found out that might / Produce his shape soe lively as to Write" (reproduced in Riggs 281). Lancelot Andrewes's posthumous volume of sermons shows Andrewes gesturing away from himself and toward a volume in his hand; the accompanying verses urge the reader not to dwell on the portrait, but to proceed immediately to the pages of divinity that follow. Marshall's frontispiece for Donne in the 1635 *Poems* carries a similar message: the portrait from Donne's youth is an altogether inadequate image of his "last, best Dayes" as a writer of divine poems. In the same vein, the title page of Randolph's poems depicts the engraved image of a young boy who looks about fourteen (the precocious Randolph who penned verses while his fellows were playing with nuts and apples) yet the inscription places the poet's age at the time of his death as twenty-seven. Here again, the art is not to be trusted. The lot of an English engraver was not a happy one. Insofar as such craftsmen undertook frontispieces and title-page portraits, they were laboring in a craft fated to be undermined within the volume itself in favor of the superior portraiture of language.

Milton's title page needs to be imagined as part of the same somewhat playful tradition. The frontispiece offers two or more "false" portraits of the author—the effigy which is too old and unlike, the shepherds outside the window who are too distant and too generalized to be Milton. The "real" Milton peers out at us only through the Greek of the inscription. Once again, words win out against the visual as a true portrait of the author. I can imagine that Marshall himself might have been in on the joke, at least to the extent that he collaborated knowingly in his own preempting when he carved out the inscription. As a side note, I might mention that later engravers sought to rectify "botching" Marshall's "mis-attempt." Of the four copies of the 1645 *Poems* at the University of Texas, two have the original frontispiece. The other two have frontispieces af-fixed later—probably around 1700. One of these later renderings of Marshall shows Milton's face with some of the lines smoothed out; the other, in addition, depicts him almost smiling. But Marshall's 1645 frontispiece establishes a true or trustworthy authorial voice—one both engagingly intimate and self-referential—from among com-peting images of the poet. The rhetoric of Mil-ton's frontispiece is thus altogether different from that of the First Folio or Du Bartas or Jon-son or Andrewes, all of which defer the reader's sense of authorial presence from the portrait to the pages of text beyond. Milton's frontispiece instead offers his learned readers a voice which is clearly established as his own before the poetry is even encountered, and which seems to extend through the volume offering explanation and judgment of the author's youthful verses in the same way that it offers judgment and explanation of the inadequate engraving on the frontispiece. The reader is enticed into a continuous measur-ing of Milton's past poetic powers against those of a nearer present, into the construction of an individual history of the poet's progress. In terms of the frontispiece's "botching" portrait of Mil-ton, however, I am tempted to think that Mar-shall got the last laugh: his image may look little enough like the Milton of 1645, but it is striking-ly like the portraits of Milton in his sixties en-graved by Faithorne and Dolle! Either the later engravers copied the 1645 image, or Milton in his sixties looked very much as Marshall had "aged" him earlier on. Was Marshall incompe-tent enough to fail to capture Milton's youthful visage, or prescient enough to recognize through facial structure the visage that Milton would later become?

However we may wish to answer these ques-tions, we need to recognize what a startling inno-vation the 1645 *Poems* was. At a time when many people did not even know their own age, Milton (or his "voice") meticulously provides his age at the time of many of the poems' composition. At a time when literary authorship was coming to imply a careful crafting and finishing of materials for the press, Milton supplies a poem ("The Pas-sion") that is fragmentary and self-confessedly bad: his interest in charting his own development wins out over the more usual authorial desire to place only completed, successful works in print. By arranging his own poems in developmental order, by calling repeated attention, through both the frontispiece and the comments inter-spersed in the volume, to his own poetic achieve-ment as a kind of *history*, Milton invented for England literary subjecthood as we have tradi-tionally been taught to understand it. The author is a category larger than history in that history, in the form of biography, is brought within the compass of the individual life. What the volume accomplishes is something so ordinary and recog-nizable to us that we are likely to think nothing of it, but as I have already suggested, in Milton's age it was strikingly new: the invention of an indi-vidual literary life.

The life we are offered through the 1645 vol-ume was, of course, a construct: readers of the verses are invited to forget that its author had been publicly vilified during the years immedi-ately preceding for his diatribes on the subject of divorce. A year after the publication of the 1645 *Poems* Thomas Edwards offered a rather different public image of Milton by inscribing him among the monstrous heretics and grotesques of *Gan-graena; or, a Catalogue and Discovery of Many of the Errours, Heresies, Blasphemies, and Pernicious Prac-tices of the Sectaries of This Time, Vented and Acted in England in These Four Last Years.* It is not this history that Milton calls attention to in the poems, but a personal history of artistic develop-ment that effectively closes out the cacophonies of the world at large as they impinge on his per-sonal history.

Why am I insisting so repeatedly on Milton's unusual achievement in the 1645 *Poems*? I am tak-ing a highly traditionalist tack—Milton as grand originator—but with something less than tradi-tional in mind. Let us go back to my initial point about Milton's apparent "immunity" to recent critical heterodoxies of various kinds. I would contend that if Milton appears immune to recent critical methodologies, it is in large part because of the power of his own encoding of his life as literary history. The 1645 *Poems* may be said to have inaugurated a mode of self-representation that was to become further articulated in subsequent years and subsequent literary production. As the editors of the *OED* have noted, Milton provides the first usage of several meanings for the word "individual" and its derivatives. Sometimes he used the word in its traditional sense of "indivisible," but he also inaugurated usages that emphasized the self-sameness of a discrete unit and its separateness from others. He documented his literary life by hanging on to early versions of many of his works; he saved his poems in manuscript versions that allow us to do something we can rarely do for writers before him, but can commonly do for writers who came after. We can follow the process of the poem's development from first to later and more refined versions. As David Loewenstein and James Turner have noted, in his pamphlet wars, Milton habitually aestheticizes his own history: not only does he offer himself as a "true poem" (as Jonson might have earlier) but he imagines that individual "poem" to be forged out of the crucible of contemporary events. That is not to say that Milton failed to see himself as subject to contemporary history—only that he was constantly in the process of constructing a literary vision of his own individual life that transcended contemporary history "as ever in my great task-Master's eye." Milton's ongoing "autobiographical literary history" is by no means static, but constantly in a process of stalemate, challenge, and reintegration. In fact, its vulnerability is part of its appeal. The poet's life is constructed out of anguish, out of triumph over despair.

I do not think there is anyone calling him- or herself a Miltonist who is impervious to the nobility and pathos of Milton's literary history as it has come down to us through his writings. Part of the reason that poststructuralist approaches in general, and alternative historicizations of Milton in particular, are threatening to Miltonists is that

they appear to assault the "portrait of the artist" that Milton himself constructed so authoritatively and at such personal cost. To erase Milton's own self-authorship and sense of personal development, to deny his own version of his history in favor of some other alien to him, perhaps alien to his time—that seems a much greater violation in the case of Milton than in the case of someone like Shakespeare, who had no personal "literary history" to speak of before the compilers of the First Folio began to create it for him.

But what is being violated by the new -isms that some Miltonists find so threatening to the continuing health of Milton studies? Surely not Milton himself. He has been dead for several hundred years now; however sensitive he may have been to his reputation as an author while he was alive, he is blessedly impervious to such assaults in the grave, particularly if we accept his own favored doctrine of mortalism. No, the Milton who is being defended against the various threatening -isms of late twentieth-century interpretive practice is "Milton" in quotation marks—a function rather than a man, but imagined by the collectivity of Miltonists almost as if he were still a sentient being, a being kept alive by our continuing interest in him, by our continuing fidelity to his own project of literary self-definition, and not least, by our personal identification with him. Stanley Fish has recently suggested that Milton criticism is essentially over—it has all already happened in earlier forms. All that we can do, according to this highly conservative scenario, is reenact versions of past literary history: to destabilize hierarchy in *Paradise Lost* is to repeat Blake and Shelley, to deconstruct Milton is to rediscover Milton's own undermining of traditional generic categories, to intertextualize Milton is to rediscover the "multiple voices and traditions" inscribed within the text by the "editorial apparatus of the great eighteenth-century editions," and so on (Fish; see also Fish in Loewenstein and Turner 68n27). Milton, in this version, is always his own supplement, always already outside supplementarity. No doubt there have been recurring patterns of interpretive activity within Milton criticism, just as there have been in the history of

Shakespeare criticism, or any other. In fact, the notion that Milton's "literary history" is already complete is very similar to the sense of ennui and *déjà vu* that overtook Shakespeare criticism in the sixties and seventies—just before the new methodologies began to dismantle previous collective academic visions of what constituted Shakespeare. Fish's contention that the new -isms can only repeat earlier literary history is an interesting encoding of the profoundly Miltonic ideal that one can write one's own literary history—subsequent writings will merely elaborate and extend the author's own project. Insofar as we remain within that undoubtedly fecund yet limited perspective, we will remain within Milton's literary history, in fact within a peculiarly insular version of it, since Milton's own view of his history was more developmental than cyclical.

To get outside Milton in order to rediscover Milton, as some of us would like to, we need to find other histories with which to analyze and confront Milton's own. We need to separate Milton from "Milton" and try to piece out the extent to which our energies are bound up in the latter under the name of the former. To get outside Milton's own powerful self-voicing is not necessarily to silence him or disempower him, though it may have a profound effect on "Milton" and may to some degree disempower certain groups within the community of Miltonists. Fish's caveats notwithstanding, I doubt whether any of us has the power to keep Milton static, to keep Milton from changing in ways we can only begin to imagine. The idea is disquieting, but also rather liberating. Those of us who call ourselves (or get branded as) poststructuralists or cultural materialists or feminists or new historicists or practitioners of some -ism other than critical traditionalism find ourselves in the position of the engraver Marshall vis à vis the irate extensions of authorial voice that mock our botched attempts. I have suggested, in Marshall's defense, that what he saw when he created his oddly aged figure of Milton was an uncanny prefiguring of Milton's actual visage when he reached his sixties. Marshall's image was one that the author strongly repudiated, yet later came to

resemble. Perhaps the same can be said of the various -isms that seem to threaten Milton studies today: they offer a new set of "Milton" functions that some among the present community of Miltonists find uncouth, oddly unsatisfying; they offer a set of functions that may, in time, come to signify Milton.

University of Texas-Austin

WORKS CITED

Andrewes, Lancelot. *XCVI Sermons*. 3rd ed. London, 1635.

Cowley, Abraham. *The Mistresse; or, Severall Copies of Love-Verses*. London: Humphrey Moseley, 1647.

Donne, John. *Poems*. London: John Marriot, 1635.

Du Bartas, Guillaume de Saluste. *Devine Weekes and Workes*. Trans. J. Sylvester. 3rd ed. London, 1611.

Edwards, Thomas. *Gangraena; or, a Catalogue and Discovery of Many of the Errours, Heresies, Blasphemies, and Pernicious Practices of the Sectaries of This Time, Vented and Acted in England in These Four Last Years*. London, 1646.

Fish, Stanley. "Milton's Career and the Career of Theory." Modern Language Association Convention. New Orleans, 1988.

Herrick, Robert. *Hesperides; or, The Works Both Humane and Divine*. London, 1648.

Jonson, Ben. *Workes*. London, 1616.

Loewenstein, David. *Milton and the Drama of History: Historical Vision, Iconoclasm, and the Literary Imagination*. Cambridge: Cambridge UP, 1990.

Loewenstein, David, and James Grantham Turner, eds. *Politics, Poetics, and Hermeneutics in Milton's Prose*. Cambridge: Cambridge UP, 1990.

Marcus, Leah. *The Politics of Mirth: Jonson, Herrick, Milton, Marvell, and the Defense of Old Holiday Pastimes*. Chicago, IL: U of Chicago P, 1986.

——. *Puzzling Shakespeare: Local Reading and Its Discontents*. Berkeley: U of California P, 1988.

Martz, Louis. "The Rising Poet." *Poet of Exile: A Study of Milton's Poetry*. New Haven, CT: Yale UP, 1980. 31–59.

Masson, David. *The Life of John Milton*. 7 vols. Gloucester, MA: Peter Smith, 1965.

Milton, John. *Poems Both English and Latin, Compos'd at Several Times*. London: Humphrey Moseley, 1645.

——. *Complete Poems and Major Prose*. Ed. Merritt Y. Hughes. Indianapolis, IN: Odyssey, 1957.

Randolph, Thomas. *Poems*. 2nd ed. Oxford: Francis Bowman, 1640.

Riggs, David. *Ben Jonson: A Life*. Cambridge, MA: Harvard UP, 1989.

Shakespeare, William. *The First Folio*. Prepared by Charlton Hinman. New York: Norton, 1968.

THE WRITING POET:
THE DESCENT FROM SONG IN
THE POEMS OF MR. JOHN MILTON,
BOTH ENGLISH AND LATIN (1645)

Randall Ingram

T HE RECENT DEVELOPMENT of media that provide alternates
to print have focused new attention on "the book." Jerome J. McGann,
for instance, calls for more bibliographically sensitive reading, especially of
poetry: "We must turn our attention to much more than the formal and
linguistic features of poems or other imaginative fictions. We must attend to
textual materials which are not regularly studied by those interested in
'poetry': to typefaces, bindings, book prices, page format, and all those textual phenomena usually regarded as (at best) peripheral to 'poetry' or 'the
text as such.' " By juxtaposing bibliographic data and "formal and linguistic
features," McGann implies a contrast between a formalist approach to
poetry and bibliographically informed reading. Of course, Milton's critics
have long read his books *as* books, and the critical histories of Milton's books
indicate that careful attention to McGann's "bibliographic codes" often extends rather than disrupts formalism; the book can replace the poem as a
self-contained object of close reading. For example, in his important reading
of *The Poems of Mr. John Milton, Both English and Latin* (1645), a reading
of both linguistic and bibliographic features that preceded McGann's admonition by more than twenty-five years, Louis L. Martz attempts to establish
the coherence of *Poems,* arguing that "Milton's original arrangement creates
the growing awareness of a guiding, central purpose that in turn gives the
volume an impressive and peculiar sense of wholeness. In order to regain
the significant integrity of the volume one must, now and then, go back to
the original." Martz's reading represents an expansion of formalism, an analysis of "wholeness" and "integrity" in an entire book rather than in a single
poem.[1]

But such an approach to seventeenth-century books imports the assumptions of late print into the study of early printed texts by objectifying
books that were, for their authors, publishers, and readers, far less stable
and far less sure of their format than later books. Early modern books often

contain, as Walter J. Ong and Eric Havelock have chronicled, vestiges of orality that were erased, imperfectly, in later books, and this orality continually challenges readings of individual poems or entire books as fixed, spatial objects. Ong states that "oral habits of thought and expression" remained "in Tudor England some two thousand years after Plato's campaign against oral poets. They were effectively obliterated in English, for the most part, only with the Romantic Movement two centuries later." Ong argues that poetry continues even longer to imply "a feeling that one writing is actually speaking aloud." Although critical discussion of the "speakers" of poems recognizes the remnants of orality lingering even in the most recent poetry, the transition that Ong describes can be traced in such forms as the sonnet, which shifts from the "little songs" of quattrocento Italy to the "pretty rooms" of the English Renaissance, the spatial metaphor befitting the transmission of sonnets in manuscript and print. Milton's *Poems* represents this transition in miniature, as one poet, gradually and grudgingly, comes to accept the less powerful modes of writing and print.[2]

Usually, however, Milton's *Poems*, a book with "an impressive and peculiar sense of wholeness," is said to represent a different transition. The overwhelming majority of critics who discuss Milton's first book of poetry agree that it presents a "rising poet" to an international audience. The image of the "rising poet," which Martz uses for the title of his essay on *Poems*, occurs in the source of the book's famous motto: "Baccare frontem / Cingite, ne vati noceat mala lingua futuro" ("Encircle my brow with fragrant plants so that no evil tongue may harm the future bard") (Virgil, Eclog. 7).[3] Critics regularly cite the motto's emphasis on futurity and its Virgilian source, reading the motto, and the book itself, as a promise of the epic greatness to come. For critics like Richard Halpern, the volume of 1645, coherent in itself, is also part of a "coherent poetic *career*":

As the sonnets on his blindness (for instance) suggest, Milton tends to view himself from the projected point of a later reckoning. Almost all of the early poems insist on their place within a developing order, gesturing obscurely toward the accomplishment of some greater work or task. . . . The 1645 *Poems* opens with an epigraph in which Milton declares himself a "future bard," and thus at a stroke converts the entire contents of the volume into elements in a scheme of self-preparation.

For Halpern, the motto not only signifies the single-mindedness of the book, it is a "stroke" that "converts the entire contents" into a unified presentation of a poetic career. Even when they attempt to read the motto without retrospective recourse to the later works—"to understand Milton's actions of 1645," John K. Hale warns, "we had better play down our hindsight knowledge of 1667"—critics generally invoke the motto to attribute an ambitious integrity to *Poems*.[4]

But what about the poet's vulnerability to an "evil tongue"? Though Martz quotes more fully from the eclogue, claiming that "the whole context is essential," he does so only to point out how neatly the motto anticipates the Virgilian themes of *Poems* and how it typifies the unity of the volume.[5] And yet the anxiety of the motto seems undeniable. The wreath here does not clearly denote the poetic triumph or supreme confidence of a rising poet; it is instead the talismanic safeguard of a nervous poet. The motto's imperative, *cingite*, asks for protection within an emblematic embrace. Only a readership biased by Milton's persistent popular image as a serenely self-assured titan could discuss the words *vati* and *futuro* at such length while overlooking the motto's main verbs: "Encircle so that I will not be harmed." The quotation from Virgil's seventh eclogue provides a fitting motto for *Poems,* not because both motto and book display a careerist integrity, but because the fearful image of an "evil tongue" anticipates the potency that characterizes oral utterance in the volume and the published poet's uneasy awareness of his medium's relative weakness. *Poems* complicates Milton's poetic annunciation because, especially in the English poems, it continually raises doubts about its format. This book questions books, distrusting the capacity of writing and print to capture what *At a Solemn Music* calls "divine sounds."

I. "DELIBERATE SABOTAGE"

A reader who opens Milton's *Poems* of 1645 will see, before its title page or the publisher's letter to the reader, its frontispiece, one of the most frequently discussed bibliographic details of the seventeenth century. The frontispiece features an engraving of Milton in academic robes, sitting before a window. Below the engraving is a quatrain in Greek, traditionally attributed to Milton, that invites readers to laugh at the engraver's ineptitude. David Masson's translation of the quatrain reads:

> That an unskilful hand had carved this print
> You'd say at once, seeing the living face;
> But, finding here no jot of me, my friends,
> Laugh at this botching artist's mis-attempt.

Martz describes the engraving in detail and links the frontispiece to the "theme" of "the entire volume":

The entire volume strives to create a tribute to a youthful era now past—not only the poet's own youth, but a state of mind, a point of view, ways of writing, ways of living, an old culture and outlook now shattered by the pressures of maturity and by the actions of political man. Even the frontispiece, by William Marshall, attempts to set this theme. The aim of the engraving is clearly to present the youthful poet surrounded by the Muses, with a curtain in the background lifted to reveal a pastoral landscape of meadows and trees, where a shepherd is piping in the shade, while a shepherd and a shepherdess are dancing on the lawn. The legend around the portrait identifies it as a picture of the poet in his twenty-first year—but in fact the portrait presents the harsh and crabbed image of a man who might be forty or fifty! Marshall could do better than this, as his engraving of the youthful Donne testifies; one almost suspects deliberate sabotage here.

Part of Marshall's engraving fits Martz's reading of the entire volume (the signs of nostalgic pastoral), and part does not (the "harsh and crabbed image" of the poet), leading him—or one—almost to suppose that Marshall intended to undermine the poetic authority that the volume ostensibly claims for Milton. Martz's baffled disappointment ("Marshall could do better than this") shows his discomfort with a frontispiece that mocks the poet, the engraver, and frontispieces in general. Since he cannot reconcile Marshall's engraving with his understanding of Milton's aims in *Poems,* Martz characterizes the engraving as an attempt to subvert those aims.[6]

Gary Spear also explores the tensions between the engraving and the quatrain, which figure, on a small scale, the struggle between early modern authors and countless other agents. Spear's reading parallels the work of critics like Paul Werstine who have begun to emphasize the contributions of "multiple and dispersed agencies" to Renaissance dramatic texts. Spear accordingly considers the frontispiece "a textual place where the materiality of authority and authorial identity appear as the *effects of the material circumstances* of textual production." Spear disagrees with Martz's reading of the frontispiece, making the important point that Martz attributes too much authorial autonomy to Milton: "Martz's formalist imperative compels him to see all of the features of the text including the frontispiece as a related, coherent, whole. Underlying this is the figure of Milton the author as completely autonomous: 'Milton designed his book with care.' " According to Spear, Milton attempts to prescribe the reading of a page not usually within the control of an early modern author—"The Greek epigram registers Milton's attempt to assert his own identity in this arena of authorial creation"— and Spear concludes that in early seventeenth-century England, "public identity was not always within the author's control."[7]

A belief that Milton sought to present a consistent, stable poetic identity in *Poems* informs both Martz's and Spear's readings of the frontispiece. Both assume that Milton wrote the quatrain to wrest depiction of himself from Marshall and that, as Spear puts it, "Since apparently neither Moseley [publisher of *Poems*] nor Marshall could translate it, Marshall ended up copying the character of the epigram without realizing the critical thrust of the message." Both Martz and Spear divide elements of the frontispiece between contending authors, presuming that Milton must have wanted a more accurate or flattering representation of himself and that Marshall, more craftsman than artist, must have transcribed without understanding a self-indictment in Greek. But the frontispiece does in a page what the volume does in full: it destabilizes the authority of *Poems* by undercutting the nascent conventions of print, in this case the engravings of authors that had become a conventional feature of printed literary works. Spear argues that the opening pages of the book "deconstruct the very poetic authority that it is their explicit purpose to represent," but such an argument assumes that Milton, like Jonson before him, "constructed" his authority by manipulating the semiotics of early printed books, when in fact *Poems* portrays print itself as an enormous obstacle to his authority. The compatibility of the frontispiece with the book that follows suggests that a collaborative model of authorship might better describe the engraving and the quatrain of the frontispiece: Milton, Moseley, and Marshall created a book that deliberately sabotages any reading of it as a hypostatized representation of a poet's power.[8]

The pattern established by the engraving and the quatrain of the frontispiece, a pattern of claiming the authority associated with printed books for the *Poems* then disavowing it, recurs on the next page of the book, the title page. A number of the page's features assert the book's legitimacy: it identifies an author, makes the standard claim that the poems have been "Printed by his true Copies," and states the book's compliance with prevailing laws that regulated publication, "Printed and publish'd according to ORDER," the upper-case letters of the final word reinforcing the assurance that all is in ORDER. Other features dispute the book's authority, particularly the advertisement at the center of the page:

The SONGS were set in Musick by
Mr. HENRY LAWES Gentleman of
the KINGS Chappel, and one
of His MAIESTIES
Private Musick.

Some critics, including Martz, have expressed surprise that this bit of marketing on the title page of Milton's first book of poems uses associations, however tertiary, with royalty to tantalize potential buyers.[9] More surprising, though, is that these words, set in the heart of the page that should proclaim the book's accurate representation of the poet's art, acknowledge that the "SONGS" of the volume were "set in Musick" before they were set in print, indicating that a musician can offer an alternative, if not a better, representation of the "SONGS." Like the frontispiece, which points away from the conventional engraving of the author to "the living face;" the title page points away from the printed poems to the poems "set in Musick." This pointing away from writing and print to speech and singing is a gesture of "deliberate sabotage" that the *Poems* continually reenacts, perhaps most spectacularly in the book's first poem, *On the Morning of Christ's Nativity*.

II. BREATH AND LETTER

In his preface to the *Poems,* addressed to "the reader," Humphrey Moseley describes the book as a "birth":

> The Authors more peculiar excellency in these studies was too well known to conceal his Papers, or to keep me from attempting to sollicit them from him. Let the event guide it self which way it will, I shall deserve of the age, by bringing into the Light as true a Birth, as the Muses have brought forth since our famous Spencer wrote; whose Poems in these English ones are as rarely imitated, as sweetly excell'd. Reader if thou art Eagle-eied to censure their worth, I am not fearful to expose them to thy exactest perusal.

Moseley portrays himself as a midwife, "bringing into the Light" what was "too well known to conceal." As an established publisher with a deep intellectual and material investment in print, Moseley imagines publication in strikingly visual terms, as he exposes the *Poems* to the "exactest perusal" of "Eagle-eied" readers. For Moseley, the *Poems* are a set of stable, printed works that he can reveal to the scrutiny of discerning readers.

As the first poem of the book, *On the Morning of Christ's Nativity* continues the birth imagery of Moseley's preface, employs a stanza form that, in keeping with Moseley's claim, shows the influence of Spenser, and, as a number of critics have suggested, implies a parallel between Christ's birth and Milton's own poetic nativity.[10] But the poem, like many of the English poems in the volume, undermines the print-based visual imagery of Moseley's preface, offering instead poetry that attempts to break through the limits of a printed page by emphasizing aural over visual art, song over writing. The references to song begin almost as soon as the poem itself begins. Recalling that "the holy sages once did sing" of the Nativity (5), the poet invokes his "Heav'nly Muse":

> Say Heav'nly Muse, shall not thy sacred vein
> Afford a present to the Infant God?

Hast thou no vers, no hymn, or solemn strein,
To welcom him to this his new abode . . . ?   (15–18)

The current silence of the "holy sages," the Old Testament prophets who now only "sing" in printed Scripture, and the silence of the Divine ("Infant," being derived from *infans*, Latin for "unspeaking") create the need for the poet's song. In the next stanza, the Magi, reduced to "Wisards," provide an additional competitive motive for singing, and the poet implores his Muse in the last lines of the prologue: "Have thou the honour first, thy Lord to greet, / And joyn thy voice unto the Angel Quire, / From out his secret Altar toucht with hallow'd fire" (26–28). The last line clearly alludes to Isaiah vi, 6–7: "Then flew one of the Seraphims unto me, having a live coal in his hand, which he had taken with tongs from off the altar: And he laid it upon my mouth, and said, Lo, this hath touched thy lips; and thine iniquity is taken away, and thy sin is purged." The emphasis on lips and speech is repeated in Milton's other famous allusion to the same verses, a passage from *The Reason of Church-Government* in which Milton expresses his hope of composing "a true poem." In that passage, Milton contrasts hands, "the pen of some vulgar amorist," and mouths, the purified lips of the prophet/poet.[11] The opening stanzas of the Nativity ode similarly privilege song, as they struggle against the expectations set up by the format of the printed book generally and by Moseley's preface specifically: Moseley promised to reveal something to the reader's sight, but the poet appeals overwhelmingly to hearing.

Walter Ong outlines how the shift from orality and writing to print entailed a shift from "hearing-dominance" to "sight-dominance": "Hearing rather than sight had dominated the older noetic world in significant ways, even after writing was deeply interiorized. Manuscript culture in the west remained always marginally oral." Ong argues that print finally eliminated the residual orality of manuscript culture: "Eventually, however, print replaced the lingering hearing-dominance in the world of thought and expression with the sight-dominance which had its beginnings with writing but could not flourish with the support of writing alone." The Nativity ode strains against its format because, as critics have long noticed, hearing rather than sight dominates "The Hymn." Sigmund Gottfried Spaeth concludes that "from beginning to end, the Nativity Hymn is built up on suggestions of sound. Its lyric effectiveness lies largely in this preference of the audible to the visible." Spaeth divides "The Hymn" into three parts. The first, exemplified by the fourth and fifth stanzas, "creates a background of complete silence": "But peacefull was the night / Wherin the Prince of light / His

raign of peace upon the earth began" (61–63). The celestial music announcing Christ's coming breaks the silence in the ninth stanza:

> When such musick sweet
> Their [the shepherds'] hearts and ears did greet,
>   As never was by mortall finger strook,
> Divinely-warbled voice
> Answering the stringed noise
>   As all their souls in blissfull rapture took:
> The Air such pleasure loth to lose,
> With thousand echo's still prolongs each heav'nly close.   (93–100)

The celestial music, Spaeth observes, is interrupted by the defeat of the
pagan deities which is "portrayed chiefly by the silencing of characteristic
sounds connected with their rites." After stanza xix announces that "The
Oracles are dumm" (173), the vanquished deities raise a "loud lament" of
"weeping" and "sighing" in stanza cc. The cacophony continues throughout
the retreat of "the damned crew" (228); both their ringing "Cymbals" (208)
and their singing "Timbrel'd Anthems dark" (219) are dismissed as "in
vain." But, as Catherine Belsey points out, the Nativity ode is not simply a
description of sounds; it claims itself to be a sound, a voice joined to "the
Angel Quire": "The 'Ode' is to be part of the angelic consort, a voice in
the divine polyphony which is the bond between God and human beings,
the union of heaven and earth." Moreover, the poem not only, as Spaeth
argues, prefers "the audible to the visible," the introduction of visual imagery actually forces the end of the poem: "But see the Virgin blest, / Hath
laid her babe to rest. / Time is our tedious Song should here have ending"
(237–39). Once the seeing starts, the singing stops, emphasizing with finality
the antithetical relation between song and the printed poem that reveals a
scene to the reader's eyes.[12]

The brief picture of a "Virgin" laying "her Babe to rest" brings the
Nativity ode as close as it comes to what Martz has influentially described
as "the poetry of meditation." In fact, Martz selects the Nativity ode as an
instructive contrast to that poetry, and he uses it to delineate the differences
between "the spirituality of English Puritanism and the spirituality of the
Counter Reformation." Martz remarks that in the Nativity ode, "Milton puts
last the concrete scene which would normally begin a Catholic meditation
on this subject." He compares the Nativity ode to Crashaw's "Sung as by
the Shepherds," a poem thoroughly informed by visual imagery: "Crashaw,
through the shepherds, makes himself intimately present at the manger-
scene: 'We saw,' 'I saw'—those repeated words provide the dramatic focus
and create an intimate application of senses to the scene." Although he does

not discuss it at length, Martz seems to recognize the emphasis on visualization in meditative literature. Ignatius and the authors of meditative treatises who preceded and succeeded him stress the application of all the senses, but meditation often privileges visual imagery, as the visualized birth of Christ replaces visually apprehended text describing the birth. Meditative literature and the poetry based on it generally attempt to transport the meditator to a specific scene, but the performative song of the Nativity ode brings the scene to the singer. "The Hymn," united with the song of "the Angel Quire," can, as Belsey puts it, make all time "simultaneously present," from creation to the last judgment:

> XIV.
> For if such holy Song
> Enwrap our fancy long,
>   Time will run back, and fetch the age of gold,
> And speckl'd vanity
> Will sicken soon and die,
>   And leprous sin will melt from earthly mould,
> And Hell it self will pass away
> And leave her dolorous mansions to the peering day.
>
> XV.
> Yea Truth, and Justice then
> Will down return to men.   (133–42)

Meditative poems often record exploration of the "inner world" opened by writing and print, but the singer of the Nativity ode shapes the outer world—indeed, the cosmos—through the potent orality of "holy Song."[13]

The companion poem to the Nativity ode, *The Passion*, begins with the same emphasis on song and refers directly to the ode:

> Ere-while of Musick, and Ethereal mirth,
> Wherwith the stage of Ayr and Earth did ring,
> And joyous news of heav'nly Infants birth,
> My muse with Angels did divide to sing.   (1–4)

After this reminder of the earlier song, the poet prepares for sadder music: "For now to sorrow must I tune my song, / And set my Harpe to notes of saddest wo" (8–9). The poet looks for appropriate musical instruments in the fourth stanza—"Me softer airs befit, and softer strings, / Of Lute, or Viol still, more apt for mournful things" (27–28)—but the poem soon stops describing itself as a song. By the end of the fifth stanza, the "Muse" disappeared, as has the pretense of "Ethereal" song, and an "I" appears to lament the difficulties of writing: "The leaves should all be black wheron I write, /

And letters where my tears have washt a wannish white" (34–35). Harold
Bloom's Milton is the consummate "strong poet," a source of tremendous
anxiety for his successors, but this "I" is himself anxious. As he imagines
pages blackened to suit his grief and blackened by the ink of his predecessors, he can only imagine a writing that is also a painful erasing. After the
opening stanzas, the poem is agonizingly aware of itself as a written text.
William R. Parker contends that Milton "*was writing a poem about himself
writing a poem;* in every stanza except the third he had described himself
in the process of composition."[14]

If the third stanza does not mention the process of writing the poem,
it does begin a series of visual images that bear a much closer resemblance
to other meditative poems than to the Nativity ode: "He sov'ran Priest
stooping his regall head / That dropt with odorous oil down his fair eyes"
(15–16). The poem continues to foreground "holy vision"; the sixth stanza,
for instance, depicts one of the "scenes" which "confine my roving vers"
(22):

> See see the Chariot, and those rushing wheels,
> That whirl'd the Prophet up at *Chebar* flood,
> My spirit som transporting *Cherub* feels,
> To bear me where the Towers of Salem stood,
> Once glorious Towers, now sunk in guiltles blood;
>   There doth my soul in holy vision sit
> In pensive trance, and anguish, and ecstatick fit.   (36–42)

This stanza clearly diverges from the Nativity ode's precedent: it enjoins
readers to "see see" rather than hear; the poet of *The Passion* is transported
to the site of the Crucifixion by the chariot "that whirl'd" Ezekial, but the
song of the Nativity ode brings the familiar scene, and all history, to the
present; the poet of *The Passion* sits in silence, "in holy vision," "in pensive
trance," writing rather than singing. William Shullenberger concisely summarizes the poet's struggle: "Music and masquelike ritual are abandoned for
the attempt to compose an imaginative space in which the poet can witness
the Passion." The poet never situates himself adequately to view the Passion, even though, as Shullenberger states, "Milton resorts to virtually every
strategy in the poetic repertoire in order to broach his subject."[15] After eight
stanzas the poem stops abruptly: "*This Subject the Author finding to be
above the years he had, when he wrote it, and nothing satisfi'd with what
was begun, left it unfinisht.*"

The inclusion of this fragment in *Poems* is perplexing, especially, as
Martz notes, because Milton would have had other poems available for the
collection, "the more interesting and at least completed English poems that

he added in 1673: the poem *On the Death of a Fair Infant,* and the lines from the *Vacation Exercise.*" Martz proposes that *The Passion* serves "a clear function" in the book: "to stress the immaturity of these opening pieces, to suggest the ambitious young man outreaching his powers, and achieving poetical success only when he can subject his muse to some deliberate limitation."[16] The scope of *The Passion* seems severely circumscribed, however—"These latter scenes confine my roving vers, / To this Horizon is my *Phoebus* bound" (22–23)—whereas the Nativity ode ranges freely from the beginning of human history to its end. A surfeit, rather than a lack, of "deliberate limitation" stifles the poem. *The Passion* makes explicit what is implicit in the Nativity ode: the struggle against the limits of writing. *The Passion* must end because it is smothered by the material difficulties of writing, imagined as writing on surfaces that resist inscription, black pages and rock, and because it refuses an iconic visual representation of the suffering Christ that the medium seems to encourage. Including *The Passion* discovers a fear that the Nativity ode attempts to suppress, namely, that writing will rob the poet of his poem.

Although *Poems* features no shaped poems like Herbert's "Easter Wings" or Herrick's "Pillar of Fame," works comfortable with the new visual and poetic potential of typography, other English poems, such as *On Shakespeare* and the epitaphs for Hobson, reflect less anxiety than the Nativity ode and *The Passion* about their status as written and printed texts. Crossing the divide of *Poems* into the Latin poems, readers encounter poems that, unlike the Nativity ode or *The Passion,* accept their format, distanced from the power of song.

III. Both English and Latin

Poems is, as Milton called it in his ode addressed to John Rouse, a "twin book," a book of English followed by a book of Latin poems, each complete with its own title page, commendatory poems, and pagination. Though miscellanies of poems in both English and Latin had been published often, such as *Justa Eduardo King* in which *Lycidas* first appeared, Milton's was the first book by a single author to include poems, as the title page announces, "BOTH / ENGLISH and LATIN" by a single author.[17] Despite the title of the book and Milton's reference in the Latin poem to Rouse, critical discussions of *Poems* often slight the Latin works. The Noel Douglas Replicas facsimile edition of *Poems,* published in 1926, omits the Latin poems without explanation. Cleanth Brooks and John Edward Hardy's *Poems of Mr. John Milton: The 1645 Edition with Essays in Analysis* also does not reproduce the Latin poems, even though Brooks and Hardy stress the importance of *Poems* as a whole: "The book is, in the first place, an edition of the poems which Milton chose to print in 1645. That volume was, needless to say, an important one, and from the viewpoint of literary history, there are clear reasons for preserving and emphasizing it as a volume in its own right, keeping the arrangement which Milton himself made." Brooks and Hardy include the Italian poems from the English half of *Poems*, but leave out the Latin and Greek poems that made up the second half "for obvious reasons": "Most readers simply lack the equipment to handle them as poetry, and in this edition we are interested primarily in poetry."[18] Whatever the insensitivities of twentieth-century readers to the nuances of seventeenth-century Latin poetry, and whatever the aesthetic weaknesses of the *Poemata*, the Latin works can disturb readings of *Poems* as the annunciation of a "rising poet"; the problems they raise for paradigmatic narratives of Milton's career have doubtless contributed to the Latin poems' omission from some discussions of Milton's first book of poetry.

Since Renaissance Latin developed primarily, though by no means exclusively, as a written language, it should probably come as no surprise that the *Poemata* consistently refer to themselves as written documents, most often letters. Ong's description of learned Latin—"devoid of baby-talk, insulated from the earliest life of childhood where language has its deepest psychic roots, a first language to none of its users, pronounced across Europe in often mutually unintelligible ways but always written the same way"[19]—contrasts sharply with Milton's greeting to English in the *Vacation Exercise*, added to the *Poems* of 1673:

> Hail native Language, that by sinews weak
> Didst move my first endeavouring tongue to speak,
> And mad'st imperfect words with childish tripps,
> Half unpronounc't, slide thorough my infant-lipps,
> Driving dum silence from the portal dore
> Where he had mutely sate two years before.   (1–6)

Here Milton associates English with an orality that precedes writing, but in the *Poemata* he associates Latin with conspicuously written texts. The singer of the Nativity ode claims for himself the oral force of prophetic song, but the Latin poems tend to sever song from poem. *Ad Leonoram Romeae Canentem (To Leonora, Singing at Rome)*, provides a clear instance of the separation of written texts and heavenly song in the *Poemata*:

> Angleus unicuique suus (sic credite gentes)
> Obtigit aethereis ales ab ordinibus.
> Quid mirum, Leonora, tibi si gloria maior,
> Nam tua praesentem vox sonat ipsa Deum.

Aut Deus, aut vacui certe mens tertia caeli
Pertua secreto guttura serpit agens;
Serpit agens, facilisque docet mortalia corda
Sensim immortali assuescere posse sono.
Quod si cuncta quidem Deus est, per cunctaque fusus,
In te una loquitur, caetera mutus habet.

[To every one, so let men believe, there is allotted a winged angel from out the hierarchies of heaven. What wonder, Leonora, if yours should be a greater glory, for your voice itself proclaims the presence of God. Either God, or surely a third mind that has deserted heaven, with secret power gently breathes through your throat—gently breathes, and easily teaches mortal hearts little by little to become accustomed to immortal sound. But if in truth God is all things, and is through all things diffused, yet in you alone does he speak; all the rest of his being is mute.][20]

Following, as it does, the Nativity ode, *Ad Leonoram* is almost poignant: the singer of the ode helps to unite heaven and earth with his song, but the poet of the epigram can only observe how Leonora's "voice itself proclaims the presence of God"; in the ode angelic song rings over the silenced false deities, as in the epigram the "secret power" channeled through Leonora's voice renders all creation "mute," including, presumably, the poet who responds with a written text.

Besides praising the oral performances of others, as they often do, the Latin poems can point toward the poet's own songs, but performance of those songs necessarily occurs elsewhere, outside what Ong calls the "chirographically controlled" province of learned Latin.[21] For example, like many of the Latin poems, the *Elegia Sexta*, addressed to Charles Diodati, asserts its physical existence as a written text. The headnote to the poem explains that when Diodati wrote to Milton describing how holiday festivities had sapped Diodati's creativity, *"hunc habuit responsum"* ("he received the following reply"). The poem is thus a part of a written correspondence, but at the end of the poem Milton describes a "song" usually taken to be the Nativity ode:

At tu siquid agam, scitabere (si modo saltem
Esse putas tanti noscere siquid agam)
Paciferum canimus caelesti semine regem,
Faustaque sacratis saecula pacta libris,
Vagitumque Dei, & stabulantem paupere tecto
Qui suprema suo cum patre regna colit.
Stelliparumque polum, modulantesque aethere turmas,
Et subito elisos ad sua fana Deos.

Dona quidem dedimus Christi natalibus illa,
Illa sub auroram lux mihi prima tulit.
Te quoque pressa manent patriis meditata cicutis;
Tu mihi, cui recitem, judicis instar eris.   (79–90)

[But if you will know what I am doing—if indeed you think it of consequence to know that I am doing anything—I am singing of the peace-bearing King of heavenly race, and of that happy age promised in the sacred books, of the infant cries of Jesus, and his shelter beneath the humble roof, who with his father now dwells in the realms above. I sing of the star-bearing firmament and melodious hosts in the heavens, of the gods suddenly shattered in their fanes. This is the gift that I have offered to Christ on his natal day, when the first light of dawn brought me my theme. These strains composed on my native pipes await you in close keeping, when I recite them to you, you will be my judge.] (P. 101)

Rather than affixing a copy of the ode to his letter or assuring Diodati that he will show him the poem, Milton promises to recite it later, implying that this song demands oral performance and that its ideal form cannot be captured by ink and paper. The Latin poems thus tend to distance themselves from the potency of song by ascribing it to another singer and by postponing performance.

Martz reverses the order of *Poems* in his reading of the book, considering the Latin poems first and then the English poems—significantly, the Nativity ode last. Despite his championing of "Milton's original arrangement," his discussion of the *Poems* is, in the Renaissance sense, preposterous: what should be "pre" becomes "post." Martz's arrangement lends itself easily to the narrative of a "rising poet," a poet who admires the power of song in others, looks forward to his own oral performance, and finally joins his prophetic voice to a choir of angels. The arrangement of these works in *Poems*, however, hints at the opposite story, that of a falling (and fallen) poet. If Milton's first book of poetry shows any progress—and that "if" needs much emphasis—it shows the progress of a poet not rising but descending, from angelic song to the materiality of the written or printed page.

IV. THE WRITING POET

The Latin poem *Ad Patrem* (*To My Father*) exemplifies particularly well the descent from song in *Poems*. At first the poem would seem to be an exception to the generalizations above since it calls itself *"carmen / Exiguum"* (6–7), as MacKellar translates, a "trifling song" (p. 143). But a few lines later it fixes itself firmly upon a page: "Sed tamen haec nostros ostendit pagina census / Et quod habemus opum charta numeravimus ista" (12–13) ("Nevertheless this page displays my resources, and all my wealth is set forth on this paper") (p. 143). As the poem continues, it justifies the poet's choice of career by appealing to his father's fame as a composer of music. The poem makes clear that the elements of song, words and music, have undergone a separation:

> Nunc tibi quid mirum, si me genuisse poetam
> Contigerit, charo si tam prope sanguine juncti
> Cognatas artes, studiumque affine sequamur:
> Ipse volens Phoebus se dispertire duobus,
> Altera dona mihi, dedit altera dona parenti,
> Dividuumque deum genitorque puerque tenemus.   (61–66)

[Now, if it has happened that I have been born a poet, why is it strange to you that we, so closely joined by the loving bond of blood, should pursue related arts and kindred ways of life? Phoebus, wishing to divide himself in two, gave some gifts to me, others to my father; and we, father and son, possess the divided god.] (P. 147)

In this pagan reenactment of the Incarnation, the god divides his divinity between father and son, each receiving fragmentary, separate powers— "Altera dona mihi" torn away, as in line 65, from "altera dona parenti." Rather than Incarnation, this dissolution suggests the Fall, the loss of perfect communication with the Divine. As Jacques Derrida puts it in a discussion of Edmond Jabès's *Le livre des questions*, "The difference between speech and writing is sin, the anger of God emerging from itself, lost immediacy, work outside the garden."[22] *Ad Patrem*, like *At a Solemn Music*, records how "disproportion'd sin" "Broke the fair musick that all creatures made / To their great Lord" (19, 21–22). This separation of gifts explains why the fallen poet writes: he can create words or music, but he cannot reunite the divided god in song.

If Milton imagines in *Ad Patrem* a primal splitting apart of word and music, in works like *At a Solemn Music*, *Poems* continually looks forward to a time of reuniting humanity and God, words and music:

> O may we soon again renew that Song,
> And keep in tune with Heav'n, till God ere long
> To his celestial consort us unite,
> To live with him, and sing in endles morn of light.   (25–28)

Moving from the Nativity ode, to *At a Solemn Music*, to *Lycidas*—following without mentioning it the order of *Poems*—Catherine Belsey observes how angelic song which asserts the presence of the Divine retreats from the earth into heaven between the Nativity ode and *Lycidas*. Rather than the withdrawal of the Divine, *Poems* seems to show the poet's growing awareness of the separation between heavenly song and humanity, a separation reflected in poetry from the start of the book. Belsey points out that even the Nativity ode, the work in all of *Poems* that proclaims most insistently its status as a song and its ability to make its subject present, is betrayed by an inability to transcend the limits of writing. The singer attempts to appropriate the immediate presence associated with speech, but the text repeatedly declares the singer's absence from the song's cosmic scenes. This undermining of the singer's authority is signified typographically by parentheses: "Such Musick (as 'tis said) / Before was never made, / But when of old the sons of morning sung" (117–19). "As 'tis said" indicates that the singer does not know first-hand the relation between the hymns at the Nativity and at the Creation; the parentheses deny the singer the authority of one who is present. They similarly question his ability to participate in—or even hear—the music of the spheres: "Ring out ye Crystall sphears, / Once bless our human ears, / (If ye have power to touch our senses so)" (125–27). Considering these passages, Belsey concludes that this inconsistency "within the speaking voice of the text, these uncertainties and hesitations, come close momentarily to identifying the authority of the poem as imaginary." Since the poet's fallen nature already necessarily permeates the Nativity ode, *Poems* seems to show not the opening of a chasm between human and divine, but the growing awareness of a preexisting separation and a reluctant, partial acceptance of less powerful modes of communication—writing and print rather than angelic song—that such a separation requires. *Poems* portrays not the Fall but the poet's realizing the effects of the Fall for his poetry.[23]

This realization continues in the Latin poems, culminating in *Epitaphium Damonis (Damon's Epitaph)*, the last work of *Poems*. Critics frequently read the epitaph for statements of Milton's epic aspirations. Martz concentrates on lines at the center of the poem:

> O mihi tum si vita supersit,
> Tu procul annosa pendebis fistula pinu
> Multum oblita mihi, aut patriis mutata camoenis
> Brittonicum strides, quid enim? omnia non licet uni
> Non sperasse uni licet omnia.   (168–72)

[Ah! then if life remain, you, my pipe, shall hang on some aged pine far off and forgotten, unless forsaking your native songs you shrilly sound a British theme. Why not a British theme? One man cannot do all things, cannot hope to do all things.] (P. 169)

According to Martz, "the poet is contemplating deeper themes, British themes, and themes composed in English."[24] Martz overlooks the conditional clause that begins these lines, thereby eliding the possibility that the plans that follow may not be the poet's ideal choices; given that he has an abundance of life left (the prefix *super* connotes an excess), the poet considers his options. The poem's view, however, and that of *Poems* generally, seems to extend far beyond Milton's late epics. The real exercise of poetic power within the epitaph is Damon's; because "purum colit aethera Damon" (203) ("Damon dwells in the purity of heaven"), he achieves song that *Poems*, by its very existence as a printed book, suggests cannot be sung on earth:

> Ipse caput nitidum cinctus rutilante corona,
> Letaque frondentis gestans umbracula palmae
> Aeternum perages immortales hymenaeos,
> Cantus ubi, choreisque furit lyra mista beatis,
> Festa Sionaeo bacchantur & Orgia Thyrso. (215–19)

[Your {Damon's} noble head bound with a glittering wreath, in your hands the glad branches of the leafy palm, you shall for ever act and act again the immortal nuptials, where song and the lyre, mingled with the blessed dances, wax rapturous, and the joyous revels rage under the thyrsus of Zion.] (P. 173)

These are the final lines of *Poems*, and they celebrate not the rising poet but the ascended poet; to the extent that they look forward to Milton's career at all, they look forward to his career after he leaves the earth to sing where he can "for ever act and act again the immortal nuptials" of words and music. These last lines of the book invite a rereading of some of the first lines: when is the "future" of the motto's "future bard"? Maybe 1667, but *Poems* looks forward more consistently to song "unexpressive" on earth, song that cannot be represented in writing, print, or any earthly medium.

But back on earth, near the end of 1645, the living poet John Milton used the press to circulate his poetry. *The Poems of Mr. John Milton, Both English and Latin* reveals that even before *Eikonoklastes*, when he scorned another of Marshall's frontispieces, Milton was very suspicious of the iconic potential of print. Later readers of *Areopagitica* may worship books, Stanley Fish writes, but Milton refuses to because "Milton is continually alert to the danger of reifying some external form into the repository of truth and value."[25] Consequently, his first book of poetry repeatedly calls attention to its failures: the failure of a graven image to capture even a "jot" of the poet; the failure of a spatial, visual format to reproduce the temporal, aural arrangements of Henry Lawes; the failure of print to capture the poet's song (the Nativity ode) and the failure of the poet's song to fit into print (*The Passion*); and, above all, the fallen poet's failure to escape the materiality of writing and bring heavenly song to earth. That these failures have been frequently overlooked illustrates very clearly the historical, cultural gap separating a yearning for song from an unquestioning acceptance of print and separating makers of iconoclastic books from readers of verbal icons.

Davidson College

NOTES

1. McGann, *The Textual Condition* (Princeton, 1991), p. 13; Martz, *Milton: Poet of Exile*, 2nd ed. (New Haven, 1986), p. 31. Martz's essay, "The Rising Poet, 1645," first appeared in *The Lyric and Dramatic Milton: Selected Papers from the English Institute*, ed. Joseph H. Summers (New York, 1965), but my article cites the most recent version (1986) throughout.

2. Ong, *Orality and Literacy: The Technologizing of the Word* (London, 1982), p. 26. Eric Alfred Havelock, *The Muse Learns to Write: Reflections on Orality and Literacy from Antiquity to the Present* (New Haven, 1986).

3. The version of *Poems* (1645) cited is the facsimile in *John Milton's Complete Poetical Works, Reproduced in Photographic Facsimile*, ed. Harris Francis Fletcher (Urbana, 1943), vol. I. All translations of Milton's Latin poetry come from *The Latin Poems of John Milton*, trans. Walter MacKellar (New Haven, 1930), and subsequent page references will appear in the text.

4. Halpern, "The Great Instauration: imaginary narratives in Milton's 'Nativity Ode,' " in *Re-membering Milton: Essays on the Texts and Traditions*, ed. Mary Nyquist and Margaret W. Ferguson (New York, 1987), pp. 3–4; Hale, "Milton's Self-Presentation in *Poems . . . 1645*," *MQ* XXV (1991): 37.

5. Martz, *Milton*, p. 34.

6. Masson, *The Life of John Milton: Narrated in Connexion with the Political, Ecclesiastical, and Literary History of His Time*, (London, 1896), vol. III, p. 459; Martz, *Milton*, p. 33.

7. Werstine, "Narratives About Printed Shakespearean Texts: 'Foul Papers' and 'Bad' Quartos," *Shakespeare Quarterly* XLI (1990): 86; Spear, "Reading Before the Lines: Typography, Iconography, and the Author in Milton's 1645 Frontispiece," in *New Ways of Looking at Old Texts: Papers of the Renaissance English Text Society, 1985–1991*, ed. W. Speed Hill (Binghamton, 1993), pp. 187, 189, 192, 193.

8. Spear, "Reading Before the Lines," pp. 193, 188.

9. Martz, *Milton*, p. 34.

10. See, for instance, C.W.R.D. Moseley, *The Poetic Birth: Milton's Poems of 1645* (Aldershot, 1991).

11. *Complete Prose Works of John Milton*, 8 vols., ed. Don M. Wolfe et al. (New Haven, 1953–82), vol. I, pp. 820–21.

12. Ong, *Orality and Literacy*, pp. 119, 121; Spaeth, *Milton's Knowledge of Music: Its Sources and Its Significance in His Works* (Princeton, 1913), p. 92; Belsey, *John Milton: Language, Gender, Power* (London, 1988), p. 4.

13. Louis L. Martz, *The Poetry of Meditation: A Study in English Religious Literature of the Seventeenth Century* (New Haven, 1954), p. 165; Belsey, *John Milton*, p. 2.

14. Parker, *Milton: A Biography* (Oxford, 1968), vol. I, p. 72.

15. Shullenberger, "Doctrine as Deep Structure in Milton's Early Poetry," in *A Fine Tuning: Studies of the Religious Poetry of Herbert and Milton*, ed. Mary A. Maleski (Binghamton, 1989), pp. 198–99, 196.

16. Martz, *Milton*, pp. 50–51.

17. Hale, "Milton's Self-Presentation in *Poems . . . 1645*," 38.

18. Brooks and Hardy, *Poems of Mr. John Milton: The 1645 Edition with Essays in Analysis* (New York, 1951), p. vi.

19. Ong, *Orality and Literacy*, p. 113.

20. *The Latin Poems of John Milton*, p. 111.

21. Ong, *Orality and Literacy*, p. 113.

22. Derrida, *Writing and Difference*, trans. Alan Bass (Chicago, 1978), p. 68.

23. Belsey, *John Milton*, pp. 31, 22.

24. Martz, *Milton*, p. 38.

25. Fish, "Driving from the Letter: Truth and Indeterminacy in Milton's *Areopagitica*," in *Re-membering Milton*, p. 236.

THE PATTERN OF MILTON'S *NATIVITY ODE*

Arthur Barker

I

"THE Puritans," writes Professor Woodhouse, "(though in different degrees) were men who had undergone a religious experience, whose effect was to bestow a new unity of feeling upon their thoughts."[1] As he observes, this experience of a sudden renewal of spirit, mind and purpose, after confusion and paralysis of will, animated the apparently cold formulations of Puritan theology. Indeed, so important was it in the Puritan scheme that it inevitably received its own formulation, patterned on the experiences of Moses, Elijah, and St Paul, and vividly, yet still typically, presented in Bunyan's *Grace Abounding to the Chief of Sinners*. After a life of cynical carelessness, the sinner was oppressed by a terrifying sense of human corruption and of his own especial depravity; he contemplated with horrified fascination the torments to which he felt himself justly damned—a symbol of his torturing mental paralysis; he then began hopelessly to desire peace through God's mercy and to shift the weight of his oppression by striving to accept the divine will, whatever it might be; ultimately, if he were one of the chosen, the weight was removed by his recognition of the significance of Christ's incarnation and vicarious suffering, and he experienced a transporting illumination of spirit which neutralized his self-accusation and produced the calm certainty and the unity of purpose which made the Puritan a dangerous and inflexible opponent. From the moment of his illumination he dated his spiritual rebirth; and he might prove his claim to saintship (or be called upon to prove it) by giving an account of his experience and of the precise occasion on which he was illuminated.

Like so much in Puritanism, this process merely intensified an experience common in the seventeenth century. At a time of religious, intellectual, political, economic confusion, when the aspiring enthusiasm of the Renaissance had given place to the feeling (expressed by Donne) that man's world was "all in peeces, all cohaerance gone, All just supply, and all relation," it was

[1]*Puritanism and Liberty*, ed. A. S. P. Woodhouse (London, 1938), p. [38].

natural that many should escape from their oppressive sense of frustration by turning for reassurance and direction to a power beyond themselves, and that they should describe the renewal and re-integration of their energies in the terms employed by others during the decline of Jewry and later of Rome. If the experience was not always as sharply defined as the Puritan's conversion, it was nevertheless common to men as different as Bunyan and Donne himself. Donne's poetry is a record of his conversion; Walton took pains to emphasize the same pattern in the *Life of Herbert;* Henry Vaughan presented his variation in the preface to *Silex Scintillans;* the process carried Richard Crashaw to Rome. With the metaphysical poets, no less than with Bunyan, the experience was the prime source of inspiration; and it would not be too much to say that a conversion, in one form or another, lay behind most of the important literary products of the middle years of the century.

It is obvious that the greatest of the seventeenth-century poets shared this experience to some degree. Is it possible to be more precise and to point to some particular occasion when Milton experienced an illumination corresponding to the typical exaltation of the Puritan? Professor Haller thinks not: "We are not told in Milton's spiritual autobiography the precise moment when he first felt the conviction of grace. The sense of personal election seems to have been his from the start."[2] Certainly Milton seems never to have doubted his own importance; yet there is nothing in his poetry or prose before his twenty-first year which suggests that he found a deeply personal significance in the Puritan theory of election. In the prose of his middle period, however, he constantly uses the doctrines in which the Puritan formulated his experience, writing of the glorious privileges of the saints with enthusiasm, and (in the pamphlets of 1659 especially) of the "far surpassing light" of the Spirit with a depth of conviction comparable to Bunyan's. How were the formulae of theology thus animated for him? He nowhere describes an experience precisely like the typical conversion of the tinker. Nothing in his youth exactly corresponds to the depravity Bunyan emphasized; it is difficult to believe that he ever trembled at the thought of the punishments of the damned;

[2]William Haller, *The Rise of Puritanism* (New York, 1938), p. 297.

and, however else his self-esteem was expressed, he never described himself, with Bunyan and Cromwell, as "the chief of sinners." Yet he repudiated (though he printed) the more sensuous of his early poems;[3] and the Hell of *Paradise Lost* is the product of a vivid sense of evil which expresses itself throughout his works. His life was no fugitive and cloistered serenity, but a series of frustrations both private and public. His Puritan contemporaries found a constant source of reassurance in the fruits of their religious experience; he found a similar source in the genius which enabled him to rise imaginatively above despair. In that fact lies the explanation of the sense of personal election which he shared with them.

The autobiographical passages Professor Haller seems specially to have in mind are those in the pamphlets of 1641 and 1642 in which Milton defends his right, though a layman, to meddle in ecclesiastical matters.[4] Somewhat incongruously, they deal chiefly with his poetical development and plans; but the incongruity is only apparent since he regarded himself by then as a poet-prophet of special calling, whose inspiration was from God. This conviction is, as Professor Hanford remarks, "the centre of his spiritual biography."[5] But it was not his from the start; it is not suggested in his poetry or prose before 1629; and its impact on his imagination is the experience which corresponds to the conversion of his Puritan associates. The moment of impact is fixed by his *Ode on the Morning of Christ's Nativity*, composed in December, 1629, near his twenty-first birthday. This poem strikes a note altogether new in his poetry, includes an implied rejection of his earlier manner,[6] and records a vision which produced a confident and harmonious purposefulness by overcoming the forces of gloom and confusion. It is to be regarded as the testimony of Milton's religious experience, but with this difference, that he thenceforth thought of himself not simply, like Bunyan, as a saint but as a poet sacred to the gods and their priest, whose inmost soul and lips breathe

[3]In the lines appended to *Elegia Septima* in the 1645 edition of his *Poems*.

[4]Especially *Reason of Church Government*, *Works* (Columbia), III, pp. 235-9; and *Apology*, *Works*, III, pp. 301-7.

[5]"Milton's Mosaic Inspiration" (UNIVERSITY OF TORONTO QUARTERLY, VIII, p. 147).

[6]The first stanza of "The Hymn" clearly refers to the sensuous imagery of *Elegia quinta*, *In adventum veris*.

out Jove.[7] For the experience which produced the *Ode* was unlike Bunyan's in being essentially aesthetic. I propose to show that the recognition of the significance of Christ's incarnation and sacrifice recorded in the *Ode* was coupled with a recognition of the potentialities of a peculiarly complex poetical symbol, and that these recognitions together bestowed a new unity of feeling upon both Milton's thought and his art.

II

Milton emphasized the importance of his *Ode* by setting it at the beginning of the section devoted to English verse in the *Poems* (1645). *Lycidas* (November, 1637) concluded this section, and clearly marks the end of a period in Milton's development of which the *Ode* is the beginning. Hitherto Ovid had been his chief model; after 1629 his tone was more severe. He noted this departure in an account of his development written in 1642,[8] and more significantly in *Elegia Sexta*, composed shortly after the *Ode*, when he spoke for the first time of the rigorously disciplined virtue required of the poet who would write of cosmic and epic themes, and referred to his Nativity poem as, by implication, an earnest of his intentions.[9]

The self-dedication of the *Ode* and the *Elegy* have often been noted;[10] the nature of this dedication has not, I think, been precisely explained because the quality of Milton's art in the *Nativity Ode* has not been fully comprehended. Its charm and freshness have been praised, but (apart from a few lines of swelling grandeur) it has been said to lack the distinctively Miltonic excellences so fully apparent in *Lycidas*. Mr Tillyard, for example, thinks *Lycidas* "one of the greatest poems in English"; but he finds the *Ode* less satisfactory since, though it has a "beautiful diversity," its heterogeneous elements are only "harmonized by a pervading

[7]*Elegia sexta*, ll. 77-8, translated.

[8]*Apology, Works*, III, p. 303.

[9]*Elegia sexta*, ll. 55 ff.   He had already expressed his ambition to write upon such themes in *At a Vacation Exercise*, but without speaking of the required discipline.

[10]See J. H. Hanford, "The Youth of Milton" (*Studies in Shakespeare, Milton and Donne, University of Michigan Publications, Language and Literature*, I, pp. 122-4); E. M. W. Tillyard, *Milton*, pp. 35-42; W. Haller, *op. cit.*

youthful candour" and superficially unified by the fact that at the beginning Milton hastens to prevent the Wise Men whose arrival (as he thinks) is indicated at the end.[11] The impression made on my mind by the *Ode* has, however, a unity which could not be produced simply by a pervasive charm or the provision of a frame for the picture. In this respect it is not unlike the impression created by *Lycidas*. I believe one can show how Milton's architectonic power is exerted with impressive results in both poems, and how in the case of the *Ode*, as more obviously in *Lycidas*, its influence helps to define mood and significance.

Since *Lycidas* is in many respects the type in little of Milton's peculiar genius, it provides a suitable standard for judging the earlier *Ode*. As Mr Tillyard has made clear, the elegy is essentially a personal poem, the ostensible subject making possible the resolution of the emotional problems created by Milton's disciplined devotion to poetry.[12] Like his great poems, it performed a cathartic function for the poet himself, was indeed the very process through which a balanced calm was brought out of emotional disquiet. The achievement of this calm is expressed through the poem's achievement of a symmetry of structure which Mr Tillyard might have emphasized more heavily. Dr Johnson recognized the excellence of "the design" in *Paradise Lost*, but he was prevented from discerning the same quality in *Lycidas* by what seemed to him the trivial character of the pastoral fiction. It is just Milton's balanced manipulation of this convention to throw into relief the resolution of his own problems, which gives the poem its serene power.

Lycidas consists of an introduction and conclusion, both pastoral in tone, and three movements, practically equal in length and precisely parallel in pattern. Each begins with an invocation of pastoral muses (ll. 15, 85, 132), proceeds with conventions drawn from the tradition of the pastoral elegy (the association of the lamented and the poet as shepherds, the mourning of nature, the

[11]*Op. cit.*, pp. 37, 85. Similarly G. W. Knight (*The Burning Oracle*, 1939, p. 64) thinks the *Ode* "somewhat fluid in its addition of stanza to stanza: there is no complex inter-knitting, that is, of central action with design, nor is such necessary." A similar failure to recognize the design of *Lycidas* leads Professor Knight to describe that poem as "an accumulation of magnificent fragments" (p. 70).

[12]*Op. cit.*, pp. 80-5.

questioning of the nymphs, the procession of mourners, a flower passage,[13] and the reassurance), and ends with the formulation and resolution of Milton's emotional problem. The first movement laments Lycidas the poet-shepherd; its problem, the possible frustration of disciplined poetic ambition by early death, is resolved by the assurance, "Of so much fame in heaven expect thy meed." The second laments Lycidas as priest-shepherd; its problem, the frustration of a sincere shepherd in a corrupt church, is resolved by St Peter's reference to the "two-handed engine" of divine retribution. The third concludes with the apotheosis, a convention introduced by Virgil in *Eclogue* V but significantly handled by Milton. He sees the poet-priest-shepherd worshipping the Lamb with those saints "in solemn troops" who sing the "unexpressive nuptial song" of the fourteenth chapter of *Revelation*. The apotheosis thus not only provides the final reassurance but unites the themes of the preceding movements in the ultimate reward of the true poet-priest.

It is the cumulative effect of its three parallel movements which makes *Lycidas* impressive; the return to the pastoral at the beginning of each makes possible three successive and perfectly controlled crescendos. The gathering up of the first two in the last gives the conclusion its calm finality; and the balanced unity of the design appropriately represents the calm achieved through the resolution of emotional conflicts. The problems are solved for Milton by the apotheosis because he regards himself as a poet-priest who can hope that his "destin'd urn" will bring the same reward.

The *Nativity Ode* resolves no pressing problems, but it expresses profound feeling and calm determination in much the same way as *Lycidas*. It seems architectonically inferior because its parts are not held together by the same strictness of formal design. But it produces a unified impression because it is built upon another kind of design. The four introductory stanzas apart, and

[13]Mr Tillyard, finding it "difficult to describe the function" of this passage (ll. 133-64), regards it as a transitional interlude, the third movement of the poem beginning with line 165. But the invocation of Alpheus in line 132 clearly marks the beginning of a third movement, and the flower passage performs for this movement exactly the same function as the similarly conventional passages of the preceding movements.

the brief conclusion, it too consists of three equal movements, held in relation, not by the repetition of a structural pattern, but by the variation of a basic pattern of imagery. The first eight stanzas of the "Hymn" describe the setting of the Nativity, the next nine the angelic choir, the next nine the flight of the heathen gods. The conclusion, the last stanza, presents the scene in the stable. A brief analysis will show that the three movements each present a single modification of the simple contrast, preserved throughout the poem, between images suggesting light and harmony and images of gloom and discord.

The Nativity setting is described in a series of negatives whose effect is to reduce light and sound to a minimum while subduing all discordant elements. There is no colour because Nature has "doffed her gaudy trim" and covered her face with "a veil of maiden white."[14]   Peace has stilled the din of war; the air is "gentle"; the winds "smoothly the waters kiss't" while "birds of calm sit brooding on the charmed wave." The scene is dimly lit by the "glimmering orbs" of the stars standing "fixt"; the sun (as we are told in the first and seventh stanzas) withholds his "inferior flame." The eighth stanza completes this peacefully hushed and faintly illuminated scene by introducing the shepherds "simply chatting in a rustic row." It also serves as a link with the second movement, for there breaks upon their ears, with a suddenness for which the poet has carefully prepared, the enrapturing harmony of the angelic choir:[15]

> When such music sweet
> Their hearts and ears did greet,
>   As never was by mortal finger strook,
> Divinely-warbled voice
> Answering the stringed noise,
>   As all their souls in blissful rapture took:
> The air such pleasure loath to lose,
> With thousand echoes still prolongs each heav'nly close.

The harmony is such as might bind heaven and earth "in happier union"; and it is accompanied by an intense but not formless brilliance—"a globe of circular light"—revealing the

[14]The unhappy personifications of Peace and Justice contain the only touches of colour in the first two movements.

[15]Milton wisely omits the announcement of Luke's single angel which would have reduced the sharpness of the contrast.

angels "in glittering ranks." This association of light with harmony
and order is emphasized in the succeeding verses with reference
first to *Job* 38.7, and then to the Pythagorean music of the spheres.
The music is such as was heard "when of old the sons of morning
sung" and God, setting his constellations in the heavens, brought
order out of chaos in creating the "well-balanc't" world. The
"crystal spheres," representing the order of nature, are urged to
ring out their ninefold "silver chime" to "make up full consort
to the angelic symphony." The possible effect of the harmony
on men is elaborated by the two following verses in terms of light:
"the age of gold" may return, and "speckl'd vanity" and "leprous
sin" give place to Mercy, "thron'd in celestial sheen," and Justice,
wearing "th' enamel'd arras of the rainbow."

This vision is dissipated by the thought of the Cross, and the
movement comes to an end with a reference to the last judgment
which prepares for the third movement by introducing ideas of
dissonance and gloom in sharp contrast with the harmony and
order of the second. The trump of doom must "thunder" with
"a horrid clang" such as was heard amid the "smouldering clouds"
of Sinai, and with a "blast" shaking the earth "from the surface
to the centre."

The last movement is full of discordant sounds, distorted forms,
and shadows. The old dragon thrashes with his "folded tail";
one hears the "hideous hum" and "hollow shriek" of the oracles,
and "a voice of weeping" and "loud lament"; with "flow'r-inwoven
tresses torn" the nymphs sorrow in "twilight shade of tangled
thickets"; the lars and lemurs "moan with midnight plaint"; "a
drear and dying sound" affrights the flamens; Moloch leaves his
"shadows dread" and "burning idol all of blackest hue." "The
rays of Bethlehem" blind the gods, and the Babe can "control the
damned crew."

Light and order return with these phrases, and gloom and
confusion make way for them as the "shadows pale" disperse and
the fairies leave "their moon-lov'd maze." The poet strives for
striking brilliance through the unhappy image of "the sun in
bed" which, if less clumsy, would have reminded the reader that
day-break was withheld in the opening movement. Even so, the
verse prepares for the final picture of the nativity:

66

> But see! the Virgin blest,
> Hath laid her Babe to rest.
>   Time is our tedious song should here have ending;
> Heav'n's youngest teemed star
> Hath fixt her polisht car,
>   Her sleeping Lord with handmaid lamp attending:
> And all about the courtly stable,
> Bright-harness'd angels sit in order serviceable.

This scene has often been compared with the simply but definitely composed fifteenth-century nativities; but its effectiveness depends on more than its own composition. It catches up the pattern underlying the preceding movements, bringing order after confusion and reflecting the peaceful hush and the brilliant harmony of the first two movements. It is pervaded by the clear and steady brilliance of the new star's "handmaid lamp," and enclosed by the "order serviceable" of the "bright-harness'd angels." Its static quality fixes with appropriate firmness the pattern of light and harmony on which the poem has been composed.

The effect of the *Nativity Ode* is thus produced by its reiteration of a pattern of imagery, variously presented in the three movements, and impressed with finality in the concluding verse. The balanced contrast between the first and third movements serves to throw the central movement into sharp relief. This emphasis defines the poem's significance for Milton. It was at about this time that he was, in his own phrase, "confirmed in this opinion, that he who would not be frustrate of his hope to write well hereafter in laudable things ought himself to be a true poem; that is, a composition and pattern of the best and honourablest things. . . ."[16] The *Nativity Ode* is his first achievement of composition and pattern in the full Miltonic sense, and it is so because it expresses his achievement of composition and pattern in himself through the harmonious illumination resulting from his recognition of the significance of the Incarnation. It is the first of Milton's inspired poems; and the angelic choir is the symbol of his inspiration.

III

The imagery of the *Ode* is of course no more original than the pastoral conventions of *Lycidas*.[17] The effect again depends on

[16]*Apology, Works,* III, p. 303.

[17]See the annotations by Verity (Pitt Press Series), Hughes (*Paradise Re-*

Milton's handling of traditional elements. The emphasis on the intense brilliance and divine harmony of the angelic choir has in itself no peculiar personal significance, for it was a commonplace in seventeenth-century poetry—to go no farther. Milton knew, for example, Giles Fletcher's reference, in *Christ's Victorie in Heaven*, to the time

> When, like the starres the singing angels shot
> To earth, and heav'n awaked all his eyes
> To see another sun at midnight rise
> On earth.

Nearly the whole of Milton's conception is implicit in these unmusical lines; but they are not a source, for the ideas were simply part of the consciousness of a century whose metaphysics were shot through with symbolic light. They occur repeatedly in the work of poets who neither knew Milton nor were known to him in 1629. George Herbert concluded his second *Christmas* with a typically metaphysical association of the sun and harmony:

> His beams shall cheer my breast, and both so twine,
> Till even his beams sing, and my music shine.

His mystically-minded disciple, Henry Vaughan, used the idea of nature's harmony in *The Morning Watch:*

> Thus all is hurl'd
> In sacred hymns, and order, the great chime
> And symphony of nature. Prayer is
> The world in tune.

Richard Crashaw made the idea that the Nativity was the "bright dawn of our eternal day" the centre of *In the Holy Nativity*, and his *In the Glorious Epiphany* associated harmony with light through the idea that the sun is symbolic of the sin which prevents man from hearing the heavenly music:

> This daily wrong
> Silenc't the morning-sons, & dampt their song.
> Nor was't our deafness, but our sins, that thus
> Long made th'harmonious orbes all mute to us.

These examples will suffice to indicate that Milton's imagery is not unique, and also to suggest what I believe could be proved by an extensive examination of seventeenth-century poetry, that none of his contemporaries developed the idea and its varied

---

gained . . . , *Minor Poems*), and Cook (*Transactions of the Connecticut Academy of Arts and Sciences*, XV, pp. 307-68).

associations with anything like the controlled complexity of the central passage of the *Ode*. Behind the symbol of the choir and the spheres lies an intricate fusion of traditions. The connection of angels with stars is suggested by such passages as *Revelation* 9.1, 11; 12.4; *I Kings* 22.19; *Judges* 5.20. It also owes much to the Greek idea, recorded by Plato (*Republic* 621B) and Aristotle (*Nicomachean Ethics* 6.7), and frequently employed by Milton's former model Ovid, that the stars are divine beings. This leads inevitably to the association of the songs of praise sung by the angels in heaven with the music of the spheres (as in Crashaw), the bringing together of passages like *Job* 38.7, and the Pythagorean doctrine expressed, for example, by Plato (*Republic* 617) and by Cicero (*De re publica*, 6.17, 18). Nine was the number of spheres usually given (as by Cicero). This is the number of the Muses, identified by Plutarch with the spheres (*Symposium* 9). The Muses can thus be connected with the angels, who (according to Pseudo-Dionysius the Areopagite) are divided into nine orders. Moreover, the music of the spheres is represented by the pipe of Pan, who is in love with Echo, another symbol of the music. Pan is sometimes identified with the universe, sometimes with the sun; and he is a shepherd who controls the flocking stars and preserves their harmony. The early Christians associated Pan with Christ, as does Milton in the eighth stanza of the *Ode*; but the full significance of Milton's association is only apparent from the description of the choir which follows. Christ is the reason for the angelic music and the source of the music of the spheres, which, at his birth, should harmonize with the choir and produce in men the harmony of their first perfection. These harmonies are not only described but echoed in Milton's verse. Of the music of the spheres Cicero wrote: "Some learned men, by imitating this harmony with strings and vocal melodies, have opened a way for their return to this place; as all others have done who, endued with pre-eminent qualities, have cultivated in their mortal life the pursuits of heaven."[18] This becomes the function of Milton's verse for the first time in the *Nativity Ode*; and the incarnate Christ is not only the subject of his poem, but the source of his inspiration.

It is thus the symbol of illumination and harmony provided

[18]*De re publica*, 6.17; see S. G. S. Spaeth, *Milton's Knowledge of Music*, appendix v.

by the choir and the spheres which fuses the heterogeneous particles of the *Ode* and gives it its controlled power. It does so because it enables the poet to draw on a vast reservoir of pagan and Christian suggestion while transcending the conflict between the two traditions, and consequently to express something approaching the totality of his literary experience. The fruit of this experience is his sense of divine inspiration. From "the Samian teacher"[19] he had learned of the stern discipline required of the poet who would reproduce the music of the spheres; for the Christian the aim of such discipline must be to echo the angelic hymn of communion with God through the incarnate Christ. The central symbol of the *Ode* represents the achievement of this inspiring communion.

IV

It is significant that there is no reference to the celestial music in Milton's poetry before 1629. His attention seems to have been drawn to it when he had to compose his second academic prolusion. Here he examines the opinions of Plato and Aristotle on the Pythagorean allegory, and observes: "Hence arose the story . . . of how the Muses dance before Jove's altar day and night; hence too the attribution to Phoebus . . . of musical skill. Hence the belief . . . that Harmonia was the daughter of Jove and Electra, and that at her marriage to Cadmus all the choirs of heaven sang in concert."[20]   The mythological references to God, the sun, harmony, and light, suggest that this is the germ from which the *Ode*'s pattern developed; its significance is indicated by the assertion that man cannot hear the music because "the presumption of that thief Prometheus" has left him "buried in sin," though "if our souls were pure, chaste, and white as snow . . . , then indeed our ears would ring and be filled with that exquisite music of the stars in their orbits; then would all things turn back to the age of gold, and we ourselves, free from every grief, would pass our lives in a blessed peace. . . ."

[19]Pythagoras, *Elegia sexta*, l. 59.
[20]*Milton: Private Correspondence and Academic Exercises*, trans. P. B. Tillyard, p. 66. The prolusion cannot be dated, but since Milton placed it second in the group it probably belongs to the beginning of his Cambridge career. Its connection with the *Ode* leads E. M. W. Tillyard to place it about 1629 (*ibid.*, pp. xxvi-xxix).

The force with which this idea struck Milton's imagination is indicated by the fact that from the *Ode* to *Lycidas* he was almost incapable of writing on a serious subject without introducing the music. *Il Penseroso* echoes the phrasing of his prolusion; *The Passion* and *Upon the Circumcision* begin with references to the music of the *Ode*. *At a Solemn Music* is constructed upon its central conception, with this significant variation, that the place of the Nativity angels is taken by the hundred forty and four thousand "not defiled with women," who sing before the Lamb in *Revelation* 14. In 1642 Milton recorded the impression made on his youthful mind by this passage.[21] Its song provided a more suitable angelic counterpart for the music of the spheres than the Nativity choir since the latter belonged to a particular occasion while the former was constant. In *Arcades* "the celestial siren's harmony" marks the climax of the speech of the Genius, though there is no reference to its scriptural counterpart. Superficially this is also true in *Comus*; but the Renaissance habit of speaking of God and Christ in mythological terms indicates the significance of the prologue's opening lines and of the epilogue's exhortation to love virtue since

> She can teach you how to climb
> Higher than the sphery chime.

Finally in *Lycidas* the destiny of the poet-priest is fulfilled as he hears "the unexpressive nuptial song" sung by

> all the saints above,
> In solemn troops, and sweet societies,
> That sing, and singing in their glory move.

This is the appropriate resolution of the problems involved in the elegy's lament; for in his youthful defence of poetry, *Ad Patrem*, Milton envisaged for himself and his musical father the same reward: "When we return to our native Olympus . . . we shall walk . . . through the temples of the skies, and with the harp's soft accompaniment we shall sing sweet songs to which the stars shall echo and the vault of heaven from pole to pole. Even now the fiery spirit who flies through the swift spheres is singing his immortal melody and unutterable song in harmony with the starry choruses."[22]

[21] *Apology, Works*, III, p. 306.
[22] Hughes' translation, ll. 30-7. Cf. the apotheosis of Diodati in *Epitaphium Damonis*.

This is the reward of the poet who seeks his inspiration from the "Heav'nly Muse" of the *Ode*'s introductory verses.[23]   Here Milton calls on his muse to present a gift to the Christ who has laid aside "that glorious form, that light unsufferable," and to prevent with her offering the star-led wizards:

> Have thou the honour first, thy Lord to greet,
> And join thy voice unto the angel quire,
> From out his secret altar toucht with hallow'd fire.

This hallowed fire from God's altar, about which the angelic muses eternally sing and singing in their glory move like stars, is the fire with which the seraph touched the lips of the prophet Isaiah.[24] The product of this inspiration is the glorious form and light unsufferable of the symbol thrown into relief by the patterning of the *Ode* whose beauty surpassed anything Milton had hitherto written because it expressed with perfect adequacy and complete control a new and profound religious emotion.   Like that Englishman of whom Bede tells "a marvellous and very pleasant anecdote," Milton "suddenly by an act of God became," not simply "a poet," but a poet with a peculiar purpose and peculiar gifts.[25]

It was this experience, at once aesthetic and religious, which crystallized Milton's conviction of special poetical calling and provided him with a definition of his function.   Its effects correspond in general to the effects of the Puritan conversion.   He then determined to forsake the ways of his youth and (as *Elegia sexta* implies) the masters of the *elegia levis*; the new pattern imposed on his thought and feeling drove out these masters as the Babe drove out the pagan gods.   But as his experience was essentially aesthetic and immediately produced the harmonies of the *Ode*, so it differed from the experience of his Puritan contemporaries in involving a recognition, not only of the personal significance of the Incarnation, but also of its relationship to the classical and humanistic doctrine of harmonious perfection symbolized by the music of the spheres.   Of this perfection divinely inspired poetry seemed

[23]On the Renaissance identification of the muse of astronomy with the Holy Spirit as the inspirer of Christian poets, and on the place of Milton's *Paradise Lost* invocations in this tradition, see Miss L. B. Campbell, "The Christian Muse" (*Huntingdon Library Bulletin*, 8).

[24]Cf. *Reason of Church Government*, *Works*, III, p. 241.

[25]Translation of a Latin note in Milton's Commonplace Book, *Works*, XVIII, p. 139.

to him the supreme expression. Thus the *Ode* helps to explain the enthusiasm with which he found in the Calvinistic doctrine of grace a satisfactory expression of his sense of peculiar calling, and also his devotion to the ideal of a harmonious society reproducing "the old and elegant humanity of Greece." The delicate balance represented by the *Ode*'s central symbol was difficult to preserve; but the main effort of his life was directed towards its preservation in himself and its reproduction through poetry and in the life of men. When his efforts for society were frustrated and he himself was cut off by blindness, it was to the far surpassing light of his inspiration that he turned for the harmony of spirit expressed in the Christian doctrines and the classic composition and pattern of his great poems.

stands to Milton in place of what the Puritans called "conversion" (73). Despite Rosemond Tuve's cautions against "over-personal" readings of the poem (44), this view of the Ode as, in Barker's phrase, "the testimony of Milton's religious experience" (170) has gained wide currency in recent discussions. According to Patrick J. Cullen, for instance, the *Nativity Ode* "is structured so that the meditator himself experiences a conversion from pagan illusion to the new Christian truth of the babe in the manger" (1568). In much the same vein, I. S. McLaren argues that the poem enacts "the process by which the narrator gradually perceives the significance of both God's offer of grace through the Son and man's responsibility for response entailed in that offer" (194). And Georgia B. Christopher defines Milton's subject as "the revolution that grace makes in the consciousness of the poet" (23).

All these readings of the poem as a kind of confessional autobiography seem to me to be based upon a patently false assumption: namely, that there is an individualized human presence in the text—whether Cullen's meditator, McLaren's narrator, or Christopher's poet—to be converted. In fact, as I hope to show, the *Nativity Ode* is the most rigorously depersonalized of all Milton's nondramatic works. It is a poem that faces not inward but outward, a poem that casts the reader rather than the poet in the role of the convert.

The very form in which Milton chose to cast his poem militates against autobiographical interpretation. For whether we follow Robert Shafer, George N. Shuster, Carol Maddison, and Paul H. Fry in identifying *On the Morning of Christ's Nativity* as an ode or Philip Rollinson in reading it as a hymn, the genre of the poem automatically implies a choric rather than an individual speaker. In the performance of Pindar's odes, Shafer reminds us, "the chant of the chorus still held undisputed the place of first importance" (17), while the hymn, Fry remarks, is almost by definition "a choir-poem that harmoniously effaces the individual" (44). Sensitive as he always was to generic expectations, Milton created accordingly a voice that is essentially choric in nature. As the final lines of the proem make clear, the "hymn"

A Poem of Absences

J. Martin Evans

In an influential article published in 1941 Arthur E. Barker argued that the *Nativity Ode* records an experience in Milton's life "which corresponds to the conversion of his Puritan associates" (170). Amplifying on Barker's point, A. S. P. Woodhouse claimed two years later that "taken together, the *Nativity Ode* and *How Soon Hath Time* give evidence of an experience which

(17) is sung by the heavenly muse in concert with "the Angel Choir" (27)[1]—hence the insistently plural pronouns in the latter part of the poem— "our" ears (126), "our" senses (127), "our" fancy (134), "our" song (239). Far from belonging to an individualized poet or his surrogate, the voice we hear performing the "humble ode" (24) is public rather than private, communal rather than personal, celestial rather than human.[2]

In this respect it is instructive to compare *On the Morning of Christ's Nativity* with its intended companion piece, *The Passion*. The latter poem is almost literally suffocated by the poet's self-consciousness:

Befriend me Night, best Patroness of grief,
Over the Pole thy thickest mantle throw,
And work my flatter'd fancy to belief,
That Heav'n and Earth are color'd with my woe;
    My sorrows are too dark for day to know:
The leaves should all be black whereon I write,
And letters where my tears have washt, a wannish white.   (29-35)

During the course of this one stanza Milton refers to himself no fewer than six times, and the poem as a whole is obsessively self-referential. The *Nativity Ode*, on the contrary, contains not a single "I," "me," or "my" in its thirty-one stanzas. If *Lycidas* is "a poem nearly anonymous" in John Crowe Ransom's famous formulation, the *Nativity Ode* comes as close as a poem can to being wholly anonymous.

This lack of personal involvement stands out in marked contrast to most other representatives of the Nativity tradition. If we compare the *Nativity Ode* with almost any celebration of Christ's birth written in the sixteenth or seventeenth centuries, what strikes us immediately is the absence of any reference to the effect of Christ's birth upon the poet himself. At the end of "New Heaven, New Warre," for example, Robert Southwell turns from the manger scene to exhort his own soul to remain loyal to his Savior:

My soul with Christ joyne thou in fight,
Sticke to the tents that he hath pight;
Within his Crib is surest ward,

This little Babe will be thy guard;
If thou wilt foyle thy foes with joy,
Then flit not from this heavenly boy.   (43-48)

In the sestet of his sonnet on the Nativity, John Donne, after addressing the Christ child throughout the octave, suddenly shifts his attention to his personal spiritual concerns:

Seest thou, my Soule, with thy faiths eyes, how he
Which fills all place, yet none holds him, doth lye?
Was not his pity towards thee wondrous high,
That would have need to be pittied by thee?
Kisse him, and with him into Egypt goe,
With his kinde mother, who partakes thy woe.   (9-14)

And in a similar vein, Ben Jonson, in the concluding lines of "A Hymne on the Nativitie of My Saviour," meditates upon the significance for himself and his readers of the events he has just described:

What comfort by him doe wee winne,
Who made himselfe the price of sinne
    To make us heires of glory.
To see this Babe, all innocence;
A Martyr borne in our defence;
    Can man forget this Storie?   (19-24)

There is nothing even remotely corresponding to these sentiments in the *Nativity Ode*, and indeed it is hard to see how there could be. The poem does not contain anyone who could experience them.

The presence of a poet or his surrogate in the text of a poem does not, of course, depend exclusively upon the use of the first-person pronoun. It can also be implied by a direct, second-person address to a character in the poem. Thus George Herbert in his sonnet on "Christmas" after lines of pure narration suddenly turns in the sestet to pray to the child whose birth he has been describing:

O Thou, whose glorious, yet contracted light,
    Wrapt in nights mantle, stole into a manger;
Since my dark soul and brutish is thy right,

To Man of all beasts be not thou a stranger:
Furnish & deck my soul, that thou mayst have
A better lodging then a rack or grave.
                                        (9–14)

And Henry Vaughan, after celebrating Christ's
birth and its impact on the natural world, devotes
the final two stanzas to confessing his own inadequacy and sinfulness:

I would I had in my best part
Fit Roomes for thee! or that my heart
Were so clean as
Thy manger was,
But I am all filth, and obscene,
Yet, if thou wilt, thou canst make clean.
                                        (19–24)

Milton, on the contrary, never addresses the
child directly. Jesus is consistently referred to in
the third person—"Nature in awe to him" (32),
"he her fears to cease" (45), "His reign of peace"
(63). As a result, there is nothing in the *Nativity
Ode* to parallel the agonized yearnings of Herbert
or Vaughan for personal regeneration. It is difficult, therefore, to agree with Barker when he
claims that the effects of the experience recorded
in the poem "correspond in general to the effects of the Puritan conversion" (181), for there
is no conversion in the poem to be affected.

At first sight this lack of any subjective presence might seem strange in a work by a Puritan
poet, but I believe it is part of an overall strategy
which is quintessentially Puritan. We may begin
by noting that although the poet is the most
notable absentee he is by no means the only one.
For whereas most representations of the Nativity
in art and literature focus on the presence of the
wise men and the shepherds at the manger, Milton sets the scene before their arrival. The magi
are still on their way to Bethlehem:

See how from far upon the Eastern road
The Star-led Wizards haste with odors sweet:
O run, prevent them with thy humble ode,
And lay it lowly at his blessed feet;
Have thou the honor first, thy Lord to greet.
                                        (22–26)

And the shepherds in turn are still in the fields
with their flocks:

The Shepherds on the Lawn,
Or ere the point of dawn,
    Sat simply chatting in a rustic row. (85–87)

The heavenly muse has "prevented" them all.
When we encounter the child in the manger
there is no one standing between us.

What is more, Mary and Joseph have been
effectively banished from their traditional positions. The former eventually makes a brief appearance in the final stanza; the latter never
appears at all. As Blake failed to notice when he
illustrated the poem (see especially Blake's first
illustration in Keynes's edition), the only figures
we encounter in the early stanzas are the personified abstractions of Nature, Peace, Truth, Justice,
and Mercy. The entire scene, one could say without exaggeration, has been completely dehuman-
ized. The space which in so many Nativity representations was crowded with observers is totally
empty. Even the traditional ox and ass have been
omitted. The *Nativity Ode* is a poem of absences.

Milton's strategy of erasure is too consistent to
be accidental. It reflects, I believe, the Puritan dis-
taste for allowing any intermediary to intrude
between the individual soul and its maker. By purg-
ing the scene of all the traditional witnesses of the
Nativity, Milton forces us to respond to the Nativity
not vicariously through the experiences of the wise
men and the shepherds but directly. Nobody, not
even the poet, stands between the reader and the
babe in the manger. To a greater degree than in
any other Nativity poem, we encounter the Christ-
child face to face. One might well say of Milton, as
Ruskin once said of Giotto, that "the most significant thing in all his works ... is his choice of moments" (Herbert, *The Art* 248).[3]

As Lowry Nelson has noted, moreover, Milton
heightens this sense of immediacy by fusing the
tenses in the poem in such a way that the events
seem to be taking place in a kind of eternal present, both then and now. From the opening stanza
of the hymn onward, the verbs alternate between
past and present so frequently—"was" (29), "lies"
(31), "was" (35), "woos" (38), "Sent" (46), "strikes"

(52)—that the narrative finally seems to transcend chronology. We are simultaneously looking back at the Nativity across history and witnessing it as it happens.

Seen in such a temporal context, Milton's choice of a moment has theological as well as narrative significance. For the narrative is so organized that although the child has been born when the poem begins he has not yet been welcomed or accepted by the world. The induction insists that the sky, "by the Sun's team untrod, / Hath took no print of the approaching light" (19-20). Literally, of course, this refers merely to the fact that the scene takes place before sunrise. Metaphorically, however, it suggests that the world is still "untrod" by the Son; the approaching light of Christ has not yet risen. As the sole human witnesses of the scene, we, too, by implication, have not yet been illuminated by the arrival of Christ. Like Nature in the opening stanza of the hymn, we are unregenerate, unenlightened, still trapped in a pre-Christian stage of our history. The shepherds' lack of awareness that the "mighty *Pan*" has "kindly come to live with them below" (89-90) interprets retrospectively our position as the poem begins. By implication, our "silly" (92) thoughts, too, are preoccupied with other matters.

In a sense, then, one might say that the *Nativity Ode* is about *our* conversion, *our* dawning awareness of the new birth and its overwhelming consequences. By creating a spatial and temporal vacuum between his audience and the "Heav'n-born child" (30), Milton draws us into the poem no less surely than he transforms the spectators of *A Maske Performed at Ludlow Castle* into participants. Like the women of Canterbury in *Murder in the Cathedral*, we are forced to bear witness, to experience as if for the first time the Savior's entry into this "darksome House of mortal Clay" (14). My disagreement with Barker thus has to do not so much with the nature of the experience recorded in the poem as with its location. If indeed a personal conversion takes place during the course of the *Nativity Ode*, it is the reader's, not the poet's.

Stanford University

NOTES

[1] In order to maintain her thesis that the poem is spoken by a "poet-swain" Georgia Christopher is forced to rewrite line 27 to read "and join [his] voice unto the Angel Choir" (23). Similarly Michael Lieb asserts that: "the speaker desires to 'lay' his 'humble ode' 'lowly at [Christ's] blessed feet' " (352).

[2] The way Milton retroactively defines the speakers of the *Nativity Ode* in the companion poem *The Passion*—"My muse with Angels did divide to sing" (4)—may suggest at first that the muse sings some sections of the poem, the angel choir other sections. However, the word "divide" was a technical Renaissance term used to describe polyphonic music in which the various voices perform simultaneously.

[3] It has become almost obligatory to compare Milton's verbal representation of the Nativity with paintings of the scene (see Tillyard 35-42 and Stapleton, for example). The closest visual analogue I have found is the triptych by Grunewald in which the Virgin is portrayed alone with the child and a string orchestra of angels in the central panel.

WORKS CITED

Barker, Arthur E. "The Pattern of Milton's *Nativity Ode.*" *University of Toronto Quarterly* 10 (1941): 167-81.

Christopher, Georgia B. *Milton and the Science of the Saints*. Princeton, NJ: Princeton UP, 1982.

Cullen, Patrick J. "Imitation and Metamorphosis: The Golden Age Eclogue in Spenser, Milton, and Marvell." *PMLA* 84 (1969): 1559-70.

Donne, John. "Nativitie." *Donne: The Divine Poems.* Ed. Helen Gardner. Oxford: Oxford UP, 1952.

Fry, Paul H. *The Poet's Calling in the English Ode.* New Haven, CT: Yale UP, 1980.

Herbert, George. "Christmas." *The Works of George Herbert.* Ed. F. E. Hutchinson. Oxford: Clarendon P, 1941.

Herbert, Robert L., ed. *The Art Criticism of John Ruskin.* New York: Bantam, 1964.

Jonson, Ben. "A Hymne on the Nativitie of My Savour." *Ben Jonson*. Ed. C. H. Herford and Percy and Evelyn Simpson. 11 vols. Oxford: Oxford UP, 1925-52. 8:130

Keynes, Geoffrey, ed. On the Morning of Christ's Nativity: *Milton's Hymn with Illustrations by William Blake*. Cambridge: Cambridge UP, 1923.

Lieb, Michael. "Milton and the Kenotic Christology: Its Literary Bearing." *ELH* 37 (1970): 342-60.

Maddison, Carol. *Apollo and the Nine: A History of the Ode*. Baltimore, MD: Johns Hopkins UP, 1960.

McLaren, I. S. "Milton's *Nativity Ode*: The Function of Poetry and Structures of Response in 1629." *Milton Studies* 15 (1981): 181-200.

Milton, John. *Complete Poems and Major Prose*. Ed. Merritt Y. Hughes. Indianapolis, IN: Odyssey P, 1957.

Nelson, Lowry. *Baroque Lyric Poetry*. New Haven, CT: Yale UP, 1961.

Ransom, John Crowe. "A Poem Nearly Anonymous." 1933. Rpt. Lycidas: *The Tradition and the Poem*. Ed. C. A. Patrides. New York: Holt, 1961. 64-81.

Rollinson, Philip. "Milton's Nativity Poem and the Decorum of Genre." *Milton Studies* 7 (1975): 165-88.

Shafer, Robert. *The English Ode to 1660: An Essay in Literary History*. Princeton, NJ: Princeton UP, 1918.

Shuster, George N. *The English Ode from Milton to Keats*. New York: Columbia UP, 1940.

Southwell, Robert. "New Heaven, New Warre." *The Poems of Robert Southwell, S. J.* Ed. James H. McDonald and Nancy P. Brown. Oxford: Oxford UP, 1967.

Stapleton, Laurence. "Milton and the New Music." *University of Toronto Quarterly* 23 (1954): 217-26.

Tillyard, E. M. W. *Milton*. London: Chatto and Windus, 1930.

Tuve, Rosemond. *Images and Themes in Five Poems by Milton*. Cambridge, MA: Harvard UP, 1957.

Vaughan, Henry. "Christs Nativity." *Vaughan's Works*. Ed. L. C. Martin. Oxford: Oxford UP, 1957.

Woodhouse, A. S. P. "Notes on Milton's Early Development." *University of Toronto Quarterly* 13 (1943): 66-101.

Expectation and Prematurity in Milton's *Nativity Ode*

DAVID QUINT

Yale University

The inaugural poem of Milton's career, *On the Morning of Christ's Nativity*, tells the story of great expectations that fail to be realized in the way that they are initially projected. Much is anticipated from the fresh start to history, both sacred and literary, promised by the poem. Overturning its classical models—and I shall propose that a Euripidean subtext governs the poem's shape—the *Nativity Ode* expects from the newborn Christ a reign of truth that will replace and banish earlier pagan error once and for all; it expects, moreover, the restoration of a sinful nature and humanity to their original purity. Written in dialogue with other works of Milton of the same period, notably his Latin *Elegies V* and *VI* and the *Second Prolusion*, the poem also suggests what the new poet expects of himself: a purified poetry that separates itself from a fleshly, pagan inspiration. These double projects of the *Nativity Ode* are, at best, only partly fulfilled, and the course of the poem reveals them to have been mistakenly conceived in the first place, the products of the young poet's wishful thinking. But the wishes are felt, nonetheless, particularly insofar as they express a longing to escape from or put an end to history and death. Milton's first great poem succeeds by staging the failure of its fondest dreams.[1]

---

1. "Ay, me, I fondly dream!" the swain will cry out in *Lycidas* (line 56), as he hopes that poetry might grant an exemption from death. For commentary on *On the Morning of Christ's Nativity*, see Albert S. Cook, "Notes on Milton's Ode on the Morning of Christ's Nativity," *Transactions of the Connecticut Academy of Arts and Sciences* 15 (1909): 307–68; A. S. P. Woodhouse and Douglas Bush, *A Variorum Commentary on the Poems of John Milton* (New York, 1972), 2, pt. 1:34–110; and the notes of Winifred Maynard in John Milton, *Odes, Pastorals, Masques*, ed. John Broadbent (Cambridge, 1975), pp. 6–44. Some important critical treatments of the poem are Paul Fry, *The Poet's Calling* (New Haven, Conn., 1980), pp. 37–48; J. B. Broadbent, "The Nativity Ode," in *The Living Milton*, ed. Frank Kermode (London, 1960), pp. 12–31; Rosamund Tuve, *Images and Themes in Five Poems by Milton* (Cambridge, Mass., 1957), pp. 37–72; Don Cameron Allen, *The Harmonious Vision: Studies*

I

On the Morning of Christ's Nativity celebrates in a hymn the birth of a
new oracle of truth in the world, the silencing of the old false oracles,
and the expulsion of those oracles' gods. However unprecedented the
sacred event it describes, Milton's version is modeled closely on an
earlier classical poem which tells a nearly identical story. In verses
1234–82 of the *Iphigenia in Tauris* (see Appendix), in a passage which
the young Milton annotated in his copy of Euripides, the chorus sings
of the birth of Apollo on Delos, how the infant god next leapt out of his
mother's arms, slew the serpent guarding the shrine at Delphi, and in-
stituted his oracle.[2] Here the choral ode divides in two, and its second
half, its antistrophe, recounts that there was already an oracle at Delphi
that Earth had reserved for her daughter Themis, an oracle that sent its
prophecies forth in the form of nighttime dreams and phantasms—what
the Latin translator, Wilhelm Canter, in Milton's edition, calls "spectres"
("spectra," for the Greek *phasmata*)—and "nocturnal imposture" ("imposturam / Nocturnam"). The baby Apollo appeals to his father Zeus,
who silences the nighttime voices—*enopas*—of the rival, female oracle
and expels its phantom dreams—*oneirous*—from Delphi.

Euripides's two-part ode is hymnal, and it appears to be a much con-
densed version of the *Homeric Hymn to Apollo*, a poem that has recently
been linked to the *Nativity Ode* by Stella Purce Revard.[3] The Homeric
hymn similarly divides into two major parts split between the cult sites
of Delos and Delphi, the story of the god's birth on Delos and the account of his slaying at Delphi of the serpent who was the foster mother
of the monstrous Typhaon. The serpent's rotting away beneath the
rays of Helios gives the place the name of Pytho and Apollo the epithet
of Pythian ("the rotter"); in subsequent tradition the serpent is herself
named Python as in the first book of Ovid's *Metamorphoses* (1.438),
though she is sometimes confused, in a kind of rhyme or typographical

---

in Milton's Poetry (1954; enlarged ed., Baltimore, 1970), pp. 24–40; Arthur Barker, "The
Pattern of Milton's *Nativity Ode*," *University of Toronto Quarterly* 10 (1941): 167–81. I. S. Mac-
Laren provides a bibliography of criticism at the end of his "Milton's Nativity Ode: The
Function of Poetry and Structures of Response in 1629 (with a Bibliography of Twenti-
eth-Century Criticism)," *Milton Studies* 15 (1981): 181–200. I cite the texts of *On the
Morning of Christ's Nativity* and of other poetic works of Milton from *The Poems of John
Milton*, ed. John Carey and Alastair Fowler (London, 1968). I cite Milton's prose works
from *The Works of John Milton*, ed. Frank Allen Patterson et al., 18 vols. (New York, 1931),
hereafter referred to as *Works*.

2. For Milton's annotations, see Milton, *Works*, 18:311.

3. Stella Purce Revard, *Milton and the Tangles of Neaera's Hair* (Columbia, Mo., 1997),
pp. 64–90. Revard's arguments and my own overlap at several points; she is particularly
intent on relating Apollo to the classicizing culture of Papal Rome.

inversion, with her foster child, Typhon.[4] The young Milton evokes the myth at the end of his *First Prolusion*, where he remarks of the defender of night over day: "Surely worthy is he that the Sun slay him with the adverse strokes of its rays, like a new Python."[5] The Euripidean version of the hymn is notable on two scores: first, Apollo is still a baby when he kills the serpent at Delphi and institutes his oracle; second, he displaces a preexistent, nocturnal oracle on the spot: there is some suggestion—at least in Canter's translation—that this was a false oracle. Both of these variations anticipate the *Nativity Ode.*

Apollo is the first of the pagan gods to be silenced when the oracles become dumb at the birth of Christ in stanza 19 of Milton's poem; he leaves shrieking from the Delphic shrine which he had founded in the Homeric hymn.[6] Typhon is the last to go in stanza 25:

> Nor all the gods beside,
> Longer dare abide,
>   Not Typhon huge ending in snaky twine:
> Our babe to show his Godhead true,
> Can in his swaddling bands control the damned crew.

(Lines 224–28)

The emergence of Typhon here seems to be suggested by the story of Osiris that precedes it, for there were at least two Typhons, one the Egyptian god who slew his brother Osiris—a story that Milton famously recounts again in *Areopagitica*.[7] But the size and snaky body of this Typhon seem to identify him with the Greek Typhoeus-Typhon—the Typhon who will later appear in the opening simile of *Paradise Lost* to suggest the size of Satan (1.199). We may also note that Milton's epic gives us our last view of Satan with a simile describing him as "whom the sun / Engendered in the Pythian vale on slime / Huge Python" (10.529–31) as he and his followers are transformed into snakes. This is the Typhon-confused-with-Python of whom Natales Comes writes in his

---

4. On this lore, see Joseph Fontenrose, *Python* (Berkeley and Los Angeles, 1959), pp. 70–93. For the relation of the Python tradition to Spenser's Error, see James Nohrnberg, *The Analogy of "The Faerie Queene"* (Princeton, N.J., 1976), pp. 135–51; Nohrnberg discusses Milton's use of Python in *The Reason of Church Government* on p. 145.

5. Milton, *Works*, 12:147.

6. For the tradition of the silencing of the oracles, derived largely from a Christianizing reading of Plutarch's *On the Obsolescence of Oracles*, see C. A. Patrides, "The Cessation of the Oracles: The History of a Legend," *Modern Language Review* 60 (1965): 500–507. Plutarch's treatise lies behind the reference to Christ as "the mighty Pan" at line 89. The silencing of the oracles is featured in Milton's more proximate model for *On the Morning of Christ's Nativity*, Tasso's canzone, "Mira devotamente, alma pentita," lines 73–90, written to celebrate the crèche in the chapel of Sixtus V in Santa Maria Maggiore in Rome; see Torquato Tasso, *Opere*, ed. Bruno Maier, 5 vols. (Milan, 1963), 2:412–17.

7. Milton, *Works*, 4:338.

83

influential *Mythologiae*: "Homer wrote in his hymn to Apollo that Apollo was called Pythian because he killed Typhon with his arrows: who, rotted away by the heat of the sun, hence gave to Pythian Apollo his name."[8] Milton plays on the multiple Typhon myths in order to frame the parade of dispossessed pagan gods on both ends with the story of Apollo. He inverts and runs backward the stories of the Homeric and Euripidean hymns to Apollo in which the god kills the monster at Delphi before instituting his oracle: here Apollo leaves his shrine before the Christ child overcomes Typhon with the rest of the damned crew. The "snaky twine" of Typhon's body may suggest snaky twins, the two serpents sent by Hera whom the infant Hercules strangled in his cradle in Pindar's first Nemean Ode: this is the mythic parallel noted by previous commentators. But the feat of "our babe" equally repeats the victory of baby Apollo over the serpent of Delphi, the Python-Typhon, in Euripides's account of the god's birth-myth. The overcoming by Christ of both Apollo and Typhon discloses, of course, that there is no difference between the pagan god and the monster he defeated, even if the poem puts them on either end of its catalog of the "damned crew": from the perspective of the new, true religion, they are equally monstrous.

The model of the ode in the *Iphigenia in Tauris* is especially felt in the following, penultimate stanza 26 of Milton's poem, where the pagan gods are reduced in simile to shadowy nocturnal ghosts and fays fading away at sunrise:

> The flocking shadows pale,
> Troop to the infernal jail,
>   Each fettered ghost slips to his several grave,
> And the yellow-skirted fays,
> Fly after the night-steeds, leaving their moon-loved maze.
>
> (Lines 232–36)

This final simile is like the simile that ends book 1 of *Paradise Lost* and analogously compares and diminishes the devils—devils whose future enshrinement as pagan deities in the Holy Land and on the "Delphian cliff " (1.517) has just been cataloged—to faerie elves dancing in the moonlight whom "some belated peasant sees / Or dreams he sees" (1.781–88). Both suggest a rationalist understanding of paganism that explains away gods and devils as so many phantoms of benighted superstition or of a literally lunatic imagination. The insubstantial fays may be harmless enough, even charming; they, like the gods themselves, have their uses for poetry—as Milton will demonstrate in *L'Allegro* (lines 100–116). But the dismissal of paganism from the earth and from the poem in the form of ghosts and fays that may be indistinguishable from

---

8. *Natalis Comitis mythologiae sive explicationis fabularum libri decem* (Padua, 1616), p. 189.

the shadows of night repeats the banishment and silencing of the nocturnal larvae of Themis at the advent of Apollo. In fact, all of the pagan gods who are silenced at the birth of Christ are characterized by nighttime activity and darkness: "nightly trance" (line 179), "twilight shade" (line 188), "midnight plaint" (line 191), "temples dim" (line 199), "shadows dread" (line 205), "dismal dance" (line 210), "anthems dark" (line 219). The light of truth disperses the shades of pagan error, just as Apollo's oracle replaces the voices and dream-specters of the night.

By a later period of antiquity, Apollo had become a sun god; reading back from this perspective, his displacement of the night-oracle of Themis can be characterized as the victory of solar light over darkness, and it thus conforms even more closely to Milton's final simile of the rising sun expelling the shadowy ghosts and fays of night. The model of Euripides's revised hymn to Apollo fits into the larger pattern of solar imagery that critics have observed in Milton's ode.[9] The sun, the paramour of Nature, is dismissed in the first stanza of the hymn and sees in stanza 7 "a greater sun" (line 83) appear with the birth of the Son. The English language pun reinforces the typology of Christ as the Sun of Righteousness.[10] Apollo is merely the first of a series of banished pagan gods in Milton's poem—Baal, Hammon, Thammuz, Moloch, and Osiris—who are solar deities or have solar associations, all of whom are shown to be false suns eclipsed in darkness when the "rays of Bethlehem" (line 223) begin to shine.[11]

Milton would have known that the Christmas feast had itself replaced pagan festivals of the birth of the sun at the winter solstice, and his hymn recalls another pagan hymn to the sun god: Julian the Apostate's long prose hymn to King Helios written to celebrate the new solar year in January.[12] In the *Apology for Smectymnuus*, Milton would later mention

9. See, esp., Mother M. Christopher Pecheux, "The Image of the Sun in Milton's *Nativity Ode*," *Huntington Library Quarterly* 38 (1973–74): 315–33.

10. For the tradition, see Franz Dölger, *Sol Salutis* (Münster, 1925).

11. Pecheux mistakenly asserted that Moloch is the one god in Milton's list of expelled pagan deities who does not have associations with cults of sun worship (p. 331). John Selden's *De diis syris*, Milton's source for the gods of the ancient Near East, argues that Moloch was a solar deity and assimilates him with Mithras; see Selden, *De diis syris syntagmata II* (Amsterdam, 1680), pp. 103–5. The one deity in Milton's list whom Selden does not treat as a sun god is Dagon, "that twice battered god of Palestine" (line 199).

12. Eduard Norden has studied this tradition, which could alternately place the birth of the sun on December 25 or January 6 (the Christian feast of Epiphany) and which Norden places behind the announcement of the birth of a wonder-child in Virgil's *Fourth Eclogue*. See Norden, *Die Geburt des Kindes* (Leipzig, 1924), esp. pp. 14–50. Crashaw exploits the same tradition of the sun's birthday in his "Hymn in the Glorious Epiphanie," published in 1648 and possibly written shortly earlier, where the pagan religions that Christianity will replace are characterized as solar cults. Compare the announcement of the end of the pagan rites (lines 85–86) to the silencing of the oracles in Milton's ode. For a critical discussion, see George Walton Williams, *Image and Symbol in the Sacred Poetry of Richard Crashaw*

the "hymne in prose, frequent both in the Prophets, and in humane authors," and he probably has Julian in mind among the latter.[13] While Julian suggests that all the Olympian gods are manifestations of the power of the invisible sun, Helios, he particularly identifies Helios with Apollo, both as imperial patron (153d) and as divine interpreter and oracle (144b; 152d); Helios "is himself Apollo, the leader of the Muses." Julian, it is worth noting, represents a first attempt to bring back pagan error—under the form of pagan illumination—as a substitute for the Christian truth that has superseded it. At the beginning of his hymn, he refers to his former Christianity as itself a period of darkness—*skótous* (131b)—from which he has emerged to the true worship of the light of Helios.[14]

II

The Christian revelation is thus paralleled both before and after by false Apollonian enlightenments that similarly claim to chase away the shadows of untruth; the institution of the unique oracle of Christ can appear to fall into a historical series. The double problem posed to Milton's poem by its models and analogues—that its celebration of the birth of the true God repeats the pattern of a pagan nativity hymn, that pagan error has the potential to return after it has supposedly been definitively banished—is, in fact, built into its subject and unfolding argument. The *Nativity Ode* hesitates at a moment of premature apocalypticism or fullness of meaning at its center when "wisest fate says no" (line 149), and then must turn to the dispelling of residual error. The prospect of a still incomplete purification has implications not only for the poem's religio-historical ideas but for the poetic project of the young Milton intent on writing a noncarnal or virginal verse in this inaugural poem of his career: and we shall see that this project, too, involves the rejection of, and attempt to move beyond, Apollo as leader of the Muses. Both a pure poetry and a pure religion face checks that provide the drama of the poem.

Milton's ode was written between and in dialogue with his fifth and sixth Latin elegies.[15] In *Elegy VI*, Milton informs Charles Diodati that he has written or at least begun the *Nativity Ode.* The poem also announces

---

(Columbia, S.C., 1963), pp. 60–83. If Crashaw wrote his poem between the 1646 and 1648 editions of his *Steps to the Temple*, he could have known the *Nativity Ode.*

13. Milton, *Works* (n. 1 above), 3.1:343.

14. *The Works of the Emperor Julian*, trans. Wilmer Cave Wright, 3 vols. (Cambridge, Mass., 1980), 1:354.

15. The relationships among Milton's works in this period are discussed in A. S. P. Woodhouse, "Notes on Milton's Early Development," *University of Toronto Quarterly* 13 (1943–44): 66–101.

Milton's taking leave from elegiac poetry, a poetry that is written under the aegis and inspiration of Apollo. Diodati had sent some of his own Latin verses to Milton; he asked to be excused for their quality because the Christmas festivities he was enjoying with his friends had not allowed him to give successful attention to the Muses. Milton replies that, to the contrary, both wine and dance music—especially pretty girl musicians—are occasions for the poetic inspiration of Apollo:

> Massica foecundam despumant pocula venam,
>   Fundis et ex ipso condita metra cado.
> Addimus his artes, fusumque per intima Phoebum
>   Corda, favent uni Bacchus, Apollo, Ceres.

(Lines 31–34)

[Your Campanian cups foam with a fertile vein of poetry, and you pour your store of verses out of the very winejug. To all this we add the arts and Phoebus infused through your inmost heart; to you, uniquely, Bacchus, Apollo, and Ceres shed their favor.]

> Crede mihi, dum psallit ebur, comitataque plectrum
>   Implet odoratos festa chorea tholos,
> Percipies tacitum per pectora serpere Phoebum,
>   Quale repentinus permeat ossa calor;
> Perque puellares oculos digitumque sonantem
>   Irruet in totos lapsa Thalia sinus.
> Namque elegia levis multorum cura deorum est,
>   Et vocat ad numeros quemlibet illa suos.
> Liber adest elegis, Eratoque, Ceresque, Venusque,
>   Et cum purpurea matre tenellus Amor.

(Lines 43–52)

[Believe me, when the ivory plectrum plays on the strings, and the festive dancers, to its accompaniment, fill the perfumed halls, you will perceive Phoebus silently insinuate himself through your breast like a sudden heat that permeates the marrow; and through a girl's eyes and sounding finger Thalia will rush into and fill your bosom. For the lightsome elegy is the care of many gods, and she can call whom she will to her numbers. Bacchus, Erato, Ceres, and Venus are at hand to elegies, and with his rosy mother tender little Cupid as well.]

Diodati, his friend Milton tells him, really has no excuse for not producing elegiac verses in his festive surroundings. Many gods patronize this poetry of the fleshly senses—the gods and muses of wine, food, music, and love—but their leader is Apollo. This is the same Apollo who is the major protagonist of *Elegy V*, Milton's poem on the coming of spring, and who is welcomed ecstatically at the beginning of the poem as "Delius" when he fills the poet with divine poetic furor:

> Delius ipse venit, video Peneide lauro
> Implicatos crines, Delius ipse venit.

(Lines 13–14)

[Delius himself comes—I see his locks wreathed with the laurel of
Daphne—Delius himself comes.]

This Apollo is invoked with the name of his birthplace, Delos; his approach here coincides with the new season of rebirth and with the rekin-
dling of the poet's own powers of song. *Elegy V,* that is, is a kind of nativity
poem in its own right.[16] At its center is the love song of Earth, Tellus, to
the sun, Phoebus: she invites him twice to pour his light into her lap—
"Huc ades, et gremio lumina pone meo" (line 88; see also line 94)—
and she brings forth her fertile gifts. This cosmic lovemaking provides an
analogue for the act of Apollonian inspiration and penetration that sets
the elegy going: both poet and poem are filled with a creative force that
is both sexual and part of a natural cycle of regeneration. This carnal
force is essentially pagan, and the elegy ends with a further summoning
of lesser deities—lusty satyrs and sylvan gods pursuing less than reluctant nymphs—that gives a presence, both numinous and sexual, to
nature itself:

> Dii quoque non dubitant caelo praeponere sylvas,
>   Et sua quisque sibi numina lucus habet.
> Et sua quisque diu sibi numina lucus habeto,
>   Nec vos arborea dii precor ite domo.

(Lines 131–34)

[The gods, too, do not hesitate to prefer the woodlands to heaven, and
each grove possesses its deity. And may each grove long possess its deity,
and I pray to you, oh gods, do not leave your sylvan home.]

The poet ends by wistfully hoping for a return of the Golden Age, or
at least that Phoebus will draw out the spring and summer.

Elegy V was written in the spring of 1629. By the next Christmas Milton had just reached his twenty-first birthday, and from this moment of
maturity he would look back on the elegy and reject its Apollonian poetics in the first stanza of the hymn of *On the Morning of Christ's Nativity.*
He writes of a personified Nature:

> It was no season then for her
> To wanton with the sun her lusty paramour.

(Lines 35–36)

16. For the tradition of the return of spring as the birthday of the world, see Norden,
pp. 14–18.

Furthermore, the last section of the poem sends packing the deities invited into Nature at the end of *Elegy V:*

> From haunted spring, and dale
> Edged with poplar pale,
>   The parting genius is with sighing sent,
> With flower-inwoven tresses torn
> The nymphs in twilight shade of tangled thickets mourn.

(Lines 184–88)

The winter that *Elegy V* had, at its end, begged Apollo to hold off has come nonetheless and with it the removal, perhaps to warmer, non-English climes, of that poem's eroticized sun and pagan gods. The turnabout between spring and Christmas of 1629 is occasioned by Milton's taking up of sacred song, a song in English rather than in the language of the pagan classics and dependent upon an entirely different kind of inspiration. Milton explains this difference to Diodati in *Elegy VI* before he announces his new poem on the birth of Christ. Banquets and wine are fine for poets of elegy. But the poet of higher ambition and maturity, the poet of epic wars and of an adult Jove—"At qui bella refert, et adulto sub Iove caelum"—is a pure and chaste poet:

> Ille quidem parce Samii pro more magistri
>   Vivat, et innocuos praebeat herba cibos;
> Stet prope fagineo pellucida lympha catillo,
>   Sobriaque e puro pocula fonte bibat.
> Additur huic scelerisque vacans, et casta iuventus,
>   Et rigidi mores, et sine labe manus.
> Qualis veste nitens sacra, et lustralibus undis
>   Surgis ad infensos augur iture deos.

(Lines 59–66)

[Let him live sparingly according to the conduct of the Samian teacher, and let greens furnish his innocent food. Let pellucid waters stand near him in a beechwood bowl, and let him drink sober draughts from a pure source. Beyond this his youth should be chaste and free from crimes, his morals strict and his hand without stain. As you, o priestly augur, when shining in your holy vestments and lustral waters, you rise to go before the angry gods.]

All of twenty-one, Milton declares his poetic adulthood, leaving behind childish things—the wine, women, and profane song of elegy, which he somewhat condescendingly encourages Diodati to continue to enjoy in order that his friend may keep his poetic vein flowing. Yet the vegetarian virgin that he aspires to be seems less like a step toward adulthood than what William Kerrigan has called Milton's prolongation of his latency period, a postponement of sexual maturity in exchange for poetic power—and the unstained hand of this priestly poet seems pointedly to rule out masturbation.[17] Milton's period of principled chastity, associated with his years of retirement at Horton, may begin here, where he is clearly already interested in what we may call a chaste or noncarnal poetics.[18] The rejection of the solar, Apollonian inspiration of the elegy entails a separation of poetic imagination from the appetites of the flesh and a resulting poetry that purifies itself of carnal images—the forms of Nature and the human body. In the *Nativity Ode*, this purified poetry attempts to reduce itself to the state of pure light and music. It aspires to nothing less than the music of the spheres to which Pythagoras, the teacher from Samos, could listen, as Milton wrote in his *Second Prolusion*. In that text Milton invites the soul of Pythagoras, the beneficiary of Pythagoras's own doctrine of metempsychosis, to transmigrate into his own soul, for "if we possessed hearts so pure, so chaste, so snowy [*nivea*] as once upon a time Pythagoras had, then indeed would our ears be made to resound and to be completely filled with that most delicious music of the revolving stars; and then all things would return immediately as it were to that golden age; then at length, freed from miseries, we should spend our time in peace, blessed and envied even by the gods."[19] The fantasy of listening to the music of spheres lies at the very center of Milton's hymn and, with it, the idea of overcoming original sin, which the prolusion has a few sentences before allegorized in the crime of Prometheus. It is a fantasy devoutly felt and dispelled by the *Nativity Ode*, which itself seeks to approximate divine melody.

17. William Kerrigan, *The Sacred Complex: On the Psychogenesis of "Paradise Lost"* (Cambridge, Mass., 1983), pp. 38–56.

18. So E. M. W. Tillyard suggests in his appendix, "The Doctrine of Chastity in Milton," in *Milton* (1930; rev. ed., New York, 1967), pp. 318–26. Tillyard, p. 323, links the shift in Milton's attitude toward sexuality with the *Nativity Ode*, and he further relates it, as I shall do, to the myth of the music of the spheres in the *Second Prolusion*. This literary-biographical scheme should not be drawn too neatly. Where, for example, does *Elegy VII* fit in this picture, the most erotic of Milton's Latin poems and one that seems to draw precisely on the Apollonian poetics he attributes to Diodati's verse in *Elegy VI*? It is dated by Milton to the same year as the *Nativity Ode* in the *Poems* of 1645. And *L'Allegro* celebrates the same festivity and "store of ladies" which the Diodati of *Elegy VI* is said to enjoy. The poetics of chastity represent one dimension, for some time dominant, but not exclusive, of the young Milton's literary thought and endeavors. On Milton's retirement at Horton, see J. Martin Evans, *The Road from Horton: Looking Backwards in "Lycidas"* (Victoria, B.C., 1983). Whether Milton actually made a commitment to sexual abstinence has been recently challenged by John Leonard, "Milton's Vow of Celibacy: A Reconsideration of the Evidence," in *Of Poetry and Politics: New Essays on Milton and His World*, ed. P. G. Stanwood (Binghamton, N.Y., 1995), pp. 187–201. Leonard does not take into account *Elegy VI*.

19. Milton, *Works*, 12:157.

III

The hymn begins by trying to clear both its visual and aural fields. Nature has not only "doff 't her gaudy trim" (line 33) of vegetation in the first stanza but has also blanketed herself—and virtually disappeared— beneath innocent snow. This "saintly veil of maiden white," with its reference to the white robes of the saints in Revelation 3, already announces the premature and illusory apocalypticism of the poem. Nature is no virginal maiden—she does not have the snowy heart of Pythagoras— but a lady with a shady past, and the "foul deformities" that are covered up here will return, like the return of the repressed, in the monstrous forms of the pagan deities who parade through, if out of, the hymn's last section. But this snow cover is also a white or blank page: the poem's imagination cleansing itself of images—images of nature, bodily images, images above all of a pagan, literary past—in order to prepare itself for the unprecedented event of the birth of Christ. One need not have recourse to Mallarmé; Milton would in the next year invoke a similar, if inverted, idea of the black page in the unfinished *The Passion*:

> The leaves should all be black whereon I write,
> And letters where my tears have washed, a wannish white.
>
> (Lines 34–35)

And much later, he would describe his blindness as a "Universal blank / Of nature's works to me expunged and razed" that seems to be a precondition for the divine inspiration of *Paradise Lost* that allows him to see "things invisible to mortal sight" (3.48–55). In *On the Morning of Christ's Nativity*, this blankness is willed, a clearing away of the carnal imagination in anticipation of a new kind of vision. Similarly, an expectant silence takes over the hymn in stanzas 4 and 5 as Peace, in a glance at the tradition that the Pax Augustea coincided with the Nativity, places a hush over the world: "No war, or battle's sound / Was heard the world around" (lines 53–54); "The trumpet spake not" (line 58); the "kings sat still" (line 59); the winds are "whist" with wonder (line 64) and whisper to a calmed Ocean (line 66). This initial silencing of nature and history will turn out to be just as provisional as the snow cover that repristinates the poem's field of vision, and it, too, is belied in the last section of the hymn, where, in spite of the fact that their oracles are now "dumb" (line 173), the dispossessed pagan deities make a loud exit.

The silence and blankness are the preparations for the music and the globe of light that descend on Bethlehem. The music of the angelic choir in stanza 9 is matched by the stanza's own musical effects. Milton pulls out all the stops:

> When such music sweet
> Their hearts and ears did greet

> As never was by mortal finger strook,
> Divinely-warbled voice
> Answering the stringed noise,
>   As all their souls in blissful rapture took:
> The air such pleasure loth to lose,
> With thousand echoes still prolongs each heavenly close.

(Lines 93–100)

The pronounced assonance and internal rhymes—"answering/ stringed"; "echoes/close"—in the fifth and eighth lines of the stanza enact the answering and echoing they describe, as the final alexandrine in line 8 formally enacts their prolonging. But these are only the most obvious instances of sound play. In the second line there is a visual rhyme in "hearts and ears" that refers back to the opening "Their," itself repeated in the play between "their" and "the air" in lines 6 and 7. "Mortal" associates with "warbled," "finger" with "stringed," "rapture" with "pleasure." The final ell-sounds in line 6—"all," "souls," "blissful"—are reversed in line 7 in "pleasure loth to lose," as are the very words "souls/lose."

Milton's poetry is thus turning into the pure music that it describes, the "unexpressive notes" of line 116: a music that lies, in fact, beyond the poet's abilities to express its nature, a music that expresses or represents nothing but itself. It is not clear whether the music at Bethlehem is identical to or merely like ("Such music" [line 117]) the anthems that the angels sung as God created the earth and stars in stanza 12, but the question is crucial. Does the birth of Christ constitute a new creation or restoration of the universe, the occasion that would justify the speaker's subsequent calling upon the spheres in stanza 13 to ring out and for "once bless our human ears" (line 126)? The music of Milton's hymn cannot express an angelic music, the music of divine mediation, that itself points to a still more unexpressive, unheard Platonic music of the heavens—a music that is now invoked to make a "full consort to the angelic symphony" (line 133). The fantasy or "fancy" (line 134) of this fullness occupies the three central stanzas, 13–15, of the 27-stanza hymn. Repeating the terms of Milton's *Second Prolusion*, it relates pure music or the purity of music to a distinctive theology of the Incarnation: the return of created nature to a prelapsarian purity, to a Golden Age.

These terms are spelled out in stanza 14 in a series of wishful thoughts:

> For if such holy song
> Enwrap our fancy long,
>   Time will run back, and fetch the age of gold,
> And speckled vanity
> Will sicken soon and die,
>   And lep'rous sin will melt from earthly mould,

And hell itself will pass away,
And leave her dolorous mansions to the peering day.

(Lines 133–40)

Critical commentary has not, I think, done justice to the radical nature of the yearnings expressed in this stanza, nor considered why they should occupy the very center of Milton's hymn. The return at the birth of Christ of the golden age of Virgil's *Fourth Eclogue* is a commonplace.[20] The notion that time will run backward is a much odder idea. Milton appears to owe it to a passage in the *Statesman* of Plato that describes how at the end of a great historical cycle time will reverse itself.[21] The attendant effects on humanity are startling:

> All mortal beings halted on their way to bent and hoary age, and each began to grow backwards, as it were, towards youth and ever greater immaturity. The white hairs of the older men began to grow dark again; the cheeks of bearded men grew smooth once more and restored to each the lost bloom of his youth. The bodies of the young men lost the signs of manhood and, growing smaller every day and every night, they returned again to the condition of newborn children, being made like to them in mind as well as in body.[22]

The enrapt fancy in the *Nativity Ode* is ready to imagine what Nature in stanza 10 cannot be quite persuaded—she is "almost won" (line 104)—to think, that the Incarnation is already her "last fulfilling" (line 106). But it imagines this apocalyptic state as a return of creation to its condition before the Fall—to a world, like the Christ child himself, "yet in smiling infancy" (line 151). What the poet sees in fancy is a form of regressive "infancy," and the poem must subsequently remind him that, instead, the Last Judgment will involve the destruction of "the aged

20. For the tradition, see Domenico Comparetti, *Vergil in the Middle Ages*, trans. E. F. M. Benecke (1908; reprint, Hamden, Conn., 1966), pp. 96–106. In Jacopo Sannazaro's brief Neo-Latin epic on the birth of Christ, the *De partu virginis* (1526), the shepherds of Bethlehem cite the *Fourth Eclogue* virtually verbatim (3.196–232). Charles G. Osgood ("Paradise Lost 9.506; Nativity Hymn 122–153," *American Journal of Philology* 41 [1920]: 76–80) draws attention to the fifth book of Lactantius's *Divine Institutes* for the identification of the Golden Age with the worship of Christianity itself.

21. A modern editor of the *Eclogues* suggests that Virgil has the *Statesman* passage in mind in the *Fourth Eclogue* when it predicts "the regression from Iron to Heroic to Golden Age." See the *Eclogues*, ed. Robert Coleman (Cambridge, 1977), p. 141, and Coleman's commentary to *Eclogue* 4.36. It is possible that Milton's version of time running backward derives simply from an attentive reading of the *Fourth Eclogue*, a model repeatedly invoked by the *Nativity Ode*—that the *Statesman* is not present here at all. The succession of ages in lines 18–45 of Virgil's poem is, however, notoriously difficult to construe, and I have not seen a Renaissance commentary on Virgil that understands the verses to refer to a reversal of time like the one in Plato's myth.

22. *Statesman*, 270e, quoted from Plato, *The Collected Dialogues*, ed. Edith Hamilton and Huntington Cairns (Princeton, N.J., 1963), p. 1036. I am grateful to Michael Murrin for pointing this Platonic myth out to me.

earth" (line 160), a creation that will die to be reborn. Sickness and death may appear as well in the vision of fancy, but they are applied to the sinful pride of human nature, while the disease of sin itself is cured. It melts away, obviating the need for Hell, which similarly falls into disuse and ruin. The divine Mercy whose personification descends as in a court masque in the following stanza 15 seems to have completely prevailed over her companion Justice. Here, too, the ensuing stanzas correct fanciful expectations. The "trump of doom" (line 154) that will wake the dead at the true end of time recalls the thunder and lightning of Sinai and the giving of the Law that convicts mankind of sin; it announces the "last session" (line 163) of God's tribunal and the divine judgment it will hand down. Hell, it appears, will still be open for business.

The doctrine that Hell will "pass away" (line 139) — or, for that matter, may not even exist—has a long history that is particularly associated with Origen and his Platonizing Christianity.[23] In the same tradition, Gregory of Nyssa could describe the blessed life as a restoration of the state of Eden accomplished by retracing backward the history of the Fall—the starting point on this path is virginity—and speak of the redemptive process in terms of a new creation.[24] The teachings of the Greek fathers were revived by Italian humanists, particularly by writers in Rome before the sack of 1527. Much as Milton seems to do at this moment of the *Nativity Ode*, they emphasized the moment of Incarnation to the relative playing down of the sacrifice of the Crucifixion and saw in the divinization of humanity the redemption and restoration of the universe as a whole.[25] Christ is hailed as cosmic creator and savior— "opifex rerum, vastique salutifer orbis" in Vida's *Christiad* (6.797), a poem that, as *The Passion* attests (line 26), appears to have been much on the young Milton's mind.[26] Related ideas were to reemerge in the writings of the Cambridge Platonists toward midcentury. Benjamin Whichcote would argue that grace allowed human sin to be "reversible" through repentance; he declared that "the recovery of Christ is a restoration, and further confirmation of all the principles of God's creation."[27] As D. P. Walker has shown, Whichcote's fellow Platonists at Cambridge, Peter

23. See D. P. Walker, *The Decline of Hell* (Chicago, 1964).

24. Jean Daniélou, *From Glory to Glory: Texts from Gregory of Nyssa's Mystical Writings*, trans. Herbert Musurillo (New York, 1961), pp. 112–17, 273, and *Platonisme et Théologie Mystique* (Paris, 1944), pp. 110–23.

25. See John O'Malley, *Praise and Blame in Renaissance Rome* (Durham, N.C., 1979), pp. 138–52; and Charles L. Stinger, *The Renaissance in Rome* (Bloomington, Ind., 1985), pp. 314–19.

26. See Mario di Cesare, *Vida's "Christiad" and Vergilian Epic* (New York, 1964), pp. 222–23, 274–79; cited in Stinger, p. 397.

27. *The Works of the Learned Benjamin Whichcote, D.D.*, 4 vols. (Aberdeen, 1751), 1:239–40 (Discourse 14) and 1:388 (Discourse 23); for Whichcote's remarkable discussion of the relationships of these "principles" and grace, see 1:370–73 (Discourse 23).

Sterry, Jeremiah White, and Henry More, rejected or cast doubts upon the idea of an eternal Hell.[28] Whichcote was a year younger than Milton and a year behind him at their university.[29]

There may have been something in the air at Cambridge. But these various doctrines that resemble or bear some relationship to the vision of redemption deeply yearned for at the center of Milton's hymn do not normalize that vision but rather suggest its strangeness and heterodoxy. The platonizing, musical poetics of the hymn—the chaste poetics announced in *Elegy VI* and effected in the reduction of the first part of the *Nativity Ode* to music and to a sound-and-light show—are linked to a platonizing theology that the subsequent argument of the *Nativity Ode* will acknowledge to be overly optimistic, the product of fancy. We are confronting a private myth of Milton's, the myth of the *Second Prolusion.* It will later reappear in *At a Solemn Music,* where music can present to the "high-raised Phantasy" (line 5) an angelic music that mankind once heard before the Fall and "disproportioned sin / Jarred against nature's chime" (lines 19–20), the same "silver chime" of the spheres that are called upon to ring out once again to human hearing in the middle of the *Nativity Ode.* It is the myth of the son of John Milton, Sr., musician and composer, but it seems to be something more.[30] If timeless divine music prompts the fantasy that time will run backward instead of forward and turns the poem away from Christ's growing up and dying on the "bitter cross," it also suggests the desire of the young poet, on reaching his adulthood at twenty-one, to grow up no further. Kerrigan has acutely argued that Milton's embracing of virginity was intertwined with "the wish to be exempt from death," and already in *Elegy VI* chastity is the apparent precondition that makes possible the sacred song of the *Nativity Ode*: the Milton of the elegy who aspires to be a mature poet, the poet of an "adult Jove," nonetheless does not want to move beyond the infant Christ.[31] The vision of sin simply melting away through the ability

---

28. Walker, pp. 104–34.

29. A. N. Wilson makes some brief but indicative remarks on the intellectual climate of Milton's Cambridge in *A Life of John Milton* (1983; reprint, London, 1996), pp. 22–23.

30. See *Ad Patrem*, lines 30–37, where the poet looks forward to an eschatological heaven in which he will be singing antiphonally to the music of the spheres, only to claim that he already sings among the starry choirs; such song, the poem suggests (lines 56–66) blends his own poetic art with the music of his father. See Laurence Stapleton, "Milton and the New Music," *University of Toronto Quarterly* 23 (1953–54): 217–26. For *At a Solemn Music*, see John Hollander, *The Untuning of the Sky* (1961; reprint, New York, 1970), pp. 323–31.

31. Kerrigan, *The Sacred Complex*, p. 37. See also William Kerrigan, "The Heretical Milton: From Assumption to Mortalism," *English Literary Renaissance* 5 (1975): 125–66, for an astute discussion of the relationship of Milton's early interest in bodily assumption into heaven to his later embrace of mortalism, both, Kerrigan argues, ways to avoid the experience of the body's decay in death.

of nature to participate in divine music—in the timeless goodness and truth that it mediates—contains the same idea: without sin there is no death, nor was there death before the Fall. It would be possible then to avoid the fate of the earth that will grow "aged" before the Last Judgment, to avoid judgment itself by the divine father: Hell passes away. The intensity and central position of this vision suggests a core of feeling that may not simply be gainsaid by the doctrinal correction that follows in the poem. Not unlike most of us, the young Milton would prefer not to die. (The same core of feeling—a sense of the injustice of death—still haunts the older Milton's project to justify God's ways in *Paradise Lost*.) [32]

This wish overlaps with the poet's declared desire to achieve priority over his tradition and history. "O run," he tells himself as he introduces the hymn of *On the Morning of Christ's Nativity*, to "prevent," to come before the magi and all others in welcoming the Christ child:

> O run, prevent them with thy humble ode,
> And lay it lowly at his blessed feet;
> Have thou the honour first, thy Lord to greet,
>   And join thy voice unto the angel quire,
> From out his secret altar touched with hallowed fire.

> (Lines 24–28)

The desire to be first—to be there at the very dawn of the morning or new day celebrated by the ode—is tied here to the subsequently developed idea of a poetry of pure music and transcendence. The poet's voice would join the singing of the angels, and it would also partake in prophetic initiation, as is suggested by the allusion to the touching of Isaiah's lips with the coal from the divine altar (Isa. 6:6–7). His running in order to be in at the beginning anticipates the regressive fantasy of a Time that will run back and fetch the age of gold. The poet would outrun all precursors to be precursor himself, the runner who comes in first and takes the honors. The anxiety of influence he expresses is another version of the desire to be exempted from history—and hence from death. [33] Such anxiety complements or could indeed

32. The fallen Adam of *Paradise Lost*, facing the unbearable prospect of death, gives voice to what looks like a later, more knowledgeable and aware—and for that very reason, more markedly regressive—version of the wish of the *Nativity Ode*: "How gladly would I meet / Mortality my sentence, and be earth / Insensible, how glad would lay me down / As in my mother's lap? There I should rest / And sleep secure; his dreadful voice no more / Would thunder in my ears" (10.775–80).

33. "Poetic anxiety implores the Muse for aid in divination, which means to foretell and put off as long as possible the poet's own death, as poet and (perhaps secondarily) as man. The poet of any guilt culture whatsoever cannot initiate himself into a fresh chaos; he is compelled to accept a lack of priority in creation, which means he must accept also a failure in divination, as the first of many little deaths that prophesy a final and total extinction" (Harold Bloom, *The Anxiety of Influence* [Oxford, 1973], p. 61). Milton is

produce the ambition to write a chaste, sacred poetry—a purified, perhaps Puritan poetry—that would start anew with a fresh page, distill itself into Neoplatonic, heavenly music, and be purged of the marks of history, notably of the instrument of history, the sexualized human body that is fated to die.

I V

"But wisest fate says no." *On the Morning of Christ's Nativity* stages the foundering of this ambition against the fact of the historical embeddedness of both the poet and the religion he celebrates. The vision at the center of the hymn is already belied by the way that its image of sin melting from earthly creation revises and inverts the earlier conceit of Nature clothing herself in a winter veil of "innocent snow." When that snow melts, it will reveal the "guilty front," "naked shame," and "foul deformities" of a sin that has only been provisionally covered over: nature has a body, and a diseased one, after all. The connection between the two figures is underscored by the adjective "lep'rous" used at line 138 to describe the sin that the poet's fancy subsequently hopes will fall away at the Incarnation. For in the Bible leprosy is "like snowe" (Ex. 4:6; Num. 12:10; 2 Kings 5:27) in its whiteness.[34] Milton's two images mutually expose each other's wishful thinking: the supposed purity of the snow cover—the "saintly veil of maiden white"—may be a sickly excrescense of the sinful Nature it is supposed to cover; the imagined melting away of sin, like snow from the earth, misconceives the nature of sin that does not merely overlie but is deeply rooted in a fallen creation, infecting it with death. By the same token, if the earlier image of snow cover suggested a fresh beginning for the virginal poetic imagination—its inversion here exposes as illusory the notion that the young Milton can escape his historicity and mortality, his relationship both to his literary precursors and to his own body: to an original sin that he is not aware of having committed and from which he seeks to exempt himself.

This Milton does not appear able to come to terms imaginatively with the very event of Incarnation he describes, the godhead who "chose with us a darksome house of mortal clay" (line 14) and to die alongside human beings.[35] Far from being able to sing of an "adult

---

the hero of Bloom's book, particularly Milton the modern poet embodied in his Satan who struggles against a God who "is cultural history, the dead poets" (p. 21). On the fourth stanza in the *Ode on the Morning of Christ's Nativity*, see Fry (n. 1, above), who links the sense of rivalry with the Magi with the appearance at line 74 of Lucifer—already, for Fry, a figure of a Satanic Milton (pp. 44–45).

34. I am grateful to James Nohrnberg for pointing out this likeness.

35. In one of the best critical assessments of the poem, Broadbent complains: "The language of Milton's poetry is notoriously deficient in 'body' " ("The Nativity Ode" [n. 1 above],

Jove," Milton forsook *The Passion*, the sequel to the *Nativity Ode* he undertook the following spring, later acknowledging that he found its subject "to be above the years he had when he wrote it." In the last section
of *On the Morning of Christ's Nativity*, the poetic mind that cannot face
a dying incarnate god expels that god's demonic surrogates—a whole
series of moribund, embodied deities. These fleshly gods were idols,
defined by Paul in Rom. 1:23: "They changed the glory of the incor-
ruptible God into the likeness of the image of a corruptible man, and
of birds, and of fourfooted beasts and of creeping things." Milton will
recall this Pauline text in book 1 of *Paradise Lost*, just before the epic enters into its catalog of demonic pagan gods—Moloch, Baalim, Ashtaroth, Thammuz, Dagon, Osiris, Isis, Orus—in a passage that clearly
looks back on the *Nativity Ode*:

> By falsities and lies the greatest part
> Of mankind they corrupted to forsake
> God their creator, and the invisible
> Glory of him that made them, to transform
> Oft to the image of a brute, adorned
> With gay religions full of pomp and gold.

(1.367–72)

The now dethroned pagan gods of the *Nativity Ode* suggest the idolatrous progression into bestiality described by Paul in the sequence that
leads from classical Apollo to the "brutish gods" (Horus the hawk, Osiris
the bull) of the Egyptians and to snaky Typhon. But Christ, too, took the
image of corruptible man, and we may feel that the poem's iconoclasm,
its attempt to purify its field of vision and to remove the last vestiges of
profane idolatry, risks throwing out that fleshly image as well, the holy
babe with the pagan bathwater. The Christ child is only briefly glimpsed
in the hymn that celebrates His coming into the world.

And because time does not stop with the coming of Christ, error can
creep in once more. The false gods in the poem's last section are brought
back into the picture even as they are expelled. What begins as Apollo's
shriek (line 178) and the sighing (line 186) and moaning plaint (line
191) of the dispossessed gods has modulated by the end of the sequence
into music—the "anthems dark" (line 219) of Osiris's priesthood—and
suggests a rival, pagan poetry, the Classical Tradition itself, that continues to echo in time and perpetuate its falsehoods after its historical

---

p. 17)—a position that would be hard to extend, as Broadbent appears to do, to *Paradise
Lost* and to the two most famous naked bodies of world literature—and that the *Nativity
Ode* shares "so much of learned, Platonizing Christian Humanism's partial apperception
of the gospel" (p. 30). This high-church Eliotism—the Metaphysicals are, of course, to
be preferred to the Puritan—grasps well the limitations of the *Nativity Ode*, but it does
not register the poem's own recognition and dramatization of those limitations.

supersession by Christianity. One false tradition leads to another. Critics have generally understood that the gods embody not only the carnal, pagan superstition that Jesus is uprooting but also the superstitious Christianity of Catholicism, into which the idolatrous remnants of pagan religion have returned—even the Christianity of the English Reformed Church, which, so Milton and other Puritan believers thought, had itself been incompletely purged of the remnants of Catholicism and now, under Laud, was indeed welcoming them back.[36] Cleanth Brooks and John Edward Hardy saw in "mooned Ashtaroth / Heaven's queen and mother both" (lines 200–201) a reference to the cult of Mary decried by reformers.[37] The priests of Osiris who carry the image of the god "within his sacred chest" (line 217) suggest priests with ciborium or pyx: "sabled-stoled" (line 220), they wear the Catholic *stola* that, Barry Spurr has pointed out, the Church of England had suppressed, to perform a literal black magic—or black mass.[38] The "consecrated earth" of line 189 has a similar force for the poet who in *Paradise Lost* will declare that "God attributes to place / No sanctity" (11.836–37). Milton had anticipated this depiction of pagan cult as proto-Catholic sacramentalism three years earlier in *In Quintum Novembris*, his poem on the Gunpowder Plot, where he describes a papal procession in Rome as a similarly dark pagan ritual:

> Reddiderant dubiam iam sera crepuscula lucem,
> Cum circumgreditur totam Tricoronifer urbem,
> Panificos Deos portat, scapulisque virorum
> Evehitur, praeeunt submisso poplite reges,
> Et mendicantum series longissima fratrum;
> Cereaque in manibus gestant funalia caeci,
> Cimmeriis nati in tenebris, vitamque trahentes.
> Templa dein multis subeunt lucentia taedis
> (Vesper erat sacer iste Petro) fremitusque canentum
> Saepe tholos implet vacuous, et inane locorum.
> Qualiter exululat Bromius, Bromiique caterva,

36. See Michael Wilding, *Dragon's Teeth: Literature in the English Revolution* (Oxford, 1987), pp. 12–17. Wilding suggests that the publication of the *Ode on the Morning of Christ's Nativity* in the *Poems* of 1645 was a conscious intervention into the religious debates of the period; by carefully dating the poem to 1629, Milton, Wilding argues, attributed to it a kind of prophetic premonition of the crisis of the 1640s.

37. Cleanth Brooks and John Edward Hardy, *Poems of Mr. John Milton: The 1645 Edition with Essays in Analysis* (New York, 1951), p. 101. Ashtaroth and her "tapers' holy shine" (line 202) bring to mind the complaint of a character in Erasmus's dialogue, "A Fish Diet" ("Ichthyophagia"): "How many there are who put their trust in the Virgin Mother's protection, or Christopher's, rather than that of Christ himself! They worship the Mother with images, candles, and canticles. Christ they offend recklessly with their wicked life" (*The Colloquies of Erasmus*, trans. Craig R. Thompson [Chicago, 1965], p. 355).

38. Spurr, "'Sable-stoled Sorcerers,'" *Milton Quarterly* 26 (1992): 45–46.

Orgia cantantes in Echionio Aracyntho,
Dum tremit attonitus vitreis Asopus in undis,
Et procul ipse cava responsat rupe Cithaeron.

(Lines 54–67)

[Now the shades of evening brought back the twilight, when the bearer of the triple crown circulated through the entire city, and carried his gods made of bread, and he is carried on men's shoulders; kings on bent knees and a very long line of mendicant friars proceed before him. Blind as they are, born and dragging out their lives in Cimmerian darkness, they carry wax tapers in their hands. They go into temples lit with many candles (for it was the Eve sacred to Peter) and the noise of their singing repeatedly fills the vacuous domes and empty places. They howl, just like Bacchus and his band of Bacchants singing in Theban Aracynthus, while the astonished Asopus trembles in its glassy stream, and far away even Cithaeron answers from its hollow cliff.]

This scene of nocturnal worship—with its procession, its carrying of the god's image in the form of eucharistic wafers, its noisy music, above all its darkness, both physical and spiritual—suggests the topical model behind all the various pagan rites evoked by the *Nativity Ode* even as the poem announces their supersession and silencing.[39] They are not silenced so easily, Milton acknowledges, but have returned in the false traditions of the Church of Rome. If the poem has a double time scheme, in which Christ's birth represents both the Incarnation with the expulsion of pagan error and the Reformation with the rejection of Catholic superstition and idolatry, it may describe a still further "reforming of Reformation it self," of the kind that Milton would later announce was at hand in *Areopagitica.*[40] The *Nativity Ode* might be the work of one who, as *Areopagitica* puts it, "would write and bring his helpfull hand to the slow-moving Reformation which we labour under";[41] yet the poem, in the voice of wisest fate, also warns against thinking that Reformation can be speeded up to the point of completion, that is, to an escape from a past tradition of error.

V

Reformation—whether of poetry or of religion—is an ongoing, repeated process in history, a series of new beginnings. So Milton's poem lets us infer by its very imitation of the earlier pagan revelation of Apollo at Delphi. It is not only that the *Nativity Ode* finds itself repeating

39. Revard (see n. 3 above) also connects the *Nativity Ode* to this passage in *In Quintum Novembris* (p. 86).
40. Milton, *Works* (n. 1 above), 4:340.
41. Ibid., 4:350.

the Euripidean hymn, even as it disenshrines Apollo. Even in that earlier hymn, the false enlightenment of Apollo struggled to dislodge a still earlier cult that was already in place, the benighted phantoms of Themis. There is always a precursor, a sin at the origin that is dispelled only to return in different forms. The prospect of an infinite regress is the demonic counterpart of the regressive infancy—the pure origin of divine creation, the infancy of the world—for which the poet of *On the Morning of Christ's Nativity* seems at first to yearn and from which he must be weaned away by the progress of the poem. For such infancy is, as its etymology suggests, without speech, its notes "unexpressive"; it is hardly less "dumb" than the false pagan oracles it silences (lines 173–75).[42] There is, in fact, little future in a purified poetry of music and light, and, in pursuing it, the young Milton may have painted himself into a corner. The poem written on the poet's reaching the age of adulthood expresses, to the contrary, the pathos of prematurity. It is a pathos felt in his other great early poems, in the paralysis of the Lady in *Comus*, in the swain seeing himself in the dead Lycidas cut short before his time, in the complaint of sonnet VII that the speaker's "inward ripeness doth much less appear" (line 7) than his outward semblance of manhood. But it is most starkly confronted here, where Milton may literally have nothing to say. He corrects himself with the voice of wisest Fate—the "Fatum" which is both speech and authentic oracle—even if this is also the voice of paternal negation, the "no" that knows human limits and mortality. Ready or not, Milton comes to similar knowledge.

Yet the poem does achieve a measure of readiness and composure in its final stanza. The temporal suspension it has variously invoked and yearned for is momentarily realized in the sleep of the Christ child. The hush and quiet at the beginning of the poem return now that "the virgin blest / Hath laid her babe to rest" (lines 237–38). All of the preceding poem, both the angelic hymn and the discordant music of the defeated gods, has turned into a lullaby that now ceases as the child falls asleep. The stars that stood "fixed" (line 70), stopping time, at the Nativity are now replaced by the single star of Bethlehem, newborn— "youngest teemed" (line 240)—like the babe, which has "fixed her polished car" to wait upon him with "handmaid lamp" (lines 241–42). The ministering star accompanies the heavenly ministers of the poem's closing alexandrine: "Bright harnessed angels sit in order serviceable." The poet had sought to join his song with the angel choir: looking back on the *Nativity Ode* in *The Passion*, he says, "My muse with angels did divide to sing" (line 4). Here he joins them as they merely sit around the Bethlehem stable, inactive but full of potential, able and ready to serve.

---

42. Compare the "inennarabile carmen" (line 37) of the angelic choir of *Ad Patrem* and the "unexpressive nuptial song" (line 176) of the saints in *Lycidas*.

101

The pose is recognizably Miltonic, most famously repeated in sonnet XIX on his blindness, where Milton again compares himself to the thousands of angels who speed at God's bidding and to those like himself who "also serve who only stand and wait" (line 14). It is the other side of the sense of impasse in his early poetry, understood not so much as a negative prematurity, but as a positive gathering of forces and patient waiting for the time when his poetic task will be ripe and his true subject be found.[43] So Milton will covenant with his reader in the second book of *The Reason of Church Government* (1642): "At mine own perill and cost I refuse not to sustain this expectation from as many as are not loath to hazard so much credulity upon the best pledges that I can give them."[44]

On the Morning of Christ's Nativity thus ends by recovering a note of expectancy even after it has corrected Milton's premature expectations. He has expected too much of himself, too much of poetry itself. But even as it dramatizes the nonfulfillment of his initial, cherished hopes, the bravura performance of the ode has proved him serviceable.[45] The poem forces him to confront his own future death as he moves from youth to adulthood; it dispels the deeply felt fantasy at its center of an escape, a backward retreat from time. Yet the ode is simultaneously a pledge—one of the best—that he was to achieve a style that, in the words of *The Reason of Church Government*, "by certain vital signs it had, was likely to live."[46] Like the birth of Christ, the poem is a pledge of greater things to come: a poetic career. The shape of that career must still reveal itself to the waiting Milton—"but now begins" (line 167).[47] A star is born.

---

43. This double view of Milton's development becomes a retrospective view in the fiction of *Paradise Regained*, which features a Jesus repeatedly tempted to premature action. For a fundamental critical reading that shapes the terms of my essay, see James Nohrnberg, "*Paradise Regained* by One Greater Man: Milton's Wisdom Epic as a 'Fable of Identity,'" in *Centre and Labyrinth: Essays in Honour of Northrop Frye*, ed. Eleanor Cook et al. (Toronto, 1983), pp. 83–114. See also Kerrigan, *The Sacred Complex* (n. 17 above), p. 133, and, more largely, the chapters on *Comus* and *Paradise Regained* (pp. 22–126), which form a kind of diptych in Kerrigan's study.

44. Milton, *Works*, 3:241.

45. Wilson (n. 29 above), calls the poem "a turning-point in Milton's life. For, after this, he knew that he was a great poet" (p. 33).

46. Milton, *Works*, 3:235.

47. Compare the anaphora at the end of Virgil's *Fourth Eclogue*: "Incipe parve puer, risu cognoscere matrem / (matri longa decem tulerunt fastidia menses) / incipe, parve puer" (lines 60–62).

APPENDIX

I present here the choral ode in the *Iphigenia in Tauris* (1234–83) in the modern English translation of Richmond Lattimore (Oxford, 1973). It is followed by the Latin translation of Wilhelm Center (1542–75) that appeared in Milton's text of Euripides, *Euripidis Tragoediae quae extant* (Geneva, 1602), pages 217–19. There are some slight variants in the Greek text of the 1602 edition with respect to the modern edition of M. Platnauer (Oxford, 1973); most notable is the substitution at line 1277 of "oneirous" for "enopas"—"dreams" for "voices"—probably an attempt to avoid the repetition, probably the result of a corrupt text, of "enopas" at line 1273.

Beautiful was the child
Leto bore in the grain-giving valley on Delos.
A god with golden hair,
skilled in the lyre, and with him the sister who glories
in marksmanship with the bow. His mother
carried him from the island ridge,
leaving the storied place of birth,
to the mountain, Parnassos,
celebrant of Dionysos,
place of the streaming torrents.
There a great snake, spangled
of back, bright of eye,
coiled in the dark shadow
of laurel leafage,
a monster out of primeval earth, controlled
the chthonic oracle.
You, Phoibos, still only a child
in your mother's arms leaping,
you killed it, and mounted the sacred oracle.
You sit on the golden tripod, on the throne that never is false,
dealing out the prophetic answers to mortals
from the inner chamber, neighbors to Kastalian springs, keeping
your house at the world's center.

When Apollo, going to Pytho,
had driven Themis, daughter of Earth, from that sacred
oracular place, then Earth
produced the Dreams, nocturnal apparitions,
and these to mortal multitudes divined
things primeval, things of the time of telling,
and what she would bring to pass,
by incubation in sleep under the dark ground.
Earth, angry in her daughter's cause,
took from Phoibos his privilege.

But Lord Apollo ran on swift
feet to Olympos,
clung with his infant hand
to the throne of Zeus, pleading
that the grudge of the earth goddess be taken away
from the Pythian temple.
Zeus laughed because his child
had come in haste for the spoils with their golden treasures,
and shook his curls to affirm the surcease of the night voices,
took away truth from what was shown men in night visions,
restored to Apollo his privileges,
and to mortals at the throne thronged with strangers gave
    confidence
in his oracular poems.

Praestanti indole *est* Latonae filius, quem olim
Deliacae *terrae* in fertilibus
Vallibus auricomum
Phoebum citharoedum peritum,
Et *Diana*, quae propter iaculandi
Peritiam exultat,
Tulit ipsos à scopulo marino,
Puerperii locum inclytum relinquens, non
Stillantium, *at immotarum,* mater aquarum,
Ad consecratum Baccho
Parnasium cacumen,
Ubi maculosum tergum habens, & cruentam faciem draco,
Sub opaca aereus, *i. dentibus aereis minax,*
Frondosa lauro, telluris
Immane monstrum, cu-
stodit oraculum terrestre, *vel subterraneum.*
Adhuc ipsum, adhuc infans, adhuc charae
In matris ulnis saliens
Interfecisti ô Phoebe. oracula verò ini-
Isti divina, tripodéque in aureo
Sedes, in mentiri nescio throno,
Oracula mortalibus edens,
Divinis meis adytis,
Super Castaliae fluenta,
Vicinus, tenens medium terrae locum.

Themin verò Terrae filiam *Phoebus* invadens eiecit,
Ex divinis oraculis, *ubi* nocturna
Terra peperit spectra, *filiosque produxit,*
Qui multis mortalium,
Et praeterita, & praesentia,
Et quaecunque sunt futura,

In somno, sub obscura terra,
In lectis dicebant. Terra enim
Vaticinio privaverat honore
Phoebum invidia filiae *ex oraculis ab eo pulsae.* Celeri pede
Autem in Olympum contendens Rex,
Manum inanem *sibi esse* dixit ad Iovis thronum.

     Quare oravit ipsum,
Pythiis *ex* templis
Terrestrem ut auferret
Deae *Telluris* iram, nocturnáque responsa.
Risit autem *Iupiter,* quod filium statim *ad se* venisset,
Opulentos cupiens obtinere cultus.
Postquam autem concussit comam,
Fecit cessare nocturna somnia,
Et imposturam
Nocturnam exemit hominibus:
Et *pristinos* honores, iterum dedit Phoebo.
In celebri autem, & hospitum frequen-
tia claro solio fiduciam hominibus
Oraculorum carminibus *suppeditat.*

MILTON MEDITATES THE ODE

JOHN K. HALE

A NTIQUITY OFFERED MILTON a range of exemplars for his ode-writing. Of these, Pindar was the most highly esteemed. Milton, accordingly, emulated Pindar, and was compared by contemporary readers with Pindar, who enjoyed a vogue in Milton's lifetime thanks to Cowley and others. Nonetheless, it is part of Milton's differentia that he needs a wider focus if we are to understand his Pindaric. I sketch the ode traditions which he inherited before charting his agon in this arena.

CONTEXTS: ODE'S REPUTATION AND THE ASPIRATION TO PINDARIC

The Greeks of course valued the ode highly; but which Greeks, and how highly? Plato was one who, finding Homer tainted by barbarities in his portrayal of deity, wished to expel epics from his commonwealth but to retain praise-poetry; therefore ode.[1] For solider Aristotle, although ode resembled epic or tragedy in showing humankind as better than the actual, it could not match them for serious representation of a morally characterizable action.[2] Both reasons must have seemed esoteric and specialized to ordinary citizens, who venerated "Homer" in his epics and his hymns (odes) alike. Homer in both as it were told them who they were, and where they came from–cities, laws, gods, Greek itself.[3]

Pindar, the preeminent Greek odist, exemplifies exactly this sense of placing in the universe. To celebrate some victory at a religious game is to celebrate the victor's family, his city, its god; the history and exploits of them all; these humans' place before their god. It is especially to do this through a foundation-myth, retold in ode for praise. Typically Pindar dwells on how these lives all link; on why and how the whole is

---

[1] See, e.g., *Republic* 10.607.

[2] Central argument of the *Poetics* (though Aristotle himself wrote ode).

[3] The catalogue of ships, for instance, by identifying the Greek states which fought against Troy gave those states their Greek credentials.

107

good. His spirit is religious, metaphysical. And his poems are not poems in Aristotle's sense, *mimesis* = representation, fiction. They are cultic acts: sung and danced, by many persons, in structures of words to be performed in a unified act of communal joy.

But once the Greek city-states lost their independence, and once the cultic surroundings disappeared and only the words remained, Pindar became a magnificent enigma. He was just that to the Romans, to Horace for example.[4] As early as Callimachus, ode had become a different, smaller thing; not just to the extent that later epic is called "secondary" epic, or Attic tragedy in performance is spoiled already for Aristotle,[5] but ode has become an indoors and elucubrated action.

What lasted, nonetheless, was a memory, or dream, of restoring the "greater ode." To emulate Pindar, or to achieve a Pindaric in his spirit, became an aspiration for Greeks, then Romans, then for the Renaissance. It beckoned to Ronsard and Chiabrera in Europe. It attracted almost every poet in the English seventeenth century.[6]

The English vogue for "Pindaric" can be seen in a recently unearthed comment by John Beale, corresponding with John Evelyn about the state of poetry in the 1660s.[7] Beale deplores Milton's politics and religion, and is non-committal about *Paradise Lost.* (The devil's lines are too dangerously interesting for him.) But Milton "was long agoe an excellent Pindariste," meeting the criteria of being "pure," "bright," and "wonderful" (= arousing wonder). Oh let him replace Cowley, just deceased, with odes or Pindaric "upon some honest argument"– preferably a defence of the new Royal Society against its detractors.[8] The mind boggles; and Evelyn demurred. But Beale is thinking of Milton's odes printed early on in *Poems, 1645*; perhaps also of *Lycidas* and sundry epicedia. The point is, he admired Milton's few performances in a genre which commanded much seventeenth-century debate.

As for Milton, we find him in two minds. When the Trinity Manuscript lists numerous possibilities for a poem of high seriousness, one and all are either epic or tragic: Milton concurs with Aristotle about *spoudaiotatēs* of *mimesis*, does he? Yet in parts of his poetic practice,

---

[4] *Odes* 4.2. cf. Gilbert Highet, *The Classical Tradition* (New York: Oxford U Pr, 1949), 225-226 and n.10.

[5] *Poetics* (25.1461b.30).

[6] Highet (above, note 4) ch. 12, 219-254 is my main source. Doubtless Milton knew the English attempts at Pindaric, yet in this respect as in much else Italian precedent may have been more formative. Tasso will be mentioned. An Italian friend, Francini, composed an ode for Milton himself, which he kept and printed in *Poems of Mr John Milton* (1645; hereafter cited as *Poems, 1645*): it is not Pindaric in form or appearance.

[7] See Nicholas von Maltzahn, "Naming the Author: Some Seventeenth-Century Milton Allusions," in *Milton Quarterly* 27 (1993): 1-19, esp. 10; and Nicholas von Maltzahn, "Laureate, Republican, Calvinist: An Early Response to Milton and *Paradise Lost (1667)*," in *Milton Studies* 29 (1992): 181-198.

[8] Maltzahn, "Laureate, Republican, Calvinist" (above, note 7) 184, 185, 183.

and in remarks he made about ode, he dreams the dream of a Christian Pindaric. This paper narrates the zigzag story of this "dreaming," this slowly-recognised agon.

MILTON'S OWN REMARKS ABOUT ODE AND PINDAR

The aspiration is ringingly set out in *Reason of Church-Government* in 1642. After stating how he hopes to write a poem for his own time and nation which should do for them what the best Greek, Roman, Italian, or Hebrew poets did for theirs, he reviews possibilities. These include epic; tragedy; sacred drama (as in Origen's view of the Song of Solomon or Paraeus' of Revelation); "or if occasion shall lead to imitat those magnifick Odes and Hymns wherein *Pindarus* and *Callimachus* are in most things worthy, some others in their frame judicious, in their matter most an end faulty: But those frequent songs throughout the law and prophets beyond all these, not in their divine argument alone, but in the very critical art of composition may be easily made appear over all kinds of Lyrick poesy, to be incomparable."[9] Such abilities "are the inspired gift of God . . .and are of power . . . to allay the perturbations of the mind, and set the affections in right tune."[10]

We should note the sequence and wording. First, though odes come fourth, the order is an ascending one: Milton waxes yet more exalted after the sketch of catharsis with which my extract closed ("to celebrate in glorious and lofty hymns the throne and equipage of God's almightiness"–for "glory" is a key concept in Milton's thinking, here as everywhere). Secondly, odes are like hymns, "magnifick": they make their subject great, they express its greatness, or enlarge the spirit of the listeners/worshippers. Thirdly, Pindar is named first. Callimachus stands for all the successors to Pindar: an Alexandrian odist, of the secondary not cultic sort. "Some others" may mean only lesser Greeks, or Romans, or Renaissance emulations too. But fourthly, all are inferior to the odes within the Hebrew Bible; inferior in construction, technique, beauty ("the very critical art of composition"), as well as in doctrinal truth or efficacy. Finally, such poems depend upon the poet's own "critical art" if they are to have an impact of sanctified catharsis.

This programme might seem airy, or overshadowed by the fictions preceding, or sidelined by the narrative and dramatic sketches in the

---

[9] *Complete Prose Works of John Milton*, ed. Don M. Wolfe et al., 8 vols. (New Haven: Yale U Pr, 1953-1982), 1: 815-816; hereafter cited as *Complete Prose.*

[10] Ibid., 1: 816-817. As the cathartic effect is discussed in my next paragraph, this may be the place to record Milton's general conviction that ode was beneficial. *Areopagitica* declares that Lycurgus, the lawgiver of the Spartans, "sent the Poet *Thales* from *Creet* to prepare and mollifie [soften] the *Spartan* surlinesse with his smooth songs and odes, the better to plant among them law and civility" (*Complete Prose*, 2: 496). This (anachronistic) story hinges on a Platonic axiom, that ode by its nature could uplift a whole community.

Trinity MS. Not so. It suggests a Christian Pindaric, having biblical subject and style, and requiring strong self-critique by the poet, to achieve a holy restorative impact. The remarks match (and explain) Christ's preference in *Paradise Regained* over the "Dorian lyric odes" which Satan recommends, of "All our law and story strewed / With hymns, our psalms with artful terms inscribed, / Our Hebrew songs and harps in Babylon."[11] "Artful" means artistic, technically skilled. Moreover, these principles are exemplified in the odes incorporated into *Samson Agonistes.*

But if Pindar (Satan's "Dorian lyric odes") is finally eclipsed, he provided Milton with much that he needed on the long march. Milton would Christianize Pindar's glory as "Heaven," the hope and apprehending of it. He would not seek to recover Pindar's technique. Not even the clear triadic structure (strophe, antistrophe, epodos: Ben Jonson's "Turn," "Counter-Turn," and "Stand" in the splendid "Morison Ode" [*To the Immortal Memory, and Friendship of that Noble Pair, Sir Lucius Cary, and Sir H. Morison*]). His emulation would be one mainly of spirit; exploiting mythos and imagery and swift transitions of thought rather than inherited forms, so as to probe behind the given physical. A rending of the veil, to transfigure what is.

MILTON'S ODES

Milton's experimental development, which I have variously imaged as zigzags, an agon, a dreaming and a "long march," comprises: poems entitled "Ode" in English; the more spasmodic attempts in Italian and Greek; an oblique attempt, in *Lycidas*; whereupon, multilingually again, Pindaric in Latin. A silence follows, for his sonnets of the 1640-60s are few, and though they do express occasions for praise, they do it ruminatively rather than with passion. But then ode enters into his English epics, as a sub-genre, incidental or episodizing (like those "songs throughout the Law and prophets"). Finally, odes become overt in his biblical dramatic poem, as the choric odes of a Grecian tragedy, and dominate its ending.

EARLY ODES IN ENGLISH

When Milton assembled his poems of twenty years into the elegant volume of *Poems, 1645*, he placed his "Nativity Ode" [*On the Morning of Christ's Nativity*] first of all. Whether or not he wanted to present a pious self to a public who only knew him as a notorious divorcer, we can infer he gave the ode pride of place because he took pride in it. He speaks in equivalent tones of enthusiastic joy about his poem in a letter

---

[11] *Paradise Regained*, 4.257 and 334-336, respectively. All verse quotations come from *The Poems of John Milton*, ed. John Carey and Alastair Fowler, Longman Annotated English Poets Series (London: Longman Group, 1968); hereafter cited as *Poems.*

to his friend, Diodati, straight after having composed it. His subject is
the "king who brings peace to men, God who bawled in a stable."[12] The
subject came to him before dawn, near Christ's birthday (and his own
twenty-first).

Intrinsically as well as circumstantially the ode is his first major
deliverance. In its form it owes nothing whatever to Pindar, being
modelled on Italian ode, specifically Tasso's "Nel Giorno della
Natività." In its address, however, its narratives, and its entire tone and
tenor, it is Christian Pindaric; seeking by Pindar's spirit to outdo him.
To illustrate briefly.

First, odes address an occasion, and the "Nativity Ode" boldly urges
itself to become a birthday present to Jesus: "Say heavenly Muse, . . .
Hast thou no verse, no hymn, . . . To welcome him to this his new
abode?" Then he bids the Muse, or is it himself now, to "run, prevent
them [= beat the wise men to it!] with thy humble ode, / And lay it lowly
at his blessed feet" (lines 15, 17-18, 24-25).

Secondly, the whole ode thereafter is narrative. Not as in Pindar,
myths to illustrate an insight: the whole is insight, epiphany, *the*
Epiphany. Furthermore, he sets smaller myths inside the main one: the
vision of the music of the spheres (stanzas 11-15), the departure of the
ancient gods (stanzas 19-25).

Thirdly, tone is governed by the rhythmic drive. Pindaric, to achieve
conviction, must fly strongly. It should do this not despite but because
of the irregularity or asymmetricality of line-length. As a strong bird
flies: Peace "strikes a universal peace through sea and land" (52).

Lastly, tenor is governed by imagery. Norwood[13] urges that any ode
of Pindar's derives unity from a single controlling image. Be that as it
may, some of Milton's do: the book's journeys in "Ad Ioannem
Rousium," the assembling icon here.[14]

After such a start upon ode, where next? Very interestingly, he
tackled a second ode soon after, on *The Passion*. Since its opening
refers to the "Nativity Ode," this would have been composed at the next
Passiontide (in 1629-1630 Old Style). It is unfinished, and a flop, and
he thought so too: "This subject the author finding to be above the years
he had when he wrote it, and nothing satisfied with what was begun, left
it unfinished." Then why did he publish it in *Poems, 1645*? To say,
perhaps, "I shall try again later." Though no explicit poem on the

[12] "Vagitum Dei," *Elegia Sexta*, line 83 (*Poems*, p. 117). I note a deliberate breach of
decorum in the service of Christian paradoxes here, a Latin epigram pointing to the
paradox of the English Ode, that Heaven comes on earth by the Nativity.
[13] Gilbert Norwood, *Pindar*, Sather Classical Lectures, 19 (Berkeley: U of Cal Pr,
1945).
[14] Imagery assembles into Nativity icon, then icon radiates energy—just as in Botticelli's
Nativity. For ode's paramountcy of image, thrusting plot aside, compare Gerard Manley
Hopkins's *The Wreck of the Deutschland*.

Passion of Christ did eventuate, the attempt to find meaning in pain
pervades all his best later work. And why the present failure? Because
as a meditation it is too Catholic-influenced to be successful or
congenial?[15] Because its baroque conceits are frivolous or frigid, like
the final one of Milton begetting "mourners on some pregnant cloud"?–
totally unvisualizable, or making Milton an Ixion (line 56). Because the
long lines and torpid movement of the thought have proved
unprepossessing to the poet? While recognising some truth in all three
diagnoses, I find the act of self-critique itself highly commendable.
Milton has judged that, Ode being a high-risk genre (that is its appeal),
this one should go no further but remain on record as generic self-
admonition.

His next ode, still on the life of Christ, but perhaps responding to the
third of the above diagnoses, varies the line-lengths much more, and for
the first time has a Pindaric look: *Upon the Circumcision* observes
complete responsion. It is a10 b10 c10 b10 a10 c10 c10 d6 d6 c10 e10
f3 f3 e3, twice over. Because it has a more exact responsion than he ever
again used, and is moreover typologically neat rather than personally
passionate, I regard this ode as mainly technical experiment, trial that
proves to be error. It remains revealing that he devoted three odes to
events in the life of Christ; and what it "reveals" is a sustained interest
in *literally* "Christian" Pindaric.

Other odes of this early period are more transcendent than the three
on Christ: *On Time, At a Solemn Music*. The latter, especially, leaps at
once to its transcendent object: "Blest pair of sirens, pledges of heaven's
joy, / Sphere-borne harmonious Sisters, Voice and Verse" (1-2). Poetry
and Music are sister goddesses, born of the spheres and embodying the
promise of the unitative dance of heaven. An exorbitant claim, but we
do not flinch: the syntax has not allowed us to, and we follow, if we can,
where the vision goes next. It is very Pindaric, only not so much through
myth as through pageantry, the pageant of the company of heaven. A
very congenial mental act, this one, and a very pure ode.[16]

In such poems, then, Milton is in love with transcendence. His odes
rise up to it, or bring it to the earth without diminution. "An excellent
Pindariste" indeed: "pure," "bright," and "wonderful," as Beale had put
it, a most worthy emulator of Pindar. Yet Milton gave it up, in English.
Why? One might give either a psychological or chronological answer.

---

[15] As argued by Louis L. Martz, in *The Poetry of Meditation: A Study in English
Religious Literature of the Seventeenth Century* (New Haven: Yale U Pr, 1962).

[16] No wonder that the composer Parry went far above his usual form when he set it to
music: the work is half done, by the spirit, the energy, the ryhthmic spontaneity, the
whole way that the structure mirrors the thought–not by symmetry, then (which would
be merely a crude onomatopoeia), but by embedded following of vision by words
including their size-embodiment, in a line-length which follows the thought not a preset
scheme.

A psychological answer is implied by John Broadbent. He finds all these early English odes a "search for some immunity," an "'adjuring verse' uttered to ward off the thickening of age, the closing down of intimations of immortality," a "habitual tactic" of making ode an "expedition to another realm."[17] The tone is faintly pejorative. The first remark seems alien to the "Nativity Ode" at least, and forgets the abortive "Passion"; the second has got Wordsworth spilled over it; the third seems unhistorical, oblivious of the vogue for Pindaric. But still what does one do after emulating Pindar successfully? Having perceived that "Schicksallos, wie der schlafende / Säugling, atmen die Himmlischen," ["Immune from fate, the celestials breathe like sleeping infants"] what *does* one do in life, in poetry, in ode?

Milton's answer was to pursue the original aspiration by other means, or subdue it to contemplation of mortality (having decided from *The Passion* that mortality did not suit Ode, or not yet). In the Ludlow "Masque" [*A Masque Presented at Ludlow Castle*] odes abound, but as explicit songs. Even if this masque makes the words a more senior partner in the wedding of voice and verse than was usual in that mode (witness Jonson versus Jones), the music still takes over when the songs are being sung. For once, we have the music to compare and so can test this proportioning. Lawes's excellent music shows how words and songs collaborate, taking turns, not vying, as a "blest *pair* of sirens" (*Solemn Music*, 1). In *Lycidas*, the paragraphs and line-lengths and rhymes in their counterpoint follow Italian ode. Yet the dramatic transitions, the energy of rhythm, the structure obeying thought, are all Pindaric. Still, the pastoral is paramount, as it should be where the whole point is that "Et in Arcadia ego." Now if ode has begun to *contribute*, as servant not master, I see a consonance between this change of direction of the later 1630s and what he declares about ode within the Bible in 1642 in *Church-Government* ("those frequent songs throughout the law and prophets," where "frequent" =-"interspersed, recurrent").

ODES IN MILTON'S OTHER LANGUAGES

However, this provisional summation looks different when we turn to Milton's poems in his other languages. He wrote one small ode in

---

[17] John B. Broadbent, in *Odes, Pastorals, Masques*, in the Cambridge Milton for Schools and Colleges series, with himself as General Editor (Cambridge: Cambridge U Pr, 1975), 3. He quotes the excerpt from Hölderlin, *Hyperions Schicksalslied*, which I draw in here. After two stanzas on beatitude, the third one plunges: humans, by contrast, are "hurled like water from precipice to precipice down through the years into uncertainty" ("Wie Wasser von Klippe / Zu Klippe geworfen, / Jahr lang ins Ungewisse hinab"). This excellent ode is an inverted Pindaric: short stanza first, then two matching nine-line stanzas (triadic structure but inverted); rhymeless, the short lines dart diagonally across the page.

Italian; one major one in Greek; several in Latin, mostly not Pindaric; but his last of all, in 1647, was his most Pindaric of any attempt. And it was his last such attempt.

The Italian one is the little *Canzone* which punctuates the small sequence of Italian love-sonnets. Its presence reminds us of similar punctuatings in Dante. Formally, it is not a full ode: it is fifteen lines, through-composed. It has the Italian *commiato*, or envoi addressed to the ode itself. Its meaning is pride in love: though the writer risks absurdity by writing in Italian, so what? His lady says that Italian is Love's own language. He will therefore speak it (after all, her remark is distinctly encouraging). There is a proud joy, or moral pride, about this little peripeteia which Longinus–or Pindar–might have approved.

Milton's Greek ode is free of paradox, wit, and slightness equally. He translates into Greek Psalm 114, the great Exodus psalm "When Israel came out of Egypt." In a letter he explains that he has translated this ode (hanc *Oden*) of the "divine poet" [David], "upon a vague impulse," "before daybreak."[18] Thus had he written the "Nativity Ode," and thus would his Muse visit him when working on *Paradise Lost*. Savour the exultation of a biblical Pindaric, as he hands over the close to imagery, the image of God saving Israel in the wilderness by striking water from the desert rock:

> Ὅς τε καὶ ἐκ σπιλάδων ποταμοὺς χέε μορμύροντας
> Κρήνην τ᾿ ἀέναον πέτρης ἀπὸ δακρυοέσσης.

[God is the one who, as in the exodus of Israel] "poured forth sounding torrents from the crags, and an everflowing spring from the rock, making it weep."[19]

Milton expands the sense to appropriate it; and (despite a little gilding of the lily therewith) we note how the resounding magniloquent adjectives–"ever-flowing spring," "weeping rockface"–seize the Hebraic parallelism within the hexameter, energizing the nouns' plainness. A "magnific" ode, with its magnifying process for once visible.

Latin odes by comparison[20] are quiet or tangential–till 1647. In that year, however, and once again in winter, he wrote his most explicitly, that is, formally and structurally, Pindaric ode.

The ode *Ad Ioannem Rousium* is a verse-letter to Bodley's Librarian accompanying a copy of *Poems, 1645* to replace one sent but lost

---

[18] In a letter to Alexander Gil, 4 December 1634 (*Complete Prose* 1: 321-322).

[19] Carey, in *Poems*, 230 (with his translation adapted).

[20] He uses ode metres for obituary pieces on a Vice-Chancellor and a Bishop of Ely (*Poems*, 24-30), probably tasks set him at university rather than voluntary writing. "Epitaphium Damonis" closes the Latin part of *Poems, 1645*, balancing "Nativity" which opens the English part; but it is less of an ode than *Lycidas*, even more of a pastoral (in fact Vergilian to the core).

earlier. It comes to us complete with a prose discussion of its structure
and metres. This discussion notes that whereas the stanzas observe
responsion, the individual lines and sections (cola, limbs, the sub-units
of odal strophe) do not. (And though it has three strophe/antistrophe
pairings, it has only the one, final epodos.) Lines are set out for ease of
the reader, not from adherence to any ancient versification. This kind of
writing ought to have been termed "monostrophic" (through-composed).
The metres being partly correlated (between units) but partly freed from
that constraint, the ode's form is fundamentally eclectic, a free
expression; one to be judged, accordingly, by its own rules.[21] The
explanation, then, keeps Pindar in view by declaring how freely it
departs from him. This paradox infuses the whole jeu d'esprit.

As structure, so texture, for instance allusion. Thoughts from Pindar
and Horace and many more combine. The most extended allusion is to
Euripides (whose text Milton was re-reading and carefully editing in
this period of his life):

> Teque adytis etiam sacris
> Voluit reponi quibus et ipse praesidet
> Aeternorum operum custos fidelis,
> Quaestorque gazae nobilioris,
> Quam cui praefuit Iön
> Clarus Erechtheides
> Opulenta dei per templa parentis
> Fulvosque tripodas, donaque Delphica
> Ion Actaea genitus Creusa.
>
> (52-60)

Rouse wanted you [= my book of poems] to be placed in those holy
sanctuaries over which he himself presides, as the faithful guardian of
immortal works, custodian of a treasure richer than the one which
famous Ion superintended—Ion of the race of Erechtheus, Ion the child
of Actaean Creusa—in the sumptuous temple of his father, Apollo, with
its golden tripods and its gifts brought to Delphi.

As Merritt Hughes puts it, "Milton thought of the atmosphere of
charmed magnificence thrown around Apollo's Delphian temple in the
first act."[22] The allusion reminds us that some of the greatest of all odes
come within tragedies, sung and danced by the chorus: I return to this
point. Neatly, wittily, Milton seizes a point of conjunction between
Euripides and Pindar: Pindar wrote odes for the Pythian Games (those
of Apollo, resident at Delphi), while Euripides' *Ion* is a paternity-quest

---

[21] The text gives a summary of Milton's explanation (*Poems*, 303 for its Latin, 304
for full translation). The explanation was first printed in 1673 for the reissue of the
Poems, *1645*. I do not know when it (as distinct from the Ode itself) was composed.

[22] Merritt Y. Hughes, ed., *John Milton: Complete Poems and Major Prose* (New
York: Odyssey Pr, 1957), 148.

by Ion who guards the shrine at Delphi for Apollo, a quest which moves through bitterness against the god into wonder.

Nonetheless, Pindar looms largest: spirit; structure; myth; image as centring; rhythm; occasion. Take for example the scholars of Oxford seen as a "thyasus sacer" (21), a sacred band of Bacchus-worshippers. Whether serious, whimsical, or ambiguous, it is pure transmuting image. Or take the sense of occasion. Odes relate to shrines, to festivals, to celebration in joy of peaceful games-playing, by mortals seeking excellence under a benign heaven. Oxford, Bodley, is a treasury of human wisdom become divine. (And if that sounds excessive, or false, think of your own favourite research library, and imagine it wiped out by a civil war.) Milton's has just survived intact (God knows how!) through the years of the siege of Oxford: why should he not be writing an ode of *passion*, including relief? It is a shout of victory, an epinician ode, to the one who has done the most to keep it all safe, celebrating the shared joy we take in books.

Make no mistake: Milton is jubilant. Hence the extraordinary conjunction of genres, ode with verse-letter. To repeat, it is an epinician, about a civilised victory. Victory over the enemies of promise, over civil war, over oblivion; for now Milton's *Poems* will be placed in the company of Bodley's treasures (61-87). The Bodleian is being celebrated, as a treasury like that of Apollo at Delphi. A civilised, and civilising permanence is glimpsed–much like the epinicians of Pindar, except that there is bound to be some winner in a chariot-race, but there is not necessarily a Bodleian Library. Milton's stakes are higher.

Hence the more-than-Pindaric sweep and swirl of rhythm. It moves like the sprung rhythm of Hopkins. To codify it is self-defeating, because only sound and pulse matter. Energy lurks in momentum, not in notional units analysed to a standstill. Seventeen years after his "Nativity Ode," Milton embraces the needs of a different occasion– living in the world of experience now, not innocence–to scale a new odal peak.

The paradox emerges, that precisely because Milton does *not* use Greek (though Rouse would have understood it), and moves *away* from Pindaric responsion, we register the bold abandon of Pindaric. "Pindaric" means "high-risk," even "bordering on perversity," here. Like Hölderlin, Milton stands on the shoulders of the giant, upside down and wiggling his toes victoriously.

ODE AS SUB-GENRE

After 23 January 1647 he fell as silent in Latin odes as he had already done in English. Had he given up poetry for prose? Or were his poetic energies already flowing into *Paradise Lost*? Or should we take his sonnets of those years (15-23) as substitutes for ode, Horatian meditations replacing Pindaric exclamations? We cannot say, without fresh evidence emerging. Two things stand out, at any rate, one negative, one positive. Negatively, his mind seems far removed from odal ecstasy if we look at the psalms he translated in 1648 and 1653: gone is the excitement of Psalm 114, for these read like liturgy and experimentation respectively.[23] But positively, whenever it was that he devoted himself to *Paradise Lost*, odes play a notable part in it, locally, for special effect.

Such odal "sub-plots" include prayers, hymns, and love-songs. Naturally, they are in blank (heroic) verse, and dispense with most of the formal features which acknowledge Pindar as model. We perceive Pindaric, rather, in rhythm and repetition and imagery; in the sense of soaring or deepening; in the mimesis of aspiring.

Till they fall, Adam and Eve speak first and foremost in praise-poetry; to God in prayer, to each other in ceremonious love. But even this habit of rapture is not all: at *PL* 4.641 Eve goes a notch or two higher, in that following her usual honorific apostrophe ("My author and disposer, etc." [635f.]) she expresses an upsurge of her feeling for him: "Sweet is the breath of morn . . ." and so on for nine lines, following which praising of the world simply for existing she says in seven more lines that not one of all these things "without thee is sweet" (656). Overwhelming, loving emphasis on "thee." The passage is marked off from the surrounding high style by several things, amounting to a Pindaric heightening of the register: wealth of circular or completive rhetorical figures[24]; abounding of images, all sensory-innocent, none metaphorical; ecstatic varying of pauses, like the flight of a bird in a hurry; the numerical balance of nine lines with the answering, countervailing six. Pindaric without the formal accoutrements, it is one of Milton's best Pindaric creations within *Paradise Lost* to make an Aristotelean episode out of pure feeling (of this, more in a moment).

More routinely elsewhere, Milton composes hymns to God for the choirs of heaven. Take 3.372-415, heaven's praising of the Son's self-offering for mankind. Image-laden and myth-telling, it moves out of theological discourse into more or less straight psalmody, as marked by the appearance latterly of the psalmist's personal-corporate "I."[25] More inventively again, because returning towards drama, he writes varying prayers for Adam and Eve. Others, he writes for himself: the four

---

[23] I have discussed his Psalms 80-88 and 1-8 in John K. Hale, "Milton as a Translator of Poetry," *Renaissance Studies* 1 (1987): 238-256.

[24] Fowler, in *Poems*, 650.

[25] "The copious matter of my song . . . never shall my harp thy praise / Forget . . ." (3. 414-415) do not (as Fowler thinks, ad loc.) allude to Milton's own art, even as an overtone. Besides obliterating the link to psalmody, that would to my mind upset the epic voice's reminder following, "Thus *they* in heaven . . ." (my emphasis). We are up there, not down here, during the hymn.

invocations (1, 3, 7, 9) are similar as speech-act. (Pindaric touches epic at many points, amongst which is the fact that both find a place for reflections upon the poet's own role, its rights and duties.)

Ode-like alterations to the register, then, whether by the narrator or characters, vary and heighten the already high blank-verse style. Ode is subdued, certainly, to the needs of the epic. But so it becomes integral to the poem's varying voice, and a source of its episodizing. By "episodizing" I mean, obviously not Aristotle's technical sense of any unit of a play that comes between two choruses, nor that of a unit of action integral to it, but within epic's greater length a distinguishable happening which has its own unity but also some clear connection or at least relation to the central action. To put it more simply, odes as episode do what the odes of the Bible do in their surrounding narratives. Witness the Magnificat: it raises the Annunciation-narrative to a much higher power. Milton touches on the Magnificat and other gospel canticles in his last two poems, *Paradise Regained* and *Samson Agonistes*. Having already referred to Christ's praising of biblical odes in the former, I close with a sampling of the latter work, its tragic ode.

THE ODIC VOICE IN *SAMSON AGONISTES*

Far more salient, prolonged debts to ode appear in *Samson Agonistes*. They appear throughout it, like the odes "throughout the law and prophets." They have every right to do so, of course, in that Greek tragedy involved chorus verses, in triadic structure, danced and sung. But choruses had lost their song and dance long since, and had died out of English tragedy (where a "Chorus," if there is any, is normally a solo speaker, uncharacterized). Reviving them, Milton rejuvenated (if he had ever lost) his interest in ode. We know so, because in his preface to *Samson* he describes the chorus' distinctive verse as "monostrophic, or rather apolelymenon,"[26] exactly as he had said of the "Rouse" ode.

But in a *drama*, how Pindaric can odes be? They must be tragic, first and last. From among Milton's rich array of choric odes, I take their last one, being the one most resembling Pindar's.

First, the Chorus seek to make sense of the report (by *exangelos*) of Samson's death. It is "revenge" yet "dearly-bought" yet "glorious": the first line writhes with paradoxes, rival meanings. Overriding all is the sense that he has done what he was born to do for Israel (1661-1663). He lies "self-killed / Not willingly, but tangled in the fold / Of dire

---

[26] The preface goes on, "without regard had to strophe, antistrophe or epode, which were a kind of stanzas framed only for the music [as] then used with the chorus that sung; not essential to the poem [the fiction], and therefore not material; or being divided into stanzas or pauses, they may be called alloeostropha [= of irregular strophes]" (*Poems*, 345). I have replaced the comma between "music" and "then" with "[as]", to keep the sense of "the music which was then used."

necessity" (1664-1666). This is the oxymoron of tragedy (Cleopatra nursing her snake-baby). It is the Hebrew paradox of God's dealings with Israel, the Christian one of strength made perfect in weakness. It is strongly Greek, too: "tangled . . . in necessity," though the words are come through Horace's ("dira necessitas," *Ode* 3.24.6). Many thoughts, many viewpoints, are being synthesized. The Chorus of Danites, clarifying the action to themselves for our sake, have moved from probing to praising. After the desolate psalmodic questioning of ealier choruses ("God of our fathers, what is man!" [*Samson Agonistes*, 667]), this is progress.

Milton has more, and needs them to sing higher. How can ode heighten its own passionate praising? One traditional way in tragedy was by splitting the chorus, for antiphony; and this Milton now does. I quote it whole, commenting as far as practicable *en courant*:

> *Semichorus.* While their hearts were jocund and sublime,
> Drunk with idolatry, drunk with wine,
>
> (1669-1670)

[change of rhythm, dactylic-ecstatic now, as the Danites revel in the nemesis that has overtaken the *hubris* and *atē* of the Philistines]

> And fat regorged of bulls and goats,
> Chanting their idol, and preferring
> Before our living dread who dwells
> In Silo his bright sanctuary:
> (1671-1674)

[While the contrast of religions is un-Greek, as is the naming of God as "living dread" (with side-glance at "living dead"), the laudatory reference to cult sites and cult practice unites Greek and Hebraic, and "bright sanctuary" is most Pindaric]

> Among them he a spirit of frenzy sent,
> Who hurt their minds,
> And urged them on with mad desire[27]
> To call in haste for their destroyer;
> (1675-1678)

---

[27] "Quem deus vult perdere prius dementat." Milton's English does not allude to this formulation, but rather it thinks the same thought, in a way that lights up a convergence of Greece, Rome, and Israel in the perception. Typically of the chorus' idiom and role in *Samson*, and also of Pindar: both evince Coleridge's "coadunativeness" of imagination, seen in most pure form in ode (as Coleridge's quotations in chapter 18 of the *Biographia Literaria* confirm–prolific in Pindar, and Greek ode).

[condensed prolepsis: Greek locution, but endemic in ode's conciseness]

> They only set on sport and play
> Unweetingly importuned
> Their own destruction to come speedy upon them.
>   (1679-1681)

[onomatopoeic alexandrine, with corroborative dactylic hustlings. Now, following the exultant critique comes the more sombre, because universal and human apothegm]:

> So fond are mortal men
> Fallen into wrath divine,
>   (1682-1683)

["It is a terrible thing to fall into the hands of the living God," Hebrews 10.31.]

> As their own ruin on themselves to invite,
> Insensate left, or to sense reprobate,
> And with blindness internal struck.
>   (1684-1686)

[A thematic directive: Samson's blindness now is *not* "internal."]

There is noticeably little rhyme in this first hemichorus. I say "noticeably," not only because the second one (as we are about to see) rhymes more and more, so as to intensify the thought into a more ode-like rapture, but because this first one attempts or approaches rhyme: sublime/wine, desire/destroyer, them/men. Half-rhyme is used thematically, to suggest broken order, then a move towards order.

Conversely, when the answering hemichorus takes over it at once rhymes with a key word of the first, "invite [ruin]" (1684). Carrying on that sound and idea to contrast Samson's response to the Philistines' hubris, rhyme resounds: sight/quite. Rhyme then recedes, before resurging; again thematically. Rhyme behaves now like a bird learning, or re-learning, to fly. A phoenix-flight in the line-endings accompanies the sudden eruption of imagery, and the steady strong bell-beat of the wings of the rhythm. Nothing here is *precisely* Pindaric; but everything which stands out in the style is Pindaric in spirit, as Milton rejuvenates his hitherto more tortured and plainer style; for a climax, which is an ode. (A two-part chorus, for two emphases of the emergent sense.)

> But he though blind of sight,
> Despised and thought extinguished quite,
> With inward eyes illuminated
>   (1687-1689)

[the blindness theme pointed out again in its converse]

> His fiery virtue roused
> From under ashes into sudden flame,
>   (1690-1691)

[now images become the foreground, first this metaphor then simile, which at once accretes further figures]

> And as an evening dragon came,
> Assailant on the perched roosts, [scan perched, ´x]
> And nests in order ranged [monosyllable]
> Of tame villatic fowl; but as an eagle
> His cloudless thunder bolted on their heads.
>   (1692-1696)

[This prosopopoeia transforms the gory present into new scenes. Do snakes attack at evening? Is the snake a python, with even a glance at Apollo as Python-slayer and the "Pythian" Games? The sudden Latinizing coinage "villatic" wrests attention to the victims. Dragon versus fowls becomes Samson "as an eagle," one vehicle within another; and he "thunders," Zeus-like; metaphor now, higher-aspiring still. The register goes on climbing, or rather–thanks to the gallery of airborne species now dominating attention–flying. Last comes the creature unique among flyers, the phoenix, here personifying virtue:]

> So virtue given for lost,
> Depressed, and overthrown, as seemed,
> Like that self-begotten bird
> In the Arabian woods embossed,
> That no second knows nor third,
> And lay erewhile a holocaust [sacrifice, fire-consumed],
> From out her ashy womb now teemed,
> Revives, reflourishes, then vigorous most
> When most unactive deemed,
> And though her body die, her fame survives,
> A secular bird, ages of lives.
>   (1697-1707)

[Countless heightening devices cluster here: rhyme, line-length, rhythm, and the joining of all three; multilingually-derived neologism; startling switches of register in diction; transitions of thought (as in the gendering of the phoenix); and the rapid shifts between tenor and vehicle (I counted four). The flight of fancy becomes more and more startling; deliberately, functionally so, as revival and eternity are felt on the pulses. Incipient self-reflexiveness of the poet is also felt.]

121

Did Milton ever before compose such risky verse? Or come so close
to the spirit of Pindar? For[28] the sense and thought and the words and
images all alike fly close to crashing, skate on the thinnest of ice. Not
just with the innate aberrancy of all verse that is ambitious, as in
Wordsworth the good and bad cohabit or fuse. We are viewing here the
authentic odic bardic frenzy, which nests on a precipice. It lives
dangerously. Not despite but because of its greatness it might at any
moment plunge into the ludicrous awful.

Even this soaring is not quite the whole sense of an ending. After
Manoa has spoken his own victory tribute, hard-won and still precarious
(as in his final clauses he resumes grumbling about Samson's
"unfortunate nuptial choice," 1743), the Chorus speaks its final word.
What is left to say? And how, after that Pindaric upsurge, will they say
it without anticlimax? Milton finds a way, and once more with a glance
at ode, now more broadly viewed.

> All is best, though we oft doubt,
> What the unsearchable dispose
> Of highest wisdom brings about,
> And ever best found in the close.
> Oft he seems to hide his face,
> But unexpectedly returns
> And to his faithful champion hath in place
> Bore witness gloriously; whence Gaza mourns
> And all that band them to resist
> His uncontrollable intent,
> His servants he with new acquist
> Of true experience from this great event
> With peace and consolation hath dismissed,
> And calm of mind, all passion spent.
>
> (1745-1758)

Observe the interrelated thought and medium here. The thought
summates the will of God in the action, then its emotional impact,
which is catharsis. The medium is a total surprise, being a sort of
sonnet. Shakespeare had occasionally employed sonnets as a formal
heightening and summarizing device for tragedy (especially in *Romeo
and Juliet*). Now here Milton evokes Shakespeare, since his rhyme-

---

[28] This is what everyone encounters when reading Pindar, or enthusing about him.
"Water is indeed very good, and gold which shines like blazing fire in the night is far
better than all the riches which make men proud. But, my spirit, if you do desire to sing
of contests, do not look for any star brighter than the sun during the day in the empty
heavens, nor let us sing any contest more illustrious than Olympia." What on earth is
going on? Why does literal rendering of Pindar make him sound like an idiot, yet he
carries conviction in Greek, associatively / excitedly? This criticism is brilliantly
stated, and answered, by Highet (above, note 4) 271-272 and 239 respectively.

scheme is an unparalleled special effect. It almost alludes to Shakespeare, being **ABAB, CDCD** at first–like Shakespeare, unlike Milton elsewhere.[29] Being a surprise, this "sonnet" bespeaks surprises–theophany, catharsis, salvation; for sonnets like to sum up reversal as witty paradox. We are being *guided* by all the special and surprising features, to a clarifying and purifying of experience; to a conclusion about the way things are; to metaphysical bondings glimpsed through the physicality of a human crisis.

CONCLUSION

Milton's lifelong meditation on the ode and Pindaric issued in these very surprising, late,[30] experimental flowerings. The close of *Samson* is continuing the experimental urges which prevail throughout Milton's ode-making, subdued now to tragic ode or encouraged by it. His latest work contains his most odes.

Tragic ode empowers him, to fuse Greek and Hebrew–as insight and texture–within his new, strange English. The work's earlier choruses stay closer to tragic exemplars. The last two wax more Pindaric. But all alike are "Sion's songs," the sort of ode which by being biblical and (for Milton) true overgoes even Pindar.

A final conundrum. Longinus, developing his ideas about *hupsos*, irresistable sublimity, instances Pindar only once.[31] Though Longinus' text is mutilated, the fact remains surprising. But as for Milton, his poems appealed equally to conservative and progressive tastes as "sublime," and Pindaric. His own conception of poetry altered drastically, from the early odes to the great late works which are *sui generis*. Their conceptions and aspiration remain "high-flying," risky, Pindaric where it counts, namely in spirit. He became more, not less, Pindaric–by practising distances from direct imitation of Pindar himself.[32]

UNIVERSITY OF OTAGO, NEW ZEALAND

---

[29] The rhyme-scheme is alternating throughout, ABAB,CDCD,EFEFEF. Thus its first eight lines do not form Milton's usual octave, but work like Shakespeare's preferred form. Then, unlike Shakespeare's form, the six lines also alternate, reverting to a sestet which keeps to one of Milton's own most frequent schemes. The impact of the whole is to that extent less sonnet-like, which suits the location by *hinting* at sonnet without insisting on it. The line-length equally *approaches* sonnet: 6 x 4, then 2 full pentameters; then 3 x 4, 2 pentameters, 1 more tetrameter. I infer this to make us think of sonnet virtues–paradox, division of mind, resolving at the close–whilst feeling the shortfall too, the more simple and declarative gnomic of the short lines à la Greek chorus.

[30] If a 1640s dating for *Samson* (as adopted by John Carey in *Poems*) turned out to be correct, the development I have inferred would need alteration. It would become a more

linear progression of Milton's ode, from the Rouse Ode of 1647 into an adjacent odic
work, of opposite passions but similar metrics; followed by a departure into epic sub-
genre, and no late return. I think my more sinuous line of development more interesting
and more credible. In any case all we *know* is that *Samson* was published in 1671 along
with *Paradise Regained.* It is certainly for the reading public a work of that year.
Perhaps also the final breakthrough of Pindaric in the closing chorus has the mark of a
great artist's last and victorious experimentation (Titian, Beethoven, Shakespeare).

[31] Longinus, *On the Sublime* 33.5.

[32] The distance can be perceived, despite obvious communality of approval, in his
sonnet about the worth of poets: he reasons that Pindar's odes were so great that
Alexander the Great spared his house, whereas Euripides' tragic ode saved a whole city.
Euripides, by the first chorus in his *Electra*, gets the last word:

> Captain or colonel, or knight in arms,
> Whose chance on these defenceless doors may seize,
> If deed of honour did thee ever please,
> Guard them, and him within protect from harms,
> He can requite thee, for he knows the charms
> That call fame on such gentle acts as these,
> And he can spread thy name o'er lands and seas,
> Whatever clime the sun's bright circle warms.
> Lift not thy spear against the muses' bower,
> The great Emathian conqueror bid spare
> The house of Pindarus when temple and tower
> Went to the ground: and the repeated air
> Of sad Electra's poet had the power
> To save the Athenian walls from ruin bare.
>
> (*Poems*, 285)

DAVID M. MILLER

From Delusion to Illumination: A Larger Structure for *L'Allegro-Il Penseroso*

MOST modern critics of Milton's "twin" poems find the old divisions between day and night, between the solitary and the social man, between youth and age unsatisfactory.[1] Both poems are more complex than such categories indicate, and together they yield a sense of unity that is not just the unity of complement. Cleanth Brooks finds light to be a unifying principle. Kester Svendsen and Nan C. Carpenter find musical continuums. D. C. Allen sees the towers as providing thematic unity.[2] There still persists, however, the idea that the two poems are, ultimately, separate worlds between which Milton does not judge, and that they are "exercises," apart somehow from the moral vision of the later works.

In a sense they are exercises. Almost all of Milton's early effort was, more or less consciously, a preparation for the great argument, and it is useful to note specific kinds of experimentation. But the conclusion that such work is devoid of moral judgment need not follow. Milton asserts that he was assigned the topic for prolusion seven, but it is difficult to believe that he could have, whatever the assignment, written the prolusion in favor of ignorance, or that he would have preserved such an effort had he done so. I find *L'Allegro* and *Il Penseroso* to be more nearly a single structure than has generally been recognized, and that, far from being amoral, the poems are a gentle fusion of the rival claims of God and of the world, a fusion that forecasts the rigorous harmony that informs Christ's attitude toward Greek culture in *Paradise Regained*.

At the onset, a disavowal may be in order: I do not suggest that Milton felt the silent life always and intrinsically superior to the life of society, nor that there are not sober pagans and manic Christians. But the pattern of Milton's major poetry, from *Lycidas*, to the Lady of *Comus*, to the Christ

of *Paradise Regained*, indicates that Milton would quite likely have found the close of *Il Penseroso* superior to anything accomplished in *L'Allegro*. Such a preference has nothing to do with black and white puritans who smash organs. As the seventh prolusion asserts, Milton's test of value, even in youth, was the usefulness of a particular action in man's movement toward God.[3]

The seeming separateness of the two poems is a part of Milton's strategy: both play and study are given full and fair treatment before they are incorporated into a unified vision. Initially the two poems appear to be neatly balanced: either mirth or melancholy is satisfactory. Man may sometimes have one, sometimes the other, or some men may choose study, some play. Milton may here be employing the kind of wit that Stanley E. Fish sees as the mode of *Paradise Lost*.[4] Milton takes a common argument—which is superior, the life of careless ease or of diligent study?—an argument that his readers would expect to be solved in favor of study. He upsets that expectation by presenting both courses so favorably that initially there appears to be a standoff. Then, at the end of *Il Penseroso*, he provides a key that upsets the balance in favor of melancholy, and the reader can then go back to discover the limitations of mirth. Eventually he should see that the virtues of *L'Allegro* have been incorporated into the second poem, and that both mirth and melancholy have been ordered into service for the progress of the soul. The two poems are made up of parallels that are at the same time contrasts; the activities of Il Penseroso complement those of L'Allegro, but at each point they are nearer to the contemplation of God. There is something of the Neoplatonic ladder that organizes Spenser's four hymns. The progress of the poems culminates in the contemplation described in the final section of *Il Penseroso*, a description that has no parallel in *L'Allegro*.

Such a vertical structure encompasses a number of subsidiary organizations. Image patterns range from humor psychology to music, and from hermeticism to topology. And these several patterns of images are further organized into a number of parallel thematic units. Chief among these are the education of a superior mind, the subordination of flesh to mind and of mind to spirit, the syncretic nature of Christian vision, and the progress of the mind and soul through the complementary disorders of black melancholy and vain deluding joy. All come together in the conclusion of *Il Penseroso*. When Milton writes of what we would now call psychotherapy he is also speaking of education; when he writes of education he also speaks of moral progress. And the portrait that emerges of the poet-scholar-seer-mystic, one cannot but feel, is one that Milton would have wished of himself.

On the surface the poems appear to be primarily graceful descriptions of generalized activity —descriptions made the more graceful by their jarringly antithetical introductions. But the descriptions have both a dramatic and a didactic function. The poems are at once a pattern and an example, without ceasing to be poems. The details are generalized to suit the idyllic pastoral tone of *L'Allegro* and the idealized Platonism of *Il Penseroso*. It is clear that Milton is keeping a number of balls in the air at the same time; in this complexity we may find an explanation for the sense of completeness, of being profoundly "finished," that eludes the endless comments that have been made upon the poems' individual parts and internal patterns.

The opening of *L'Allegro* introduces black melancholy, and the remainder of the poem is, for one thing, an antidote for that disease. The opening of *Il Penseroso* sets forth what is apparently the obverse of black melancholy, "vain deluding joys." The second poem then proceeds with a pattern for curing that disorder. These parallels suggest a vertical structure. In *L'Allegro* it is man's tendency to return to the chaotic stuff of which he is created that must be resisted. In *Il Penseroso* thoughtless excess must be controlled lest man abdicate the responsibilities of his amphibious nature. Milton finds both extremes reprehensible, though the second is less painful, less dangerous, and perhaps morally superior to the first.

In his discussion of *Il Penseroso* Lawrence Babb isolates two kinds of melancholy: "Black" and "Golden tinged with purple."[5] He suggests that black melancholy is primarily a medical concept derived from Greek physicians, particularly Galen. Ficino's description of another sort of melancholy, whose colors are royal, Babb traces to Aristotle. Golden melancholy was the concern, not of physicians, but of poets. And its products were not despondency amid madness, but the highest of man's artistic achievements. That the two were not often clearly distinguished Babb admits, and their confusion is documented by Leishman.[6] It would appear, however, that Milton does distinguish between the two and that he plays one off against the other. The Galenic, or black melancholy, he calls "loathed": the Aristotelian, or golden melancholy, he names "divinest."

The fulminating lines that open *L'Allegro* carry a moral as well as a psychological implication. The condition described is the worst possible state of man on earth. The black melancholiac has for psychic parents the dog of hell and the formlessness of uncreated darkness. The vapors of his excess, cold and dry, discolor his instruments of perception so that all images are black and funereal. He has horrible dreams. Because he is the enemy of the sun, he seeks grots and caves for his misanthropic solitude. Among the delusions from which the black melancholiac may suffer is the belief that he has no head—that the seat of his reason is gone. In short, he lives in hell and chaos, or as close to them as man may come without dying. The formless, painful discord of the black melancholiac's existence is exactly what Milton exorcises.[7] The verse of the opening with its alternating trimeter and pentameter and its rhyme scheme that rests in neither quatrains nor couplets projects a state of mental disorder. Black melancholy is the devil's bath. In terms of progress of the soul, the opening of *L'Allegro* represents a start at nearly zero. Man can sink no lower on earth—one step down and he is in hell. In terms of humor psychology, the opening represents a classic diagnosis of black melancholy; for a man so afflicted, neither education nor spiritual progress is possible.

The body of *L'Allegro* is made up of a description of Mirth (ll. 11–40) and the supposed activities of a man under Mirth's influence (ll. 41–134). The description of Mirth may be considered a prescription, after the manner of Galen, for the treatment of black melancholy with its opposite. The alternative genealogies of Mirth are both heavily sensual. Venus and Bacchus, the first parents proposed for Mirth, are the most earthy of classical gods, and though the second pair, Zephyr and Aurora, are much less anthropomorphically sexual, Milton insists upon their substance in the specificity with which he describes Mirth's conception. The opposite—hence medicinally effective—of the deadened, deluded torpor of the black melancholiac is to be found in a thoroughgoing sensuality. Milton qualifies this corrective in exactly the way we might expect. The "Liberty" of line 36 is not license, and the pleasures are "unreproved."[8]

The center of the poem is (among other things) a generalized case history of a black melancholiac undergoing Galenic therapy. The supposed activities of L'Allegro are strikingly like those recommended by Burton for the treatment of melancholy:

To walke amongst Orchards, Gardens, Bowers, Mounts, and Arbors, artificiall Wildernesses, and greene thickets, Arches, Groues ... Pooles, Fishponds, betwixt wood and water, in a plaine, or runne vp a steepe hill, or sit in a shady seat, must be a delectable recreation ... To see some Pageant, or sight go by, as at Coronations, Weddings, and such like solemnities, to see an Embassadour or a Prince met, receaued, entertained with Masks, shows, fire-works &c ... The Country hath it's Feasts, Wakes, & merry meetings to solace themselues ... *Dancing, Singing, Masking, Mumming, Stageplayes,* hosoeuer they be heauily censured by some seuere Catoes, yet if opportunely and soberly used, may iustly be approued ... To read, walke and see Mappes, Pictures, Statues, old Coynes of severall sorts in a fayre Gallery, artificiall perspectiue glasses, old reliques, Roman antiquities, variety of colors.[9]

Burton's recommendations are not only like Milton's in detail, but they are "unreproved pleasures free"; even the control of Mirth has the authority of Burton.

As we shall see, the activity of L'Allegro differs from that of Il Penseroso in that it is largely amoral. The real tournament lacks the moral significations of Red Cross Knight's battles where "more is meant than meets the ear." Milton would not expect the comedies of Shakespeare and Jonson attended by L'Allegro to provide the depth

of insight available in the plays of Aeschylus and Sophocles that Il Penseroso reads. It is significant that Il Penseroso reads, rather than views, the plays. He uses them as materials for meditation, rather than as entertainment. The same is true of his "spelling" of herbs and stars. It is internal vision that he seeks.[10]

The last section of *L'Allegro* (ll. 135–50) represents a state from which black melancholy is completely eliminated. Presumably, such a condition is that required before further education, intellectual and moral, can take place. The disease described at the opening of the poem has been eliminated, but the climb from hellish melancholy is but to a neutral, amoral state. The "Lydian Airs" that lap L'Allegro with "linked sweetness long drawn out" are not heavenly music of sphere and angel; are in fact enervating.[11] Their function, as Milton indicates by the segment of Orphean myth he chooses to recall, is to deliver the soul from hell. The music L'Allegro desires would free the "half-regain'd Eurydice," and is thus presumably superior to the music of Orpheus that ultimately failed to do so, but at best Eurydice is returned to earth, quite a different accomplishment from approaching the gates of heaven.. The spirit of L'Allegro (which is here equated not with Orpheus, but with Eurydice) is rescued from infernal regions, but its highest climb is to earth. There is a hint of dissatisfaction in the tentativeness with which Milton approves Mirth:

These delights *if* thou canst give
Mirth, with thee I *mean* to live.[12]

The subjunctive, when examined in the context of both poems, suggests that only limited spiritual health is possible under the best of non-Christian religions. The virtuous pagan may perhaps avoid spiritual deformity, may not be a black melancholiac, but he cannot attain true spiritual health. And the activities of L'Allegro have not even searched the limits of non-Christian wisdom: the profundities of epic, of tragedy, and of philosophy remain untouched. The pattern, the lesson, the education, and the cure are incomplete.

The Christian dispensation, however, opens a new dimension to man. Lydian airs may save man from misanthropic, desperate black melancholy, but there is a progress, a Platonic ladder, that begins where the avoidance of deformity ends. The Mirth that both Milton and the reader welcomed in *L'Allegro* is, when set against the vision of God, most unsatisfying: the pleasures of this earth in innocence are exquisite, but if they become the goal, they are, for the wayfaring Christian, only "vain deluding joys." *Il Penseroso* shows a progress from the neutral middle ground achieved at the close of *L'Allegro* to a more positive state: as near to the contemplation of God as man can achieve on earth.

The opening of *Il Penseroso* is, in form, the exact counterpart of the bombastic introduction to *L'Allegro*: the distraught search for a higher good is reflected in groping rhyme and meter. But the lines are much more restrained, the imagery is only mildly pagan, and nothing is said of hell. Morpheus is the only god named, and his powers, illusions, operate upon earth. The faults of mundane joy are negative. They are · "vain," "deluding," "fickle" dreams, of no more account than motes of dust dancing in sunlight, but they *are* in the sun, rather than in hell. They harm man only insofar as they prevent him from desiring a higher state. The description that opens *Il Penseroso* is of an earthly, rather than an infernal, malaise. The difference between the two is emphasized by the genealogy of the diseases; the parthenogenetic children of folly are meanly descended, but better no father than Cerberus.

The description of "divinest Melancholy" that follows is a corrective for the imperfect mental and spiritual health that was achieved at the end of the first poem, and it also sets forth a higher curriculum. Whereas the Mirth of *L'Allegro* is characterized by things earthly, elevated only by the deities of earth, the description of "divinest Melancholy" is consistently suggestive of a superior world: she is a "goddess," "holy," "Saintly," and, like God, too bright for human sight. Her blackness is like that of "Memnon's sister" or of Cassiopeia who was raised to the stars. Her parentage, too, is less mundane than that of Mirth, going back to the golden age "While yet there was no fear of Jove." The pastoralism of *L'Allegro* is thus incorporated and then surpassed. The age of Saturn may even be a mythic version of the Garden of Eden.[13] Rather than tripping, she steps sedately with eyes raised, experiencing a momentary commerce with the skies through ecstasy.[14] Her body, like those of Donne's lovers, is a sepulchral statue. The incorporation of *L'Allegro*'s virtues continues. The chief com-

panion of Melancholy, the "Cherub Contemplation," combines Christian vision and human intellectual effort. Not only is she superior to the happy troupe which joins Mirth, but since prime requirements for contemplation are leisure and freedom, *L'Allegro*'s mountain nymph, "sweet Liberty," is incorporated.

The prescription set by Mirth in *L'Allegro* had to be tempered in its application, but the pattern given Il Penseroso is more precise—is in fact the exact path to be followed. In *L'Allegro* the movement from personification to generalized activity (from prescription to therapy) is clearly signaled by the change from "Liberty" to "lark." But there is hardly a break between the description of Melancholy and the activity of Il Penseroso:

> And mute Silence hist along,
> 'Less *Philomel* will deign a Song,
> In her sweetest, saddest plight,
> Smoothing the rugged brow of night.
>
> (ll. 55–58)

By calling the nightingale "Philomel" Milton suggests something more than the bird and something less than the myth. The unified vision toward which Il Penseroso climbs sees God in the world, and as is usual with Milton, the Christian vision does not exclude the glory and achievement of the classical world. But the classical accomplishment is dwarfed by setting it in perspective against the glories of God.[15]

The state described at the opening of *Il Penseroso* is one that can be improved by education. And the therapy for "vain deluding joys" is just that. There is a surprising similarity in point-by-point statement between prolusion seven and the body of *Il Penseroso*, but more important, both reveal the rigorous but humane attitude toward study that is to fill *Of Education*. If *L'Allegro–Il Penseroso* is a consideration of two happy states, the title of the seventh prolusion suggests which Milton is likely to prefer: "Learning Makes Men Happier Than Does Ignorance." Once again Milton makes use of parallels that are actually contrasts. The education of Il Penseroso through study is radically different from the education of L'Allegro through observation. The similarities in form serve to insist upon the differences in substance.

The first requirement that Milton sets forth in the seventh prolusion is a lack of pressure:

"The truth is that nothing has fed my mind or contributed more to its health than intelligent and liberal leisure" (p. 622). The chief companion of Mirth is of course "sweet Liberty," but this sounds more like Il Penseroso's "retired Leisure." The advantages of retirement are set forth plainly: "There among the fields and in the depths of the woods I seemed to myself to have achieved some real growth in the season of seclusion" (p. 622). And the theme of incorporation and subordination could not be more clear: "Therefore nothing can rightly be considered as contributing to our happiness unless it somehow looks both to that everlasting life as well as to our life as citizens of this world" (p. 623). The hierarchy between God and the world, between body and spirit, is explicit: "contemplation is . . . the only means whereby the mind can set itself free from the support of the body and concentrate its powers for the unbelievable delight of participating in the life of the immortal gods." But such contemplation is *not* anti-intellectual: "Yet without learning, the mind is quite sterile and unhappy, and amounts to nothing" (p. 623). This might almost be a paraphrase of the last section of *Il Penseroso*, and when we set "Scrutinize the face of all the world in whatever way you can. . . . The more deeply we search into its marvelous plan . . . the more we honor its Creator with our admiration and follow him with our praise" (p. 623) beside

> Where I may sit and rightly spell
> Of every Star that Heav'n doth shew,
> And every Herb that sips the dew;
> Till old experience do attain
> To something like Prophetic strain,
>
> (ll. 170–74)

the religious context of Il Penseroso's accomplishment can hardly be doubted. In both cases it is "the approval of the Almighty" that leads to happiness. Milton designates learning *and* virtue as the proper goal for man, but if a choice must be made, he picks virtue.

The conversation that Milton praises in the prolusion is not that of checkered shade and peasant story but of study, like the efforts of Il Penseroso to unsphere "The spirit of *Plato*." "The delights," the prolusion tells us, "that are the secret of study and learning . . . easily surpass all others." The curriculum for such learning set forth in the prolusion is almost as close to Il Penseroso's activity as Burton's therapy is to L'Allegro's:

How much it means to grasp all the principles of the heavens and their stars, all the movements and disturbances of the atmosphere, both its awful fulmination of thunder and the blaze of its comets, which terrify dull minds, and also its freezing into snow and hail, and its soft and gentle precipitation of dew and rain. How much it means to get an insight into the fluctuating winds and the exhalations and gases which the earth and sea emit, and . . . finally—into the divine powers and faculties of the spirit, and whatever knowledge may be accessible to us about the beings that are called household gods and genii and daemons. (p. 625)

Finally, the prophetic strain of Il Penseroso's accomplishment is clearly the goal set forth in the prolusion: "And shall I ignore a satisfaction to which no parallel can be found? To be the oracle of many people, to have one's home become a shrine" (p. 625). Like *Il Penseroso* the seventh prolusion reaches its climax in heaven as both knowlege is spread before the worthy, but in both cases, Milton returns the reader to earth, for it is of this world he speaks, and the pattern he sets forth is for humans, not saints.

It is true that Milton was assigned the topic for prolusion seven, but the reality of its assertions does not therefore seem suspect. Whether or not the prolusion is a "source" for *Il Penseroso* is relatively unimportant. The significant thing about juxtaposing the two pieces is that they are thus both seen to approximate Milton's later thought. The humane schoolmaster envisioned in *Of Education*, the confident purity of the Lady in *Comus*, the tutorial relationship between Raphael and Adam, the supreme vision of Christ, and the dawning self-awareness of Samson are all implicit in both works. Too, there is the fatal curiosity about the stars that signals danger in *Paradise Lost*. Certainly the poems must be considered as poems, not as interesting anticipations of later work, but it would be surprising to find them in conflict with Milton's virtually lifelong moral stance.

The superiority of the pattern set by *Il Penseroso* is signaled by the use Milton makes of the Orphean myth in the two poems. In *L'Allegro* the accomplishment of Orpheus, the supreme though flawed achievement of the classical world, concludes the poem. In *Il Penseroso* Orpheus is placed as only one of many who might be raised through meditation. Still, in *Il Penseroso* the emphasis is upon the power of Orphean music; in *L'Allegro* it is upon

Orpheus' failure to return Eurydice to the world.[16] Il Penseroso's retreat into "virgin wood" is a turning inward for meditation; L'Allegro in his walks turns outward for observation. Even Il Penseroso's dreams are "mysterious" in sharp contrast to the youthful poet's dreams in *L'Allegro*. The discovery of such patterns and contrasts seems to indicate a vertical structure for the poems. The achievement of L'Allegro, pleasing though it is, may be for Il Penseroso vain deluding joy. If such is the case, three, not four, not two, qualities are represented in the two poems: black melancholy, golden melancholy, and careless ease. The ease differs in the two poems because the perspective of *L'Allegro* is that of innocent, amoral pastoralism, and that of *Il Penseroso* is striving Neoplatonic Christianity. The quality remains the same; the criteria change.

Il Penseroso's way is not without its temptations; as he stares at "glowing Embers" he revels in "the sweet self-sufficiency of the melancholy mood."[17] In its own way, this state is as limited as that of careless ease. Put most simply, any state that is not useful as a movement toward God, any state that becomes an end in itself, is unsatisfactory. The activity of Il Penseroso within "some high lonely Tow'r" is that of the *vita speculativa sive studiosa*, the Renaissance counterpart of the *vita contemplativa sive monastica*. Milton is fully aware of the attractiveness of such a life, but here he recognizes the dangers more fully than he had in prolusion seven. Il Penseroso is returned to nature, "To arched walkes of twilight groves," there to retreat in sleep from the willed ratiocination of study. The life of the mind is not so much rejected as incorporated—and then superseded.

The music that awakens him, "Sent by some spirit to mortals good," is parallel to the Lydian airs that close *L'Allegro*, but it is but a preparation for the Christian music that is to produce rapture.[18] Il Penseroso, purified of sensuality, freed from worldliness, even from secular study, is able to receive the higher sights and sounds of Christianity. The combination of studious cloister, organ music, and religious light is prelude to ecstasy. All that which is good and beautiful is incorporated in his vision as Milton develops the Christian connotations of divinest Melancholy. The line "And bring all Heav'n before mine eyes" indicates that Il Penseroso has fulfilled the pattern set by Melancholy's "looks commercing with the skies." The poems, the lesson, the pattern, and the therapy are complete. Il Penseroso will spend the remainder of his life meditating upon the creations of God, secure from both the torments of black melancholy and the vanities of the world. "Something like Prophetic strain" is the best that can be achieved in this world. As Contemplation incorporates Liberty, so too "old experience" gathers all of human life—from tripping on the toe to the mysteries of Hermes Trismegistus—in its devotion to God. Il Penseroso has reached the top rung of the earthly Platonic ladder. One more step would place him in heaven. A difference in degree of subjunctive may not seem important, but the superiority of Il Penseroso's accomplishment is subtly asserted by the relative security of the closing lines:

These pleasures Melancholy give,
And I with thee will choose to live.
(ll. 175–76)

There is no doubt that Melancholy can give such pleasures; there is some question of Mirth's power. In context, the difference between the "mean to" that closes *L'Allegro* and the "will choose" of *Il Penseroso*'s last line is indicative of the difference between classical and Christian virtue.[19]

The major problem must still be the relative value that Milton places on the two patterns, if indeed he "values" them at all. It is clear that *L'Allegro* makes use of humor therapy for its texture, and equally clear that *Il Penseroso* develops the same educational pattern set forth in the seventh prolusion. It is reasonable to expect that the mental health described at the end of the first poem, neutral though it may be, is a requirement for the study directed in the second. Finally, a setting of the poems beside the comprehensive moral vision that Milton reveals in his mature work suggests that they too recommend an incorporation of everything—study, play, food, fast, health, leisure, delight in the world, meditation—into man's progress toward God. The delights of L'Allegro are real and valued, but like the glories of Greece they cannot stand against the ecstasy of Christian contemplation. Partial truth is inferior to complete truth. It is Il Penseroso who represents the proper Christian pattern.

Purdue University
West Lafayette, Indiana

Notes

[1] Summaries of the principal critical positions with regard to the relationships and sources of the two poems are: J. B. Leishman, " 'L'Allegro' and 'Il Penseroso' in Their Relation to Seventeenth-Century Poetry," *Essays and Studies*, 4 (1951), 1–36; and Eleanor Tate, "Milton's 'L'Allegro' and 'Il Penseroso'—Balance, Progression, or Dichotomy," *MLN*, 76 (1961), 585–90.

[2] D. C. Allen, *The Harmonious Vision* (Baltimore, Md., 1954), notes the Platonic elements of *Il Penseroso*, sees the poems as moving from "dissatisfaction to an ultimate gratification" (p. 9), and finds the "structure of the poems rests on the rising stairs of the tower" (p. 18). Kester Svendsen, "Milton's 'L'Allegro' and 'Il Penseroso,' " *Explicator*, 8 (1950), No. 49. Nan C. Carpenter, "The Place of Music in 'L'Allegro' and 'Il Penseroso,' " *UTQ*, 22 (1953), 354–67. Cleanth Brooks, "The Light Symbolism in 'L'Allegro' and 'Il Penseroso,' " in *The Well Wrought Urn: Studies in the Structure of Poetry* (New York, 1947), pp. 47–61.

[3] William Madsen, *From Shadowy Types to Truth* (New Haven, Conn., 1968), suggests that Milton not only supersedes the sensuous, but rejects it. See pp. 124–44.

[4] Stanley E. Fish, *Surprised by Sin* (London, 1967). The dangers inherent in Fish's approach are clear; anything may be proven if the critic is granted to have an insight into the poet's intention *and* into the "reader's" response, and if it is further assumed that the poet is manipulating affective responses, a sophisticated impressionistic criticism may result. Fish seems to me to be generally right about *Paradise Lost*; Wimsatt's cautions in *The Verbal Icon* (Lexington, Ky., 1954), however, are in order. I do not here insist on an intentional-affective stance, but rather wish to suggest a possibility.

[5] Lawrence Babb, "The Background of 'Il Penseroso,' " *SP*, 37 (1940), 257–73. Babb finds that "The Melancholy of the Aristotelian tradition was never more completely described or more beautifully celebrated than it is in 'Il Penseroso.' " He does not, however, note what I consider to be the progression from Black to Golden Melancholy through a state of Mirth. An argument for Milton's awareness of Golden Melancholy is given by Raymond Klibansky, Erwin Panofsky, and Fritz Saxl in *Saturn and Melancholy* (New York, 1964), Pt. III, Ch. iii.

[6] " 'L'Allegro' and 'Il Penseroso' in their Relation to Seventeenth-Century Poetry." Klibansky supports Leishman: "the fusion of the characters 'Melancholy' and 'Tristesse' in the fifteenth century brought about not only a modification of the notion of melancholy . . . but also, *vice versa*, of the notion of grief, giving it the connotations of brooding thoughtfulness and quasi-pathological refinement." "This new melancholy could . . . rise to sublime renunciation of the world, or be dissipated in mere sentimentality" (*Saturn and Melancholy*, pp. 231–32).

[7] Geoffrey Bullough. *Mirror of Minds* (Toronto, 1962), sets forth the commonplaces of Renaissance humor psychology that seem to underlie Milton's suggestion of hierarchy, and William J. Grace (see n. 8, below) sets forth many details from Burton that Milton seems to echo.

[8] Grace, "Notes on Robert Burton and John Milton,"

SP, 52 (1955), 579–83, finds the same distinction between two kinds of Melancholy as does Babb. He contends, however, that the Mirth of *L'Allegro* is as different from the "joys" of *Il Penseroso* as are their respective melancholies.

[9] Robert Burton, *The Anatomy of Melancholy*, 1621 ed., Pt. II, Sec. 2, Memb. 4, pp. 341–51, quoted by Leishman and in part by Grace.

[10] For an argument in favor of Milton's choice of word over sight see Madsen, *From Shadowy Types to Truth*, pp. 166–80.

[11] Carpenter ("The Place of Music in 'L'Allegro' and 'Il Penseroso' ") disagrees with Hughes's quote (p. 71; see n.12) that seems to deny the pejorative implications of "Lydian." She writes ". . . the Lydian being soft, effeminate, beguiling, even lascivious, unlike the manly Dorian . . ." (p. 355). Hughes's source for the rescue of Lydian is Cassiodorus, through James Hutton, "Some English Poems in Praise of Music," *English Miscellany*, 2 (1951), 1–63. Neither Cassiodorus nor Hutton seems to recommend the Lydian as anything except a kind of tranquillizer. Since the implications of Lydian are important to my argument, I quote at length from Hutton:

The commentators inform us that Milton dissents from Plato's condemnation of the Lydian mode; but that is beside the point. Milton is merely reproducing Cassiodorus, who in reviewing the effects of the modes decides that "the Dorian bestows chastity . . . the Ionian sharpens the intellect and turns the desires heavenward . . . the Lydian restores us with relaxation and delight, being invented against excessive cares and worries (*contra nimias curas animaeque taedia repertus*)." Joined with immortal verse, these Lydian airs will perform their effect by penetration, the soul of the singer being met by the soul of the hearer . . ." (p. 46).

The ranking implied by Cassiodorus and the discrete function he attributes to Lydian is exactly that which I suggest as functioning in *L'Allegro*.

[12] All citations of Milton are from *John Milton: Complete Poems and Major Prose*, ed. Merritt Y. Hughes (New York, 1957), p. 72, ll. 151–52; my italics.

[13] A. Bartlett Giamatti, *The Earthly Paradise and the Renaissance Epic* (Princeton, N. J., 1966), illustrates the commonplace link between the Age of Saturn and the Garden of Eden. See pp. 11–86.

[14] The connection between melancholy and ecstasy is noted by Burton: "Ecstasis is a taste of future happiness, by which we are united unto God, a divine melancholy, a spiritual wing" (p. 394). Klibansky finds "her leaden downward cast" to be "nothing but the reverse side of a condition of ecstatic, visionary trance" (p. 230). Rosemond Tuve, "Images and Themes," in *Five Poems by John Milton* (Cambridge, Mass., 1957), denies this connection for Melancholy: "the ecstasies of apprehending relations and harmonies are not those of the mystical union with the divine." Since she writes that "contemplation leads to . . . . the mystical union" (p. 30), the difference seems to be based on interpretations of "skies."

[15] Klibansky finds a similar ordering and incorporation: "Milton renounced the profound and ingenious plan of concealing the tragic face beneath a comic mask . . . he combined all the aspects of the melancholic: the ecstatic and the contemplative, the silent and Saturnine no less than the musical and Apollinian, the gloomy prophet and the idyllic lover of nature, and welded their manifoldness into a unified picture, mild on the whole rather than menacing" (p. 236).

[16] Carpenter finds a parallel difference between the two uses of Orpheus: " 'L'Allegro Orpheus' is chiefly a musician—the Orpheus of 'Il Penseroso' adds words and vision" (p. 357).

[17] Klibansky, p. 232.

[18] Svendsen ("Milton's 'L'Allegro' and 'Il Penseroso' ") approaches this idea when he observes of the music that transports Il Penseroso: "This religious experience contrasts with the pagan myth at the conclusion of 'L'Allegro' but is in the same continuum, as it were." Carpenter explicates the details of the music that closes "Il Penseroso": "High" service is the "Great Service" using polyphonic, rather than homophonic. music. The "anthem" that takes the place of the old Latin motet is a complex form for many voices (p. 559).

[19] Although she finds *L'Allegro* to be cyclical, Carpenter seems also to see a progression: "In 'L'Allegro' the sophisticated pleasures of the active life culminate in secular dramatic song which can tear out one's heart and cause one's soul to meet the soul of music itself. But in 'Il Penseroso' the superior pleasures of the intellectual life as found in a university atmosphere reach a peak with sacred music, symbolized by the organ and the full voiced choir; and it is by means of this music that one can become immersed in contemplation of the Divine and through that contemplation attain finally divine wisdom, even prophecy —the ultimate *raison d'être* for a poet" (p. 366).

THOMAS M. GREENE

The Meeting Soul in Milton's Companion Poems

M OST criticism of "L'Allegro" and "Il Penseroso" could be said to fall into one of two interpretive schools. The first of these assumes a pair of opposed but complementary temperaments, already knowable and known as we begin to read, already defined by dictionary and by convention. Members of this school begin by assuming these pre-existent qualities and then perceive each to be exemplified by the myriad stock details of its poem. Thus J. B. Leishman writes that "exemplification . . . was to provide the main substance of [Milton's] poems."[1] This is a view which might be described as Platonic, and indeed one scholar, Phyllis MacKenzie, uses Platonic language to formulate it: "In a classical poem such as 'L'Allegro' we should regard the natural details as a Platonist looks at the parts of the universe. They are the multiple bodyings-forth of an Idea in the mind of the poet."[2] This is essentially the view of Rosemond Tuve, who writes that Milton "portrays . . . that bodiless thing itself which the freely delighting mind or the meditative mind tirelessly seeks to ally itself with." This bodiless thing sounds distinctly Platonic. Later Tuve writes that "the subject of *L'Allegro* is every man's Mirth, our Mirth, the very Grace herself with all she can include. Therefore its images are not individualized."[3] The Platonic reading with its upper-case "Mirth" is bound to produce an argument for generalized images, since to find particularizing imagery would reveal a Milton betraying the abstract purity of the ideal quality.

1. J. B. Leishman, *Milton's Minor Poems* (London, 1969), p. 129.
2. Phyllis MacKenzie, "Milton's Visual Imagination," *University of Toronto Quarterly* 16 (1946–1947), 19.
3. Rosemond Tuve, *Images and Themes in Five Poems by Milton* (Cambridge, Mass., 1957), pp. 15, 20.

135

Among twentieth-century critics this reading seems to have had a strong appeal.[4]

On the other hand one can distinguish an opposite critical tradition going back to Doctor Johnson and Thomas Warton, critics who stress the particularity of Milton's mirth and melancholy. They seem not to find an idea of mirth in "L'Allegro" but rather a specific mirth, tinged in this case with a peculiar melancholy. Doctor Johnson writes: "The author's design is . . . to shew how . . . among the successive variety of appearances, every disposition of mind takes hold on those by which it may be gratified." Here the phrase "every disposition of mind" seems to permit an indefinite number of dispositions, and this assumption is confirmed when Johnson writes: "His Chearfulness is without Levity, and his Pensiveness without asperity . . . No mirth can, indeed, be found in his melancholy; but I am afraid that I always meet some melancholy in his mirth."[5] This famous remark leads us a long way from Tuve, and not least in the use of the possessive adjective: *his* Cheerfulness, *his* Pensiveness, *his* melancholy, *his* mirth. For Johnson the subject of "L'Allegro" is not "every man's Mirth, our Mirth"; it is an individuated mood with special nuances and private shadings. It corresponds to no Platonic idea. Warton sensitively develops Doctor Johnson's insight into the specificity of "L'Allegro's" tone. "Even his landscape, although it has flowery meads and flocks, wears a shade of pensiveness; and contains russet lawns, fallows gray, and barren mountains, overhung with labouring clouds. Its old turreted mansion peeping from the trees, awakens only a train of solemn and romantic, perhaps melancholy, reflection. Many a pensive man listens with delight to the milkmaid singing blithe, to the mower whetting his scythe, and to a distant peal of village bells."[6] Warton perceives, anti-Platonically, that each poem offers a particular-ized "disposition of mind" which harmonizes with the other. In our century Don Cameron Allen has sustained this attention to specificity. Rather than beginning with an idea or an archetype and moving out deductively to its predictable, conventional, generalized exemplifica-tions, this school begins with a recognition of the images' peculiarities,

4. See also David M. Miller, "From Delusion to Illumination: A Larger Structure for *L'Allegro–Il Penseroso*," *PMLA* 86 (1971), 33: "The body of *L'Allegro* is made up of a description of Mirth (ll.11–40) and the supposed activities of a man under Mirth's influence (ll.41–134)."

5. Quoted in *A Variorum Commentary on the Poems of John Milton*, II, Part One, ed. A. S. P. Woodhouse and Douglas Bush, (New York, 1972), p. 242.

6. Quoted in the anthology of criticism appended to the edition by Elaine B. Safer and Thomas L. Erskine: John Milton, *L'Allegro and Il Penseroso* (Columbus, Ohio, 1970), p. 29.

their idiosyncratic overtones and special resonances, and then infers inductively a corresponding unique sensibility.

This latter move seems to me to produce more interesting readings and to correspond more nearly to the two poems' elusive workings. I have to confess, alas, that l'allegro's mirth is not my mirth; I only wish it were. It is not predictable and conventional; it is inimitable. Some images and motifs in each poem, to be sure, can be traced back to earlier texts and conventions, and modern scholarship has shown how particularly rich was the tradition produced by the Renaissance interest in melancholy. But "Il Penseroso" asserts its own removal from that tradition very markedly, both from the Galenic self-destructive type of melancholy and from the milder Aristotelian-Ficinian type which associated this temperament with genius. Aristotle himself insisted on the range of personalities which an excess of black bile could create.[7] For him (or for the pseudo-Aristotle, author of the *Problemata*) there was no single melancholic personality. If one looks at the works which allegedly anticipate "Il Penseroso," one is struck by how much of the convention it excludes.[8] Some of Burton's allegedly melancholic experiences turn up as mirthful in "L'Allegro." Even if Milton did draw to some degree on the literature of melancholy, that literature was abundant and amorphous enough to leave plenty of room for choice within parameters. Milton's respect for these parameters should not blind us to the choices he made in both poems—culling, recombining, reformulating, replacing emphases, refining, adding (above all adding)—choices which essentially produced two distinctive, carefully modeled sensibilities. In several cases a reader could not predict a priori in which poem a given image might appear. Thus the "Bee with honied thie, / That at her flowry work doth sing" could not, out of context, predictably be placed where it is found, in "Il Penseroso."

7. The discussion of melancholy in *Problemata*, XXX, 1 is summarized and in part quoted by Lawrence Babb, *The Elizabethan Malady* (East Lansing, Mich., 1951), p. 59.

8. Warton cited a poem by Beaumont on melancholy which many scholars have regarded as a model for "Il Penseroso" and which is quoted by the editors of the *Variorum Commentary* (pp. 240–41). Beaumont's poem mentions bats and owls, "A mid-night Bell, a parting groane, . . . folded Armes and fixed eyes, / A sigh that piercing mortifies / . . . A tongue chain'd up without a sound." Except for the eyes, none of these motifs appears in "Il Penseroso." The opening of "L'Allegro" exorcises much of the conventional claptrap of melancholy—Burton's "ghosts, goblins, fiends," "thousand ugly shapes," "doleful outcries and fearful sights"—and we never hear of them again, any more than we hear of the "ghosts and spectres and fearsome goblins" of Milton's own first Prolusion. The one (rather amiable) goblin who turns up appears in "L'Allegro."

The proper reply to T. S. Eliot's comment that the ploughman and the milkmaid are generalized is that while they may be in themselves, they participate through context in a larger whole which is not generalized but subtly individuated. They are units in a long series of objective correlatives to a progressively emergent consciousness, and that consciousness is not general but special. The ploughman, the milkmaid, and their companions belong, in Johnson's phrase, to "the successive variety of appearances" which this "disposition of mind takes hold on" so that "it may be gratified" and so, one might add, that it may be defined. Even if another poet had had the genius to write something like these poems, his would have had a different variety of appearances and thus a subtly or obviously different disposition. If Eliot wanted specification he could have found it in these poems; he looked at single "appearances" and not at the consciousness they sub-tend.[9]

In *Saturn and Melancholy,* the most exhaustive history of the tradition behind "Il Penseroso," Klibansky, Panofsky, and Saxl single out the originality of the poem's revisions. The authors stress the modernity of the "enhanced self-awareness, since the ego is the pivot round which the sphere of joy and grief revolves." They find in late Renaissance melancholy a "singularly complex, affective condition of the soul," "a special kind of emotion, tragic through a heightened awareness of the Self."[10] If tragedy is named in "Il Penseroso," the poem itself is not tragic, but it is aware of an intensely realized selfhood. The true subject of each poem is named in passing near the conclusion of "L'Allegro."

> Lap me in soft Lydian Aires,
> Married to immortal verse
> Such as the meeting soul may pierce
> In notes (136–39)[11]

The *meeting* soul demonstrates its receptivity by advancing, coming out to the music halfway, moving forward to encounter and correspond. But

9. It may not be irrelevant to point out that in the *Asclepius* of Hermes Trismegistus, one of il penseroso's favorite thinkers, special emphasis is placed on human beings as individuals. "Though each living being has in all respects the form which is proper to its kind, the individuals . . . yet differ among themselves. For instance, though the human race has a common form, so that we can know from a man's appearance that he is a man, at the same time individual men . . . differ from one another . . . . The type persists unchanged, but generates at successive instants copies of itself as numerous and different as are the moments in the revolution of the sphere of heaven" (III, 35).

10. Raymond Klibansky, Erwin Panofsky, and Fritz Saxl, *Saturn and Melancholy* (New York, 1964), pp. 231–32.

11. Quotations from Milton are taken from *The Poems of John Milton*, ed. Helen Darbishire (London, 1961).

this metaphorical meeting understates the Stevensian role of the soul in the poem as wholes; it goes out to select and apprehend and order and assimilate and thus to create itself. The soul is not simply meeting what Johnson called "appearances" but calling itself into being by means of the controlled conjunction.

Thus in the companion poems we come to know each consciousness as it defines itself through its predilections, its choice of sensations and activities, and through its formulation of these predilections in language. An affinity for the moon may have been characteristic of the melancholy temperament, but it is only this melancholic who sees it "Riding neer her highest noon, / Like one that had bin led astray / Through the Heav'ns wide pathles way" (68–70). We learn a little about the moon from that, but a great deal about the perceiving sensibility responding to it and evoking it metaphorically. A couplet in "L'Allegro" is exemplary: "Streit mine eye hath caught new pleasures / Whilst the Lantskip round it measures" (69–70). The two verbs need to receive their full force. The eye *catches* the pleasures it chooses for itself; it takes what it wants and remakes the pleasure in the process of assimilating it. It *measures* the landscape, "surveys and composes the scene" as one editor paraphrases;[12] it organizes and assigns relationships, as when a few lines below "Towers, and Battlements it sees / Boosom'd high in tufted Trees" (77–78). This perception of trees as tufted and as embosoming reflects the dynamic acts of measuring, composing, relating, and comparing.

The human mind is of course incapable of pure description. It cannot leave appearances alone. One can only ask what kinds of interference the mind imposes, how intrusive and how rigorous is its control. "L'Allegro" can be compared to a poem by Nicholas Breton which begins:

> Who can live in heart so glad
> As the merry country lad?
> Who upon a fair green balk
> May at pleasure sit and walk.
> And amid the azure skies
> See the morning sun arise

Milton's poem is more rewarding than Breton's partly because its interpositions are more skillfully intrusive, more self-conscious, more strictly controlled and more singular; they bear a signature. They consistently offer more information than Breton's about the mind moving through the landscape. In Milton but not in Breton the mind's serial acts

12. Lorna Sage edits the companion poems in John Milton, *Odes, Pastorals, Masques,* general editor J. B. Broadbent (Cambridge, Eng., 1975), p. 75.

of perception are self-constitutive and self-identifying. They are also represented with insidious calculation, with wanton heed and giddy cunning; the art of the mind's self-definition in both companion poems does not yield easily to the mind of the inquisitive reader.

II

This art is perplexing in part because the being of the "appearances" remains unsettled. These appearances only seem to possess hard edges and firm substance. Both poems have a trick of altering retrospectively the ontological status of a given appearance. We meet what looks like a sketch of external phenomena, and then the phenomena are internalized, prove to be elements in a private reverie so that we are led to question retroactively how much independent reality they ever had. A passage in "L'Allegro" (117ff.) evokes "Towered Cities" with their "busie humm of men," an apparently concrete, objective description, then modulates to "throngs of Knights and Barons bold" in the next line, already a shift away from the concrete towards fanciful romance, then at line 125 introduces an explicitly fictive divinity—the god Hymen with his traditional accouterments, and then after visions of "antique Pageantry" reaches the unexpected and astonishing couplet "Such sights as youthfull Poets dream / On Summer eeves by haunted stream." That couplet forces us to consider the possibility that the revelry and the triumphs and ladies and barons bold, even the urban hum of men, have all been fictions of a "dream." Perhaps the towered cities please us only in fancy; perhaps we have never left the countryside with its streams haunted by fantasies.

One could cite other examples of retrospective internalization. A particularly subtle modulation appears in "Il Penseroso" beginning at line 139.

> There in close covert by som Brook,
> Where no profaner eye may look,   140
> Hide me from Day's garish eie,
> While the Bee with Honied thie,
> That at her flowry work doth sing,
> And the Waters murmuring   144
> With such consort as they keep,
> Entice the dewy-feather'd Sleep;
> And let som strange mysterious dream,
> Wave at his Wings in Airy stream,   148
> Of lively portrature display'd,
> Softly on my eye-lids laid.

We begin with a brook which we are led to take as quite simply external, move to "the Bee with Honied thie," which we take to be equally external despite the intrusion of the metaphorical thigh; then move to the waters murmuring which we begin to assimilate to the preceding phenomena until we reach "the dewy-feather'd Sleep," and we are obliged to shift levels of reality; we are obliged to admit more allegoresis into the landscape than we were prepared for. This shift is followed by the slightly mysterious imagery of lines 147–50 which has troubled editors and is rather hard to visualize, but which now seems to locate an "Airy stream" within a dream of the drowsy speaker. That modulation into the fanciful and dreamlike again blurs retrospectively the status of what precedes. As we move from "brook" (139) to waters enticing the personified Sleep (144–46) to the "Airy stream" (148), the firm external-ity of the brook is undermined. It is not even clear what an "Airy stream" is; the phrase sounds like an oxymoron, fusing elements as a dream will do. These local modulations into the subjective (and there are other examples[13]) act out sequentially what happens less obviously everywhere in the poems. Even the images which are not obviously internalized are still there as objective correlatives, as pieces of informa-tion about the viewer. Even so concrete an object as a book, a work of Hermes Trismegistus or Chaucer or Aeschylus, ceases to be a fixed object, begins to lose its determinacy, begins to be subtly transformed by the play of fancy and personality.

It is characteristic of the companion poems that they play elusively with inside and outside, description and allegory, perceptions and dreams. An uncertainty of substance hovers throughout them both, an uncertainty which is intensified by the conspicuous options and hesita-tions. The poems are filled with alternative versions of truth, alternative names and genealogies, optatives, conditionals, concessions, contrary-to-fact constructions, all of them thickening the haze of half-realities. As precise evocations of places, the poems might be said to fail; as represen-tations of a dreaming fancy, they succeed. Impressions fade into limbo while we take them in. Light counterfeits a gloom, we read, "Far from all resort of mirth, / Save the cricket on the hearth, / Or the Belmans drousie charm" (81–83). *Are* we far from mirth or are we not, with that cricket chirping and the bellman singing his blessing? Apparently not, if we agree that those sounds are indeed mirthful. But we would be

13. Note for example how the word "perhaps" subjectifies the description at A79. Note also A136ff. and P69–70.

unlikely to meet them in "L'Allegro." They are part of the atmospheric penumbra, the half-light of a qualified gloom, a limbo where two temperaments overlap. Both poems are full of concessions like this one, and in fact they concede so much that often we are left unsure how much remains. The personification "Silence" is said to accompany the goddess Melancholy, "'less *Philomel* will daign a Song," that chauntress who is "most musical, most melancholy." If "musical" and "melancholy" seem almost interchangeable in this line, what has happened to Silence? She too seems in limbo. That abbreviated "unless" is characteristic of the poems' play with options and concessions. When l'allegro asks for soft Lydian airs, we have no immediate reason to doubt that he can hear them, until, as the poetry imitates them with progressively ravishing sweetness, the very existence of such enchantment becomes open to question. It is harmony such that "*Orpheus* self may heave his head / From golden slumber" and "hear / Such strains as would have won the ear / Of Pluto, to have quite set free / His half regain'd Eurydice" (145–46; 147–50). This would be music more potent than Orpheus', music which would succeed where he failed, music such as has never been heard, sounding only in a limbo of the imagination. Perhaps all the images of both poems should be understood to reside there. Again we are moved inward, away from concrete actuality to a specific embracing consciousness.

The haziness of things is further blurred by a vagueness of syntax unparalleled in Milton's poetry. The reader's movement forward is eased by a magisterial art of elision which lubricates transitions and disguises shifts of attitude, exploiting a fluidity of syntactic connections. The major transition in both poems is from invocation to promenade; and in both, the elision is managed so as to be almost imperceptible. "L'Allegro" follows its catalogue of Mirth's companions,[14] the last of whom is

---

14. Modern editors generally print in lower case the nouns "cranks," "wiles," "becks," and "smiles," from the following passage, words which seventeenth-century editions give in upper case.

> and bring with thee
> Jest and youthful Jollity,
> Quips and Cranks, and wanton Wiles,
> Nods, and Becks, and Wreathed Smiles,
> Such as hang on *Hebe's* cheek,
> And love to live in dimple sleek. (A25–30)

Read in upper case, these nouns must be understood as at least semi-personified; this impression is strengthened by the "love to live" in line 30, attributing feelings to "Wreathed Smiles." Again the ontological status of these semi-personifications is ambiguous.

Liberty, with a conditional clause on which a very great deal will be made precariously to hang.

> in they right hand lead with thee,
> The Mountain Nymph, sweet Liberty;
> And if I give thee honour due,
> Mirth, admit me of thy crue
> To live with her, and live with thee,
> In unreproved pleasures free;
> To hear the Lark begin his flight
>
> .   .   .
>
> Then to com in spight of sorrow,
> And at my window bid good morrow (35–41, 45–46)

We can note in passing that the conditional addressed to Mirth at line 37 is precisely the contrary of its counterpart in the poem's final couplet, to which I shall return. What needs stressing here is the grammatical obscurity inhibiting our understanding of who it is who feels sorrow or bids good morrow,[15] an obscurity which persists through the long sentence which in the 1673 edition ended only at line 56. The reader is led to forget that the last eighteen lines of the sentence depend upon a conditional clause, just as he or she is led to overlook the dangling participle at line 53 ("Oft list'ning how the Hounds and horn"). The next "sentence" is itself hung upon another dangling participle ("Som time walking not unseen") which has to serve as the closest thing to a main verb. Only at line 69 does a declarative verb actually affirm unconditional enjoyment ("Streit mine eye hath caught new pleasures"), although formulated in a somewhat disorienting past tense. An elision at line 131 again omits the main verb ("Then to the well-trod stage anon"), an omission which facilitates the important shift away from the indicative to the imperative at 136 ("Lap me in soft Lydian airs"). The imperative will be needed for the challenge of the concluding couplet to make sense ("These delights, if thou canst give"). Thus a syntactic blur informs l'allegro's activity with something of the same haziness we have already found in the appearances around him.

"Il Penseroso" is somewhat less cavalier with its syntax[16] but its

15. The *Variorum Commentary* summarizes the long controversy. More contributions to it are cited in an amusing summary by Stanley Fish in his essay "What It's Like to Read *L'Allegro* and *Il Penseroso*," *Milton Studies* VII (1975), pp. 77–80.

16. But see ll.25–28. The *Variorum* editors also raise a question concerning the syntax of "hist" in line 55, p. 319. The syntactic function of "awght else" at line 116 is vague at best. It is not clear what noun is modified by the participle "ending" at line 129.

elisions are equally artful and the status of action or event at least as uncertain. The shift from Melancholy's train of companions to il pense-roso's promenade is wrought through that abbreviated conjunction "'less" we have already noticed: "the mute Silence hist along / 'Less *Philomel* will daign a Song. . . . Thee Chauntress oft the Woods among, / I woo to hear thy Eeven-Song" (55–56, 63–64). That elision, marvelously deft, introduces a series of il penseroso's preferred activities in the indicative mood, a series which breaks off in this poem quite early, after only twenty lines, in favor of optatives and imperatives which continue uninterrupted up to the final conditional couplet. The shift away from the indicative is subtly elided by the conjunction "or" at line 84 suggest-ing a false parallelism ("Or let my Lamp at midnight hour, / Be seen"). One important series of the optatives that follow is phrased so as to cast doubt on their possibility ("But, O sad Virgin, that thy power / Might raise Musaeus from his bower" 103–04), so that many of the events envisaged seem contrary to fact. In "Il Penseroso" quite as much as in its companion it is not easy to gauge the reality of what does or might or might not happen. Process as well as objects are bracketed as virtual in a world whose ideality and subjectivity call its being into question.

III

Up to this point I have been speaking of the companion poems as though they were more or less interchangeable. Many readers have shared Doctor Johnson's opinion that they are insufficiently distin-guished, but they nonetheless swerve away from each other in important ways. It is not without significance that "L'Allegro" sustains the indica-tive far longer than "Il Penseroso." But perhaps the main distinction can best be formulated in terms of an open wakefulness in the meeting soul. Allen remarked that rather than "cheerful man" or "pensive man," both speakers could best be described as an "alert man."[17] Yet one is bound to note how often the soul is made to drift away from waking alertness, towards dreams (like those of the "youthfull Poets" or the "strange mysterious dream" laid softly on il penseroso's eyelids) or the drowsiness of the Bellman's charm, or the outright sleep of the fabulous Goblin by the chimney and of the rustics who tell of him ("By whispering Windes soon lull'd asleep," A116) or the "golden slumber" of the dead Orpheus (A146) or the rapture of the goddess Melancholy, forgetting herself to

17. Don Cameron Allen, *The Harmonious Vision: Studies in Milton's Poetry* (Baltimore, Md., 1954), p. 7.

marble, or the "extasies" which dissolve il penseroso (165) as he hears the full-voiced choir. Both poems seem intermittently to want to pull away from the alert wakefulness of daylit humanity, as though their speakers envied "The immortal mind that hath forsook / Her mansion in this fleshly nook" (P91–92). But "L'Allegro" successfully holds off this temptation so that some kind of reciprocity between outer appearance and inner consciousness remains possible. "Il Penseroso" partially yields to the seduction of innerness, covering the unbearably bright with dark, almost resisting sensation in its faintly glimmering bowers.

The soul in these poems is solicited on the one hand by appearances, however problematic their status, and on the other hand by golden slumber. The covert drama of the poems lies in the tug between these opposite solicitations, and the poems distinguish themselves according to their stronger resistance to one or the other. At the electrifying opening of l'allegro's experience the song of the soaring lark startles the night and sleep, and it will not distort the poem, I think, to read into that startling lark an allegory of the birth of sensation in the erstwhile sleeping soul. The cock who "Scatters the rear of darknes thin" (50) confirms this birth, fully waking the soul to the solicitations of things outside it. Mirth is the daughter of Aurora. The image of solar magnificence as the day's regal progress begins (59–62) befits a poem that privileges waking lucidity. Mirth becomes the name of a joyful, cyclical interchange between appearances and the meeting, measuring, assimilating, and articulating soul emergent in the poem. That soul is not immune to the seduction of dreams but it maintains through most of its life its temperate, daylit exchange of reception and creation. It is tempting to liken the cycle of raw appearances under the reign of Mirth to a goblin at work in the mind with his "shadowy Flale," who then falls asleep with the receptive ego before issuing forth at daybreak, nourished and filled, as the mind returns to formative wakefulness. The last image of "L'Allegro" echoes its beginning by evoking another awakening, as Orpheus heaves his head from slumber. The Nods and Becks that follow Mirth beckon to an ideal watchfulness. If the exorcism of Melancholy (A1–10) scorns her solitude, "forlorn" in a desert or her uncouth (desolate) cell, the exorcism of Mirth (P1–10) scorns the volatile receptiveness of the mind filled with toys. The reader of "L'Allegro" may see this volatility as the caricature of a virtue.

The glimmering shades of "Il Penseroso" can be read as a resistance to the beckoning of appearances, perhaps a clearer perception of their uncertain substantiality. Here the "dimm religious light" (160) recalls a line of Donne—"Churches are best for Prayer, that have least light"—from a poem that yearns for non-being (the Germany Hymn). There is no startling in this poem; in its twilight groves "the rude Ax . . . was never heard the Nymphs to daunt" (136–37). In this emergent sensibility the charm of appearances, although exquisitely registered, yields more quickly to the pressure of desire for the invisible. Melancholy's looks are "commercing with the skies" (39), although the moon's example will demonstrate the risk of getting lost in "the Heav'ns wide pathles way" (70). Thus the optatives quickly replace the descriptive indicatives. Externals break in less forcefully in a sensibility prone to bookish solipsism and attracted fitfully by power. Hermetic knowledge, the lore of demons and correspondences, is a knowledge of secret power, like that of "the vertuous Ring and Glass" (113) of the *Squire's Tale*. The fantasy of conjuring seems to exceed even the goddess' limits: "But, O sad Virgin, that thy power / Might raise *Musaeus* from his bower, / Or bid the soul of *Orpheus* sing" (103–05). The ultimate wish is for the power of prophecy. Into this hermetic sensibility appearances come as from a solemn distance, like "the far off *Curfeu* sound, / Over som wide-water'd shoar, / Swinging slow with sullen roar" (74–76). The curfew seems to knell the death of the visible. Melancholy becomes the name for this relationship between a world of dim or invisible phenomena and a unique sensibility treasuring its solitude and its aspiration to dominion. Melancholy unbalances the reciprocal interchange between appearance and soul in favor of a withdrawn soul wanting to absorb, transform, and transcend. Yet this is not a driven soul, manic or obsessive. Its spell lies in the languor of its rhythms. It has not yet reached Marvell's proto-modern will to annihilate; it is best located at the precise point where the sound of the brook is transmuted into an airy stream reflecting an antic fantasy. Analogous meetings of soul and world take place in both poems, in the name of both goddesses, but each poem produces a separate pattern of homogeneous response.

IV

The most difficult lines in each poem are found in their respective final couplets, and it is a little odd that they have not attracted more critical attention. They pose undeniable hermeneutic problems for the reader; in fact they oblige him or her to reconsider radically the foregoing text. Each final couplet introduces a conditional whose irresolution seems to reach backward and embrace the whole poem. I want to argue that these conditionals are there in both poems, that they are important, and that any complete interpretation has to take them into account. "L'Allegro" ends: "These delights, if thou canst give, / Mirth with thee, I mean to live" (151–52). Although the couplet in "Il Penseroso" contains no "if," its conditional character is clearly present: "These pleasures Melancholy give, / And I with thee will choose to live" (175–76). I take this to mean "*If* you can give these pleasures and do give them to me, then I will choose to live with you." The construction in itself expresses the conditional, and if there were any doubt, the parallel with the close of "L'Allegro" would suffice to dispel it. Moreover, as everybody knows, both couplets echo Marlowe's poem where there is a double conditional in the two final quatrains: "If these pleasures may thee move, / Come live with me, and be my love" and "If these delights thy mind may move, / Then live with me and be my love." Marlowe's two central nouns, "pleasures" and "delights," are precisely those that reappear in Milton's final couplets. The deliberate allusion is unmistakable, but there is also a striking difference from Marlowe and from the usual erotic situation: Marlowe's shepherd promises pleasures to the nymph to attract or seduce her: "*If* these pleasures move thee, then come live with me." Milton's speaker is rather issuing a kind of challenge: "If *you* can supply these pleasures, then I will consent to live with you." The male speaker is no longer the provider of the pleasures but the potential recipient; the female figure is openly invited to please *him*. In "L'Allegro," as we have already noted, this challenge reverses and supersedes the more conventional appeal of the invocation.

> if I give thee honour due,
> Mirth, admit me of thy crue
> To live with her [Liberty], and live with thee,
> In unreproved pleasures free. (37–40)

Thus the Marlovian pattern is introduced only to be abandoned.

One must ask who is this "I" of the final couplets who will consent to cohabit with one or the other of the goddesses if the conditions are right? He cannot be the figure we have been following in each of the poems, neither l'allegro who hears the lark startle the night and visits meadows trim with daisies pied, nor il penseroso who listens to the nightingale and frequents the arched walks of twilight groves. Each of these figures has already received many of the pleasures corresponding to his temperament. The "I" of the last couplet has *not* received them, has not yet given himself to one or the other goddess; he waits to see if such delights will be forthcoming. The figure who issues a challenge or proposes a bargain in the final couplets is a figure we are not prepared for and about whom we know little. Is it the same figure at the close of both poems? The near-identity of the two challenges suggests that both are made by the same individual. Apparently we have to assume that the same persona issues an invitation to Melancholy who has already issued one to Mirth. He is neither l'allegro nor il penseroso but a third presence susceptible to the charm of the existence of each.

This third presence who emerges abruptly at the very end of each poem does undeniably create problems for the reader. The reader believes that he or she has been hearing a frank, unqualified celebration of a specific sensibility and its peculiar attendant pleasures; the reader has supposed that the invocations to Mirth and Melancholy were unreserved, only to learn that there *is* a reservation. The ending reinforces the insubstantiality of the pleasures; it makes explicit the possibility that the challenges will *not* be met, that neither goddess can produce the pleasures which have just been evoked. In fact the very status of these pleasures is further undermined by the final retrospective conditional; the external realities serving to define a sensibility become still more remote. They are nowhere available firm realities but hypothetical delights which each sensibility may or may not be capable of attaining. The ontological character of these delights is distanced at one further remove as the reader is obliged to adjust his conception of the images he has just been savoring. But so must the reader adjust his conception of the meeting soul who seeks them out, the consciousness emergent from the images and defined by them; this ideal consciousness in each case becomes itself hypothetical, a consciousness this third presence might come to resemble were the respective goddesses fully able to satisfy him. Both sensibilities, both l'allegro and il penseroso, seem to be creatures in a reverie of this single embracing mind, constructs of his dreaming bookish imagination. Those closing conditionals which put so much in doubt even blur the actuality of the two figures we thought we had seen moving through two hazy landscapes.

For the literal-minded reader there is still a further problem: what if this third presence has promised too much? If both the goddesses were to provide the pleasures he wants, he would be incapable of responding equally to both; he could only choose one of them. Thus in this twofold challenge there lies a certain degree of negativity; at the very least one of the two sets of pleasures will have to be foregone.

It is not altogether clear what role in fact the goddesses are called upon to play in the poems. If these are read as experiments in ideally harmonious individuation, it is not clear why the goddesses are necessary. It would appear to be their presence that has misled the Platonizers. One might pose this question in structural terms by asking how the invocation should be understood to relate to the following description, a question Milton's art of elision seems calculated to suppress. One answer would be that Mirth and Melancholy serve to provide two spectrums of temperamental range upon which l'allegro and il penseroso respectively can locate themselves. Each offers a vague psychological field, a primary delimitation, which initiates, but only initiates, the process of individuation. Each goddess is an enabling figure who makes self-definition possible. The invention of a fresh parentage for Mirth/Euphrosyne, in despite of mythography, and the invention of a boldly incestuous parentage for Melancholy are both indications that a re-imagining is at work. By the end of each poem, it is the goddess who *may* bestow those pleasures just evoked; in another sense it is she who incarnates them if and when one chooses to live with her. Union would symbolize attainment of the pleasures. Mariann Regan writes: "The lyric text, like the self, can be . . . a construct woven with both the longing for fusion and the energy of individuation."[18] In Milton's poems the energy of individuation leads at the very end to a hypothesis of fusion.

It remains inherently unclear of course what precisely living with one or the other goddess means. The final couplets constitute good examples of the young Milton's filtered or displaced sexuality. The invitation by Marlowe's shepherd to "live with me, and be my love" is frankly and unambiguously erotic. The voice in Milton challenges the female divinities to win his consent to live with each, but although one of them is notable for her wanton wiles, we are not encouraged in either case to dwell on the erotic possibilities of cohabitation. The seduction remains chastely metaphorical, "unreproved," so that we are not led to wonder why the goddess Melancholy, the "pensive nun, devout and pure," should want to win anybody to live with her. Even to raise the subject of sexuality in these airy streams of enchanted language seems like a crude violation. Yet the poems would be radically altered if the personifications were male rather than female. This is another area where the poetry betrays a delicate and fleeting ambiguity.

18. Mariann Regan, *Love Words: The Self and the Text in Medieval and Renaissance Poetry* (Ithaca, N.Y., 1982), p. 76.

We seem to be left with a pair of essays in temperament, playful experimentation with two invented sensibilities by an invisible third presence who is tempted by each but committed to neither. He tries on each sensibility in turn, and through it the set of pleasures, the set of phenomena which in each case helps to construct it for him and for us. These phenomena are delightful partly because their silhouettes seem sharp and their impressions in focus, but we are never allowed to count on them. They serve as fragments in the reveries of a genius experimenting with moods and styles of apprehension. To read the poems in this way as the artifacts of sublime playfulness is not to deny them intellectual seriousness or moral idealism, but to see the idealism held at a cool presentational distance. Many of Milton's youthful poems end with a movement upward towards heaven. The last line of "At a solemn Musick" for example, seems deliberately to sublimate the last lines that have concerned us: "till God ere long / To his celestial consort us unite, / *To live with him*, and sing in endles morn of light." A song from "Arcades" extends an invitation to nymphs and shepherds.

> From the stony *Maenalus*,
> *Bring your Flocks, and live with us*,
> Here ye shall have greater grace,
> To serve the Lady of this place. (102–05)

The companion poems are distinguished by their *teasing* welcome, modulating between levels of reality and degrees of receptivity as though their writer understood the insidious equivocality that attends the proposals we make for union.

YALE UNIVERSITY

WILLIAM McCARTHY

The Continuity of Milton's Sonnets

MILTON WROTE his sonnets over thirty years, from about 1628 to 1658, and he could not have conceived them originally as a sequence. He published them in 1673, however, in an order that shows many marks of sequence. E. A. J. Honigmann, their latest editor, has argued that the sonnets constitute, though not a Petrarchan cycle, a loose unity for which precedents occur in the odes of Horace and the sonnets of Shakespeare as well as in other seventeenth-century collections like Crashaw's *Steps to the Temple* and Donne's *Songs and Sonnets*. Their unity derives sometimes, Honigmann says, from continuity of subject, as in Sonnets 11 and 12, both occasioned by the reception of Milton's book, and sometimes from theme, as in 18 and 19, which both "celebrate God's terrible way with His chosen." More pervasive are "various verbal, tonal and allusive 'rivets,' " such as the word *taught*, which, carried over from Sonnet 12 to a similar context in 13, "mortises these two sonnets together."[1] Some of these connections have always been seen; others, the "rivets," had to wait for Honigmann's microscopic eye. My own view of the sonnets is macroscopic. They are a sequence by virtue of large patterns, patterns large enough to subsume these details. The patterns are not narrative, nor need they have been: A sonnet sequence does not have to tell a story. A structure of imagery having thematic implications, a group of themes developed by one "implied author"— these may make pattern enough and may tell their own "story."[2]

One pattern in the sonnets is visible to even the casual eye. Whether we read them in *Poems*, 1673, or in the modern editions based on the Cambridge Manuscript,[3] we can see that the sonnets dispose themselves into three groups. First is the Italian group (2 through 6 and the Canzone), concerned with love as an inspiration to poetry and introduced by "O Nightingale," in which the poet dedicates himself to love and poetry; these are poems of youth, the poet presenting himself

throughout as what he calls himself in Sonnet 6, "giovane piano, e semplicetto amante" ("young, gentle and simple lover").[4] The second group, Sonnets 8 ("Captain or Colonel") through 18 ("Avenge O Lord"), comprises poems of maturity: Here the poet exerts his powers on public and private themes such as concern serious-minded adults, and we feel ourselves in the company of a strenuous moral activist and master of rhetoric's heavy guns. The third group, Sonnets 20 ("*Lawrence* of vertuous Father vertuous Son") through 23 ("Methought I saw my late espoused Saint"), gives us the poet in retirement. The winter imagery of Sonnet 20, the avuncular tone of the first sonnet to Cyriack, the conscious looking-back on his career in 22 all suggest old age, and calm wisdom achieved at the end of life.

We can also see that the points of division between these groups are turning points in their poet's career. Sonnet 7 ("How soon hath Time") registers the poet's anxious dismay at having arrived at maturity: He finds himself no longer the young, gentle, and simple lover but all at once a grown man who has to act in a world governed by time. Sonnet 7 is about choosing a vocation, and thus it introduces the second group of sonnets, which illustrate the poet's vocation—illustrate, that is, what Renaissance apologists for poetry, including Milton, took to be the poet's vocation. Sonnet 19 ("When I consider how my light is spent") corresponds to 7 at the other end of the poet's career: It registers his shock at finding himself out of work and seemingly laid by as useless. We watch the poet recovering from that shock in Sonnets 20 through 23.

This pattern, then, is a human career in its three conventional phases of youth, maturity, and old age. Because it is the ground plan of the sonnets as I construe them, its status—whether it is intrinsic or extrinsic to the poems—is a crux of interpretation. We do better, I think, to call this career a paradigm of a career than Milton's own career, even though the sonnets do at times refer to his career. Knowing that Milton printed the sonnets approximately in the order he had written them, scholars have concluded either that the sonnets have no unity—that they are unrelated results of unrelated occasions, a birthday, a death, a detraction, a massacre—or that they take their unity from the form of Milton's public and private life: They "chronicle," as Honigmann puts it, Milton's "reactions to the events and individuals of his time," their unity "centring, in the last resort, on the writer's definitive personality" (pp. 72, 74). In either of these views, to discern a career in the sonnets is to see no more than the order in which Milton wrote them, an order extrinsic to them and intrinsic only to Milton's life.

And yet the order that I have described is indeed intrinsic to the sonnets, if to be "intrinsic to the sonnets" means to be inferable from traits undoubtedly present in the texts. This order is inferable from just such traits as I have mentioned: that the speaker early calls himself a young and simple lover; that he later says that he has reached age twenty-three, and that he thereafter speaks of things only adults of a certain character would speak of: that the periods of life implied by his speeches are supported by images customarily associated with them (spring with youth, winter with age). To recite the whole inventory of traits would be, of course, to repeat the poems themselves, but we may remind ourselves of some and mark in doing so how consistent a picture of this speaker the sonnets give us. To begin with, he is consistently a poet: He vows to serve the Muse (Sonnet 1), he sings of a lady (3) and cultivates Italian for that purpose (Canzone); like other poets, he can "call Fame on . . . gentle acts" (8); he cares that verse be well set to music (13); and, of course, what sounds redundant as soon as one says it, he performs as a poet all the while—performs in ways that make us feel he is conscious of this role and in modes that Renaissance poets (we know from other sources) thought right for poets. The range of his concerns, the values he holds to, once again are coextensive with the sum of the poems. Values implied early are never violated later: The man who praises virtue in his "donna leggiadra" (2) is mutatis mutandis the same man, we are moved to say, who praises virtue in the Lady of Sonnet 9, in Fairfax (with whatever reservations), and in the Alpine saints. He stays true even to small details

of his character, loves music in Sonnet 20 ("To hear the Lute well toucht") as he had in 13, and retains his youthful mastery of Italian (20 again, "Warble immortal Notes and *Tuskan* Ayre").

The portrait I have been sketching has much in common with John Milton, of course, and on these resemblances rests the tradition that the sonnet speaker is "Milton himself." But if "Milton himself" means the man from whom these utterances issued, neither the sonnet speaker nor any other Miltonic speaker can be identified with that man. If the "man himself" be defined as the sum of his utterances (and the definition ought also to include his actions), not even all the Miltonic speakers taken together will yield us that man: There will still remain the utterances that Milton uttered "in his head," as when considering lines for poems, or uttered only by mouth. The only utterances from which we can infer the man are the relatively few he committed to paper, and what we infer from them is biographically a fragment though it be esthetically and ethically a whole.

The Milton in the sonnets, as in all the works, is thus an implied author, a figure whom Wayne Booth calls "an ideal, literary, created version of the real man" (p. 75). In one sense, it is indeed right to identify the sonnet author with Milton: It is right if we mean that he is not a persona, that there is no intended ironic distance between him and his maker. Of course there is none; he is a character whose beliefs we are desired to adopt and whose judgments we are meant to approve.[5] As he resembles in some particulars Milton the man, so the sonnet author resembles in many implied authors of Milton's other works. But again, he need be collapsed into those other authors no more than into the flesh-and-blood author of them all. He shares the affliction of blindness, for instance, with the implied authors of *Paradise Lost*, the *Second Defense*, and the letter to Leonard Philaras, and shares not only blindness, but similar attitudes toward it (attitudes that, no doubt, were also Milton's); yet his and their voices remain distinguishable from one another. The author of the *Defense* cites famous examples of gifted blind men; this suits his polemical purpose and differentiates him from the authors of Sonnet 19 and the letter. For their part, Sonnet 19 and the Philaras letter both affirm faith despite affliction, but the letter's implied author, perhaps because he addresses a foreign admirer, displays a buoyancy of faith—he is as steadfast in it as if he had the eyes of Lyncaeus—denied, at that point, to the sonnet author.

But if we can make such fine discriminations as these, should we not make them also among the different sonnets? How do we, after all, know that the sonnets do not speak in twenty-three quite independent voices? It is true that we hear different tones throughout, that they change. Yet the course of their change is intelligible, with help from other intrinsic features such as subject and imagery, as the career I have described. My argument is necessarily circular. But it is not entirely circular, for the sonnets possess, besides the traits I have mentioned, two more which are fundamental to them and them alone: They are all sonnets, and sonnets that Milton grouped together in numbered sequence. To discriminate the sonnet author from other Miltonic authors is therefore an act based in part on a real, in this case a formal, difference, while to ascribe the various sonnet tones to one implied author is an act based in part on real likenesses, likenesses unduplicated outside the sonnets and brought by Milton deliberately to our attention.[6]

Because we can ground their tones in the voice of one implied author, a poet who passes from youth to maturity to old age, we can say that the sonnets do possess an intrinsic order. Yet we cannot suppose that Milton in 1628 designed them that way, and we must wonder how the order got into them. I shall soon suggest that it got into them in the "natural" course of Milton's writing career, a career that was at once personal to Milton, in that he pursued it, and conventional, in that it followed a pattern well known to professional writers (as, indeed, do all writing careers). It is, I shall suggest, the conventional aspect of Milton's career that gave the sonnets the main lines of their order and is itself reflected in them. There is also another point to consider, Milton's choices in arranging the sonnets for print.[7] He had to decide on some principle how to arrange them, and the principle had to be public if the arrangement was to appear an arrangement. Why not distribute Sonnets 1 through 6 across the whole series, or put 23 first and 1 last? Because such arrangements would not "make sense." One possible grouping was generic—sonnets of praise in one group, of dispraise in an-

other, of love in a third—and generic grouping does indeed appear in Milton's arrangement. But why put the groups themselves in this order instead of another, and why punctuate them with Sonnets 7 and 19 rather than putting 7 and 19 together? Even a merely chronological arrangement has to be public if it is to be seen as chronological. Since in 1673 no sonnet bears a date, the reader could not have known that Milton arranged them chronologically (if that was Milton's aim) except by prior knowledge of conventions. And he could only guess the applicable conventions by reference first to traits of the sonnets themselves—including their sequence.

This appeal to sequence suggests that we might search the conventions in other sonnet sequences. Can we find, among the spawning permutations of the English sequences, any particular principle whereby poems are connected? Taken as a whole, Milton's sonnets are obviously not a Petrarchan sequence of the type that raged in the 1590's—a type itself comprising many types—though we note that Spenser's *Amoretti* supply an instance of chronological order, the order of the calendar. Other English sequences show great variety of ordering principles: sometimes thematic or topical, as in Donne's religious and Chapman's philosophical sonnets; sometimes modal, as in the satirical "Gulling Sonnets" of Sir John Davies; sometimes formal, as in the coronal device of linking sonnets by repeated lines. In England at least, the idea of a sonnet sequence seems from the start to have implied unstable hybrids of experiment and copying; in a remark upon the elasticity of the concept, David Kalstone has said that " 'sonnet sequence' depends for its definition upon the practice of individual poets, upon the advantages poets may find in setting sonnets in tandem."[8] Readers, for their part, must have learned to expect in a sequence *a* principle of order, but no one particular principle, and not necessarily a principle exclusive to sonnet ordering. (Spenser's *Amoretti*, for one, share their calendar order with, of course, *The Shepheardes Calender*.)

For Milton's sonnets two principles of order prove applicable, and neither, certainly, is peculiar to the ordering of sonnets. The first is a broad scheme which, like commonplaces in rhetoric, could be used to order many sorts of utterance: the stylization of human life into distinct "ages." Jaques's speech about the "seven ages" of man in *As You Like It* (II.vii); Titian's *The Three Ages of Man* (c. 1510); Holbein's title-border to the *Lexicon Graeco Latinum* (Basle, 1545); this sentence from Milton's own *Seventh Prolusion*: "Taceo de arte quod sit pulcherrimum juventutis honestamentum, aetatis virilis firmum praesidium, senectutis ornamentum atque solatium" ("I shall not say that knowledge is the most beautiful ornament of youth, the strong defense of manhood, and the adornment and comfort of old age")[9]—all these, various as they are, build upon this one schematic idea. Milton's sonnets have little in common with any of them, except the schematic idea. But that idea is one convention that Milton could depend upon his readers to know. Another was the set of conventions, both practical and ideal, directing the career of the poet. This is familiar ground, but for clarity I briefly retrace it.

The aspiring major poet in the Renaissance was expected to follow a career corresponding to the ladder of genres from pastoral or love lyric at the foot, up (if he rose so high) to epic or tragedy at the top. Spenser's E. K. greets "our new Poete" as the latest of a series who "deuised" the pastoral genre "at the first to trye theyr habilities: and as young birdes, that be newly crept out of the nest, by little first to proue theyr tender wyngs, before they make a greater flyght" (*The Shepheardes Calender*, prefatory letter). Describing his own version of the career in *An Apology against a Pamphlet*, Milton starts from his youthful reading of "the smooth Elegiack Poets, . . . which in imitation I found most easie." In *The Reason of Church-Government* the career begins with Milton's school exercises and ascends through years of "intent study" to the literary role he aspired to fill, the role of "interpreter & relater of the best and sagest things among mine own Citizens throughout this lland in the mother dialect"; Homer, Virgil, Tasso, and the Old Testament prophets are named or implied as models. One's progress up the ladder signified not only technical gains but improvements in wisdom and virtue. Having learned to admire Dante—presumably the *Vita Nuova*—and Petrarch, Milton perceived that whoever "would not be frustrate of his hope to write well hereafter in laudable things, ought him selfe to bee a true Poem, that is, a composition, and patterne of the best and honourablest

things"; and once arrived at this insight, he was ready to betake himself "among those lofty Fables and Romances, which recount in solemne canto's the deeds of Knighthood founded by our victorious Kings" (*Works*, III, 1931, 235–37, 302–04).

The counterpart in the sonnets to this career, their reflection of it, is the progress from Sonnet 1 to Sonnet 18, that is, from amatory verse "which in imitation I found most easie" to verse that interprets and relates the highest concerns of the poet's culture. Once again, we know that this career was Milton's and that the sonnets do document his progress in it. But even if we did not know this we would still be able to read their order as an illustration, a series of "moments," in such a career, for they follow a typical course. The implied author of the sonnets shares continuously with John Milton two traits: He is a poet and a Christian. For expository purposes these traits can be treated separately, and when they are they appear to yield two careers—the typical human one, which for Milton was the Christian career, and the more specialized one of the poet. These careers proceed concurrently and are ultimately inseparable, being joined by the very dialectic according to which the true poet must become a true poem or pattern of virtue. Although Milton knew that pagan poets too could attain to virtue, the pattern of virtue relevant to the sonnets is Christian, and in them the making of the poet goes hand in hand with the making of the Christian. But for descriptive convenience I start with the poet's career. As we traverse the sonnets we will see that one of their chief concerns is the use of the poet and of poetry itself.[10]

Sonnets 1 through 6 may be called "the poet's awakening." In them the poet exercises himself two ways, both prerequisite to future success. First, he learns to distinguish the beauties and virtues of his "donna leggiadra" (2); this is really an exercise in distinguishing goodness itself, in learning sensibility and judgment, and it breeds the capacity to write poems of praise like Sonnets 9, 10, and 14. Second, the poet schools himself in service of a higher power, the power that calls forth language from him and so makes him a poet, but also marks him as a person apart and imposes on him burdens not imposed on ordinary people. In Sonnets 1 and 6 the poet affirms his service to Love and the Muse. Sonnet 3 ("Qual in colle aspro") considers the ambiguous nature of the poet's gift. Love wills him to write, and to write in a language—Italian, but also the language of poetry itself—alien to his community. The main image in this sonnet, a mountain, suggests at once supremacy and isolation, and the poem likens the mountain to the poet's tongue, the organ of poetry. This mountain is pastoral, but as a scene of growing and lonely virtue it foretells later mountains, such as the Hill of heavenly Truth in Sonnet 9, which show that to serve is to endure distinguished suffering. In the Canzone the poet's isolation is dramatized in a scene of mockery, light enough to be sure, but still the first of others, more terrible, to come. Here the poet is surrounded by youths and maidens who ask why he wastes time on Italian when he ought to be seeking the fame that awaits him in English. As mockery this can hardly hurt, yet its germ is that of greater mockery: incomprehension by those who do not serve of those who do. The mockers do not understand that the terms of poetic service demand Italian before English, for only by serving first in Love's language can the poet fit himself for future service in his own.

Sonnet 7 ("How soon hath Time") marks the end of the poet's apprenticeship and the start of his adult career. Pivotal because it represents at once a consummation and a new beginning, the sonnet dedicates him to whatever work his "great task-Master" assigns, and thus it corresponds to Sonnet 1, but on a new level. The rhetoric of Petrarchan devotion, of "serving" Love, presents an analogy to the rhetoric of religious devotion, and the difference between Sonnet 1 (service to Love) and Sonnet 7 (service to God) is the difference between the analogy to a thing and the thing itself. In Sonnet 7 the analogy finds its consummation in the thing itself. Here we enter the "real" world, the world of ordinary human life where people are called to work. The sonnet defines the poet's mature task as the service of God in the world of human work.

Sonnets 8 through 18 are virtually a syllabus of the topics on which, by exerting his powers, a poet was conceived in the Renaissance to serve God. Collectively they illustrate Milton's description in *Church-Government* of the power of poetry,

beside the office of a pulpit, to inbreed and cherish in a great people the seeds of vertu, and publick civility, to allay the perturbations of the mind, and set the affections in right tune, to celebrate in glorious and lofty Hymns the throne and equipage of Gods Almightinesse, and what he works, . . . to sing the victorious agonies of Martyrs and Saints, the deeds and triumphs of just and pious Nations doing valiantly through faith . . . , to deplore the general relapses of Kingdoms and States from justice and Gods true worship. (*Works*, III, 238)

In these sonnets the poet considers himself the spokesman and conscience of his community, his task being to rouse his community into redemptive action by interpreting and illustrating to it its own ideals. The arrangement of poems in this group moves up and down an ethical ladder, giving us images of action, public and private, at various levels of regenerancy. First a group of three sonnets embodies three ideals of action: art (8), sainthood (9), and government (10, in part). From these we plunge into the actualities of a society that has forgotten its ideals (11 and 12). A society that forgets its ideals brutalizes itself, and "I did but prompt the age" presents a veritable zoo of animal images—owls, cuckoos, asses, apes, dogs, frogs, hogs. The London setting of "A Book was writ of late" seems a prototype of the London of *The Dunciad* or even of *The Waste Land*: It is a city of ignorant stall-readers and phantom Scotsmen whose cacophonous names "would have made *Quintilian* stare and gasp"; its jeering hatred of letters makes it an intellectual Sodom. In the sonnet to Lawes and in Sonnet 14 ("When Faith and Love") we again behold ideals; and we drop again in the sonnets to Fairfax and Cromwell, now into the usual world of war and politics, where intentions are hard to scan and virtue may succumb to self-interest. In the Vane sonnet this world is shown as it would be if all politicians were unambiguously servants of God: civil society in its perfection. In withering juxtaposition to this is the slaughter of the Alpine saints: civil society as holocaust. Throughout these sonnets contrasting groups or pairs show what is to be sought and what shunned, images of desire and of loathing. These oppositions generate within the sonnets also: the Lady against her detractors; the integrity of Sir James Ley against the perfidy of Charles I; "*Latona's* twin-born progenie" against the railing hinds; the soul of Sir John Cheke against an age that hates learning; that life to which the soul in Sonnet 14 has departed against "this earthy load / Of Death, call'd Life; which us from Life doth sever." The character of all these sonnets is their energetic making of distinctions.[11]

To rouse people is to change them, to make actual into possible, or at least to imagine the possible in the actual and disclose it. This is what Milton's poet wants to do; Sonnet 8 ("Captain or Colonel") beautifully illustrates how it is done, at least by a Renaissance poet. This sonnet is Milton's "Defense of Poesy," a charming enactment of what Sidney meant when he wrote that poets "range . . . into the divine consideration of what may be, and should be," and so deliver a golden world in place of nature's brazen one. The poem opens with a disarming avowal of the poet's defenselessness: Like anyone else he is subject to the chance brutalities of war, and, locked in his house, he cannot even know who will assault him. But though defenseless himself, he is the little master of an art stronger than himself, and we see him turn the tables on his would-be conqueror. Against the "harms" of this world the poem opposes the "charms" of poetic power, and their magic expands the poem's horizon. The poet has all at once made his hypothetical captain famous for an act not yet even done, and behold! captain and poet fade into the legend of Pindar and Alexander, London into classical Athens. The sonnet does what it says it can do. Poets, as their Renaissance apologists liked to claim, record human action; but since they also conventionalize what they record, they turn today's captain into an Alexander if he gives the least hint of acting like one. Turned into poetry, today's actions become lasting images of action; and these images have ethical power, for they can induce good action in those who contemplate them, as Pindar's praise of heroes induced Alexander to spare Pindar's house.

The soldier of Sonnet 8 was an unknown quantity to begin with, of course, and Milton's poet may be said only to have exercised over him the privilege of fiction. Nevertheless, the transforming power shown there works also in sonnets whose subjects are historical. Milton does not merely attach epithets to real people; he remakes the people into "true Poem[s]," that is, compositions and patterns of the best and most honorable things. His artistry with them must, to be sure, be assumed mimetic: He assuredly wants us to

believe that the originals of figures like the Lady in Sonnet 9 did attain to the virtues for which he praises them. We do believe it, but our warrant for believing it begins and ends with the poems themselves: We believe the figures the poet so confidently makes, and makes, as it seems, before our eyes. Thus in Sonnet 9 ("Lady that in the prime of earliest youth"), once he has named the Lady in line 1 he sets to work to make an image of her. He classes her "with *Mary*, and with *Ruth*"; he endows her with a lamp; and by the poem's end he has changed her from a virtuous adolescent into one of the Biblical Wise Virgins prepared to enter eternity with the Bridegroom. Sonnet 10 performs a like transformation with tactful virtuosity. The poet first addresses a "daughter to that good Earl," then leaves us wondering what he will say to her while he writes an elegy on the Earl himself. He moves from the present, as yet barely identified, to an example of virtue in the recent past, and from it again to a classical example of the same virtue, service to liberty. "That Old man eloquent," Isocrates, is by simile made parallel to Ley, and the parallel creates a tradition—the "line of Isocrates," as it were. From the poet's place in history, both men, Isocrates and Ley, appear as heroic legends; he has been born in an age too late to have known either, it seems. But no: For turning at last to the present, he sees in the daughter all that the Earl had been. Her own virtuous oratory—"So well [her] words his noble vertues praise"—revives the tradition, and in the poem's last line she achieves identity with honor. To name but one more instance, the sonnet to Vane begins with a natural fact—that Vane is "young in yeares"—and ends with an emblematic representation of Vane as a wise "eldest son" upon whose hand religion, like an aged parent, "leanes / In peace." In all these sonnets, and in the sonnet to Lawes, Milton's strategy is to start with the historical person and then transform the person into an image of the virtue for which the sonnet praises him or her.

The sonnets to Fairfax and Cromwell have a different dynamic, for the actions they praise are, properly interpreted, incomplete, and the business of these poems is to make that incompleteness manifest. Although there is no doubt that Fairfax and Cromwell have acted, or that their acts were needed and were right, they are summoned now to bring those acts to fulfillment. Will they do so? In both sonnets a resurgence of bestial images—hydras, wolves—signals encroaching depravity; "serpent" (15) and "cloud" (16) suggest the ethical tangles and ambiguities among which warriors and statesmen move. In this mingled world there is room to doubt intentions, or, if not intentions, understanding; a question as to one or both inheres in Milton's exhortations, diplomatic though these are, and perhaps extends even into his praise of Fairfax. Fairfax' "vertue ever brings / Victory home," but is it moral virtue as well as military *virtus*, valor? Fairfax and Cromwell are men of demonstrated power to work for good, and up to now have worked for good, whatever their intentions; but working for good now means making distinctions: freeing truth and right from violence, clearing public faith from the shame of public fraud, perceiving that peace has victories not less renowned than war. To make these distinctions is to be as Henry Vane, who firmly knows "the bounds of either sword"; not to make them is to acquiesce in a cycle of carnage and tyranny, the worst form of unregenerate action: "For what can Warr, but endless warr still breed, / Till Truth, and Right from Violence be freed" (15). The sonnets call Fairfax and Cromwell to a Last Judgment upon themselves by setting before them the work undone. To this unfinished work Milton subordinates their past achievements and their praise—subordinates them in the very syntax of the sonnets, especially of the Cromwell, it being almost entirely a set of dependent clauses which resolve only at the last minute in the main clause, "helpe us. . . . "[12] In both sonnets the poet knows that victories have been won, "and when they conquer that had the right cause, who will not gratulate their victory, and be glad of their peace? Doubtlesse those are good, and Gods good guifts." His questions concern the uses to which victory will be put, and how it will be valued by those who won it; for, to use again the Augustinian terms,

if the things appertaining to that celestiall and supernall Citie where the victory shall be everlasting, be neglected for those goods, and those goods desired as the onely goods, or loved as if they were better then the other, misery must needs follow, and increase that which is inherent before. (*De Civitate Dei* xv.4, trans. John Healey, 2nd ed., London, 1620)

In Sonnet 3 the poet had experienced, together with his awakening as a poet, a sense of isolation; and in the Canzone he had been mocked. These were intimations of what must be suffered by those who serve. In the middle sonnets the role of the servant, its peculiar eminence and danger, is developed with growing intensity. As a public voice of conscience the poet identifies with his community's ideals: with the Lady of Sonnet 9, Margaret and her father, Henry Lawes, the redeemed soul of Sonnet 14, Henry Vane, and the Alpine saints. This identification requires that he often oppose his community and in turn be persecuted by it, for although communities invent ideals nothing is more common than for communities to lapse from and persecute them. The Lady in Sonnet 9 is being persecuted by them "that overween, / And at [her] growing vertues fret their spleen"; Sonnet 8 began with the poet anticipating the sack of his house; and in "I did but prompt the age" he finds himself reviled by the people he meant to help. As we approach Sonnet 18 the feeling grows that human society is no secure place for the just person: Lawes, who is just, is conspicuously exempted "from the throng"; and the redeemed in Sonnet 14 is envied (if that is the right word) for having escaped "this earthy load / Of Death, call'd Life." Sonnet 17, indeed, gives us a society in which the just can live; but lest anyone forget that it is still the earthly city, Sonnet 18 ("Avenge O Lord") makes a forcible reminder. Much of the power of Sonnet 18 accumulates from these premonitory images of persecution, of potential martyrdom at the hands of a depraved people. When the poet speaks of flying "the *Babylonian* wo" it is hard to feel that he means only the Papacy; he means also human society itself.

That Sonnet 18 is the climax of the sonnets every reader must feel: Its intrinsic power is palpable, its rhetoric torrential. I disparage neither of these by suggesting that the sonnet also gains force, and some significance, from its position. It constitutes a node in the sonnets and gathers up so much that it is difficult to speak of analytically. For expository convenience I have separated the poet's career from the Christian's, but in Sonnet 18 the speech of the poet is so manifestly a mode of Christian speech that the separation becomes inconvenient. Of this poet we ought really to say, varying Johnson's phrase, that he is perpetually a Christian, but a poet only by talent. Still, Sonnet 18 is where that talent finds its fullest use. In the sonnets up through 17 the poet's career has taken him through a series of increasingly strenuous public performances in which he has acted hortatory and epideictic roles. Sonnet 18 resoundingly closes this public career—which, we must again recall, is not to be taken for the specific career of John Milton (that, of course, in 1655 had not yet reached its glory), but for a typical career. The poem closes it by speaking on still a higher level than its predecessors, the highest any Renaissance poet could aspire to: prophecy. Its breadth of reference, its sense of historic meaning—the event, properly construed, breaks upon all at least of Protestant Christendom—its sheer eloquence of indignation, all befit the prophet's role.

Prophecies reveal final truths, or the ground of all truth, and Sonnet 18, alone among the sonnets, delivers such revelations. It reveals the ultimate form of persecution of the human ideal, of those who serve, and so consummates the series of evil adumbrated in Sonnet 3. It is also the moment, an apocalyptic moment, when the poet addresses by name the power he has all along been serving. And again, it is the moment when that power reveals itself most directly to man. That power reveals itself in the poet's utterance, like the voice of the Old Testament God in his prophets; it reveals itself still more in the poet's strength of imagination, the strength to interpret the slaughter providentially ("that from these may grow / A hunderd-fold, who having learnt thy way"). Here, precisely, is where the separation of poet and Christian dissolves. The strength of a poet, at least of a poet like Milton, is certainly to imagine, in the face of the greatest possible loss, the greatest possible recompense. This also is the strength of the good man, who makes himself most completely human when he becomes capable of providential interpretation, or wresting good from evil. This capability, at once imaginative and moral, we may call in speaking of Milton the "Christian imagination" (its later, secular version would be the Romantic imagination or one of its varieties), and it is the ground on which poet and Christian join. When the poet addresses God he addresses the source of his imagination; but this

is no privileged communion with a Muse, or rather, if it is, it is a privilege he shares with every man of good imagination.

For the poet as a poet, however, this height of speech fulfills his training, and his public role finds its end in its fulfillment. Hence Sonnet 19 retires him, and does so with the only touch of irony to be found in the whole sequence. Remembering Milton's other versions of his blindness, those aggressive wrenchings of good from evil in the *Second Defense* and the Philaras letter, one would like to find in this sonnet the same triumph; but the sonnet does not work that way. It presents what seems to the poet an inscrutable disaster. Retrospectively, in Sonnet 22, he will be able to construe this "disaster" in providential terms, just as in 18 he had construed the slaughter providentially. Yet the position of Sonnet 19 permits us to construe providentially what the poet himself cannot; for we know that no matter how "bent" his soul to serve, he could not do more than he has done: Though his natural light has been spent, his Talent, far from being "useless," has been richly invested. But for him, conscious yet of the will to serve, imagination has temporarily failed: he is reduced to murmur a querulous version of the question Sonnet 7 had asked, What can I do of any use now? The answer given by patience—"God doth not need / Either man's work or his own gifts"—reminds us that the question was egoistic and is a hard answer for the pride of a visionary poet just arrived at his peak. Yet to accept this answer, to "only stand and waite," is part of what it means to serve. However reluctantly, the poet must now study the wisdom he had praised Margaret's father for learning in Sonnet 10, the wisdom of leaving public life "more in himself content."

Sonnets 20 and 21 are exercises in learning to be content. Sonnet 20 ("*Lawrence* of vertuous Father vertuous Son"), indeed, performs on the poet himself a transformation like those that 8, 9, and 10 had performed on their subjects. It opens on a wintry scene—"Now that the Fields are dank, and ways are mire"—and the poet, a touch of winter in his mind, wonders how to "wast a sullen day." Put this way, the question does not promise a good answer; better to ask "what may be won / From the hard Season gaining," which directs attention to redeeming, not wasting,

time. Reconceiving his question at once permits
him to imagine answers: He can wrest some good
from winter's evil in humane conversation and in
study of the humane pleasures. It restores to him,
too, his providential sense of time: "Time will
run / On," Favonius will "re-inspire / The frozen
earth" and bring again "the Lillie and Rose, that
neither sow'd nor spun." With time now on his
hands, the poet needed to learn the wise passive-
ness that imitates the lily and rose; the action of
Sonnet 20 shows him learning it.

Sonnet 22 ("*Cyriack*, this three years day these
eyes") affords the true counterpart in the sonnets
to Milton's other affirmations of faith despite
blindness. Where Sonnet 19 has only bedrock patience for consolation, here are "heart" and
"hope." The sonnet presents a final stocktaking,
the poet's review of his lot, his achievement, his
state of mind. Ledgerlike, it tots up the evil
(blindness) and the good (consciousness of having done his work) and strikes a balance: "content though blind." The mood, too, is balanced,
countering moderate regret of the evil with not
immoderate cheerfulness at the good. If there
is a bit of boasting in the thought that "all *Europe*
talks from side to side" of the poet's accomplishments, the boast is chastened by the thought that
this world is, after all, a "vain mask"; and the
poet ends by reposing faith in his "better guide."

Thus the poet's career makes one pattern in
Milton's sonnets. The other is a Christian career
which unfolds against the background of traditional cosmology. As a Christian, the poet is a
typical fallen man trying by virtuous action to
make his life as good as is humanly possible and
expecting supernatural aid to make up what
human power can't supply. His career conforms
in little to the traditional Christian pattern of
human history, a fall from original innocence into
a state of bondage which he is obliged to struggle
against with the hope of eventual redemption.
The two careers, we have noted, can be syn-
chronized in the sonnets because the virtues
thought necessary to the Christian are also
necessary to the poet, and because poetry itself is
a mode of virtuous action. Poetry assists in the
redemption of the poet himself, and of his society, if his society heeds it.

The cosmology of the sonnets comprises four
levels of existence.[13] Familiar categories though
these are, we must review them yet once more if we

are to see how they help to order the sonnets. The
highest level, of course, is heaven, the supernatural. The sonnets allude to it prospectively, as
a promise (9 and 23), and as that "Life" from
which "this earthy load / Of Death" severs us
(14). But the ordinary human world is always
under its direction, a fact sometimes signally, if
paradoxically, revealed in events like those of
Sonnets 18 and 19. The second and highest natural level is Eden, the level of human innocence.
In the sonnets this is represented by the Petrarchan group. They remind us of Eden because
their world is pastoral and playful, its inhabitants
are a nightingale, a shepherdess, youths, and
maidens, and time in it seems never to change
from the May evening of Sonnet 1. They remind
us of Eden too, perhaps, because their world is
fragile, like the fragile blossom of the poet's
language in Sonnet 3. Their very playfulness,
such as the poet's delight in his newfound tongue,
is mixed with anxiety, such as his feeling of
alienation; and Sonnet 3 ends with a sigh and a
hope that he "who plants from Heaven" will find
the poet's "slow heart and hard bosom as good a
soil" as Love had found his tongue. When in
Sonnet 7 the poet enters adulthood we wonder if
this thought was a foretaste of what was to come,
like Eve's anxious dream before the Fall.

Eden is also the state of youthful innocence
before one comes to mature consciousness. When
one does that, as the poet does in Sonnet 7, one
enters the third level, the level of human life in the
context of ordinary fallen nature. This is the
world of time and the seasonal cycle—the late
spring of Sonnet 7, the approaching winter of
Sonnet 20—and of time's companion, mortality.
Our feelings about entering this world are
ambivalent, as they are at the end of *Paradise
Lost*: We fall, yet we also rise to it, for while we
find that we need redemption we also find that
we have the power to participate in our redemption by working at it. Looked at from this level,
Eden appears as an ideal human state which can
in some measure be regained through virtuous
action. We saw that a prime purpose of Sonnets 8
through 18 is to illustrate human ideals, that is,
to give images of virtuous action. Sonnet 9 images
its Lady's virtue as a laborious climb up a steep
hill. This would be the equivalent of Dante's
Mount of Purgatory, which Milton mentions in
Sonnet 13 when he sets Lawes higher on it than

Dante set Casella. Purgatory fills the space between our ordinary fallen world and Eden, and to act virtuously is metaphorically to climb Purgatory. Not only the Lady and Lawes, but the Alpine saints must be set there too, for having "kept thy truth so pure of old." Moreover, if poetic action, a poem's treatment of its subject, can be equated with poetic imagery, then the transformations in these sonnets of actual into ideal, of people into poems, themselves enact the climb.[14]

Our feelings about the fallen world are ambivalent not only because our fall into it is both loss and gain, but also because this world partakes of sin. It is a world of appearances which may be deceptive, like the poet's immature appearance in Sonnet 7, and in which motives are hard to know, as Fairfax' and Cromwell's are. In this world it is constantly necessary to distinguish real good from disguised evil, and at this task the poet is a specialist, for his job is to praise real good when he finds it, to castigate evil, and to exhort waverers in the right way. It is because the poet's task is only a more intense version of the Christian's that the sonnets can synchronize the poet's career with that of fallen man.

Below this mixed world is the level of pure evil, of unregenerate action. This lowest level is plumbed by Sonnets 11 and 12, which together make the dead center of the sequence somewhat as Dante's Hell makes the center of the earth. Here all action is brutish: We noted how full of animal imagery Sonnet 11 is. The inhabitants of these poems have lost touch with all the humane arts, and having lost these disciplines they have lost all conception of liberty as well. The undistinguishing crowd "bawle for freedom in their senceless mood, / And still revolt when truth would set them free" (11). Mindless revolt is of course not freedom but bondage. These two poems are satires, and what their satire expresses is the poet's "sense of looking down on a scene of bondage, frustration, or absurdity" (I borrow Northrop Frye's words from *Anatomy of Criticism*, Princeton: Princeton Univ. Press, 1957, p. 34).

Given the ambiguous character of the third of these levels, we should expect to find that the poet's human career through them partakes of both fall and rise, the Christian (and eminently Miltonic) paradox that one must go down in order

to go up. Through the first half of the sequence the poet's professional career rises, as we have seen. Humanly, however, we should have to say that he has fallen, as he has lost Eden. Yet clearly this was a fortunate fall, like Adam's: Great things have come from it. The Renaissance poet, we remember, ascends a ladder that is both generic and ethical; Milton's prose description of it may make the ascent sound like a dialectic of reading and writing only, but Milton, we also know, was never one to praise a merely bookish virtue. Where else does the Christian learn ethics? From his descent into the world, from experience of evil. In the sonnets from 1 through 12 the poet's human career takes him downward, his experience of evil in the two last of these sonnets affording a reminiscence of Dante's. The image of the poet environed by beasts in Sonnet 11 recalls the image of Dante environed by beasts at the start of the *Commedia*. There Dante is midway on his life's journey, he is suddenly conscious of sin in himself, and he is about to enter Hell. Here the poet is midway on his journey—midway through the sequence—and he is in Hell, or its earthly analogy, a depraved city. The sin that Milton's poet has become conscious of is not in himself, however, but in his community, and he is not its agent but its victim. It has two facets. First, it is a sin against the human ideal, the sin of persecution. Second, it is a sin against one's own liberty, the sin of self-enslavement. The two facets go together, for it is precisely the self-enslaved who are apt to persecute. For Dante, again, the journey down was the necessary start of the journey up, as sin must be confronted and understood before it can be overcome. Likewise for Milton's poet: Having explored the depths of Sonnets 11 and 12, he concerns himself in the later sonnets with ascension from bondage through the exercise of liberty.

The juxtaposition of Sonnets 11 through 14 illustrates that concern. This group moves between extremes, with the sonnet to Lawes (13) filling the middle ground. Literally, the poet commends Lawes for understanding the proportion of short to long in English prosody: His song is "well measur'd." Measure is an artistic virtue, but for Milton, as we know, artistic and ethical virtue go together. In both art and ethics, measure is the harmonious proportion of lesser to greater, awareness of the relative values of things, and adjustment of one's desires to their proper limits. Coming after the bestial disorder-- the "licence" --of Sonnets 11 and 12, the praise of "measur'd Song" has powerful redemptive implications: It is measure that makes us human.[15] Like others of the sonnets that praise people as embodiments of virtues, this one treats its subject to a progressive perfecting. Lawes is first exempted "from the throng" of the unmeasured, then promised fame "to after-age," and finally set somewhere above "the milder shades of Purgatory." This upward motion continues through the scene change, as it were, and when Sonnet 14 opens, a human soul, "ripen'd" in due course by Faith and Love, has gone "to dwell with God." The purgatorial restraint of 13 modulates here to "joy and bliss for ever," for here are no limits to be observed: The redeemed may "rest / And drink [her] fill of pure immortal streams." Denial of limit is the condition of sin, freedom from limit the privilege of eternity. The aspirant to virtue in this life must aspire, as Lawes and the poet do, to measure.

Redemption from bondage is the theme of the public sonnets as well. Fairfax, we saw, is asked to "free" Truth and Right from the bondage of cyclical violence; Cromwell, to "save" free conscience from devouring mouths. In Henry Vane we see measure, still the redeeming virtue, embodied in the statesman. His counterimage is the "triple Tyrant" of Italy, from whose bloody immoderation others must learn "early [to] fly the *Babylonian* wo." In these sonnets the bondage to be escaped both is and is not society itself. The Vane sonnet is there to show us that society is capable of its own kind of perfection and to encourage pursuit of that perfection as a proper object of man so long as he must live in society. Yet in the Christian scheme of history society is indeed bondage, the earthly city in its perfection being still the earthly city, still bonded to time. Hence the images of society given us in Sonnets 15 through 18 should remind us of Michael's narrative to Adam in the last books of *Paradise Lost*, where human history is foreseen as a cycle of dubious victories (as in the Fairfax and Cromwell sonnets), brief reestablishments of good (such as the Vane sonnet presents), and subsequent relapses into evil. "So shall the World goe on," Michael forecasts,

To good malignant, to bad men benigne,
Under her own waight groaning, till the day

Appeer of respiration to the just,
And vengeance to the wicked.　(XII.537- 41)

In the sonnets it is Sonnet 18 that corresponds to this prophecy. One more way, and the most evident, in which Sonnet 18 is apocalyptic is that it resonates of the Book of Revelations, where a society permitted its last confirming act of desperate wickedness is then brought to an end and swept aside. This will be man's general release from bondage, and having foretold it the poet turns in Sonnet 19 to work his own release from the seeming bondage of enforced idleness.

It is not from blindness so much as from impatience and then sullenness that the poet needs redemption. The first lines of Sonnet 20 identify the illness suffered commonly by retired people—a sickened sense of time, which imagines the day as something that can only be wasted. Redeeming the time is thus the theme of Sonnet 20, and in its companion ("*Cyriack*, whose Grandsire on the Royal Bench") the poet, having learned to redeem it, counsels Cyriack "to measure life." Other kinds of measure, too, can be learned in domesticity: bodily temperance (Sonnet 20 invites Lawrence to a feast that is "neat," "light," and "choice") and pleasure in such humanly small things as "the Lute well toucht" (20) and "a cheerful hour" (21). Readers who can attend to nothing in Milton but the Sublime are in danger of undervaluing these sonnets for their seeming triviality; the joke, insofar as there is one, would be on them. Poor earnest Cyriack, deep in his Euclid and Archimedes, sounds like some Victorian images of John Milton. Milton's poet is wiser, and in these sonnets he discloses the just relation in time of small things to great. His achievement of this wisdom: his anticipation, in Sonnet 20, of returning spring, of "the Lillie and Rose, that neither sow'd nor spun"; his invitation in Sonnet 21, to "drench" deep thoughts " in mirth, that after no repenting drawes"—all these betoken a recovery of innocence like that which Michael promises Adam: "A Paradise within thee, happier farr" (XII.587).

The Christian career finds its resolution, all passion spent, in Sonnet 22. There the poet rests his faith in his "better guide," and his faith is rewarded in Sonnet 23 by the vision of his late espoused saint. The old and, one hopes, discredited reading of Sonnet 23, which makes of it entirely a lament for a dead wife, also makes it a most un-Miltonic close to the sonnets: On that reading the dreamer's expulsion into lonely "night" has no human counterpart anywhere else in Milton's poetry. Interpretation of this sonnet must recognize that although the saint is originally Milton's wife she has been assimilated, as Leo Spitzer observed, to a *donna angelatica* of the same type and function as Dante's Beatrice; but it must then emphasize, as the poem does, besides the pain of temporal separation the certainty of eternal reunion with her.[16] Like a musical coda, the sonnet affords a last review of the levels through which the poet has passed: first Hell (in the form of the Classical underworld whence Alcestis was rescued, "pale and faint"); then Purgatory ("Purification in the old Law"); and last, the Edenic vision of the bright but veiled saint. Redemption can go no higher in this life, but in the next the veil will be removed and the poet, fully redeemed, will see "without restraint" just as the redeemed in Sonnet 14 can "drink [her] fill." The poet's dream is a promise and a reminder: a promise of bliss to be granted in the next world and a reminder of how inferior this one is. His pain on waking is the pain of having to wait for the dream to fulfill itself.

"Milton's first and last Sonnets," Todd remarked, "display . . . the sweetness and tenderness of Petrarch."[17] Sonnet 23 does indeed bring us round again to the beginning of the sequence, to the poet's Petrarchan dreamland and his "donna leggiadra"; but with the same difference that exists between Eden before the Fall and the throne of God surrounded by saints after the Last Judgment. These, Eden at one end, the Apocalypse at the other, are of course the two images to which Milton's literary mind gravitates. In *Paradise Lost* they enclose the entirety of human history. In the sonnets they enclose the whole of a human career, stylized into a paradigm of all human careers and an analogue of human history. When we consider that Milton wrote many, perhaps most, of his sonnets during the years when he was thinking of *Paradise Lost*, we are not surprised to find motifs from his epic washing into them. "Washing into them," though, suggests a cause-effect relation which is surely too simple; some concept like the participation of the Many in the One seems needed to describe the sort of all-involving devotion that produces a *Paradise Lost* and its satellites. That such a de-

votion is personal, a trait of the man Milton, no one doubts. That it is also literary, a devotion to literary kinds of order, is a main premise of this essay. Indeed, I am tempted to call it inevitable that Milton would order his sonnets in the shape of his favorite myth.

This essay has now given several hypothetical explanations of how the sonnets received their order, and it may be well to review them. Milton, then, could not in 1628 have conceived the series he eventually wrote; this acknowledges the obvious truth that he could not have foreknown the particularities of poems to be occasioned by future events. He could, and did, envision a certain kind of career for himself in which certain kinds of efforts were to be made in a certain order; he could, and presumably did, conceive Sonnets 1 through 6 as early steps on that ladder. As he pursued the career, rising to public themes and roles in his work of the 1640's and 1650's, he wrote these themes and roles into the sonnets as well. Did he write the sonnets with consciousness of their accumulating effect and with a view to preserving it? All that we know of Milton's single-mindedness in general, and of the sonnet manuscripts in particular, at least permits us to imagine that he did, although in a sense the question cannot be answered because we lack access to Milton's consciousness at any of the moments when he perceived a connection or made a decision. (Indeed, to state this is to see how wrongly conceived the question is. Were we obliged to answer for the author's interior consciousness, could we ever construe any work or speech or act?) We can be sure, however, that some concept of order, of putting this before that, came into play perforce when Milton published the sonnets. That he published them in the order of their writing is a fact which, I should like to emphasize, implies of itself no one interpretation: The traditional "biographical" interpretation and its traditional alternative, the denial of unity, are both as much hypotheses as the one offered here. None can claim self-evident truth, but the "literary" hypothesis has this advantage of its rivals, that it construes the order of the sonnets in terms more appropriate to literature, to Renaissance literature, and to Milton's other works.[18]

Iowa State University
Ames

Notes

[1] *Milton's Sonnets* (London: Macmillan, and New York St. Martin's, 1966), pp. 62–68. The sonnets are quoted from this text.

[2] "Implied author" is Wayne Booth's term: See *The Rhetoric of Fiction* (Chicago· Phoenix Books, 1967), Ch. III.

[3] The chief difference between *Poems* and MS is that Milton omitted from *Poems* four sonnets, 15 through 17 and 22, whose politics had become dangerous to him. They are restored to the sequence by John S. Smart (1921) and Honigmann in the order in which they appear in MS. The absence of Sonnet 22 from *Poems* does not materially affect my argument in this paragraph.

[4] Translations of Milton's Italian are by Smart, as reprinted in Honigmann.

[5] For the restricted definition of "persona" which I am using here, see Irvin Ehrenpreis, "Personae," in *Literary Meaning and Augustan Values* (Charlottesville: Univ. Press of Virginia, 1974), esp. p. 57. Ehrenpreis protests against the fashion of seeing personae indiscriminately, arguing that what is often praised as "artifice" is rather a necessity of expression: "this kind of rhetorical pose is absolutely inseparable from all language and communication. One could never reveal the whole truth about oneself, even supposing one knew it. . . . One cannot speak without selecting a limited number of remarks from among possible remarks" (p. 51). It is in just this necessity for selection among possible utterances that the concept of "implied author" finds its justification. Although Booth's language ("an ideal . . . version") seems to grant the implied author a sort of Platonic excellence, he perhaps means only that good writers use necessity to advantage—in short, select well.

[6] A sign that Milton wanted to mute the occasions of the sonnets is his treatment of their MS titles: See Honigmann, pp 71–72, and n. 7 below

[7] That Milton did not in 1628 set out to write the series he eventually wrote is not strictly true, for Sonnets 1 through 6 and the Canzone, all composed probably between 1628 and 1630, must surely have been intended as a sequence. Milton first arranged sonnets for print in 1645 (*Poems*) and in doing so established two principles which he followed more or less closely thereafter. First, the order of the ten sonnets in 1645 is chronological (but whether strictly or loosely so has been debated). Second, four of these sonnets —7 through 10 —appear in the Cambridge MS.; here they lack numbers, but 8 and 10 are titled. In 1645 all ten are numbered, and none is titled; with three exceptions, this pattern of converting titles to numbers is maintained in 1673. In composing new sonnets Milton continued the numbering initiated in 1645, but whether higher number always means later date of composition has been often doubted. Since, however, no one doubts that in general the series is chronological, and since my interpretation stands in no need of scholarly latitude regarding individual sonnets, I frankly embrace the straight conservatism of Maurice Kelley ("Milton's Later Sonnets and the Cambridge Manuscript," *Modern Philology*, 54, 1956, 20–25), who argues that Milton's MS numbering represents exactly the order in which the later sonnets were composed. Between 1646 and 1652, as Kelley reconstructs it, Milton or his copyist entered Sonnets 11 through 17 and "On the Forcers of Conscience" in what were

then two adjacent leaves of the MS, pp. 43- [44] and 47 [48]. These were Milton's sonnet workshop during those years: The leaves contain nothing but sonnets and drafts of sonnets. We may reasonably imagine, therefore, that as Milton composed new sonnets he had the old not only in view (until his blindness), but also in mind.

In 1655 (Kelley again) Milton began a new transcript of these later sonnets, noting at the top of p. 1 (present p. [46] in MS) that they were to follow the ten in the printed book. Half of this transcript is lost, but Kelley believes it contained all the later sonnets including "Forcers." The next document is 1673 itself. Here "Forcers" is divorced from the numbered sonnets, 11 and 12 are reversed, and 15 through 17 and 22 are suppressed (see n. 3). Although early MS drafts of Sonnets 11 and 13 through 17 have elaborate titles, the surviving part of the 1655 transcript shows the titles dwindling away, and in 1673 just three sonnets are titled: 12, "On the same" (i.e., as 11); 13, "To Mr. H. Lawes, on his Aires"; and 15 (i.e., 18), "On the late Massacher in Piemont." I concur with Honigmann (p. 72) in taking these more as footnotes to allusions than as real titles.

From this review it appears that Milton ordered his sonnets chiefly in the process of writing them, that he made most --though not all—of his choices as he went. He may never have asked himself the questions I proceed to ask in this paragraph. But that is only to say that a poet may do by "instinct" things a critic must do by argument.

[8] *Sidney's Poetry· Contexts and Interpretations* (1965: rpt. New York: Norton, 1970), p. 133. For a survey of ordering techniques, some of them used perhaps but once, in the very earliest sequences, see William O. Harris, "Early Elizabethan Sonnets in Sequence," *Studies in Philology*, 68 (1971), 451–69.

[9] Milton, *Works*, ed. Frank A. Patterson, XII (New York: Columbia Univ. Press, 1936), 260. The Holbein woodcut, used more than once as a title-border, allegorically presents the course of human life from birth to redemption; reproduced in Thomas P. Roche, Jr., *The Kindly Flame: A Study of the Third and Fourth Books of Spenser's* Faerie Queene (Princeton: Princeton Univ. Press, 1964).

[10] The following description requires many cameo explications of individual sonnets. These are instrumental to its purpose, but, although they contain here and there a new reading, in general I make no claim for their originality. I attend to the parts for the sake of their sum.

[11] Latent in these oppositions and in the historical pattern described later is Augustine's dialectic of the Two Cities. I do not think the sonnets are designed to illustrate it; rather, it enters into them as part of their general "set" on the world. But *De Civitate Dei* XV.4 does have special application to Sonnets 15 and 16, discussed below.

[12] The syntax of Sonnet 16 is described by Taylor Stoehr, "Syntax and Poetic Form in Milton's Sonnets," *English Studies*, 45 (1964), 289–301.

[13] They are four in the many descriptions Northrop Frye has given of Renaissance poetic cosmology. They can also be collapsed into two, as by A. S. P. Woodhouse in "The Argument of Milton's *Comus*," *University of Toronto Quarterly*, 11 (1941), 46–71, and "Nature and Grace in *The Faerie Queene*," *ELH*, 16 (1949), 194-228. I have gone for my ac-

count to two essays by Frye, "Nature and Homer" and "New Directions from Old" (1958 and 1960; rpt. in *Fables of Identity*, New York: Harcourt, 1963, pp 39–66), because the four-level conception more precisely embraces the sonnets.

[14] The idea of Purgatory as a scene of personal transformation differs from the literal doctrine of Purgatory as the place where souls do penance after death. As a Protestant, Milton of course rejected the doctrine; as a poet, he found Purgatory a useful metaphor of man's aspiration to virtue. For the first point see C. A. Patrides, *Milton and the Christian Tradition* (Oxford: Clarendon, 1966), p. 264; for the second, Irene Samuel, *Dante and Milton* (Ithaca: Cornell Univ. Press, 1966), pp. 212, 218. With a change of name, the purgatorial hill can domesticate in Protestant writing: "On a huge hill, / Cragged, and steep, Truth stands, and hee that will / Reach her, about must, and about must goe" (Donne, *Satyre III*); "this hill top of sanctity and goodnesse above which there is no higher ascent but to the love of God" (Milton, *Church-Government*;

Works, III, 261).

[15] Cf. *Church-Government*: "Nor is there any sociable perfection in this life civill or sacred that can be above discipline, but she is that which with her musicall cords preserves and holds all the parts thereof together" (*Works*, III, 185).

[16] Spitzer, "Understanding Milton," *Hopkins Review*, 4 (1951), 17–25. Two readings which get the emphases right are Martin Mueller, "The Theme and Imagery of Milton's Last Sonnet," *Archiv*, 201 (1964), 267–71, and Marilyn L. Williamson, "A Reading of Milton's Twenty-Third Sonnet," *Milton Studies*, 4 (1972), 141–49.

[17] *The Poetical Works of John Milton*, ed. Henry J Todd (1809; rpt. New York: AMS, 1970), VI, 438.

[18] An early version of this essay formed part of my dissertation at Rutgers Univ. I acknowledge with pleasure suggestions given me by Carren Kaston, Linda Koenig, and Scott Consigny, and helpful criticism from Irene Samuel and Stanley Fish.

2 • That Old Man Eloquent

Annabel Patterson

> As soon as anything becomes poetic, it does transcend
> the chaos of the everyday world, and indicates an ability
> on the part of the author to transcend or transform it—
> to have his mind on consonance as well as party politics,
> and to hold action and contemplation in some kind
> of fusion where all is simultaneously ill and well.

It was not so very long ago that claims like these, for
the difference between "the poetic" (or "the literary")
and other kinds of writing, were taken as axiomatic. This
version of old New Critical doctrine, however, arrives more
intricately mediated than most. One should imagine it framed
by a double set of quotation marks, since I am here citing
Anna Nardo (in 1979) citing Joan Webber (in 1968), who
herself was adapting the anticontextual aesthetics she inherited to the subject that then engaged her—Milton's
polemical prose. As Nardo transmitted her predecessor's
dilemma a decade later, Webber wondered how Milton
"sustained his vision" of the poetic life during the years he
thrust his fighting words into the arena of church reform
and political revolution; she concluded that his vision was
sustained in the digressive spaces within those pamphlets

where Milton spoke of his poetic vocation, and thereby "evoked a timeless world where contemplation and harmony are possible."[1]

For Nardo, whose own project was to render an account of Milton's sonnets as a coherent poetic program, their origin as occasional poems notwithstanding, Webber's faith in Milton's faith in the timeless was exemplary; pondering what exactly Webber might have meant by that "kind of fusion where all is simultaneously ill and well," we might rather suspect evidentiary perversity. The intractability of the material that Webber had to deal with (in order to understand the anti-prelatical pamphleteer) breaks through the ideal hypothesis (that one can fly above the clouds) and reveals that vocationalism is itself a distillation of turbulence.

Almost a decade and a half later still, the difficulty in distinguishing between what is timeless and what time-bound appears still more intractable, not least because I write to honor a venerable Miltonist who desires that this book of essays on Milton, linking in commemoration two scholars three hundred years apart, will focus on the literary Milton. But what is literature? This question must surely provoke a rather different answer today than either that assumed by Joan Webber, or its diametrical opposite as demanded by Jean-Paul Sartre in the aftermath of the Second World War, that literature redefine itself so as to privilege political engagement.[2]

It is, of course, unfair to both Webber and Nardo to imply that their own theory of "literature" was time-bound. While the term "transcendence" irresistibly signals a poetics derived from Romanticism and given a new lease on life by certain forms of New Criticism, each took large steps in expanding the idea of the literary Milton in a direction of which Sartre might actually have approved. In Webber's case "literature" was discovered in Milton's polemical prose pamphlets by making them the subject of poetic (stylistic) analysis, and by focusing on the poetic psyche, the "Eloquent I" that Milton himself placed at their center, by his use of first-person pronouns and autobiographical excursions. In Nardo's case "literature" already existed (what can be more unequivocally literary than a sonnet?), but it was rendered more literary by the concept of an overarching intellectual program under which could shelter a seeming hodge-podge of poems, written over a quarter of a century, often in response to specific frustrations. For Nardo, there was an overarching coherence binding these fragments together, the notion of an "ideal community" of idealists, past and present. "Each sonnet," wrote Nardo, "details a unique engagement with a person, event, or partisan issue of the day, but each also asks its readers to consider this one moment in the light of man's ongoing fight against barbarity":

> At the center [of the ideal community] is an individual— free and virtuous, with a calm and humble faith. Surrounding this "upright heart and pure" are the groups of significant "others" that form the society that Milton envisioned: a beloved woman, the home, friends male and female, the nation, and Protestant Europe. Embracing all, of course, is a totally provident and beneficent God.[3]

This program has more in common, in terms of its aesthetic presuppositions, with that of Mary Ann Radzinowicz than Nardo was willing to acknowledge; for Radzinowicz was also committed to the view that Milton created that most New Critical of values, a unified structure, when he gathered his sonnets together for publication. Even though his *Poems of Mr. John Milton*(1645) contained only those sonnets now numbered 1 through 10, and even though the 1673 edition of his collected works omitted (presumably for prudential reasons) the "commonwealth" sonnets 15, 16, 17 and 22, Radzinowicz, like Nardo, believed that Milton, retroactively and quite deliberately, created a sonnet "sequence" composed of individual "clusters," whose interrelations can now be securely determined:

> Milton intended each sonnet to bear its individual meaning; he grouped the sonnets by interlinked cross-reference and wrote them at distinct periods, often several years apart, so that a thematic meaning emerges within subgroups. He then printed them retrospectively, breaking chronology for other

effects, and brought them together so that a final polyphonic harmony would be apparent in them.[4]

Radzinowicz saw the final structure as a narrative of maturation: from Milton's "youthful confident sense of the irresistibility of virtue and the certainty of election" (sonnets 1–7), to studies of the "ethics of purity" (8–10), to those of Milton's "most revolutionary period" that consider the consequences of writing the divorce tracts (11–14), to those (not quite identical with the group unpublishable in 1673) in which Milton "labored to prevent the revolution from failure" (15–18), to the last and most purely autobiographical group, which "as a whole records calm of mind and assent to the temporal circumstances of the period."[5]

No doubt for reasons of which I remain unconscious (and no doubt fortunately so) I cannot equate the "literary" exclusively with any of the values adumbrated so far: whether Webber's transcendence and consonance, Radzinowicz's "polychronic harmony," or Nardo's "free and virtuous" individual with his "calm and humble faith," secure in reliance on "a totally provident and beneficent God." For me, what constitutes the literary Milton as exemplified by his sonnets is a more embattled and less optimistic notion; though (as will become clear as I attempt to describe it) it shares with each of these three fine readings of Milton a point of convergence. With Webber I share the belief that one cannot understand Milton without taking into account the eloquence of his psychological self-presentation— although I would push psychology lightly in the direction of psychoanalysis. Milton's sonnets, like much of his mid-century pamphleteering, are full of disingenuities and repressions, whose centrifugal pressure makes their small shells always on the verge of explosion. With Radzinowicz I share the conviction that Milton's sonnets came retroactively to tell the story of his life and political career,[6] not least in the history of their printing; but their implied narrative is less a *bildungsroman*, more an undoing, than the one proposed by her five clusters. And I share with Nardo the conviction that Milton in his sonnets created the community

with which he wished to be identified; but its most important members were dead, some very long dead indeed, and
hence only available as a community in which he might
participate in a highly restricted sense; while their value to
him, as models, had itself to be constructed in a restricted,
highly selective, manner. The story that Milton made his
sonnets tell was indeed that of the "ongoing fight against
barbarity," but we learn of the defeats in that campaign as
much or more than the victories.

There is nothing casual, however, about the way that we
learn. At the center of my own argument is a definition of
the "literary" that resituates an old New Critical term,
"difficulty," in an aesthetics recharged in the 1990s with
respect for historical knowledge. One can scarcely doubt
that Milton's own aesthetics was so charged, or became so
when he entered the field of pamphlet warfare; but in the
sonnets, for reasons we will need to reconstruct with some
delicacy, he offers historical knowledge as simultaneously
a bait, the reward that will make the sonnet give up its
intellectual goods to the scrupulous and worthy reader, and,
conversely, as something finally unreliable, if not entirely
unavailable. He constructs a sonnet *sequence*, peppered with
signs that autobiography and chronology are its very themes;
but he ensures that it will remain impossible for his readers
to date them with any certainty. I take this provocative
behavior to constitute a poetics, not of the timeless, but of
sequentiality itself: of what it means, philosophically, to be
timebound, bound by what one has said and done, written
and published, previously; and bound to follow, belatedly,
those who have gone before.[7]

OCCASIONALITY

This reconnaissance of the critical tradition has perhaps
grouped too casually together ideas of sequence that should
be kept distinct. The first proposition is that Milton arranged his sonnets in strict chronological order based on the
moment of composition. This hypothesis, closely related to

the conviction that the sonnets were all "occasional," would surely not have dominated the criticism so clearly, generating only mild or sporadic dissent, without the testimony of the Cambridge manuscript, which gives firm occasions for all but two sonnets in what, looking at the final structure we ourselves have produced, is manifestly the middle of the sequence: sonnets 8, 11/12, 13, 14, 15, and 16 all carried manuscript titles that stated or implied a precise dating, one that matches the poem's position in the sequence. Yet those temporal markers that originally locked the poems into their occasions were *omitted* from the editions of 1645 and 1673. The effect is to render the occasion indistinct, the chronology harder to reconstruct, or even the referent mysterious.

Thus sonnet 8 carried in the manuscript two versions of the same title: "On his dore *when* ye Citty expected an assault," in the hand of a copyist, subsequently deleted, and below it in Milton's own hand, "*When* the assault was intended to ye Citty." Both versions contain not just a sign of time but a sign of *the times*. The precise formulation must have been important to Milton, or he would not have corrected it. The effect of the correction, while de-literalizing the poem's talismanic function, is to give the "when" more prominence. Yet (whether or not at the same time) Milton *deleted* the manuscript's marginal dating of 1642— a change of mind that inspired E. A. J. Honigmann to posit another occasion altogether, not the Royalist assault on London expected on 13 November 1642, but another alarm in May 1641.[8]

But for readers in 1645 the question was moot, since the sonnet appeared before them *almost* stripped of its uneasy ricochet between local wartime news and the claims, from time *almost* immemorial, for poetry's protective function:

> Captain or Colonel, or Knight in Arms,
> Whose chance on these defenceless dores may sease,
> If deed of honour did thee ever please,
> Guard them, and him within protect from harms,
> . . . . . .
> Lift not thy spear against the Muses Bowre,
> The great Emathian Conqueror bid spare

> The house of Pindarus, when Temple and Towre
> Went to the ground: And the repeated air
> Of sad Electra's Poet had the power
> To save th'Athenian Walls from ruine bare.[9]

I say "almost," because, with the title gone, the poem's challenge to the reader becomes better balanced. Knowledge of ancient history is required to answer the question: who was "the great Emathian Conqueror?" (Alexander) and when did he spare the house of Pindar? (during the destruction of Thebes in 335 B.C.) I submit that this act of historical reconstruction, which has to be repeated for "sad Electra's poet," generates more interesting questions about the contemporary situation and the reticence with which it, too, is described (whose "defenceless dores" are they, and why is history repeating itself?) than the question debated by Honigmann and the *Milton Variorum*,[10] of when precisely Milton would have reason to fear Royalist retribution for statements made in his pamphlets. It is not just, as Woodhouse and Bush sensibly remark, that the sonnet "uses the occasion for general reflections on the place and power of poetry in war-time," but that its withholding of historical transparency—its demand that the reader *earn* the rewards of a historical perspective—is part of its argument and its power.

Sonnet 12 (number 11 in the Cambridge manuscript) also carried an occasionalist title, "On the detraction which follow'd upon my writing certain treatises." But here the clear indication of sequentiality (the sonnet follows the detraction which followed the treatises) is accompanied by vagueness as to which treatises they were. Since sonnet 11 (numbered 12 in the manuscript, and there carrying the title "On the same") mentions by name *Tetrachordon*, published 4 March 1645, we assume that "certain treatises" referred to the four divorce pamphlets as a group; but why was Milton not more helpful, and why was even that limited helpfulness reduced when sonnet 12 appeared in the 1673 edition without the manuscript title?

Once again, without the manuscript title, the effect is not

to move the sonnet towards some transhistorical realm, but to focus attention on the mysterious structural relation between past and present, as in sonnet 8, which is arranged in reverse order of expectation in octave and sestet. Without the reference to "my writing," the passive construction of the event ("A Book *was writ* of late call'd *Tetrachordon*") generalizes the issue. Instead of a temporary need for self defence, the opening lines pose the problem of cultural innovation and the difficulty of placing a "Subject new" before a receptive audience. Moreover, there is a smaller temporal sequence invoked within the frame of the up-to-the-moment opening: a book "was writ *of late*," "it walk'd the Town a while," but "now" already it is "seldom por'd on," topical no longer. How short a time it takes for present occasion to become recent past—a troublesome concept that must inflect with slight irony the temporal marker in the opening line—"of late." That word "late," as we shall see, will acquire infinitely greater resonance when the sonnet takes its middle place in the different sequence of twenty-three.

And the last three lines are an epitome of Milton's troublemaking. Not only do they require one to know *when* it was that Sir John Cheke tutored the young King Edward VI in Greek, and the intellectual controversy generated by his changing the pronunciation of Greek at St. John's College, Cambridge (an innovation suppressed by bishop Gardiner in 1542); it is also extremely unclear what they actually assert about the relationship between the recent past and an earlier era, with respect to the climate for intellectual innovation. On the one hand Milton asserts a symmetry between the 1540s and the 1640s ("Thy age, *like* ours") and on the other his negative syntax ("Thy age . . . Hated *not* Learning") seems to require a contrast between them. The *Milton Variorum* dutifully studies this crux and the scholars who have wrestled with it;[11] but it passes lightly over what is perhaps the most interesting aspect of Milton's implied comparison of himself to Cheke—the fact that his reactionary pamphlet, *The Hurt of Sedicion*, berating the Norfolk followers of Robert Kett in 1549, had in 1641 been reissued by the Royalist Gerard Langbaine as *The True Subject to the Rebell*, with clear application now to the Long Parliamentarians.[12] If, then, Milton aligned himself with Cheke on the subject of Greek, he could only have done so by the use of a very selective memory.

Sonnet 13, appearing first as a rough autograph draft in the Cambridge manuscript, originally carried Milton's title, "To my friend Mr. Hen. Laws Feb. 9. 1645" (that is, 1646). This gives a very different chronology from that implied by the second title added by an amanuensis to Milton's fair copy: "To Mr. Hen: Laws *on the publishing* of his Aires," since Lawes' *Ayres and Dialogues* were not published until 1653; unless one posits, as does the *Milton Variorum* (399), that the poem was written in anticipation of a publishing event planned for 1646 but subsequently delayed. Critical ingenuity is required to explain the disparity; but for our purposes the most important point is that, while the 1673 edition in this rare case did retain a sonnet title, it was one innocent of dating: "To Mr. H. Lawes, on his Aires." As for sonnet 14, were it not for the survival of the Cambridge manuscript, which identified the elegy as "On ye religious memorie of Mrs. Catharine Thomason my christian freind deceas'd Decem. 1646," we would never have been able to guess that behind its baroque catalogue of religious conventions ("Purple beames/and azure wings") lurked the historical profile of *two* remarkable people: Katharine Hutton, who in the early 1630s married George Thomason, who created the great collection of Thomason Tracts, containing virtually everything that was published in England from 1640 to 1660, including unlicensed materials. Milton apparently donated several of his own pamphlets to the collection, which appear there with the words "Ex Dono Authoris." Mrs. Thomason herself owned a considerable library, and Nardo speculates that she may well have assisted her husband in the difficult and sometimes dangerous work of collection.[13]

Sonnets 15 and 16 were two of the four "commonwealth" sonnets omitted from the 1673 edition. Whose decision that was, if caution were the motive, we cannot tell. In the

Cambridge manuscript both carried specific autograph datings, in titles that never made it into print: "On ye Lord General Fairfax at ye seige of Colchester," that is to say, the summer of 1648; and "To the Lord Generall Cromwell May 1652/On the proposals of certain ministers at yr Commitee for Propagation of the Gospel." Both titles were deleted in the manuscript, indicating perhaps that Milton himself planned to publish them. In both, but especially in the sonnet to Cromwell, the erasure of the title allows a broader interpretation of the war/peace dialectic they share. In sonnet 16 the heroic references to the battles of Dunbar and Worcester (September 1650 and 1651) are allowed to set the historical context for the poem, rather than the parliamentary Committee for the Propagation of the Gospel established on 18 February 1652, of which Cromwell was a member; and the references to "new foes," "secular chaines" and "hireling wolves" in the last four lines acquire an ambiguity comparable to the famous "two-handed engine" of *Lycidas*.

The testimony of the Cambridge manuscript, then, produced the mainstay of the argument for a strictly chronological sequence: sonnet 8, dated 1642, and inviting a tighter dating of November of that year; sonnets 11 and 12, with an implied dating of 1645; sonnet 13, dated February 1646; sonnet 14, dated December 1646; sonnet 15, with an implied dating of summer 1648; sonnet 16, firmly dated May 1652. And yet the testimony of the manuscript is at odds with Milton's subsequent intentions, which include, I argue, an intention to mystify, rather than clarify, their historical context.

AUTOBIOGRAPHY

Surrounding this central group in which "signs of the times" predominate, though not exclusively, are two clusters of sonnets in which the personal, the introspective, and the autobiographical are the manifest themes: sonnets 1 and 7, framing the five Italian sonnets; sonnets 19 through 23, meditations on friendship, the late shape of his career, friendship in a "hard Season," and the death of wives. Here, apparently, Milton *started* with a decision to mystify chronology. These sonnets abound with mythical (I am tempted to say false) datings—hints of a time scheme against which the poet is measuring himself; yet they have all proved virtually impossible to date with any certainty. And what also becomes visible when the entire sequence is in place is an anxiety spreading from the ambiguous semantics of "late," as Milton deploys the word in different ambiences; an anxiety not unconnected with the fact that he conceives of his friends, male and female, in terms of their fathers or grandfathers.

On the grounds of their resemblance to Elegy 5, which Milton himself dated "Anno Aetatis 20," the Italian sonnets have been hypothetically dated 1630, at the end of which year Milton became twenty-two, though no doubt the hypothesis was influenced by their preceding sonnet 7, which locates itself in relation to his "three and twentieth year." What we don't know for certain is whether that "three and twentieth year" is 1631, at the end of which he *became* twenty-three, or 1632, during most of which he *was* twenty-three.[14] What we certainly don't know is whether sonnet 1 actually preceded sonnet 7 in terms of composition. Sonnet 1, "O Nightingale," is in one sense the most timeless of the entire sequence, in being the most conventional. In its appeal to "propitious May," to the bird of love against the "rude Bird of Hate," and its assumption that sonnets are about "success in love" or alternatively failure, sonnet 1 could be readily assigned to almost any Elizabethan sonneteer; that is, until one recognizes the peculiarly Miltonic coloring of the appeal:

> Now *timely* sing, ere the rude Bird of Hate
> Foretell my hopeles doom in som Grove ny:
> As thou from year to year hast sung *too late*
> For my relief . . .

In what sense, the poem provokes us to ask, can the traditional song ever be sung "too late"; and, as a different kind of question, why would a 22-year-old register the fear that he was too late for love, and complain, further, that his failure is of several years standing? The links between this predicament and that of sonnet 7, which complains of his *"late* spring" and his unproductivity ("no bud or blossom show'th") compared to "some more *timely*-happy spirits" cannot be overlooked once the sequence is established, suggesting a development from a sexual conception of success to a religious-vocational one; but there is theoretically nothing to obviate the possibility that sonnet 1 was written much later—[15] perhaps in the late spring of 1642, the year in whose summer Milton suddenly came home "a married man, that went out a bachelor," or even that of 1643, when, Mary Milton having gone back to her father, Milton began to write the *Doctrine and Discipline of Divorce.* Suppose that were true, we would have to recognize the order created in the 1645 *Poems* as a fiction designed to conceal. Beneath the timeless texture of nightingale and cuckoo and their ancient rivalry, behind the timebound structure of poetic auto-biography, would be *another* story in which youthful dedi-cation to the "great Taskmaster" and youthful asceticism ("strictest measure") gave way to (were followed by) adult sexual frustration; a story that would actually better explain the language of sonnet 1 ("too late for my *relief"*) and the threat of the cuckoo's song, more appropriate as a threat to the married man than to the university undergraduate who still, in all probability, considered a career in the church. This hypothesis is compatible with the theory of William Hunter, that his "three and twentith yeer" carried for Milton a special timebound force because "the age of twenty-three had been appointed by the Canons of 1604 as the earliest date for one's ordination as a deacon," and that, while fifteen of his twenty classmates had already been ordained, Milton was still hesitating over his decision.[16]

Let us now consider the opening proposition of sonnet 19: "When I consider how my light is spent,/Ere half my days." It was sonnet 19 that provoked Jonathan Goldberg's deconstructive exercise at the expense of Milton scholar-ship, which has wrestled with the problem of dating this poem only to produce at least four possibilities: 1642, 1644, 1651 and late 1655. Only the first of these hypotheses takes into account what Milton was likely to have meant by "ere half my days," which on the basis of the biblically sanctioned life span, threescore years and ten, would have implied some time before 1643, the year in which Milton became thirty-five. Indeed, if he figured a more modest longevity, such as the sixty-four years he actually achieved, this would push the sonnet back to 1639/40, when he returned from his continental tour and situated himself in London as a private schoolmaster. In such a profession, that "one Talent which is death to hide" was relatively useless; that is, if we suppose this to refer to "the strong propensity of nature" to write something truly memorable and enduring, that Milton refers to in *The Reason of Church Government* in 1642. It is the temptation to read "light" unmetaphorically and hence the assumption that when Milton declares his light "spent" and "denied" he refers to the approach of his blindness that led Honigmann to posit 1644 (the first signs of optical distress), others to posit late 1651, when his blindness became complete, and to so confuse William Riley Parker that he ricocheted back and forth between 1651–52 and 1655. On the other hand, if one assumes that the sequence is truly chronological, then sonnet 19, which follows that "On the late Massacher in Piemont," must also have been written later than the spring of 1655, when that massacre occurred, and Milton became forty-seven. If we suppose that Milton did in fact write sonnet 19 in 1640 or thereabouts (a surmise compatible with the vocational hesitations expressed in *The Reason of Church Government* but not with the conviction, expressed in the *Second Defence* of 1654, that he had already demonstrated his talents and "erected a monument that will not readily be destroyed"), we must also suppose that by rearrangement he either subordinated autobiography to a very different structure, or that he intended to live into his early nineties! Yet since the rearrangement occurs in the 1673 edition of his poems, surely prepared in the knowledge that he was running out of time in the most absolute sense, if we must choose one of these hypotheses we must choose the first. I believe we must choose. To Radzinowicz, as I have said, sonnet 19 ushers in a "final group" of autobiographical poems which "as a whole records calm of mind and assent to the temporal circumstances of the period of their composition," a sentence which now collapses under its own and Milton's ambiguities. To Goldberg, committed to the postmodern split subject and a Derridean concept of temporality, "When I consider" "would have been written and rewritten over a number of years, and could not be resolved into a single chronological placement."[17] Situating myself somewhere between them, I suggest that Milton *wrote* the sonnet in the early 1640s; but then resituated it, sometime in the late 1650s, in a sequence formed by hindsight, which is scarcely the same as a deconstructive "revision." In that hindsight, sonnet 19 becomes part of the introspective frame to the occasionalist center. The spent light becomes a reference to blindness. The vocational doubt includes the once triumphant achievement of the regicide pamphlets and the two *Defences*. Indeed, it reverberates with the vocational doubt expressed in 1655 in the *Pro Se Defensio*, that seldom-cited pamphlet in which Milton meditated aloud on the dubious fame those other contributions had brought him:

> My principle . . . is . . . that *if* as a youth in that literary leisure I then had I [sic] profited aught either from the instructions of the learned or from my own lucubrations, I would, in proportion to my poor abilities, employ all this to the advantage of life and the human race, *if* I could range so far. And *if* sometimes from private enmities public transgressions are wont to be censured and oft corrected, and *if* I have now, impelled by all possible reasons, prosecuted in a most just vituperation not merely my personal enemy, but the common enemy of almost all mankind . . . *whether* I have done this with that success which I ought . . . I do indeed hope (for why should I distrust?) that herein I have discharged an office *neither* displeasing to God, unsalutary to the church, nor unuseful to the state.[18]

In the frame of this diffident syntax, Milton's plaintive parenthesis, "Cur enim diffidam?" ("Why should I distrust?")[19]

resonates poignantly both with sonnet 19 and with sonnet 22, "Cyriack, this three years day these eys," with *its* misleading chronological marker, so seemingly precise, so open to subsequent conjecture.[20]

Given the reverberations between "late" as a marker of historical topicality and as a confession of belatedness or retardation, what are we to think of the "late espoused Saint" of sonnet 23, whose identity has remained in doubt because Milton chose not to specify whether it was Mary Milton or Katherine Woodcock Milton whom he mourns, and what kind of lateness is involved? Not only the woman's namelessness but Milton's syntax seems to prevent the banal reading, "My late wife," on the same level of reference, only in reverse, as the "late Massacher in Piemont" (the meaning not that his wife has come into existence at a specific moment, but at that moment been erased from history). The doubt occurs in the interposition between "late" and "Saint" of the word "espoused," of the also presumably certain date of an espousal. Were they only recently (lately) married, in which case it must have been Katherine Woodcock, whom Milton married in November 1656, and who died just over a year later? or were they married late (too late), in which case it might still be Katherine, or, by a more interesting understanding in the light of the other dating for sonnet 1, have been Mary after all, whom Milton married in June 1642, too late for his relief. Perhaps he came to adore her (late) before she died too soon, three days after the delivery of a daughter, just under a decade later. But the sonnet's reticence, not to say coyness, on the crucial question of its subject, permits every reader to indulge her personal fantasy as to how Milton resolved his relations with women.

THE POETICS OF HISTORICITY

At this point, then, we should look more closely at sonnet 10, the last of the sequence created in the *Poems* of 1645, which operates as a fulcrum between the two types of sequence discussed above: on the one hand, the sonnets that narrate, however evasively, the events that Milton thought of as symbolic or threshold moments of his personal life or his life conceived as a vocation; on the other, the sonnets that, while still autobiographical in a sense, broaden the narrative to engage the political history of his day. This sonnet is the fulcrum of my own argument also, that in constructing this sequence Milton articulated a specialized poetics, a theory of literature appropriate not only to his own personality but to his own historical moment and perhaps to ours also; that is to say, a theory of how literature cannot be understood *except* in the perspective of history, which in turn cannot be understood *except* by finessing the subjective/objective dilemma:

> Daughter to *that good Earl*, once President
> Of Englands Council and her Treasury,
> Who liv'd in both, unstain'd with gold or fee,
> And left them both, more in himself content,
> Till the sad breaking of *that Parlament*
> Broke him, as *that dishonest victory*
> At Chaeronea, fatal to liberty,
> Kill'd with report *that Old man eloquent*,
> *Though later born*, then to have known the dayes
> Wherin your Father flourisht, yet by you
> Madam, me thinks I see him living yet;
> So well your words his noble vertues praise,
> That all both judge you to relate them true
> And to possess them, Honour'd Margaret.

Here details that are inarguably literary—syntactical repetition and pointing, and the formal structure of the italianate sonnet—collaborate to reveal a failure of revelation: we learn from the closest of readings that "the text itself" is insufficient for the task of signification—that it points beyond itself to historical facts that the reader must go out and bring back if any cognitive event is to take place. This sonnet continues the theme of belatedness installed in sonnets 1 and 7, but translates it into the register invoked by sonnets 11 and 18, in which "late" points to a verifiable historical event. More precisely, the octave constructs the problem of historical knowledge as a set of interrelated questions for which there are certain answers. Like the question provoked by "my late espoused Saint"—"Which one?"—those provoked by Milton's markedly repeated "that" is also "which one?" Which good earl? (a question rendered more difficult of solution when the manuscript title, "To ye Lady Margaret Ley" was dropped). Which parliament was it whose breaking broke him? And to which old man eloquent from ancient history is Milton's good earl compared? But unlike sonnet 23, where the question, "Which one?" remains insoluble, sonnet 10 operates in the confidence that the fit reader will know what needs to be known.

Obviously, the answer to the first question is the readiest to hand, even today: James Ley, earl of Marlborough, father of the Lady Margaret to whom the sonnet is addressed. And the fact that he died on 10 March 1629 permits the certain recognition of "that Parliament" as the last of the Caroline parliaments, dissolved on 4 March 1629 by Charles I, after the demonstration, famous or notorious depending on one's own political inclinations, when the Speaker Sir John Finch was forcibly prevented from reading the royal order to adjourn until the Commons had passed resolutions against tonnage and poundage and innovations in religion. The dissolution inaugurated the period referred to either as the eleven years of Personal Rule or the Eleven Years' Tyranny, again depending on one's ideological take on these events. That Milton called it a "sad breaking" is not surprising, but the phrase admits the constitutional disaster without explicitly assigning blame to either the king or the party of Eliot, Coke, Selden and others. It is surprising, given how clearly his republican political theory had already developed, that Milton does not mention the Petition of Right; but the milder constitutionalist position was obviously more appropriate to a sonnet honoring Ley, who had made a career in the service of James I and Charles I.

Nevertheless, the third "that," requiring another historical solution from the far more distant past, adds a republican gloss. The dissolution of 1629 is the equivalent in political theory of the battle of Chaeronea in 338 B.C., when the Athenian democracy succumbed to Philip of Macedon, news of which is said to have caused the death of Isocrates, "that Old man eloquent" with whom Milton aligned himself in 1644 in the writing (and naming) of *Areopagitica*.

The rewards that accrue from restoring these facts to the spaces held open by those deictic substitutions ("that good Earl, that Parliament, that dishonest victory, that Old man eloquent") are, however, fallacious.[21] At least, the further one goes towards filling out the historical profiles this sonnet sketches so lightly, the more uncomfortable grows that knowledge. James Ley, born in the reign of Edward VI, was apparently an able municipal lawyer who had, however, first acquired a reputation at the beginning of James's reign. This was as commissioner of the great seal for Dublin, where he became generally hated for his severity against Catholic recusants. When James brought him back from Ireland to serve as attorney to the court of wards and liveries, Ley entered the profitable world of legal patronage. When Sir Francis Bacon vacated the attorney-generalship in 1617, Ley was reported by Buckingham to have offered ten thousand pounds for the vacant post, which, however, he failed to receive. At 69 years of age, and according to D'Ewes already "a decrepit old man,"[22] he married as his third wife Jane Butler, Buckingham's niece,[23] and so put himself in line for preferment from the favorite, resulting in his appointment as lord chief justice of the King's Bench in January 1621. In that capacity he presided at Bacon's trial in the House of Lords for financial corruption. In 1624 Ley retired from the bench to become lord high treasurer and a privy councillor, also under Buckingham's auspices, despite the fact that Ley had no financial experience and showed no aptitude for it.[24] He resigned the post four years later to his assistant, Sir Richard Weston, and Charles I thereupon made him president of the council. Six months later, according to Clarendon, he "was removed under pretence of his age and disability for the work."[25] He died, at 79 years of age, in the following spring. It is only on the basis of Milton's sonnet, and the coincidence between the date of his death, on 14 March 1629, that it has been attributed to political disappointment rather than simple decrepitude. The *Dictionary of National Biography* sums up Ley's career as follows:

> Ley, although a feeble statesman, was an able, erudite, and
> impartial judge . . . On the other hand, Sir James Whitelocke
> denounces him as "an old dissembler," who was "wont to
> be called 'Vulpone' " and says that he borrowed money of
> the judges when lord chief justice (*Liber Famelicus*, 108).[26]

In the ellipsis between these two contrary evaluations, the
Dictionary inserts, unconscious of any irony, the first four
lines of Milton's sonnet, with its apparent dissociation of
Ley ("unstained with gold or fee") from such venality as
Bacon had been charged with in 1622, and that led to his
disgrace.

This hole opening up in the fabric of the ideal community
under the pressure of historical inquiry is likely only to gape
wider if we also pursue "that Old man eloquent" a little
further. For Isocrates' legendary suicide after the battle of
Chaeronea could not have been, as Milton's sonnet implied,
because of its fatality to Athenian liberty, since his *Philippus*,
written in 346 after an earlier round of hostilities between
Philip of Macedon and Athens, initiated his campaign to
have Philip assume rule over a united Greece; and, as the
Oxford Companion to Classical Literature observes, this
placed him in absolute contradistinction to that other
eloquent old man who indeed lamented Chaeronea,
Demosthenes. The reason for that suicide, if truly historical,
would have been, therefore, "not that Philip had been
victorious—thus rendering practicable the chief hope of
Isocrates—but that Athens was still determined to resist
him." Again, a citation of Milton's sonnet, innocent of any
irony, appears at the end of this account; the *Milton Variorum*
acknowledges the problem, but resolves it in the most high-
minded manner possible:

> If this aspect of the matter were present to Milton, the
> implication would be quite different, namely, that the Earl's
> policy was to reconcile the King and Parliament (as his loyal
> and rewarded service of the crown would indeed suggest)
> and that his hopes, like those of Isocrates, were shattered.
> This seems better to fit the facts, while the condemnation

of Charles by the implied comparison of him to Philip seems better to suit Milton's own principles (and prejudices).[27]

The *Variorum* editors therefore chose to believe that Milton believed in the earl's idealism and integrity, while disagreeing with his allegiances; the closest they came to imagining Milton's sonnet might have been disingenuous was to wonder: "Is it possible that Milton wrote the lines in one sense and allowed Lady Margaret to read them in the other?"[28]

But what of Milton's relationship to Lady Margaret herself? Introduced by a wonderfully intricate turn from the octave, which ends with "that Old man eloquent," into the sestet, which begins with a phrase of which we should by now have learned to be suspicious, "Though *later* born ... " the relationship is itself a figure of syntactical obscurantism. Of whose belated birth are we here informed?[29] Of the daughter to whom the entire sonnet is addressed, and to the definition of whose filial excellence, by way of an account of her parent, it is, in one long sentence, dedicated? Or to the writer of the sonnet who suddenly emerges in the first person in the ninth line, in charge of the only main verb:

> Though later born, then to have known the dayes
> Wherein your Father flourisht, yet by you
> Madam, methinks I see him living yet.

In fact, one need scarcely decide which of the two is "later born," since Milton (born in 1608) and Margaret, born when her father was about sixty, were almost the same age. That being the case, and if we take the term "flourished" conventionally, implying a man at the height of his powers and reputation, we can take the idea of belatedness more literally (and more critically) than an idealistic reading of the sonnet would suppose.

In what precedes, I have only recirculated "facts" that have been known to lurk between the lines of Milton's sonnet, and that have passed from Smart's edition, through Honigmann's, to the *Variorum*. The difference resides in my own late twentieth century refusal to sweep them under the rug of a high-minded idealism, which in turn has rendered

Milton's sonnet a historical document of another sort, one supposedly capable of giving testimony as to the earl's character and the cause of his death. It is worth emphasizing again what I noted above, that both the *Dictionary of National Biography* and the *Oxford Companion to Classical Literature* incorporate lines from the sonnet as if it had acquired documentary status; whereas such other documents as we can summon to Ley's evaluation render its testimony decidedly suspect.

Perhaps we should accuse Milton of nothing worse than excessive politeness. But there is one other "historical" document that bears upon sonnet 10 and complicates the story further. In his life of Milton, Edward Phillips provided his own account of the occasion for his uncle's writing this sonnet, and placed it unmistakably during the period of temporary separation between the newly married Milton and his young wife, when Mary Powell Milton had returned to her family in Oxford and refused to return at her husband's urging. "Our Author," wrote Phillips:

> *now as it were a single man again,* made it his chief diversion now and then in an Evening to visit the Lady Margaret Lee, daughter to[Lord]Lee, Earl of Marlborough, Lord High Treasurer of England, and President of the Privy Councel to King James the First. This Lady being a Woman of great Wit and Ingenuity, had a particular Honour for him, and took much delight in his Company, as likewise her Husband Captain Hobson, a very Accomplish'd Gentleman; and what Esteem he at the same time had for Her, appears by a Sonnet he made in praise of her, to be seen among his other Sonnets in his Extant Poems (emphasis added).[30]

There are discreet signs in Milton criticism that Edward Phillips here put the cat among the pigeons—that for all its courtesy sonnet 10 barely conceals a mildly scandalous situation, which some modern readers have refused to acknowledge. What is at stake is its timing in relation to two marriages: Milton's marriage to Mary Powell in the early summer of 1642, and its almost immediate interruption (when she returned to her family in Oxford and refused to come back to her husband) which lasted until the summer of 1645;

and Lady Margaret Ley's marriage to John Hobson on 30 December 1641, which brought her into proximity with Milton in Aldersgate Street. It has therefore seemed to matter to Miltonists when precisely the sonnet was written.

If by its placement last in the 1645 volume we believe it was written after sonnet 8, "When the assault was intended to the city," sonnet 10 postdates November 1642 and therefore would fit without strain into the period described by Phillips as following Mary Milton's departure, when Milton was "as it were a single man again." Phillips' account suggests the not uncommon pattern of a newly married couple accepting the friendship of a "single" man who visits them more assiduously than neighborliness requires; he in turn, while being attracted to the wife, finds their marriage vicariously stimulating while protecting him against any serious entanglement. But William Riley Parker, whether consciously or not attempting to keep this scenario at bay, proposed that the use of Lady Margaret's maiden name in the Cambridge manuscript could mean that the sonnet was composed *before* her marriage, which would put its final placement in chronological jeopardy;[31] and Honigmann welcomed that suggestion, though "it is admittedly an open question whether every lady with a courtesy title adopted her husband's name at this time." In fact, he went further in attempting to obscure Phillips' none too obscure intimations: "As I understand him," Honigmann wrote, "Phillips merely cited the sonnet as a general illustration of his uncle's regard for Lady Margaret: that Milton's friendship with Lady Margaret only began after his wife's departure, or that the sonnet was written after that event, is by no means indicated."[32] The phrase that indicates dating, *"now as it were a single man again,"* has somehow been separated from the sonnet, lest the author we cherish might be thought to have written a sonnet less high-minded than traditional criticism would prefer.

To me, the centrality of sonnet 10 (a little off the numerical center) is a case worth making. But to make it requires a conception of the split subject that "literature," as distinct from textuality, is peculiarly equipped to accommodate. In that conception, we try to tell the truth while putting our best foot forward; an objective which requires, or ought to require, continual retrospection and stocktaking. Milton took stock, publicly, more often than most. When Milton wrote sonnet 10, probably, he was busy reconstructing his life in defiance of the mistakes he admitted in the *Doctrine and Discipline of Divorce*; when he came to publish it, as the last of the sonnets in the 1645/6 *Poems of Mr. John Milton*, a volume that Louis Martz has persuasively described as Milton's leave-taking of his moral and intellectual apprenticeship,[33] he must have been at least partly conscious that irony had accrued to his relationship with the Lady Margaret, now that his wife had returned. When he republished it in 1673, other ironies must have attached themselves to "the sad breaking of that Parlament," and the "dishonest victory . . . fatal to liberty" whose later versions Milton had tried unsuccessfully to prevent in 1659/60. As history moved on, the *words* of the sonnet, its disingenuities notwithstanding, were capable of carrying the message to the Restoration that Milton claimed he had never stopped proclaiming, "though fall'n on evil days." If he was not, as he also proclaimed, "unchang'd" over time, he registered his changes with a subtlety that deserves our continued attention. Above all, at age 63, Milton would probably have smiled over the expanding meaning of "that Old man eloquent," with whose relationship to political liberty he had taken certain liberties in the early 1640s, as in *Areopagitica* he had mystified the Isocratean position on censorship. And as in the sonnets that follow the occasionalist, activist phase Milton invited his friends to consider "what may be won / From the hard Season" (sonnet 20), or to learn "To measure life . . . betimes" (sonnet 21), so his writings in their totality (an *oeuvre* if ever there was one) will continue to invite meditation, or theorizing, on the relation between lives and works, works and days and on what, finally, eloquence is.

Lycidas, Daphnis, and Gallus

J. MARTIN EVANS

Of all Milton's English poems, *Lycidas* is perhaps the most specifically imitative. It invokes, that is to say, not only a long-established generic tradition but two particular components of that tradition: Theocritus' first *Idyl* and Virgil's tenth *Eclogue*. As generations of editors from Thomas Newton to A. S. P. Woodhouse have pointed out, the address to the nymphs in *Lycidas* echoes the question with which the formal lament begins in both the earlier works:

> Where were ye Nymphs when the remorseless deep
> Clos'd o'er the head of your lov'd Lycidas?
> For neither were ye playing on the steep,
> Where your old Bards, the famous Druids, lie,
> Nor on the shaggy top of Mona high,
> Nor yet where Deva spreads her wizard stream.
>
> *(Lycidas, 50–5)*

Where were you when Daphnis pined away, where were you, O Nymphs? Were you in the lovely vales of Peneus, or of Pindus? You surely did not haunt the mighty stream of Anapus or the steep of Aetna or the sacred water of Acis. (*Idyl*, 1. 66–9)

What groves, what glens possessed you, Naiad maidens, when Gallus was languishing with an unworthy love? It was not the mountain ridge of Parnassus or of Pindus that delayed you, nor even Aonian Aganippe. (*Eclogue*, x. 9–12)[1]

No less obviously, Triton, Hippotades, Cam, and Saint Peter have their counterparts in Hermes, the shepherds, Priapus, and Cypris, who visit the dying Daphnis in the *Idyl*, and Menalcas, Apollo, Silvanus, and Pan, who try to console Gallus in the *Eclogue*.

---

[1] I quote throughout from the translations of the first *Idyl* and the tenth *Eclogue* in Thomas P. Harrison, *The Pastoral Elegy* (Austin, 1939), and from the text of Milton's works in Merritt Y. Hughes, *John Milton Complete Poems and Major Prose* (New York, 1957).

So much is well known. Indeed, it is almost too well known, for these parallels have become so familiar that they are often taken for granted and their implications left unexamined. For example, when J. H. Hanford comes to discuss the relationship between the above-quoted passages in his classic essay on the pastoral elegy, he pauses only to assess the seventeenth-century poet's relative indebtedness to his two classical models. Milton's lines, he concludes, 'are directly reminiscent of the Greek rather than the Latin poet'.[2] I would like to suggest, however, that the whole point of the allusion lies in the *doubleness* of its reference. During the previous four verse paragraphs we have caught numerous individual echoes; now, for the space of six lines, we can hear two voices accompanying Milton's in a continuous descant, and our critical energies are more profitably occupied by the task of exploring the implications of that phenomenon than with worrying about which of the two additional voices sounds the louder.

The phenomenon itself, of course, stems from a simple fact of literary history which most of the poem's original audience would have learned at school: Virgil's tenth *Eclogue* is an imitation of Theocritus' first *Idyl*. Moreover, the features which distinguish it as an imitation are precisely those which Milton reproduces, namely the address to the nymphs and the procession of visitors. Like Plato's painted bed in the *Republic*, *Lycidas* may be defined as an imitation of an imitation. In which case Hanford's literary book-keeping is not merely beside the point. It is positively misleading, for if Milton chose to allude to those very elements which the Greek and the Latin poems have in common with each other, one can hardly escape the conclusion that he wanted us to recall both works simultaneously.

As soon as we attempt to do so, however, we encounter a major problem. Despite the verbal and structural similarities between the first *Idyl* and the tenth *Eclogue*, their respective heroes are polar opposites. To begin with the *Idyl*, most recent studies follow G. E. Gebauer in seeing Daphnis as a second Hippolytus who 'had vowed to resist love. Aphrodite was affronted and angered by such audacious arrogance and

---

[2] 'The Pastoral Elegy and Milton's *Lycidas*', reprinted in C. A. Patrides, *Milton's Lycidas, The Tradition and the Poem* (New York, 1961), p. 32.

inspired in him an overpowering passion. Rather than gratify it and thereby break his vow, Daphnis chose to languish and die.'[3] Following the example of the Greek tragedians, Theocritus dramatizes only the climactic sequence of events, the hero's final decision and subsequent death. The earlier part of the story is gradually reconstructed by the speeches of the minor characters who come, like Samson's visitors, either to divert him from his purpose or to deride him for persisting in it. Each successive encounter sheds fresh light upon the nature of his predicament until, by the time he delivers his parting words, it is fully illuminated. Thus Hermes' opening question establishes no more than the cause of Daphnis' sickness: 'Who makes thee suffer thus? With whom, my good lad, art thou so much in love?' (lines 77–8). Taken on its own, this could well suggest that the lovelorn shepherd was dying of unrequited passion,[4] but Priapus' ensuing rebuke reveals that the situation is more complicated than we might have suspected: 'Wretched Daphnis, why dost thou pine away? The maiden is roaming among all the springs, all the groves . . . searching for thee. Thou art too poor a lover and art a helpless creature' (lines 82–5). Clearly Daphnis could indulge his feelings if he wished to, so some further consideration, as yet unspecified, must be holding him back. The jeers of Cypris, who arrives on the scene shortly afterwards, disclose what it is: 'Surely thou didst boast, Daphnis, that thou wouldst throw Love for a fall; but hast thou not rather thyself been thrown by irresistible Love?' (lines 97–8). He has evidently taken a vow of chastity, and in revenge Cypris has made him fall in love with the maiden to whom Priapus referred earlier. Only now that his dilemma has been adequately defined does the hero break his silence by announcing his intention to die rather than yield to the power of Cypris. He may be 'dragged down to Hades by Love' (line 130) but even there he promises to 'bring grievous pain to Love' (line 103).

All this, it should be added, represents a radical departure from the more common version of the myth attributed to the

---

[3] I quote from the summary of Gebauer's thesis which R. M. Ogilvie provides during the course of his vigorous attempt to refute it in his article 'The Song of Thyrsis', *J.H.S.* 82 (1962), 107.

[4] In Virgil's *Eclogue*, x. 21 the shepherds put a similar question to a lover who really is in this predicament.

two Sicilian poets Timaeus and Stesichorus, according to which Daphnis was 'the child of a Nymph, who exposed him under a laurel bush from which he took his name. He became a herdsman and was loved by a Nymph, to whom he vowed eternal fidelity. A princess made him drunk and seduced him, whereupon he was blinded.'[5] Nevertheless both A. S. F. Gow in his authoritative edition and Gilbert Lawall in his full-length critical study of the *Idyls* agree with Gebauer that Theocritus completely transformed the traditional version of the story to serve his own purposes. In Lawall's words:

The nymph of the myth is simply replaced by nature herself. In the myth the nymph made Daphnis swear not to love a woman, but he was finally seduced and punished. Theocritus' Daphnis is made of sterner stuff; a true tragic hero, he resists all temptation and so pines away to his death. By retaining his chastity, he remains faithful to nature, wild animals, woods, and streams.[6]

By no stretch of the imagination could the same claim be made for the famous soldier, statesman, and poet, Cornelius Gallus, whose unhappy love affair with Lycoris is the immediate subject of Virgil's tenth *Eclogue*. He is unambiguously and unrepentantly dedicated to sexual passion, and he dies not because he refuses to indulge his feelings but because he cannot; his mistress has left him for another man. Rejecting all the conventional consolations of pastoral, he continues to love her in spite of her infidelity, and with his last words affirms the sovereignty of Eros: 'Love is victor over all. Let me too yield to Love' (line 69). The contrast between the Roman warrior and the Greek shepherd could scarcely be more extreme. Daphnis conquered love; Gallus willingly surrenders to it. As a result, although the processional figures in the *Eclogue* once again reveal the nature of the hero's dilemma, the sentiments they express during the course of their disclosures are far removed from those of their Theocritean predecessors. Whereas Daphnis' visitors came to tempt or to mock him, Gallus' are concerned only to comfort or to admonish him. Priapus, for example, urged Daphnis to pursue his beloved; Apollo urges Gallus to

---

[5] I quote from the summary of the traditional version of the myth in A. S. F. Gow, *Theocritus* (Cambridge, 1952), ii. 1.

[6] Gilbert Lawall, *Theocritus' Coan Pastorals* (Harvard, 1967), p. 25. Cf. Gow, p. 2.

forget her: 'Gallus, why art thou so mad? Thy beloved Lycoris has followed another amid snows and rough camps' (lines 22–3). Cypris exulted over the misery of an adversary. Pan advises a fellow-lover to stop grieving: 'Will there be no end of this? . . . Love cares not for such deeds; cruel Love is not sated with tears nor the grasses with streams nor the bees with clover nor the goats with leaves' (lines 28–30). The theme of the *Idyl* was heroic chastity. The theme of the *Eclogue* is the irresistible power of love.

What, then, are we to make of Lycidas' relationship to the heroes of these two very different poems? Before we can even begin to answer this question, we must first answer a prior one. How were the first *Idyl* and the tenth *Eclogue* interpreted in the sixteenth and early seventeenth centuries? Davis P. Harding and others have taught us that the 'Renaissance Ovid' was by no means identical with either the classical or the modern one,[7] and there is no reason to suppose that the same might not be true of the Renaissance Theocritus and the Renaissance Virgil. Certainly the pastoral works of both were the subject of intense scholarly scrutiny during the hundred or so years preceding the composition of *Lycidas*. The *Idyls* were annotated in considerable detail by such influential humanists as Joseph Scaliger, Isaac Casaubon, Daniel Heinsius,[8] Fredericus Lamotius,[9] and Joannes Meursius.[10] And in order to make them available to a wider audience, Theocritus' works were frequently translated into Latin. By the time Heinsius published his comprehensive collection of Greek bucolic poetry in 1604 no less than six partial or complete Latin versions were already in existence.[11]

---

[7] See, for example: Davis P. Harding, *Milton and the Renaissance Ovid* (Urbana, 1946); Don Cameron Allen, *Mysteriously Meant* (Baltimore, 1970).

[8] The annotations of all three are reprinted in Daniel Heinsius, *Theocriti, Moschi, Bionis, Simii quae extant: cum Graecis in Theocritum Scholiis & Indice copiose . . . Accedunt Iosephi Scaligeri, Isaaci Casauboni, & eiusdem Danielis Heinsii Notae & Lectiones* (Heidelberg, 1604).

[9] *Theocriti Idyllium Primum Annotationibus Frederici Lamotii illustratum* (Paris, 1552).

[10] *Ioannis Meursi ad Theocriti Syracusani Poetae Idyllia Spicilegium* (London, 1597).

[11] *Seriatim: Theocritus scripsit Philethicus Latihum* [sic] *fecit Bucolicum Carmen Res Acta Syracusis* (Rome, *c.*1480); *Theocriti Syracusani eidyllia trigintasex, Latino carmine reddita, Helio Eobano Hesso interprete* (Basle, 1531); *Theocriti Syracusani Opera Latine a Ioanne Trimanino ad verbum diligentissime expressa, locis unde Virgilius sumpsit, indicatis* (Venice, 1539); *Theocriti Syracusani poetae Clarissimi idyllia trigintasex, recens e graeco in latinum, ad verbum translata, Andrea Divo Iustinopolitano interprete* (Basle, 1554);

Virgil's *Eclogues* were even more exhaustively analysed. Antonio Mancinelli, Jodocus Badius Ascensius,[12] Joannes Pierius Valerianus, Juan Luis Vives, Helius Eobanus Hessus, Richardus Gorraeus, Philip Melanchthon, Stephanus Riccius Peter Ramus, and Thomas Farnaby[13] (who, by an odd coincidence, was Edward King's teacher)[14] all produced elaborate commentaries, while the annotations of the two best-known earlier scholiasts, Servius and Probus, were reprinted throughout the period. In addition, Abraham Fleming,[15] John Brinsley, William Lisle, and John Bidle[16] translated the *Eclogues* into English, often with extensive marginal notes. Brinsley's painstakingly literal version, 'written chiefly for the good of schools',[17] is particularly useful as an indication of the way in which the young Milton may have first encountered the poem. It is with these interpretations of both the first *Idyl* and the tenth *Eclogue* that any discussion of the relationship between *Lycidas* and its models must begin.

Moschi, Bionis, Theocriti, Elegantissimorum poetarum idyllia aliquot, ab Henrico Stephano Latina facta (Venice, 1555); Hieronymus Commelinus, *Theocriti Syracusii Idyllia & Epigrammata* (Heidelberg, 1596).

[12] I quote both Mancinelli and Ascensius from the following edition: *P. Virgilii Maronis Opera . . . cum xi acerrimi iudicii virorum commentariis* (Venice, 1544).

[13] *Seriatim*: Available in *Opera Vergiliana* (n.p., 1528); *Io Lodovico Vivis in Bucolica Vergilii Interpretatio, Potissimum Allegorica* (Milan, 1539); *Publii Vergilii Maronis Mantuani Opera* (includes 'Eclogae decem, cum Annotationibus et castigatione Helii Hessi et al.') (London, 1535); *P. Virgilii Maronis Bucolica Cum Commentariis Richardi Gorraei Parisiensis* (Venice, 1554); *Argumenta seu Dispositiones Rhetoricae in Eclogas Virgilii Authore Philip Melanchthon* (n.p., 1568); *Paraphrases, Ecphrases, succintae questiones, & brevia Scholia Textus in easdem Eclogas Authore M. Stephano Riccio* (n.p., 1568) (printed together with the preceding item); *P. Virgilii Maronis Bucolica P. Rami Professoris Regii, praelectionibus exposita* (4th edn., Frankfurt, 1582); *Publii Virgilii Maronis Bucolica, Georgica Aeneis, Notis admarginalibus illustrata a Thoma Farnabio* (London, 1634).

[14] Thomas Warton in his *Poems upon Several Occasions* (London, 1791) warns us not to confuse King's schoolmaster with the 'celebrated rhetorician' (p. 37) but the *DNB* does not distinguish between them.

[15] In fact, Fleming made two attempts, the first in fourteener couplets (1575), the second, from which I quote, in unrhymed fourteeners: *The Bucolicks of Publius Virgilius Maro . . . All newly translated into English verse by A[braham] F[leming]* (London, 1589).

[16] *Seriatim*: *Virgil's Eclogues . . . Translated Grammatically* (London, 1620); *Virgil's Eclogues Translated into English by W. L. Gent* (London, 1628); *Virgil's Bucolicks Englished* (London, 1634).

[17] Fleming also claimed that his 1575 translation was made 'for the benefit of young learners of the latine tongue'.

One of the first and most interesting facts they reveal is that the differences between the Greek and the Latin poems which I have just discussed appear to have escaped the Renaissance commentators entirely. Melanchthon, Fleming, Brinsley, and Farnaby all emphasized Virgil's debt to Theocritus without so much as a hint that he may have modified his predecessor's meaning in any way. Fleming, for instance, declared in the preface to his translation of the tenth *Eclogue*: 'Touching the argument, it is all in a maner taken out of *Thirsis*, that is, the first Idyll of *Theocritus*, who handleth the like matter in all points in his *Daphnis*.'[18] Nor was this view confined to the interpreters of Virgil. In his lecture on Theocritus' first *Idyl* Heinsius claimed that 'Virgil translated the most ancient, and to this extent the most original, material of bucolic song [in his poem] to Gallus: the whole of this eclogue . . . is a kind of imitation of the misfortunes of Daphnis'.[19] So closely were the two poems associated with each other, indeed, that they seem to have virtually coalesced in the minds of many sixteenth-century readers. The most striking evidence of this process is provided by Hessus, who incorporated whole lines from the tenth *Eclogue* into his Latin translation of the first *Idyl*, notably in his rendering of Thyrsis' address to the nymphs:

> Quae nemora, aut qui vos saltus habuere puellae
> Naiades, indigno quum Daphnis amore periret?
> Pulchra ne vos tenuisse putem Peneia Tempe?
> Num iuga Thessalici Phoebo gratissima Pindi?[20]

And when Virgil's *Eclogue* was in turn translated into Greek by Heinsius, Scaliger, and Daniel Alsworth, several of Theocritus' most striking phrases were conscripted into service to Gallus.[21] The first *Idyl* and the tenth *Eclogue* have become almost indistinguishable from each other.

[18] Op. cit., p. 29. Cf.: Melanchthon, sig. G7: 'It is written in imitation of Theocritus' first Idyl concerning Daphnis'; Brinsley, p. 93: 'All this argument is almost taken out of *Thyrsis* of *Theocritus*, where he prosecutes the like love of *Daphnis*'; Farnaby, p. 28: 'Almost all the argument is taken from the Thyrsis of Theocritus, where he relates the similar love of Daphnis.'

[19] 'Scholae Theocriticae' in Heinsius, p. 302. I am indebted to Professor A. G. Rigg throughout for his help in translating the commentators' Latin.

[20] Op. cit., sig. a8ᵛ. The borrowing establishes Daphnis' love as *indignus*.

[21] The translations of Heinsius and Scaliger are contained in the former's reissue of Commelinus' *Theocriti Syracusii Idyllia* (Heidelberg, 1603), pp. 128–31. Daniel

Needless to say, this conflation could not have taken place without a radical transformation in the character of one or other of their respective protagonists. Bearing in mind the chronological priority of the *Idyl*, we might have expected the dissimilarities noted above to have been resolved in favour of Daphnis, but in fact it was Gallus who proved to be the dominant partner. Two factors seem to have been responsible for his victory. First, there was the retrospective influence of the tenth *Eclogue* on the interpretation of the first *Idyl*. In a critical reversal of the mimetic process of composition, the Greek original was read in the light of the Latin imitation rather than vice versa, and the chaste pastoral prototype was refashioned in the image of his concupiscent elegiac descendant. Instead of producing the Theocritean Gallus we might have anticipated, the commentators of the sixteenth and seventeenth centuries thus created a distinctly Virgilian Daphnis, animated by the same all-consuming passion that had brought Lycoris' lover to his death. Second, there was the prospective influence, so to speak, of Timaeus and Stesichorus' version of the myth. For thanks to such references to it as Ovid's in Book IV of the *Metamorphoses*, the notion that Daphnis was an unfaithful lover was still very much alive in the Renaissance. For example, John Rider explained in his etymological dictionary that Daphnis was

a young man of Sicily who compacted with a Nymph whom he loved that whether of them soever should violate their faith, which they had plighted to one another, should lose both their eyes: Daphnis, forgetting his promise, fell in love with another; the gods that were called to witness in the oath, did punish the breach of it by making him blinde.[22]

In combination these two pressures (the retrospective and the prospective) were irresistible, and Theocritus' defiant virgin reverted to his original amorous persona.

The interpretative consequences of these developments are clearly reflected in the commentaries of Lamotius and Heinsius on the first *Idyl*. Both simply took it for granted that Theocritus had followed the traditional form of the Daphnis myth in his treatment of it. As Heinsius wrote:

Alsworth's was published in his *Imitatio Theocritea Qua Virgilii Eclogae, ita Doricis versibus exprimuntur* (Rome, 1594).

22 *Dictionarium Etymologicum Proprium Nominum* (London, 1648), p. 257.

Timaeus, the authority on Sicilian matters, calls this nymph Echenais, with whom Daphnis had made an agreement or resolution that he would undergo the penalty threatened by the fates if he broke faith by falling in love with someone else. . . . Parts of the speeches are assigned to this nymph in the idyl, as will be clear by the emendation of a single word.[23]

The word in question occurs during the course of Priapus' address to the dying shepherd:

Wretched Daphnis, why dost thou pine away? The maiden is roaming among all the springs, all the groves . . . searching for thee. Thou art too poor a lover and art a helpless creature. (*Idyl* I. 82–5)

The Greek verb rendered here by 'searching' is *zateusa*. This, Heinsius ingenuously insisted, made nonsense, for there was no reason that he could see why a maiden who had just been betrayed by her lover should still be searching for him. In place of *zateusa* he therefore proposed another Doric word, *zatōsa*, that is, 'speaking' or 'reproaching'. Everything thereafter, he concluded, was spoken not by Priapus, as all earlier editors had assumed, but by the nymph herself:

All this speech belongs to the nymph Echenais, who is castigating Daphnis for his promiscuity and unstable raging. By the loves of Theocritus, I swear that there is no passage that has been less understood by the scholiasts and their successors. . . . The Greek scholiast did not see how to resolve these problems, namely how she whom Daphnis had offended could be said to seek him when she ought rather to flee from him. . . . He thinks the whole speech belongs to Priapus who is consoling Daphnis, when in fact it belongs to the indignant girl whom he has betrayed and offended by his inconstancy.[24]

On the basis of this crucial emendation he then went on to summarize the lines I quoted above as follows: 'The girl is borne through springs and all the groves and *complains* [*conqueritur*] thus: "Assuredly Daphnis you are too fickle in love

---

[23] Op. cit., p. 302. Cf. Lamotius, p. 12: 'Suidas says he [Daphnis] was blinded because he had intercourse with another woman when he was drunk.'

[24] Op. cit., p. 303. The hapless '*Graecus interpres*' is a constant target of Heinsius' editorial barbs.

and too impetuous." '[25] So what in the original text had been a light-hearted piece of encouragement directed to a steadfast virgin became a deeply felt rebuke delivered by a wronged mistress. Theocritus' innocent shepherd on his way to martyrdom has turned into an unfaithful lover about to pay the just penalty of his transgression.

Virgil's tenth *Eclogue* was treated no less moralistically by the translators and annotators of the period. Servius had remarked in his commentary on the poem that 'in Gallus is exhibited the impatience of shameful love [*inpatientia turpis amoris*]'.[26] This theme was taken up and developed with evident relish by such Renaissance scholars as Melanchthon, Ramus, Riccius, Farnaby, and Brinsley. Although few of them went quite so far as Fleming, who subtitled his translation of the poem 'the mad love of Cornelius Gallus',[27] they all agreed that Virgil's amorous friend was at the very least 'fond' as another translator put it.[28] According to Brinsley, for instance, his love for the 'harlot' Lycoris was 'out of measure',[29] and as such it could bring only anguish and degradation in its train. The

---

[25] Op. cit. p. 304. It was this interpretation of the passage which Heinsius incorporated into the Latin translation of the first Idyl which he made for the 1603 reissue of Commelinus' text:

> Puella
> Per varios fontes pedibus per devia fertur . . .
> Multa movens: in amore levis nimiumque vagaris . . .
> (82–5)

But a year later, fearing perhaps that this was not clear or emphatic enough, he revised the translation of line 85 for the 1604 edition to read 'Vocibus his: Levis ah Daphni es, nimiumque vagaris . . .'. The translations of Trimaninus, Divus, and the anonymous translator all render *zateusa* by *quaerens* (seeking), while Hessus prefers *requirens* (searching). It is worth noting also that Heinsius translates *duseros* in line 85 as *levis* or 'fickle' rather than the more common 'poor at loving', thereby anticipating R. M. Ogilvie's point in 'The Song of Thyrsis', loc. cit.

[26] *In Vergilii Bucolica et Georgica Commentarii*, ed. G. Thilo (Lipsiae, 1887), p. 118. Cf. Riccius, sig. M7: 'Gallus died through the impatience of love [*inpatientia amoris*].'

[27] Op. cit., p. 29. Cf. Riccius, who throughout his *Brevia et erudita scholia* insists that Gallus was *insanis* (pp. 7ᵛ, 8ᵛ, 9ᵛ), and Hessus, who explains in his comment on lines 31 ff. that 'Fingit Gallum respondentem, ut magis ob oculos ponat hominis insaniam' (p. 14ᵛ).

[28] John Bidle, sig. C2ᵛ: 'Scorcht with Idalian Flames, fond Gallus is / Enamour'd on the Strumpet Cytheris.' Cf. Melanchthon, sig. G8: '*stulti amatoris imago*'.

[29] Op. cit. The phrase is Brinsley's addition to Servius' note. Compare Brinsley: '. . . who whenas he out of measure affected an harlot called Cytheris . . .' (p. 92) and Servius: 'hic autem Gallus amavit Cytheridem meretricem . . .' (p. 118).

apparently aimless and disconnected series of fantasies Gallus describes in lines 50–69 revealed, in Riccius' words, the 'inconstancy of love [*amoris inconstantiam*]',[30] while the work as a whole affirmed the melancholy truth that

there is no strength so great, no force of mind so powerful, even in the greatest of men, which cannot be ennervated and dissipated by the enticements of love, no vigour so great that it cannot grow languid, cannot be dominated and subjugated by the sweetness of love, which in appearance seems pleasant, delightful and gracious when in reality it is nothing but pure poison [*merum fel*].[31]

But human nature was not entirely at the mercy of Venus and her son. There was, the Renaissance commentators maintained, an external force which could give mankind the strength to resist, namely the agency invoked by Gallus himself at the height of his frenzy:

I will go, and those verses which I composed in the Chalcidian measure I will now attune to the pipe of the Sicilian shepherd. I am determined to choose suffering in the woods among the dens of wild beasts and to carve the tale of my love in the young trees. (*Eclogue* x. 50–4)

In these lines, claimed Brinsley (translating Ramus), 'Gallus propounds unto himselfe the remedies which he wil use for the curing of his love, by contrary studies. As first by giving his minde to the studie of Poetrie.' Unfortunately, however, he was already too far gone for this classic *remedium amoris* to have any effect. Just twelve lines later, Brinsley went on to note, 'the Poet suddenly disliking the former remedies, setteth out the inconstancie of love, and that no remedies can cure it, neither the pleasures of the woods, nor the study of Poetrie, no nor any musicke, nor yet any toyles can asswage the rage thereof'.[32] The time for Gallus to have sought the aid of poetry was when he felt the first stirrings of passion.

Which was just the point of Virgil's opening address to the nymphs as the Renaissance commentators interpreted it. As

---

[30] The phrase runs like a refrain through Riccius' *Brevia et erudita scholia*. It connects Gallus with Daphnis, of whom Heinsius writes, 'Obiicitur Daphnidi amoris inconstantia' (p. 303).

[31] Op. cit., sig. M7. Gorraeus agrees, but also approves (p. 154).

[32] Op. cit., p. 98. Cf. Ramus, p. 166. Brinsley evidently knew Ramus' commentary well and did not hesitate to borrow interpretations from it. Cf. sig. A4.

Servius had originally observed,[33] the locations from which the nymphs were absent while Gallus was pining away were all associated with poetic inspiration. Parnassus and Pindus were both consecrated to Apollo and the Muses while Aganippe's literary connections were too well known to deserve comment. The Naiades, it followed, were no other than the Muses, and Virgil's questions to them contained an implicit rebuke to the only power he knew which could have saved his friend from his fate: 'He seems to say this', Servius remarked, 'because, if the Muses had been present with [Gallus], that is, if he had given [himself] the task of writing songs, he would not have fallen into such amatory difficulties [*tantas amoris angustias*].'[34] In a characteristically detailed note on the same passage, Ascensius explained to his Renaissance readers the assumption underlying Servius' interpretation. 'The presence of the Muses can restrain love,' he pointed out, 'because, as the divine poet teaches in Book II of the *Aeneid*, the chaste goddesses have no dealings with Venus, whence Aeneas could not see them until Venus went away.' The Naiades were 'the goddesses of the fountains, that is, the Muses who preside over the fountains; for according to Varro the Muses and the Nymphs are the same, maidens, that is, chaste and flourishing in perpetual virginity (whence, as Catullus said, the poet ought himself to be chaste) . . .'.[35] By the time Brinsley produced his annotated translation of the *Eclogues* in 1620 this view of the episode was commonplace: 'He accuseth the Muses that they were so carelesse of Gallus', he wrote, 'to let him so to leave his studies and to perish in such unbeseeming love.'[36] Like the fourth book of the *Aeneid*, then, the tenth *Eclogue* was read in the Renaissance as an example of the distracting power of love:

So love disturbs many from their mind and sanity, and drives them

[33] Servius, p. 120. Cf. Lisle, p. 184, Brinsley, p. 95.

[34] Servius, p. 120. Riccius repeats this phrase word for word without acknowledgement in his *Brevia et erudita scholia*, p. 5ᵛ.

[35] Op. cit., p. 49. See also: J. M. Steadman, 'Chaste Muse and *Casta Juventus*: Milton, Minturno, and Scaliger on Inspiration and the Poet's Character', *Italica*, 40 (1963), 28–34.

[36] Op. cit., p. 95. Cf. Riccius, p. 5ᵛ, Ramus, op. cit., p. 161. In his *Erotemata in Decimam Eclogam*, sig. Vᵛ Riccius draws the same moral but substitutes philosophy for poetry: 'By saying this without doubt he intended to signify only that love, the most powerful of emotions, can be, if not removed, at least assuaged, by excellent precepts drawn from the recondite and hidden points of philosophy.'

either to say or to do something against the decorum of their persons. For love is a violent fire with which as long as the mind burns, it can restrain itself only with difficulty from breaking bounds. So in this *Eclogue* is set forth the picture of a foolish lover [*stulti amatoris imago*] so that by looking at this picture we may learn to avoid all the occasions and enticements by which this fire is wont to be aroused.[37]

Omnia vincit Amor was a warning, not an affirmation.

For commentators like Vives and his English translator Lisle this was all far too literalistic. 'The matter itselfe and subject of this worke', they declared, 'doth plainly witnesse in sundry places, that it is not simply, but figuratively spoken, under a shadow: which makes me admire the more at *Servius Honoratus*, who will in this booke admit of no Allegories.'[38] The dig at Servius was doubly unfair, for not only *did* he admit of allegories, both in theory and in practice,[39] but he unwittingly provided Vives with the raw material for his figurative interpretation of the tenth *Eclogue* by identifying its subject as follows:

Cornelius Gallus, the first governor of Egypt . . . was originally a friend of Caeser Augustus; later, when he had come under suspicion of conspiring against Caesar, he was killed.[40]

In Vives' *Interpretatio in Bucolica Vergilii, Potissimum Allegorica* (1539) this brief biographical sketch was transformed into the 'Argument' of the entire poem:

Cornelius Gallus, (a man of most exquisite and dextrous witt, and an admirable Poet, after hee had been preferd to Augustus and rais'd by him to the government of Ægypt), was accus'd to Caeser, to have conspir'd, and to have attempted something contrary to his mind; for grief of which accusation, hee killed himselfe: This his death Virgil deplores under the title of Love.[41]

[37] Melanchthon, sig. G8.

[38] I quote from Lisle's translation, p. 11. Cf. Fleming's letter of dedication to his 1589 translation: 'The matter or drift of the poet is meere allegoricall, and carrieth another meaning than the litterall interpretation seemeth to afford' (sig. A2ᵛ).

[39] See, for instance, his comment on line 17 of Virgil's *Eclogue*, x: 'Allegorically this says: nor should you be ashamed to write pastoral poems' (p. 121).

[40] Ed. cit., p. 118.

[41] Lisle, p. 175, translating Vives, p. 34. Cf. Fleming's 'Argument': 'How this Gallus was an excellent poet, and so familiar with Caesar, and likewise so favoured of him, that he gave and bestowed upon him the government of Ægypt. Howbeit

Political rather than erotic entanglements were thus responsible for Gallus' downfall, and Virgil's real purpose in writing the elegy was to vindicate a brilliant young statesman whose career had been cut short by the slanderous accusations of his rivals and the gullibility of his emperor. The latter, cast somewhat disconcertingly as Lycoris,[42] had adopted Mark Antony as his new favourite, leaving the hapless governor of Egypt to meditate on the perils of high office.

According to this reading of the poem, then, the address to the nymphs was a rebuke to the Muses not for letting Gallus fall in love but for allowing him to be ensnared by affairs of state:

These were the places of *Gallus* his retrait amongst the Muses, and to the study of sweete Poesie: wherein if hee had still retir'd him-selfe . . . and had not aspired to the great Imployments, and Business of state, which caus'd his ruin, hee had still liv'd.[43]

Unfortunately, like his literal counterpart in Brinsley's com-mentary, he learned his lesson too late. 'I wish now', he lamented in Vives' paraphrase of lines 35–6, 'that I had con-tinued my study, amongst my Books, and held mee to my private life, then I had proved learned like others; at least I might have had the happiness, to have been always in the company of Schollers and learned men.'[44] The love which had brought about his downfall, the love which Pan insisted could never be 'reconciled, or satisfied, with teares, and repentance'

afterwards growing in suspicion of conspiracie or treason against Caesar, he was slaine at his commandment' (p. 29). The disagreement as to whether Gallus 'killed himselfe' as Lisle believed or 'was slaine' as Fleming asserts seems to depend on whether the writer in question interprets Servius' *occisus est* as a passive or a reflexive verb. Melanchthon compromises by claiming that Gallus was ordered to kill himself (sig. G6^r).

[42] Melanchthon, on the contrary, appears to cast Gallus as Lycoris and Caesar as Gallus: 'I think that secretly the discord which had arisen between Antony and Augustus is being lamented. For Gallus was very close to both' (sig. G6^r).

[43] Lisle, p. 184, translating Vives, p. 34. Cf. Riccius, *Ecphrasis*: 'For I have no doubt that if Gallus had persevered in the study of poetry he would not have desired the friendship of the powerful to such an extent nor undertaken those affairs which brought him to his death' (sig. M8^v).

[44] Lisle, pp. 187–8, translating Vives, p. 35^v. Cf. Melanchthon: 'This signifies that a private life is sweeter than the administration of the Republic' (sig. G6^v); Riccius: 'Would that I had stayed in studies of letters and in private life, or had been erudite . . .' (sig. N^r).

was the 'love of rule and dominion'.[45] *Omnia vincit amor* was still a warning, but it was a warning against the thirst for power—hence Riccius' rendering of this famous phrase in his *Ecphrasis Allegorica in Decimam Eclogam*: 'For nothing will be able to assuage this desire of Augustus's for ruling.'[46] As Melanchthon put it in one of his comparatively rare excursions into allegory, the hero of the tenth *Eclogue* was a 'memorable example of the kind of fortune one gets at court [*memorabile exemplum aulicae fortunae*]'.[47]

Seen in this context, as I believe it should be, *Lycidas* begins to look rather less conventional than most critics have taken it to be. Far from being just another pastoral hero who died young, Edward King emerges as the exact antithesis of Daphnis and Gallus, or, more precisely, of the Renaissance Daphnis and Gallus. Unlike both, he had remained chaste all his life, thereby earning the right, reserved for those who 'were not defiled with women', of participating at the marriage of the Lamb.[48] His only mistress was his Muse. Unlike Daphnis, moreover, he did not betray her. Even though she had proved to be as 'thankless' as the cruel and fair lady of the courtly tradition, he resisted the consolations of the nymphs. Amaryllis and Neaera were never able to make him break his vow 'to scorn delights, and live laborious days'. Unlike Gallus, on the other hand, he did not abandon his studies in order to pursue a political career. Nor was he even suspected of disloyalty to the master he *had* chosen to serve. The bark was 'perfidious', not Lycidas; he had 'meditated' his Maker no less 'strictly' than his Muse.

We might well conclude, then, that Daphnis and Gallus function in this poem in much the same way that Achilles and Ulysses function in *Paradise Lost*: as counterfigures, whose pagan imperfections define the Christian virtue of Milton's hero. But I believe that there may be rather more to the matter than that. For there is one final difference between Edward King and his

[45] Lisle, p. 187, translating Vives, p. 35ᵛ.

[46] Op. cit., sig. Nᵛ.

[47] Op. cit., sig. G6ʳ. Only the first of Melanchthon's *Argumenta* treats the poem in allegorical terms. The remaining five are rigorously literal.

[48] Revelation 14, 19. Not until he wrote the *Apology for Smectymnuus* in 1642 did Milton assume that St. John's words referred only to fornication, on the grounds that 'marriage must not be called a defilement'. In the *Epitaphium Damonis*, for example, Diodati is permitted to participate in 'the immortal marriage' of the Lamb because he 'did not taste the delight of the marriage bed' (lines 212 ff.).

two classical predecessors which totally transforms the significance of all the rest: his death was an accident. It simply could not be attributed, as theirs had been, to some fatal error on his part. He had neither sported in the shade nor striven in the field. On the contrary, he had obeyed all the rules which the protagonists of the *Idyl* and the *Eclogue* had broken, yet he had still been cut off 'ere his prime'. Hence the bitterness of Milton's criticism of his own version of the address to the nymphs: 'Ay me, I fondly dream! / Had ye been there—for what could that have done?' Hence, too, the ensuing allusion to Orpheus' solitary period of abstinence after the death of Eurydice. If a life of austere dedication to poetry was no guarantee of survival, if the 'blind Fury' was as powerful and remorseless as Venus and Caesar Augustus, then what *was* the point of sexual and political self-denial, what *did* it 'boot' to 'tend the homely slighted Shepherd's trade'? The contrasts we have noted between Daphnis and Gallus on the one hand and Edward King on the other could hardly have afforded Milton much comfort, then. They may have demonstrated King's superiority over his predecessors, but they must also have called into question the very standards by which that superiority was measured.

The literary context within which Milton lamented the death of his fellow student, I would like therefore to suggest, may have served to focus his anxieties not about the possibility of suffering the same fate himself, as Tillyard has proposed, but rather about the validity of the 'fugitive and cloistered virtue' advocated by the commentators on Theocritus and Virgil, and thus about the validity of the kind of life he himself had been leading since he had come down from Cambridge in 1632. Should this suggestion be accepted, the erotic elements in the poem— Venus' myrtle in the opening line, the rathe primrose which in an earlier draft died 'unwedded', suffering the pangs of 'uninjoyed love',[49] the myth of Alpheus and Arethusa—need no longer be dismissed, as they often have been, as extraneous or inappropriate. And the 'fresh Woods and Pastures new' of the last line, in addition to standing for Italy, or the broad expanses

---

[49] Cf. the reference in the *Elegia prima* to the *puer infelix* who 'must leave his joys untasted and is torn away from his love to perish lamentably' (lines 41–2). Milton seems to have been particularly sensitive to the pathos of 'uninjoyed love'.

of the epic, may symbolize the world of sexual and political engagement which lay beyond the confines of Horton. What I am suggesting, in short, is that *Lycidas* should be read *against* the tradition of the pastoral elegy, that it was written *contra* Theocritus' first *Idyl* and Virgil's tenth *Eclogue* as the Renaissance understood them. Five years later, at all events, Milton was doing precisely what the commentators on the two classical poems had insisted a poet should not be doing: embroiling himself in the dust and heat of politics and marriage.

ONE

LYCIDAS: A POEM FINALLY ANONYMOUS
Stanley E. Fish

I. THE SWAIN SPEAKS

Much of *Lycidas* criticism is an extended answer to those who, in the tradition of Dr. Johnson, see the poem as an "irreverent combination" of "trifling fictions" and "sacred truths," or as a lament marred by intrusive and unassimilated digressions, or, more sympathetically, as "an accumulation of magnificent fragments,"[1] or simply (and rather notoriously) as a production more "willful and illegal in form" than any other of its time.[2] This last judgment—it is John Crowe Ransom's in his famous essay "A Poem Nearly Anonymous"—indicates the extent to which the poem has been brought before the bar. The indictment has included, among others, the following charges: the tenses are inconsistent and frustrate any attempt to trace a psychological progression; there are frequent and unsettling changes in style and diction; the structure is uncertain, hesitating between monologue, dialogue, and something that is not quite either; the speaker assumes a bewildering succession of poses; the lines on Fame are poorly integrated; the procession of mourners is perfunctory; the Pilot's speech is overlong and overharsh; the flower passage is merely decorative; the Christian consolation (beginning "Weep no more, shepherds") is unconvincing and insufficiently prepared for; the shift to the third person in the final lines is disconcerting and without any persuasive justification. Together and individually, these characterizations constitute a challenge to the poem's unity, and it is as an assertion of unity that the case for the defense is always presented.

Typically, that defense proceeds by first acknowledging and then domesticating the discontinuities that provoke it. Thus William Madsen observes that the voice that says "Weep no more, shepherds" at line 165 does not sound at all like the voice we have been listening to; but no sooner does he note this breach in the poem's logic then he mends it by assigning the line and what follows to the angel Michael,[3] although he fails to explain, as Donald Friedman points out, why among all the speakers in *Lycidas*, Michael is the only one who "is introduced without comment or identification."[4] Friedman himself is concerned with another moment of disruption, occasioned by the voice of Phoebus whose unexpected appearance as a speaker in the past tense blurs the narrative line and creates a "confusion about the nature of the utterance we are listening to" (13). That confusion, however, is only "momentary," at least in Friedman's argument, where it is soon brought into a relationship with "the coda in which Milton subsumes the entire experience of the swain" (13). That coda, of course, brings its own problem, for as Stewart Baker observes, the appearance, after 185 lines, of a third person narrator, constitutes a "surprise"; but after acknowledging the surprise in the opening sentence of his essay, Baker proceeds to accommodate it, and by the time he finishes, it has been removed, along with St. Peter's dread voice, as a possible threat "to the poem's unity."[5] Defending the poem's unity is also the concern of H. V. Ogden, who writes in part to refute L. C. Knight's characterization of *Lycidas* "as an effort to bind and clamp together a universe trying to fly off into separate bits."[6] Ogden cannot but acknowledge that the poem abounds in "abrupt turns in new directions," but these turns are explained or explained away by invoking the seventeenth-century principle of "aesthetic variety," and one can almost hear Ogden's sigh of relief as he declares triumphantly that "Lycidas is a disciplined interweaving of contrasted passages into a unified whole."[7]

Examples could be multiplied, but the pattern is clear: whatever *Lycidas* is, *Lycidas* criticism is "an effort to bind and clamp together a universe trying to fly off into separate bits." It is, in short, an effort to put the poem together, and the form that effort almost always takes is the putting together of an integrated and consistent first person voice. Indeed, it is the assumption that the poem is a dramatic lyric and hence the expression of a unified consciousness that generates the pressure to discover a continuity in the narrative. The unity in relation to which the felt discontinuities must be brought into line is therefore a *psychological* unity; the drama whose coherence everyone is in the business of demonstrating is mental. In the history of the criticism that coherence has been achieved by conceiving of the speaker as an actor in one of several possible biographical dramas: he may be remembering a past experience from a position of relative tranquility (the position of the last eight lines); or he may be performing a literary exercise in the course of which he creates a naive

Lycidas: A Poem Finally Anonymous

persona (the uncouth swain); or he may be in the process of breaking out of the conventional limitations imposed on him by a tradition; or he may be passing from a pagan to a Christian understanding of the world and the possibilities it offers him. These readings are written in opposition to one another, but in fact they all share an assumption that is made explicit by John Henry Raleigh when he declares that, "*Lycidas* is an existential poem. . . .it is about 'becoming,' the emergence of the ego to its full power."⁸ Given this assumption, the poem can only be read as one in which the first person speaker is a seventeenth-century anticipation of a Romantic hero.

The notorious exception to this way of dealing with *Lycidas* is John Crowe Ransom, who explains the discontinuities in the poem as evidence of a failure to *suppress* the ego, a failure to realize the proper poetic intention of remaining "always anonymous" (66). In Ransom's account, the "logical difficulties of the work" (80), the shifts in tense, the changes in tone, the interpolations of different speakers, the roughness of verse, are the intrusive self-advertisements of a poet who cannot keep himself out of his poem, who is "willful and illegal" so that "nobody will make the mistake of not remarking his personality" (80). In general the Milton establishment has not been impressed by Ransom's argument which is now viewed as something of a curiosity. In what follows, I will attempt to revive it, but with a difference. Ransom is right, I believe, to see that the shifts and disruptions in the poem reflect a tension between anonymity and personality; but I do not think, as he seems to, that the personality in the poem is triumphant because it is irrepressible. Indeed, it will be my contention that the suppressing of the personal voice is the poem's achievement, and that the energy of the poem derives not from the presence of a controlling and self-contained individual, but from forces that undermine his individuality and challenge the fiction of his control. If the poem records a struggle of personality against anonymity, it is a struggle the first person speaker loses, and indeed, the triumph of the poem occurs when his voice can no longer be heard.

That voice, when we first encounter it, is heard complaining about the task to which it has been called by "sad occasion." The complaint is all the more bitter because it takes the form of an apology. "I am sorry to have to do this to you," the speaker says to the apostrophized berries, but what he is really sorry about is something that has been done to him. The double sense of the lines is nicely captured in the ambiguity of "forc'd" in line 4 ("And with forc'd fingers rude"), which can be read either as a characterization of his own action, or as an indictment of that which has made the action necessary (he is forced to do the forcing). In the same way, "rude" is at once a deprecation of his poetic skills and an expression of anger at having to exercise them prematurely: his fingers are rude because they have been forced to an unready performance. The pretense of an apology is continued through line 5 where it is once again undermined by the phrase "the mellowing year." Warton objected to an "inaccuracy" here because the " 'the mellowing year' could not affect the leaves of the laurel, the myrtle, and the ivy...characterized before as 'never sere.' "⁹ Just so. The "inaccuracy" is there to call an ironic and mocking attention to the inappropriateness of the apology: the laurel, the myrtle, and the ivy have no "mellowing year" to shatter; what has been shattered, in different ways, are the mellowing years of Lycidas and the speaker; and it is in response to the violence (interruption) done to them that these lines are spoken. By the time we reach line 7 it is impossible to read "disturb your season due" as anything but a bitter joke. It is the speaker's season that has been disturbed and by a disturbance (the death of Lycidas) even more final; and it is with the greatest reluctance that he is compelled to give voice to this "melodious tear" (14).

This posture of reluctance is one often assumed by Milton's characters, most notably by the attendant spirit in *Comus* who is more than a little loath to leave the "regions mild of calm and serene air" (4) for the "smoke and stir of this dim spot,/Which men call earth" (6). It is also the posture in which Milton likes to present himself in the prose tracts, so that, typically he will declare with what small willingness he leaves the "still time" of his studies to engage in "tedious antiquities and disputes,"¹⁰ or announce that only in response to the "earnest and serious conjurements" of a friend has he been "induc't" to break off pursuits "which cannot but be a great furtherance...to the enlargement of truth."¹¹ The labor to which he is called in these tracts is always an *interruption*, something that comes between him and a preferred activity, a discontinuity that threatens the completion of his real work.

This is especially true of *The Reason of Church Government* where his situation, as he characterizes it, exactly parallels that of the speaker in *Lycidas*. He writes, he tells us, "out of mine owne season when I have neither yet compleated to my minde the full circle of my private studies."¹² "I did not," he says, "choose this manner of writing, wherin knowing myself inferior to myself...I have the use...but of my left hand" (808). He would rather be "soaring in the high region of his fancies with his garland and singing robes about him," where, in response to the "inward prompting" of thoughts that have long "possest" him, he "might perhaps leave something so written to aftertimes, as they should not willingly let it die" (810). It is from those exalted "intentions" that he has been "plucked" by the "abortive and foredated discovery" (820) of the present occasion ("sad occasion dear") and he knows that the reader will understand how reluctant he is "to interrupt the pursuit of no less hopes than these...to imbark in a troubled sea of noises and hoars disputes, put from beholding the bright countenance of truth in the quiet and still air of delightful studies" (821–22). In *Lycidas*, the still and quiet air of studies is punctuated by the

Lycidas: A Poem Finally Anonymous

"Oaten Flute" and by the song beloved of "Old Damaetus," but as in *The Reason of Church Government*, this is a lost tranquility now recollected from the vantage point of a present turmoil, of a "heavy change" (37). In both contexts the change is the occasion for premature activity, for the hazarding of skills that are not yet ready in the performance of a task that is unwelcome.

There is one great difference however. The Milton of *The Reason of Church Government*, like the Attendant Spirit in *Comus*, is soon reconciled to that task because he is able to see it not as an interruption, but as an extension of the activity from which he has been called away. He may be "put from beholding the bright countenance of truth," but it is as a witness to the same truth that he takes up the labor forced upon him by the moment. All acts performed in response to the will of God are equally virtuous, and "when God commands to take the trumpet and blow a dolorous or a jarring blast, it lies not in man's will what he shall say." Indeed, "were it the meanest underservice, if God by his secretary conscience enjoin it," then it is impossible for a man to draw back. It is the same reasoning that leads him in *Of Education* to accede to the entreaties of Hartlib, for although the reforming of education is not the pursuit to which the love of God was taking him, he is able to see the present assignment as one "sent hither by some Good providence" and therefore as an opportunity to manifest that same love. In *An Apology*, he has decided, even before he descends to the disagreeable business of replying to slanders and calumnies, that it is his duty to do so, lest the truth and "the religious cause" which he had "in hand" be rendered "odious." "I conceaved myself," he declares, "to be not now as mine own person, but as a member incorporate into that truth whereof I was perswaded" (871).

This conception of himself as "not. . . mine owne person" is essential to his ability to see the disrupting activity as an instance or manifestation of the activity from which he has been *unwillingly* torn. That is, the disruption looms large only from the perspective of his personal desires—he would rather be writing poetry, or reading the classics, or furthering some long term project—but from the vantage point of the truth whereof he is but a member incorporate, there is no disruption at all, simply a continuity of duty and service. It is here that the point of contrast with the speaker in *Lycidas* is most obvious: he takes everything *personally*, and as a consequence, whatever happens is seen only as it relates to the hopes he has for his own career. This, of course, is the great discovery of twentieth-century criticism, that in *Lycidas* Milton "is primarily taking account of the meaning of the experience to himself";[13] but for Milton to be *primarily* doing this is for him to be doing something very different from what he does in the prose tracts where egocentric meanings are rejected as soon as they are identified. That is, the stance of the speaker in *Lycidas* is anomalous in the Milton canon; for rather than relinquishing the conception of him-

6

Stanley E. Fish

self as "his owne person," he insists on it, and by insisting on it he resists incorporation into a body of which he is but an extending member.

Indeed, insofar as the poem can be said to have a plot, it consists of the speaker's efforts to resist assimilation. He does this in part by maintaining an ironic distance from the conventions he proceeds to invoke. As we have seen, that irony is compounded largely of bitterness, and it takes the form both of questioning the adequacy of the conventions to the occasion, and of claiming a knowledge superior to any the conventions are able to offer. Irony is itself a mode of superiority: the ironic voice always issues from a perspective of privilege and presents itself as having penetrated to meanings that have been missed by the naive and the innocent. The ironic voice, in short, always knows *more*.

In this case it knows more than the traditions of consolation; it knows that they are fictions, false surmises. The method in the opening sections is to let these fictions have their say, only so that the speaker can enter to expose their shallowness. "He must not float upon his wat'ry bier" seems as we read it to be the sentiment of someone who believes that there is something to be done, but that belief is dismissed and mocked by the first word of line 12, "Unwept." He will, in fact, continue to float on his watery bier, and the only thing that will be done is what the speaker is doing now, producing laments in the form of "some melodious tear" (14). This characterization of his own activity is slighting, but it does not mean that he is assuming a stance of modesty or self-deprecation; the criticism extends only to the means or tools, and not to the workman who finds them inadequate. It is their failure and not his that is culpable; and indeed, his recognition, even before he employs them, that they will not do the job, validates the superiority of his perception.

Even when the pastoral conventions are invoked they are invoked in such a way as to call into question their capacities. The elegy proper begins with an echo of Virgil's messianic eclogue: "Begin. . .and somewhat loudly sweep the string." That eclogue, however, specifically promises to transcend the genre and therefore to invoke it is already to assume the insufficiency of the tradition in the very act of rehearsing its tropes. One of those tropes is the recollection of past delights and it is given an extended, even lingering evocation in lines 25–36 (the lines to which Dr. Johnson so objected); but even as we listen, in the place of "old Damaetas," to this song, we are aware, with Douglas Bush, that it is "a picture of pastoral innocence, of carefree youth unconscious of the fact of death."[14] We therefore hear it with *condescension* and with an expectation that it will be succeeded by a perspective less naive. As a result, when the speaker breaks in with "But O the heavy change" (37), the tone may be elegaic, but the gesture is a triumphant one, made by someone who is able to present himself as "sadder, but wiser." What he is wiser than is the pastoral mode and all of the ways by which it attempts to render comfortable what is so ob-

212

viously distressing. One of those ways is the doctrine of natural sympathy, which would tell us that in response to the death of Lycidas, "the Willows and the Hazel Copses green / Shall now no more be seen" (42–43); but that assertion is allowed to survive only for the moment before the succeeding line at once completes the syntax and, in an ironic reversal, changes the meaning: "Shall now no more be seen / Fanning their joyous Leaves to thy soft layes." The willows and the hazel copses green will in fact be seen, but they will be seen fanning their joyous leaves to someone else's soft lays, for it is Lycidas who will be "no more." This new meaning does not simply displace, but mocks the old: "how foolish of any one to believe that nature takes notice of the misfortunes of man." Obviously, the speaker is not such a one, and as always, the superimposition of his perspective on the perspective of the convention has the effect of establishing him in a removed and superior position. He maintains this position even when he appears to be turning on himself. "Aye me, I fondly dream" (56) has the form of a self-rebuke, but the fondness is displaced onto the tradition and its representative figures, the nymphs, the bards, the druids, the Muses, Orpheus, and even Universal Nature. It is their ineffectiveness that has led the speaker to break off his performance and to exclaim, "for what could that have done; / What could the Muse herself that Orpheus bore" (57–58). What *he* can do, and very effectively, is to see and say just that and so disassociate himself from the failures he continues to expose.

I am aware that in the more orthodox accounts of the poem this questioning of pastoral efficacy has received another reading, and is seen not as evidence of egocentricity, but as a kind of heroism. B. A. Rajan, for example reads the poem as the anguished discovery by the first person voice that ritual and tradition are inadequate when confronted by the "assault of reality."[15] The poem is thus an attack on "its own assumptions" (56), an attack that is "mounted by the higher mood against the pastoral form" (54). In the struggle that ensues, "convention and elementality are the basic forces of contention" (54), and for "elementality" we may read the personal voice, characterized by Rajan, as the "cry out of the heart of experience" (62). His argument is more finely tuned than Raleigh's, but its point is the same: *Lycidas* is about becoming, the emergence of the ego to its full power; or in Rajan's more guarded vocabulary, "it is a voyage toward recognition" (63), a recognition that is won to some extent at the expense of the claims to adequacy of pastoral and other ritual or public forms.

For Rajan, then, the contest between the conventional and the real or personal is the story the poem tells; what I am suggesting is that it is a story *the speaker* tells, and that he tells it in an effort to situate himself in a place not already occupied by public and conventional meanings. It is less "a cry out of the heart of experience," than a *strategy*, a strategy de-

Stanley E. Fish

signed to privilege experience, and especially *individual* experience, in relation to the impersonality of public and institutional structures. That is why the efficacy of the pastoral is called into question, so that the efficacy of the speaker, as someone who stands apart from conventions and is in a position to evaluate them, can be that much more firmly established. In other words, the characterization of the pastoral is deliberately low and feeble in order to display to advantage the authority and prescience of the speaker when he pronounces in his own voice, as he does at line 64:

> Alas, what boots it with incessant care. . . .

Here, and in the lines that follow, the speaker is at the height of his powers, in the sense that he seems to have earned the questions he hurls at the world, questions whose force is in direct proportion to the claim (silently, but effectively made) to sincerity. Here is no mediated pastoral voice, heard through a screen of tradition and ritual; here is the thing itself, the expression of a distinctive perspective on a problem that many have considered ("Yet once more"), but never with such poignancy and perceptiveness. It is precisely what Rajan says it is, a cry out of the heart of experience, a cry which emerges from the wreckage of failed conventions to pose the ultimate question: in a world like this, what does one do?

II. THE SWAIN IS SILENCED

It is all the more startling, then, when that cry is interrupted by the voice of Apollo, a moment characterized by Ransom as "an incredible interpolation" and "a breach in the logic of composition." These are strong words, but they are in response to a very strong effect given the extent to which the speaker has, to this point, asserted his control over the poem and its progression. Here the control is taken from him in so complete a way that we as readers do not even know when it happens. The identification of Apollo's voice occurs at the beginning of line 77 ("Phoebus repli'ed"), but the identification is after the fact, with the result that there is no way of determining who has been speaking. Many editors add punctuation so as to make it "clear" that Phoebus enters with "But not the praise"; but as we read Milton's unpunctuated text, "but not the praise" seems to be part of a dialogue the first person voice is having with himself on the nature of Fame and its relationship to effort ("incessant care"). The correction supplied by "Phoebus repli'ed" does not result in a simple reassignment of the half line, but blurs, retroactively, the assignment of the lines preceding. When does Phoebus begin to speak? Is this his first reply or has he begun to respond to the first person complaint at line 70: "*Fame* is the spur. . . ."? The first person would then return in line 73—"But the fair Guerdon when we hope to find"—and *then* Phoebus would be heard to reply "But not the praise." My point is not to argue for this particular redistribution of the lines, but to demonstrate that it is possible; and because it is just one among other possibilities, and because the matter cannot be settled once and for all, the question of just who is in charge of the poem becomes a real one.

This is not the only question raised by Apollo's intervention. Because "repli'ed" is in the past tense, what had presented itself as speech erupting in the present is suddenly revealed to be recollected or reported speech. As Ransom observes, "dramatic monologue has turned...into narrative" (79); and the result in Friedman's words, "is a momentary confusion about the nature of the utterance we are listening to."[16] The confusion is not only generic (monologue or narrative), but extends to the kind of hearing we are to give to that utterance, for "if the memory of Phoebus' words is reported by the swain as part of the elegy, then what has happened to the pretense of spontaneity and present creation?" Friedman's question contains its own answer (although it is not the one he eventually gives): it is here that the spontaneity begins to be exposed precisely as a pretense, as a claim elaborately made by the speaker from his very first words: "Yet once more." Although these words acknowledge convention (by acknowledging that this has been done before) they are themselves unconventional, because they are not produced within the frame or stage setting that traditionally encloses the pastoral lament. From Theocritus to Spenser, elegiac song is introduced into a situation that proclaims its status as artifice, as a piece of currency in a social exchange (song for bowl), or as a performance offered in competition. In *Lycidas*, however, the frame is omitted, and what we hear, or are encouraged to hear, is an unpremeditated outpouring of grief and anger. When Apollo's reply is reported in the past tense, the pastoral frame is introduced retroactively, and the suggestion is that it has been there all the while. Immediately the spontaneity of the preceding lines is compromised, and compromised too are the claims of the speaker to independence. At the very moment he dismisses the pastoral, he is revealed to be a narrated pastoral figure, no longer the teller of his tale, but told by it, identified and made intelligible, as it were, by the very tradition he scorns. Moreover, he is identified in such a way as to call into question his identity. When Apollo plucks his trembling ear, he repeats an action already performed in response to another poet who also has dreams of transcending the pastoral conventions:

> When I tried a song of kings and battles, Phoebus
> Plucked my ear and warned. "A shepherd, Tityrus,
> Should feed fat sheep, recite a fine-spun song.
>   (Virgil, *Eclogue VI*, trans. Paul Alpers)

Apollo, in short, puts Virgil in his place, and by doing so establishes a place (or commonplace) that is now occupied by the present speaker.

Stanley E. Fish

That is, the desire of the poet to rise above the pastoral is itself a pastoral convention, and when the speaker of *Lycidas* gives voice to that desire he succeeds only in demonstrating the extent to which his thoughts and actions are already inscribed in the tradition from which he would be separate. Not only are his ambitions checked by Apollo,[17] but they are not *his* ambitions, insofar as he is only playing out the role assigned him in a drama not of his making.

It is not too much to say, then, that the intervention of Apollo changes everything: the speaker loses control of his poem when another voice simply dislodges him from center stage (where he had been performing in splendid isolation), and, at the same time, the integrity of his own voice is compromised when it becomes indistinguishable from its Virgilian predecessor. Apollo poses a threat to the speaker not only as a maker, as someone who is in the act of building the lofty rhyme, but as a self-contained consciousness, as a mind that is fully present to itself and responsible for its own perceptions. The speaker meets this twin threat by rewriting, or misreading, what has happened to him in such a way as to reinstate, at least for the moment, the fiction of his independence:

> O fountain *Arethuse*, and thou honour'd flood,
> Smooth-sliding *Mincius*; crown'd with vocall reeds,
> That strain I heard was of a higher mood:
> But now my oat proceeds. (85–87)

The picture in these lines is of someone who has paused to listen, no doubt politely, to the opinion of another before proceeding resolutely on *his* way (the strong claim is in the *my* of "my oat"). There is no acknowledgment at all of the violence of Apollo's entrance, of his brusque and dismissive challenge to the speaker's sentiments, of the peremptory and unceremonious manner in which he seizes the floor. Moreover, the action Apollo performs is misrepresented when it is reported as an action *against* the pastoral ("That strain was of a higher mood"). In fact, it is an action against the speaker, a rebuke, as Mary Christopher Pecheux observes, to his "rebellious questioning."[18] If Apollo's words are higher they are higher than the speaker's own; rather than supporting his denigration of the pastoral, they are precisely pastoral words, and mark the moment when the tradition interrupts the "bold discourse"[19] of one who scorns it and exposes the illusion of his control.

It is in order to maintain the illusion that the speaker sets Apollo against the pastoral, for he can then present himself as the judge of their respective assertions. But no sooner has he reclaimed the central and directing role ("But now my oat proceeds") than it is once again taken from him:

> But now my oat proceeds,
> And listens to the Herald of the Sea
> That came in *Neptune's* plea. (88–90)

Lycidas: A Poem Finally Anonymous

Suddenly the voices competing for attention, and for the position of authority, multiply and become difficult to distinguish. Triton comes, but he comes in Neptune's plea, and therefore when we read of someone who "ask'd" the waves and felon winds (91) it is not clear whether that someone is Triton or Neptune, nor when it is that whoever it is speaks (it could be that Triton reports the investigative queries of Neptune—he "ask'd," or that Triton *now* asks in the present of the narrative, but is reported as having done so in the present of the narrator, i.e. the voice that tells us that Phoebus "repli'ed"). The one thing that is clear is that the questioner is not the speaker who is now reduced to the role of a listener, as someone else conducts the investigation. Again that someone else could be Triton or Neptune or the yet unknown third person voice of whose existence we have had only hints, or, after line 96, it could be the "sage Hippotades" who brings someone's (it seems to be everyone's) unsatisfactory answers. By the time we reach the most unsatisfactory answer of all—"It was that fatall and perfidious Bark"—there is absolutely no way of determining who delivers it. A poem that began as the focused utterance of a distinctive personal voice is by this point so diffused that it is spoken, quite literally, by everybody.

Not only is the original speaker now indistinguishable from a chorus, but he is not even the object of direct address, as he was when he listened to Apollo. Whoever it is that indicts the fatal and perfidious bark, he directs his remarks to Lycidas: "That sunk so low that sacred head of *thine*." Moreover, the indictment and the entire investigation are once again proceeding in a narrated past. The fading of the speaker from the scene of his own poem coincides with the almost imperceptible slide into the past tense, and both movements are complete when we hear (we have displaced the speaker who is no longer even a prominent listener) that "last came, and last did go / The Pilot of the Galilean lake" (109).

It would seem that with this figure the poem is once again dominated by a single controlling presence, but his identity (in two senses) is perhaps not so firm as we have been taught to think. Taking up a suggestion first made by R. E. Hone, Mary Pecheux has argued persuasively that the Pilot of the Galilean lake (who significantly is not named), is not Peter, but a composite of Peter, Moses, and Christ. The speech thus dramatizes Milton's assertion in *Christian Doctrine* that revelation was disclosed in various ages by Christ even though he was not always known under that name: "Under the name of Christ are also comprehended Moses and the Prophets, who were his forerunners, and the Apostles whom he sent."[20] This splitting of the "dread voice" has the advantage, as Pecheux points out, of being "consonant with the extraordinary richness and ambivalence" of the poem, with the sense one has "of having heard a multitude of overtones difficult to disentangle from one another" (239). The details of her argument are less important than the fact that it can be made (and others are now making it) for this means that the question is now an open one, and that the Pilot's speech too proceeds from a source that is not *uniquely* identified.

That speech is also addressed to Lycidas ("How well could I have spar'd for thee, young swain"), and its "stern" message further shifts attention away from the first person voice by replacing his very personal concerns with the concerns of the church as a whole. That is, the complaint one hears in these lines is quite different from the complaint that precedes Apollo's interruption: it is not an answer to the speaker's questions ("What boots it . . ."), but a "higher" questioning in which the ambitions of any one shepherd or singer are absorbed into a more universal urgency, as rot and foul contagion spread (127). The focus of the Pilot's words is continually expanding, until it opens in the end on a perspective so wide that all of our attempts to name it are at once accurate and hopelessly inadequate. Whatever the two handed engine is—and we shall never know—the action for which it stands ready will not be in response to any cry out of the heart of experience, and in this moment of apocalyptic prophecy, the private lament that was, for a time, the poem's occasion, is so much transcended that one can scarcely recall it.

This movement away from the personal is a structural component of Milton's work from the very beginning. It is seen as early as the Nativity Ode where the poet begins by desiring to be first, to stand out ("Have thou the honor first thy Lord to greet") and ends by being indistinguishable from the others (animals, angels, shepherds) who "all about the Courtly Stable / . . . . sit in order serviceable." The glory he had hoped to win by being first is won when, in a sense, he no longer is, and is able to pronounce the glorious death of his own poetic ambitions ("Time is our tedious Song should here have ending"). While the career of the speaker in *Lycidas* is parallel, it is also different because he does not relinquish his position voluntarily. He holds tenaciously to his own song and must be forcibly removed from the poem by voices that preempt him or displace him or simply ignore him until at the end of the Pilot's speech he seems to have disappeared.

Indeed, so long has it been since he was last on stage (line 90) that when he suddenly pops up again he seems an interpolation more incredible than Apollo. He seems, in fact, a digression, a departure from what we have come to recognize as the poem's true concerns; and as a digression his gesture of reassertion is, in every sense, reactionary:

> Return *Alpheus* the dread voice is past
> That shrunk thy streams; Return *Sicilian* Muse,
> And call the Vales and bid them hither cast
> Their bells and Flourets of a thousand hues. (132–35)

Once again the return of the speaker is marked by a rewriting that is a misrepresentation. He acts as if all had been proceeding under his direction, as if the voices in the poem require his permission to come and go, a permission he now extends to the pastoral, which is characterized as if it were a child that had been frightened by the sound of an adult voice. His strategy is two pronged and it is familiar. He opposes the pastoral to the speech of the Galilean Pilot (as he had earlier opposed it to Apollo) and thus denies it the responsibility for documenting ecclesiastical abuses, a responsibility it was given in the Scriptures. In effect, it is he, not the Pilot, who shrinks, or attempts to shrink, the pastoral stream, and he does it, characteristically, in a denial of the extent to which his own stream has been shrunk in the course of the poem. It is a classic form of displacement in which he attempts, for the last time, to project a story in which he is a compelling and powerful figure. It is as part of that story that he calls the role of flowers, a gesture intended not so much to "interpose a little ease," but to set the stage for still another assertion of pastoral inadequacy:

> Let our frail thoughts dally with false surmise. (155)

As before what is presented as self-deprecation is an act of self-promotion. The "frail thoughts" are detached from the speaker—he merely dallies with them—and identified with the failure of the convention; if, in some sense, he can do no better, at least he is able to recognize a false surmise when he sees one, and that ability in itself is evidence of a vision that is superior even if it is (realistically) dark:

> Ay me! Whils't thee the shores and sounding Seas
> Wash far away, where ere thy bones are hurl'd. (154–55)

This is, of course, exactly what he has said before, when he breaks off his address to the nymphs to exclaim, "Aye me, I fondly dream," and again, when his rehearsal of Orpheus's death (he also was hurled by shores and sounding seas) is followed by a bitter question: "Alas! What boots it with incessant care?" What is remarkable about the speaker is how little he is affected by those sections of the poem that unfold between his intermittent appearances. Higher moods and dread voices may come and go, but when he manages to regain the stage, it is to sing the same old song: Ay me, alas, what am I to do? What's the use? it's all so unfair. As the poem widens its perspective to include ever larger considerations (eternal fame, the fate of the Church, the condition of the Christian community, the last judgment), he remains within the perspective of his personal disappointment, remains very much "his owne person," and therefore he becomes, as I have said, a digression in (what began as) his own poem. While he has been busily exposing the false surmises of pastoral consolation, the poem has been even more insistently exposing the surmise that enables him (or so he thinks) to do so, the surmise that his vision is both inclusive and conclusive, that he sees what there is to see and knows what there is to know. What he sees is that there is no laureate hearse (only the "wat'ry bier" he saw at line 14), and what he knows is that there is neither justice nor meaning in the world. He seems to have heard in the Pilot's speech none of the resonances that have been reported by so many readers. His words remain determinedly bleak, and therefore, they are all the more discontinuous with the call that is sounded at line 165:

> Weep no more woful Shepherds, weep no more,
> For *Lycidas* your sorrow is not dead.

These are entirely new accents spoken by an entirely new voice. It is a voice that counsels rather than complains, that turns outward rather than inward, a voice whose confident affirmation of a universal benevolence could not be further from the dark and self-pitying questioning of the swain. Everything, in short, has changed, and it has changed not even in a line, but in the space between lines. It is at this point that the orthodox reading of the poem, in which "the troubled thought of the elegist" traces out a sequence of "rise, evolution, and resolution," founders.[21] There is no evolution here, simply a disjunction, a gap, and the seekers of unity are left with the problem of explaining it. In general, their explanations have taken one of two forms. Either the change is explained theologically as "a leap from nature to revelation,"[22] and "a dramatization of the infusion of grace,"[23] or it is explained away by assigning the lines to another speaker. This is the solution of William Madsen who notes the abrupt transition from the "plaintive" and "ineffectual" to the authoritative, and concludes that the consolation is spoken not by the swain, but by Michael who responds in a fuller measure than might have been expected to the speaker's appeal ("Look homeward, Angel, now and melt with ruth"). Madsen offers his emendation as an alternative to the theological reading; but in fact there is very little difference between them, since in either reading this point marks the appearance in the poem of "a new voice." For Madsen that voice is Michael's; for Abrams and Friedman (among others) it is the voice of a regenerated (made new) swain. In either case there is agreement that the voice we had been hearing is heard no more, and that what takes its place is something wholly different. This is of course not the first time this has happened, and it is only because in Madsen's reading the event is unusual that he feels moved to assign the new voice a specific name (it is that assignment that has been objected to). In the reading that has been developed here, however, the appearance of new voices and the merging of old is occurring all the time; the speaker is repeatedly dislodged or overwhelmed or absorbed, and his disappearance at line 164 is just one in a series.

There is, however, a difference. This disappearance is the last; the speaker is never heard from again. Or if he is heard from again, it is not as his "owne person" but as a "member incorporate" of a truth from which he is now indistinguishable. That is to say, Madsen is right to hear the voice as different, but he is wrong to hear it as anyone's in particular. The accents here, as Marjorie Nicolson has observed, are "choral" as "all voices combine in virtuous crescendo."[24] If the speaker is among them, he is literally unrecognizable, since what allowed him to stand out was the "dogged insistence"[25] with which he held on to the local perspective of his own ambitions. In the end he is not even distinguishable as an addressee: the choral voice responds not to one, but to a mass of complaints; the consolation is for "woful Shepherds" and the plural noun silently denies the speaker even the claim to have been uniquely grieving; the grief is as general as the consolation and it simply doesn't leave room for anything personal. The distance that has been travelled is the distance from the melodious tear of line 14 to the "unexpressive nuptial Song" of line 176. The tear falls from a single eye; it is the poem as the product of one voice that demands to be heard, if only as an expression of inconsolability; but the nuptial song is produced by everyone and therefore *heard* by no one, in the sense that there is no one who is at a sufficient distance from it for there to be a question of hearing. That is why it is called "unexpressive" which means both inexpressible (can't be said) and inaudible (it can't be apprehended): both speaking and receiving assume a separation between communicating agents; but this song is not a communication at all, but a testimony to a joy which since it binds all need not be transmitted to any. The mistake of the first person voice has been his desire to speak, to proclaim from an analytic and judgmental distance a truth he only sees; but in the great vision of these soaring lines the truth proclaims, because it fills, its speakers, who are therefore not speakers at all but witnesses. They are in the happy condition for which Milton prays at the end of *At a Solemn Music*:

> O may we soon again renew that song
> And keep in tune with heaven, till God ere long
> To his celestial consort us unite
> To live with him and sing in endless morn of light.

The wish that we may join that choir is the wish that we *not* be heard as a distinctive and therefore alienated voice, the wish that we might utter sounds in such a way as to remain silent (unexpressive). It is a wish that is here granted the would-be elegist, whether he wants it or not, as finally, he is no longer his own person, but a member incorporate into that truth whereof he has been persuaded.

I am aware that this might seem a back door way into the usual reading of *Lycidas*, for just like any other critic I have gotten the swain into heaven or at least into a position where a heavenly vision is available to him. But if he is now one of those who sing and singing in their glory move, he could not be picked out from among the other members of troops and societies, and therefore his "triumph," if one can call it that, is

Stanley E. Fish

not achieved in terms that he would understand or welcome. As Friedman remarks, the speaker "fights *against* the knowledge" offered by the poem's higher moods; his experience is "one of active struggle" (5). My point is that it is a struggle he loses, and that the poem achieves its victory first by preempting him and finally by silencing him. Rather than the three part structure traditionally proposed for *Lycidas*, I am proposing a structure of two parts: a first part (lines 1 through 75 1/2) where the first person voice proceeds under the illusion of independence and control, and a second, longer part, where that illusion is repeatedly exposed and finally dispelled altogether. In place of an interior lyric punctuated by digressive interpolations, we have a poem that begins in digression—the first person voice is the digression—and regains the main path only when the lyric note is no longer sounded. We have, in short, a poem that relentlessly denies the privilege of the speaking subject, of the unitary and separate consciousness, and is finally, and triumphantly, anonymous.

It is anonymous twice. The last eight lines of *Lycidas* have always been perceived as problematic, because they insist on a narrative frame that was not apparent in the beginning, because the frame or *coda* is spoken by an unidentified third person voice, and because that voice is so firmly impersonal. One advantage of the reading offered here is that these are not problems at all: if the introduction of a narrative perspective suggests that everything presented as spontaneous was in fact already spoken, this is no more than a confirmation of what has long since become obvious; if the new voice is unidentified, it is only the last in a series of unidentified voices or of voices whose single identities have long since been lost or blurred; and if the unidentified voice is impersonal it is merely a continuation of the mode the poem has finally achieved. In fact, the crucial thing about these lines is that there is no one to whom they can be plausibly assigned. They are certainly not the swain's, for he is what they describe, and they describe him significantly as someone who is "uncouth" that is, unknown, someone who departs the poem with less of an identity than he displayed at its beginning; nor is there any compelling reason to assign them to any of the previous speakers, to the Pilot, or Hippotades, or Triton, or Neptune, or Cambridge, or Apollo. The only recourse, and it is one that has appealed to many, is to assign the lines to Milton, but of all the possibilities, this is the least persuasive. No voice in English poetry is more distinctive than Milton's, so much so that the characters he creates almost always sound just like him. But these lines do not sound like anyone; they are perfectly, that is unrelievedly, conventional, and as such they are the perfect conclusion to a poem from which the personal has been systematically eliminated. Indeed, if these lines were written in accents characteristically Miltonic, they would constitute a claim exactly like that which is denied to the poem's first speaker, the claim to be able to pronounce, to sum up, to say it conclusively, and once and for all. Instead

Milton gives over the conclusion of the poem to a collection of pastoral commonplaces which are not even structured into a summary statement, but simply follow one another in a series that is unconstrained by any strong syntactical pressures. (The lines are markedly paratactic and conform to what Thomas Rosenmeyer has called the "disconnective decorum" of the pure pastoral.)[26] In short, Milton silences himself, just as the first person voice is silenced, and performs (if that is the word), an act of humility comparable to that which allows him to call his nativity ode "tedious" at the very moment when its intended recipient falls asleep. Rosemund Tuve once observed that in Herbert's career we can see a life long effort to achieve the "immolation of the individual will." This has not usually been thought to be Milton's project, but the determined anonymity of *Lycidas* should remind us that the poet's fierce egoism is but one half of his story.

NOTES

1. G. Wilson Knight, *The Burning Oracle* (London: Oxford University Press, 1939), p. 70.

2. John Crowe Ransom, "A Poem Nearly Anonymous," in *Milton's Lycidas: The Tradition and the Poem*, ed. C. A. Patrides (New York: Holt, Rhinehart, and Winston, 1961), p. 71. This essay was first published in *The American Review* 4 (1953).

3. *From Shadowy Types to Truth* (New Haven: Yale University Press, 1968), p. 13.

4. "*Lycidas*: The Swain's Paideia," *Milton Studies* 3 (1971): 33.

5. "Milton's Uncouth Swain," *Milton Studies* 3 (1971): 35–50.

6. *The Burning Oracle*, p. 70.

7. "The Principles of Variety and Contrast in Seventeenth-Century Aesthetics and Milton's Poetry," *Journal of the History of Ideas* 10 (1949): 159–82.

8. "*Lycidas*: 'Yet Once More,' " *Prairie Schooner*, Winter 1968–69, p. 317.

9. Scott Elledge, ed. *Milton's Lycidas* (New York: Harper and Row, 1966), p. 259.

10. *An Apology Against a Pamphlet* in *The Complete Prose Works of John Milton*, Vol. 1, *1624-1642*, ed. Don M. Wolfe (New Haven: Yale University Press, 1953), p. 953.

11. *Of Education* in *The Complete Prose Works of John Milton*, Vol. 2, *1643-1648*, ed. Ernest Sirluck (New Haven: Yale University Press, 1959), p. 363.

12. *Complete Prose Works of John Milton*, 1: 807.

13. James Holly Hanford, *The Milton Handbook* (New York: F.S. Crofts, 1926).

14. A. S. P. Woodhouse and Douglas Bush, eds. *A Variorum Commentary on the Poems of John Milton* (New York: Columbia University Press, 1972), p. 647.

15. "*Lycidas*: The Shattering of the Leaves," *Studies in Philology* 64 (1967): 59.

16. "*Lycidas:* The Swain's Paideia," *Milton Studies* 3 (1971): 33.

17. "The Swain's Paideia," p. 13.

18. "The Dread Voice in *Lycidas*," *Milton Studies* 9 (1976): 238.

19. See *Paradise Lost*, V, 803ff: "Thus far his bold discourse without control / Had audience, when, among the Seraphim, / Abdiel . . . / Stood up."

20. "The Dread Voice in *Lycidas*," p. 235.

21. M. H. Abrams, "Five Types of *Lycidas*," in *Lycidas: The Tradition and the Poem*, p. 224.

22. Ibid., p. 229.

23. Friedman, "The Swain's Paideia," p. 19.

18
Stanley E. Fish

24. *John Milton: A Reader's Guide to His Poetry* (New York: Farrar, Straus, and Giroux, 1963), p. 110.

25. The phrase is Madsen's, *From Shadowy Types to Truth*, p. 13.

26. *The Green Cabinet* (Berkeley and Los Angeles: University of California Press, 1969), p. 33.

The Genius of the Shore: Lycidas, Adamastor, and the Poetics of Nationalism

LAWRENCE LIPKING, Chester D. Tripp Professor of Humanities at Northwestern University, has written The Ordering of the Arts in Eighteenth-Century England *(Princeton UP, 1970),* The Life of the Poet: Beginning and Ending Poetic Careers *(U of Chicago P, 1981), and* Abandoned Women and Poetic Tradition *(U of Chicago P, 1988). In 1966* PMLA *published his essay on Castiglione's* Courtier. *He is completing a book on authorship and Samuel Johnson.*

WHEN MILTON appointed Lycidas "the Genius of the shore," he was staking a claim for his nation as well as his poem. The spirit who guards the coast will cast a long shadow of British influence across the Irish Sea, translating the martyrdom of one poor soul into an opportunity for a new English poet to tame the flood and take his rightful place. Many Renaissance authors shared similar territorial interests. In an age of expansion, poets, like nations, often defined what they wanted to be by artfully redrawing or reimagining the map. Nor is this hobby innocent; as recent scholarship has insisted, map reading kindles thoughts of ownership, of empire, of routes of trade and invasion.[1] The collaboration between poetry and nationalism comes out in the open in *The Lusiads* (1572) and other imperialistic epics.[2] But it also supplies a quiet, persistent undertone to forms like the pastoral elegy of "Lycidas" (1638), which blends personal grief with a sense of how much the country has lost. Milton puts himself on the map by mourning for Britain. For one way a poet can speak for a nation—this essay will argue—is by expressing the grievances that hold it together.

The climax of "Lycidas" turns on a rescue mission. After long wandering in the sea, "the haples youth" (164) is lifted up, washed clean, serenaded, and rewarded through a direct performative speech act:

> Henceforth thou art the Genius of the shore,
> In thy large recompense, and shalt be good
> To all that wander in that perilous flood. (183–85)

A spirit now stands on guard against future shipwrecks; it is time for the weeping to stop. Yet this climax acquires its force by reversing a pattern that has run through the elegy: the theme of frustrated protection. Neither pagan nor Christian watchmen have kept harm away. The nymphs

England and Ireland (Ortelius, folio 12). According to "Lycidas," the corpse of Edward King may have drifted to the extreme north or the extreme south of the Irish Sea (154–62). The detail above on the right includes the route of King's fatal voyage. The detail below on the right shows Land's End (also called Bellerium) and St. Michael's Mount. (Photo courtesy of the Edward E. Ayer Collection, The Newberry Library)

226

and bards and muse, according to lines 50–63, were not looking after Lycidas, and had they been there, "what could that have don?" The greedy pastors of lines 113–31 neither feed their flocks nor defend them from the wolf. Even the angel Michael, "the great vision of the guarded Mount" who looks homeward from Land's End and melts with ruth (161–63), cannot offer safe harbor. Lycidas gathers all these frustrations into himself and promises help in the future—at least according to "the uncouth Swain" (186). But in the neglectful and bitter world of the poem, only an act of poetic will can salvage any hope of protecting the good.

What does Milton resent, and what does he want to protect? The questions take in the whole design of "Lycidas," its tangled poetic, theological, and geopolitical yarn. Many critics have heard a note of puritanical outrage in the poem, "the poet's anger that his countrymen should be oppressed, insulted, and tyrannized by Laud's prelates" (Radzinowicz 126), and a keen contemporary might well have felt the shiver of a coming revolution. Religion and politics join, as so often in Milton; the people of England must be protected from their government and church. Yet the poet may also have focused his thoughts more narrowly on the subject of the elegy, poor drowned Edward King, both as he was and as

he might have been. In particular, Milton tries to locate the body. The poet's fascination with atlases has long been known, and readers can hardly find their way around his globe-girdling passages without a guide like Ortelius or Camden. Evidently he responded to the death of his friend with characteristic behavior: brooding over maps (Whiting 103–07). "Lycidas" traces the path of the shipwreck from the channel of the Dee to the coast of Anglesey and sweeps the Irish Sea from north to south. However futile the search, there is comfort in navigating Camden's *Britain*, where a reader still gazes at proof that Scotland, Wales, and Ireland belong to one great commonwealth. The role of maps, and of some poems as well, can be to establish a sphere of protection—indeed, to look homeward.

Where might the angel be looking? Commentators have not had much to say about "homeward." The standard reading has pictured Michael shifting his vision 170 degrees, from southwest to due north, away from the Atlantic Ocean and the Spanish coast ("*Namancos* and *Bayona's* hold") and back toward an English protectorate, the Irish Sea, where a saint's keen eye might detect the floating speck of a body. The charm of this reading consists of the marvelous image of a rock, "St. Michael's Chaire," abruptly wheeling around with its resident spirit and melting with ruth. But the geography remains vague. Neither Milton nor the reader knows where Lycidas is, nor can we be sure that the angel knows better. Most readers, I suspect, would prefer him to look not down but up, toward the home of the saints. "Angel" surely points in that direction. Lycidas is going home, as in the spiritual or as in Clarissa's setting out for her father's house. Heaven's his destination. This reading seems inevitable, and the dolphins sustain it. But it also has flaws. It does not account well for "melt with ruth," and, perhaps more important, it seems prematurely to anticipate the turn of the following stanza, when Lycidas does rise from "the wat'ry floor" to his father's house. If heavenly trumpets ring out at "homeward," the ensuing nuptial song will sound anticlimactic. Such cavils do

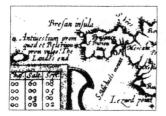

Europe (detail of Ortelius, folio 2). From the southwest tip of England, the guardian spirit Michael looks toward Spain. (Photo courtesy of the Edward E. Ayer Collection, The Newberry Library)

not eliminate the reading, yet they leave room for another, less far off the map. The youth now lost in the sea had set sail for home; both Michael and Lycidas might have looked toward that place, and grieved at his failure to reach it. Ireland, also, was his destination.

On 10 August 1637, when Edward King drowned after the ship on which he was a passenger struck a rock and sank, not far from the Welsh shore,[3] on its way from Chester to Dublin, he gave up great expectations. The Latin preface to *Justa Edovardo King*, the memorial volume in which "Lycidas" first appeared, shows just how much awaited him:

> Edward King, son of John (Knight and Privy Councillor for the Kingdom of Ireland to their majesties, Elizabeth, James, and Charles), Fellow of Christ's College in the University of Cambridge. . . . was on his voyage to Ireland, drawn by natural affection to visit his country, his relatives and his friends—chiefly, his brother Sir Robert King, Knight, a most distinguished man; his sisters, most excellent women, Anne, wife of Lord G. Caulfield, Baron Charlemont, and Margaret, wife of Lord G. Loder [Gerard Lowther], Chief Justice of Ireland; the venerable prelate Edward King, Bishop of Elphin, his godfather; and the most reverend and learned William Chappell, Dean of Cashel and Provost of Trinity College, Dublin, whose hearer and pupil he had been in the University. (Masson 651)

These were powerful connections, a family well entrenched among Ireland's ruling class. Though a younger son, Edward had reason to expect preferment in the church. Elected to a fellowship at Christ's in 1630, he had been assured by a royal mandate that Charles I, "well ascertained both of the present sufficiency and future hopes" of his promising young subject, took a personal interest in him (*DNB* 11: 128). King proved his appreciation. Almost all his Latin verses, contributed to seven Cambridge collections, celebrate royal occasions, including the king's recovery from smallpox and safe return from Scotland. The quality of these verses has been impugned, but surely they do very well as bread and butter. Had Edward met a better fate (along with his king), he would have been destined (pace Milton) to be a bishop.

Nevertheless, he had not spent much time looking homeward. Though born in Ireland, he had lived most of his twenty-five years in England and spoke classical languages but not Irish.[4] Even his college fellowship caused dispute, since he was considered, despite his Irish "home," a Yorkshireman (Fletcher 508–12). The family came from Yorkshire. Sir John King had prospered under three monarchs as one of the Protestants who colonized the Irish countryside; he had built a castle on the river Boyle and in 1613 (a year after Edward's birth) "was returned M.P. for co. Roscommon by the aid of Vice-president Oliver St. John's soldiery" (*DNB* 11: 138). Sir Robert King, the eldest son, inherited many of his father's places and fought for the king in the Irish rebellion. Later he turned to the service of the parliament, increasing his estate; and in 1650 *his* eldest son, John King, "took prisoner with his own hands the general of the catholic army, the popish bishop of Clogher" (11: 139). The family would continue to back winners. At the Restoration the same John King, a supporter of Charles II, became Baron Kingston and took his seat in the Irish House of Lords. This is a story of Anglo-Irish success, a story in which Edward King was robbed of his part.[5]

In 1637, how would Milton have viewed the story? However troubled by its royal flourishes, he would certainly not have deplored the colonizing of Ireland or denied the right of Edward King to consider it home. These were no more than justice. Whatever else Milton knew about Ireland, he knew his beloved Spenser. *A View of the Present State of Ireland* had first been published only four years earlier, in 1633, and its relentless argument for pacifying the countryside with famine and sword still seemed quite fresh. Entries in Milton's *Commonplace Book* record Spenser's call for a new settlement in which Anglo-Irish pastors like King, supported by soldiery, would wean the natives from their infidelity and paganism.[6] Moreover, the fifth book of *The Faerie Queene* gripped Milton's imagination; only outsiders could free Irena from Grantorto and bring about proper reform.[7] This view of the present state of Britain's colony would stay with Milton forever. The savage attack on prelates and papists that runs through so much of his later

pamphleteering holds Ireland especially in need of salvation. The "true Barbarisme and obdurate wilfulnesse" of the Irish renegades demand "a civilizing Conquest" (*Prose Works* 3: 304).[8] Through leniency to Catholics, according to Milton, Charles I personally incited the Great Rebellion and called down a curse *"upon himself and his Fathers House"* (3: 485);[9] to repair that division of the kingdom, Cromwell would have to serve as avenging angel. But the breach had begun much earlier. Retrospectively, when Milton gave "Lycidas" credit in 1645 for having foretold "the ruine of our corrupted Clergie then in their height" ("Lycidas," epigraph), he enlisted Edward King in the war against episcopal blind mouths and the privy popish wolf. Ireland, still more than its mother country, was being devoured. Nor could it spare the learning of scholars like King; too many Irish priests had "learn'd ought els the least / That to the faithful Herdsmans art belongs!" ("Lycidas" 120–21). This point weighed heavily in 1637. Through both precept and example. "Lycidas" celebrates the advantages of a university education, most of all when, as in Cambridge, Puritan sympathies chime with love of the classics. England had no better gift than learning to send to its poor relation.[10]

Indeed, King voyaged to Ireland like a missionary, if not a crusader. Milton was not the only friend preoccupied by that thought. Several contributors to *Justa Edovardo King* play with the same idea: Cambridge had sent out one of its own, a King (the pun was not easy to resist) to reform the world. A particularly striking instance of this missionary strain occurs in Henry King's praise for his brother's "might / Of eloquence, able to Christianize / India, or reconcile Antipathies!" (2). No place felt the want of such talent more than Ireland, the land of antipathies, and the King family aimed at reconciliation. But Milton tended to be more militant. "Angel," for him, was a fighting word; the "huge two-handed sway" of Michael's sword in *Paradise Lost* (6.251), recalling the notorious "two-handed engine" of "Lycidas," forbids any hope of a truce. Ever since the Book of Daniel, moreover, Michael had represented the ultimate nationalistic warrior-angel, Israel's champion and prince.[11] The "vision of the guarded Mount" commands a British fortress. As Michael Walzer observes, "The angelic

armies were the guardians of the elect—so important was this function to Puritan writers that they
tended to ignore all other angelic activities" (164).
And armies often crossed the Irish Sea. The angel
implored to look homeward in "Lycidas" may well
be recruited to grieve for the state of that home, be-
reft of one more guardian who would have forced
true faith on a stiff-necked people. But Ireland will
not be left defenseless. Milton provides it with a
new genius, a saintly, crusading spirit.

The geography lesson of "Lycidas" confirms this
militant, nationalistic reading. As usual, Milton's
maps cover time as well as space, identifying each
site through its historic or legendary associations.
Visiting the neighborhood where King drowned, in
lines 50–63, the poem travels back in time, to an
age when nymphs, Druids, and wizards presided
over the West Country and the landscape had been
converted to Latin—Mona, not Anglesey; Deva,
not Dee. The retrogression culminates in Orpheus,
unprotected by the Muse and Nature, at the beginning of time (Evans 36–44). What all these
sentinels and deities have in common is their inef-
fectualness. The pathos of their futility perfectly
matches the pathos of the poem that invokes them,
reciting their names in a fond dream that accomplishes nothing, least of all belief in their existence.
Like the evicted local gods of the Nativity ode,
these poetic spirits cannot survive one dash of cold
water. Perhaps the poet regrets their vanished enchantment. Yet eventually, in the *History of Britain*,
Milton would condemn the Druids as despoilers of
ancient Britain, "men factious and ambitious, contending somtimes about the archpriesthood not
without civil Warr and slaughter; nor restrein'd they
the people under them from a lew'd adulterous and
incestuous life" (*Prose Works* 5: 61). The defeat of
this "barbarous and lunatic rout" by the Romans at
the battle of Mona seems to anticipate, for Milton,
all the later struggles of pious, civilized rulers of
Britain against such barbarians and schismatics as
the Welsh and the Irish (5: 75). We cannot project
this hostility to Druids back into the dreams of "Lycidas."[12] But dreams conclude in waking. Poetic
enchantment had been no use to King, and for better protection both Wales and the shepherd-poet
would have to look to a faithful Christian god.

The circulation of Lycidas's body most fully reveals what is at stake for Milton (154–62). In their
imagined journey, the bones obey no ocean current,
but rather the extreme margins of the Irish Sea, the
limit of Britain. "Beyond the stormy *Hebrides*," it
is as if Lycidas has fallen off the world, or into "the
monstrous world" that recalls antediluvian, pre-
Christian myths or the terrors that lurk just off the
edge of the map. We veer, from that northern border, to the verge of the south. Milton invented his
own giant genius for the occasion. Though "the
fable of *Bellerus* old" suggests a prior, legendary
source, Bellerus seems in fact to have been the
poet's own backward formation from Bellerium,
the Roman name, still preserved on the maps of
Ortelius and Camden, for Land's End. Once again
we move through time as well as space. Milton
manufactures a prehistoric tutelary fable or invisible landmark, apparently for the sole purpose of
denying it any power except that of decorating a
map. But Bellerus does prepare the coming of a
greater, Christian spirit—vision rather than fable—
whose dominion near Land's End suggests that the
mandate of Great Britain derives not from a Roman
settlement but directly from heaven. Saint Michael
guards the border. Moreover, the direction of his
gaze leaves no doubt what he is guarding against.
Namancos and the castle of Bayona represent Britain's eternal enemy (Mercator, between 347 and
348), lying in wait for a chink in the armor through
which Catholic venom can pour. Milton's first published pamphlet, three years after "Lycidas," appeals to the "*Parent* of *Angels* and *Men*" to keep
the old grievances alive:

O thou that after the impetuous rage of five bloody
Inundations, . . . having first welnigh freed us from
Antichristian thraldome, didst build up this *Britannick
Empire* to a glorious and enviable heighth with all her
Daughter Ilands about her, stay us in this felicitic, let
not the obstinacy of our halfe Obedience and will-
Worship bring forth that *Viper* of *Sedition*, that for
these Fourescore Yeares hath been breeding to eat
through the entrals of our *Peace*; but let her cast her
Abortive Spawne without the danger of this travailling
& throbbing *Kingdome*. That we may still remember in
our *solemne Thanksgivings*, how for us the *Northren
Ocean* even to the frozen *Thule* was scatter'd with

the proud Ship-wracks of the *Spanish Armado*, and the very maw of hell ransack't, and made to give up her conceal'd destruction, ere shee could vent it in that horrible and damned blast.

(Of Reformation;
Prose Works 1: 614–15)*

Whirled in the sea like Lycidas, the wreck of the Armada certifies divine protection. Milton contrasts two images: the family circle of the Britannick Empire, self-contained like a throbbing, living being though in danger, through inner weakness, of suckling poisonous intruders, and the once proud, scattered enemy, her engines and explosives dispersed from frozen Thule to fiery Hell, not only visiting the monstrous world beyond the map but staying there. Contraction wins over expansion; the kingdom must draw together, into itself, to give birth to a better future. The five "Inundations"—foreign invasions of Britain—lay stress on the vulnerability of the island empire, surrounded by waves of trouble. But the greatest threat comes from a dire correspondence of inner and outer sedition, the covert alliance of prelate and papist. Only perpetual vigilance will save the nation—a vigilance that attends at once to Spain and home.

How much can one angel be expected to do? "Lycidas" does not ask him to do more than look, nor does it load him with the full burden of theological and political responsibilities. His business is melting with ruth, not arming for war. Yet

Galicia (detail of Mercator, between 347 and 348). Namancos, to the right of Cape Finisterre, and Bayona's hold, below. are kept in view by "the great vision of the guarded mount" in "Lycidas" (161–62). (Photo courtesy of The Newberry Library)

grievance does enter the poem, and Lycidas shoulders his share. His "large recompense" as genius of the shore might be read as compensation for his injuries, but might equally signify the return he will give for being blessed. In any case, this genius will be fully employed, directed to "be good / To all that wander in that perilous flood," like a celestial lifeguard. But one might question what that shore covers and how far that flood extends. Early critics, focusing on the classical genius loci, tended to think of a limited local spirit, as particular as a lighthouse, inhabiting at best one small area of the Welsh coast. The anachronism did not please them; here, as Johnson had charged, a trifling pagan fiction mingled with sacred truth (165). But modern critics have justified Milton by magnifying the scope of his genius. According to A. S. P. Woodhouse, "The 'perilous flood' is this world of chance and change, and Lycidas has already commenced to exercise his beneficent influence on those who travel through it," as on the poet himself (Woodhouse and Bush 730). Today this might be called the orthodox reading, attractive in the boundlessness of its religious and poetic faith. A more literal-minded reader, however, is likely to doubt whether Lycidas or Edward King qualifies as guardian of the whole sublunary world or of *all* that wander. The claim seems hyperbolic; Lycidas may be a Christ figure, but he is not Christ.

Perhaps a compromise is possible. If "that perilous flood" is read as the Irish Sea and the shore as the British coast that bounds it (any place where King's body might yet come to rest), both the excessively local and the excessively cosmic aspects of the genius will be moderated. The poet commissions Lycidas to watch over travelers who face the same peril to which he succumbed and offers hope for more fortunate voyages to Ireland or through life. Nor must these various readings exclude one another. Just as the angel superimposes Lycidas on Saint Michael[13] and "homeward" points toward both Ireland and heaven, so the genius fulfills many different functions. For those enamored, like the swain, with pastoral elegy and its conventions, the spirit connects the past with the present, like a new name penciled on an old map. For those, like many of the contributors to *Justa Edovardo King*, who want assurance of divine justice in a violent, sense-

less world, he restores King's religious vocation in a finer tone, more eloquent than ever after death. And for those, like Milton as he was and would become, who intend to fight for a Britain unified by true religion and the sword, the genius promises angelic sanction and victories on the other side of the "western bay." The journey will be resumed, with better success; the poet-bard makes way for the poet-saint. Twelve years later, with Milton's blessing, an English army would surge across that flood.

Does this reading seem too aggressive for "Lycidas," that tender pastoral song to an oaten flute? Some readers will always prefer a kinder, gentler Milton. But a soft spot for the amenities of the poem ought not to obscure two respects in which it differs from the elegiac norm as well as from the other verse in the memorial volume. The first is its sense of purpose. Confronted by such an untimely, calamitous death, Milton alone insists on finding not merely consolation but a meaning. "Lycidas" earns the right to conclude the book; after a long inundation of tears and metaphysical wheezes, finally one poet speaks of tomorrow. King has inspired him with "eager thought" of what is to be done (189). Conventionally, the swain and his maker collaborate on a poem about poetry and rededicate themselves to the muse. Yet several parts of "Lycidas," most notably Saint Peter's diatribe, seem irrelevant to that interpretation. The poem demands more from its readers. Verse was not King's only calling, nor was Milton the poet to separate the ambitions of art from the call of leadership and faith. The world—and more particularly Britain—needs a new reformation in which poet, saint, and soldier will join. Lycidas, once mounted high, will spend some time singing but more taking care of his flock. So will the swain, as he journeys to "Pastures new." King's mission to convert the Irish must enlist fresh recruits. Milton both justifies God's ways to men and steps out of innocence into a world that waits to be conquered, with the help of his genius. His powerful sense of purpose sets him apart.

The second difference is his emphatic sense of grievance, which sorrow alone cannot account for. To be sure, almost all the elegists in *Justa Edovardo King* sought something to blame for King's death (Williamson 132–47). Since God and providence were too high to tackle, piety usually settled on a safe alternative, like sin, storm, the rock, or (especially) the sea: "All waters are pernicious since King dy'd" (19). But Milton goes further. Not only does he indict "the blind *Fury* with th' abhorred shears," "the Fellon Winds," and "that fatal and perfidious Bark" (75, 91, 100), he also seems to hold a grudge against particular people—for instance, those who do not care enough about poetry. When father Camus poses his leading question—"Ah; Who hath reft (quoth he) my dearest pledge?" (107)—he assumes a personal culprit (*Who*, not *What*), and Saint Peter appears to reply by denouncing the faithless herdsmen, who shove everyone worthy out of the fold. In practical terms, the accused can hardly be counted responsible for Lycidas's misfortune. Yet the poet spreads his charges wide. "Lycidas" is not only lovely but sour; its berries are harsh and crude, and its rose has a canker. The blight of King's death provokes his friend to look for revenge as well as redemption. If Milton finds new strength to fight for the future, he also knows whom and what he is fighting against.

The genius of the shore will be his ally. Despite its benevolent office, both purpose and grievance contribute to the figure. The appointment of a new protector always involves a challenge to the old order. This deity will drive out nymphs and Druids, superseding the local Roman and pagan gods with a universal Christian dispensation. At the same time, the situation of the genius as guardian of the Irish Sea implies a bridge to Ireland, no longer separated from England by a perilous flood but connected by a mutual spirit. Those who "wander" will henceforth feel a force that steers them home. The Welsh and Irish might not want such protection, of course; they might reckon the cost of a colonial guard and prefer to keep their own names on the map. But Milton allows them no choice. Heaven itself ordains this recompense; Lycidas is their fate.

Most guardian spirits, in short, serve national ends, and grievances are often the mark of a nation. Too many theories of nationhood prefer to forget this disturbing historical fact. The imagined community united by bonds of sympathy and interest makes a more satisfying picture than people bound together by bitter memories and common hatreds.

America, its citizens like to think, was and remains a promise of freedom, not a complaint about taxes. Whatever the truth may be, however, an enthusiasm for the former ought not to blind a sensible person to the possibility of the latter. If recent history teaches any lesson about the rise and fall of nations—in the Balkans, for instance—it seems to be the amazing power of old resentments to endure and be revived, even after ideals have died. Nor is it only losers who feel aggrieved; the Serbs and the Afrikaners are martyrs in their stories. Poets help to keep these memories alive, with elegies as well as epics that identify great wrongs and beautiful victims. Even as Milton was mourning a friend, he also was forging a nation.

In this process, a spirit who haunts the shore can be especially useful. Even its ambiguity contributes to its value. Like any border guard, it can shift in a moment from keeping out to keeping in and is never more effective than when its territorial claims can be presented as an extension of communal goodwill. Whether warding against Catholic Spain or melting with ruth at the internal breach that has struck home, Saint Michael stands up for England. Lycidas does still more, precisely because no hint of militancy mars the grace with which he takes responsibility for a sizable chunk of the map. At the same time, his effortless combination of Christian angel with pagan genius pours balm on troubled waters. It is as if he has become a natural feature of the landscape, an eternal part of things as they are, ancient and modern at once, threatening no one no matter how large his recompense may grow. Such spirits are expansive. The comfort they offer spreads from a fringe to the whole wide world.

They also fill a gap in poetry. During the seventeenth century, as the epic gradually died, the old gods lost their positions; Milton himself evicted them and left them homeless. But the decline of classical machinery also challenged Christian poets to find some other source of interest. Conventionally, the gods were what made poems interesting. Inhabiting each river, tree, or rock, they put a human face on inhuman things and lent the mystery or fascination of a story to poor dumb nature. A shore without its genius is just a shore. How to revitalize a verse whose spirits had fled seems a concrete problem for the contributors to *Justa Edovardo*

King. Writing on classical themes in classical genres, and often in Latin, they can hardly resist the stock-in-trade of any university poet, the recycled Phoebus and Echo and Neptune and Arethusa who prove that the student has done his homework. But most of this machinery is boring. It deflects attention from the death of King without creating any narrative interest, a standstill later summarized by Johnson: "how one god asks another god what is become of Lycidas, and how neither god can tell" (164).

At the end of the century, Dryden proposed a replacement for the classical gods. What is needed, he argues, is "as strong an Engine, for the Working up Heroique Poetry, in our Religion, as that of the Ancients has been to raise theirs by all the Fables of their Gods" (19). He finds this engine in the guardian angels of kingdoms. Inspired by the Book of Daniel, as well as by the Neoplatonic eidolons who had been much in the air at Cambridge during Dryden's school days, these "Tutelar *Genij*" could battle without defying God or the truth. Unlike the wars of *Paradise Lost*, moreover, their conflicts admitted some suspense. As Dryden points out, the Lord had allowed the angels of Persia and Greece to do more than hold their own against Michael, Israel's angel. The outcome of national rivalries cannot be predicted; it rouses feverish sporting interest. And human interest could hardly be greater; real people die in these wars. Dryden believed that he had invented a better machine. If a worthy poet should arise, "I am vain enough to think, that I have propos'd a Model to him, by which he may build a Nobler, a more Beautiful and more Perfect Poem, than any yet extant since the Ancients" (21).

It is customary to say that this model was never fulfilled. From another point of view, however, it had already triumphed. By the end of the Renaissance, national mythologies and personifications were so ubiquitous in poetry as to be taken for granted, like the emblem of Britannia on a banner or shield. These guardian angels straddle the globe or are carried in the pockets of voyagers whose poems remind them of the myth they are fighting for: Bellona, Gerusalemme, the Faerie Queene. The spirits of nations transform the epic tradition. In retrospect, Homer's and Vergil's gods came to seem mere adumbrations of Dryden's territorial

angels, as if Athene had only been another name for Athens. The interest of such spirits was particularly sharp when territory was disputed. The guardian who dwells along the line, on the margin or frontier or in limbo, is always probing the limits. Here colonists encounter the unknown and strive to familiarize it with a name—Nieuw Amsterdam, New York. Eventually someone will own the shore. But in the interim, while no one knows whose genius will prevail, guardian angels have to be installed. The uncertainty of these claims is exactly what makes them so interesting. Each genius tries to establish a foothold on alien real estate and thus becomes both emblem and hostage of national glory.

In the century before "Lycidas," as nations began to define themselves by the size and sweep of their armadas, imperialistic genii flourished. Of these the great example is Adamastor. Indeed, Camões created his titan precisely to serve as a great example. Rising up at the center of *The Lusiads*, the passage competes with all the memorable episodes of world literature and demonstrates that a modern Portuguese poet can equal if not surpass them. A remarkable number of critics have concurred. "I believe, that such a Fiction would be thought noble and proper, in all Ages, and in all Nations," Voltaire decided (73), and similar encomiums have been repeated up to the present: "The invention of Adamastor would be enough by itself to put Camões among the world poets. The making of a myth is beyond the powers of all but the greatest" (Bacon 204). Such claims put pressure on the episode. What seems at stake in the greatness of Adamastor is the validation of two related enterprises, the imperialistic epic and imperialism itself.

But who or what is Adamastor? A simple answer would be the Cape of Storms (by no means, in this context, a Cape of Good Hope). As Vasco da Gama recounts the high points of his voyage in canto 5 of *The Lusiads*, he comes to a moment when a mysterious cloud blacked out the whole sky and, awestruck, he prayed to know what it portended. Instantly a monstrous figure appeared, as huge as the Colossus of Rhodes, denounced the Portuguese for violating his forbidden, outlandish retreat, and cursed them by predicting the ruin of future adventurers. Interrupted by a question, "Who are you?," he tells his story:

Eu sou aquele oculto e grande Cabo
A quem chamais vós outros Tormentório,
Que nunca a Ptolomeu, Pompónio, Estrabo,
Plínio, e quantos passaram fui notório.
Aqui toda a africana costa acabo
Neste meu nunca visto promontório,
Que pera o Pólo Antárctico se estende,
A quem vossa ousadia tanto ofende.   (5.50)

I am that secret and gigantic Cape
To which your kind has put the name of Stormy,
Never revealed to Ptolemy, Pomponius, Strabo,
Pliny, and many others long since passed away.
Here all the coast of Africa comes to a stop
In this my never-witnessed promontory,
Which toward the Antarctic pole its reach extends,
And which your insolence so much offends.[14]

"Call me Adamastor," he continues. Once he was
a titan, fighting Neptune for command of the sea.
But one day, on the shore, he saw Thetis naked and
fell helplessly in love. Lured to an assignation, he
ran to embrace her but found himself transformed
into a rock clasping a rock. He fled in shame to the
ends of the earth, but the gods pursued him and
completed his paralysis. Now, metamorphosed into
this remote cape, he is still tormented by the circling
waves, which remind him of Thetis. The story is
over. Abruptly the apparition vanishes, the cloud
breaks, the sighing of the sea is once more inarticu-
late, and the Portuguese sail on. They have rounded
the cape.

Many classical myths are recycled by this episode, particularly (as commentators have pointed
out) the woes of the cyclops Polyphemus, not only
as the savage guard of the hinterland where Odysseus trespasses but as the frustrated lover of Galatea
(Ramalho 27–44). Yet such reminiscences ought
not to paper over the wildness and strangeness of
the passage. Adamastor, in every regard, is a liminal figure. Camões takes pains to keep everything
on the edge or teetering between worlds. Even the
classical myths, Maurice Bowra notes, balance
against the ogres of fairy tales and romance (123–
26). Geographically, Adamastor stands for the place
where maps lose their potency—here be monsters;
historically, for an unknown part of the past, a legend and reality concealed from the ancients and yet
to be explored; epistemologically, for a point beyond which human perceptions fail; theologically,

for the forbidden. But above all he exists on the
border between the animate and the inanimate, between the personification that responds to human
desire and the nature whose immensity and violence reflect nothing but themselves. The difference
between his epic and all the others, Camões insisted, was that his alone told the truth. This was
hubris, of course. Yet Adamastor does emerge from
the landscape and dissolve into the elements, as if
his whole being were no more than an optical illusion. Now you see him, now you don't. His reality,
like that of the *Ding an sich*, depends on the extent
to which he cannot be apprehended.

The most impressive instance of this liminal effect occurs at his introduction, when the terrified
gaze of the mariners, enveloped by darkness, literally conjures his colossal figure out of the air, while
his voice growls from the depths of the ocean, accompanied by the creeping of Portuguese flesh. A
shudder of sublimity passes from observer to
reader. If Longinus had not been discovered, just
when Camões left on the voyage from which he
brought back his poem, this passage alone might
have inaugurated the vogue of the sublime.[15] But a
genius of the shore can also work more subtle
magic. Consider his answer to the question "Who
are you?" Translations fail to do justice to these
riddles. "I am that hidden and vast Cape which you
call Tormentório." The final word means "stormy,"
but in Portuguese as in English the sense of torment
or anguish clings to it. In fact, the Portuguese had
good reasons for using that name. Bartolomeu Dias
had christened the Cape of Storms after first rounding it, in 1488. As the spirit of the cape has already
"predicted," he will soon have his revenge on the
sailor who dared to discover him: on the Portuguese
expedition that followed da Gama's, in 1500, Dias
would die in a storm near the cape. By then King
João had renamed it the Cape of Good Hope. But
euphemism could not disguise the perils or torments of Portuguese mariners, to whom the cape
would always threaten storms. Meanwhile, the
spirit has not divulged his "real" name, which is
wrapped in darkness like the hidden or secret
(*oculto*) cape itself. Instead, he reflects the voyagers' forebodings back on themselves.

A similar finesse bears on the name he does assume. "Adamastor is my name," translators say, or

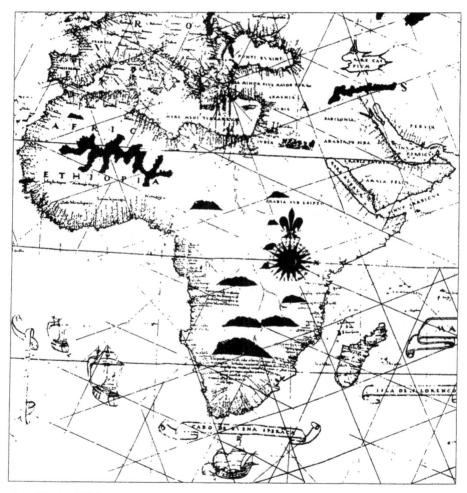

Africa (Ribeiro). This Spanish navigational map provides mariners with detailed information about the coastline; aside from a few landmarks. the interior of the continent remains mysterious. The Cape of Good Hope. conspicuously labeled. offers a passage to India and the east. In the detail of Europe, Spain dominates the Iberian peninsula, ominously leaving no room for Portugal. (Photo courtesy of The Newberry Library)

"I am Adamastor." But the text reads, "Chamei-me
Adamastor" 'Call me Adamastor.'[16] Like "Call me
Ishmael," the phrase leaves room for doubt; the
spirit might be choosing an alias. If so, he chose
cleverly, for the Greek root means "unconquerable"
or "untamed." This genius of the shore refuses to
be touched by visitors, let alone to offer them protection; even his name implies a stony resistance to
civilization. Once again the figure stands at the border of the unknown, drawing a line that can be cir-
cumvented but never crossed. At the same time, he
nurses a grievance. Torment, longing, resentment
fill his being with a wild contempt that Europeans
will try in vain to conquer or tame. Whatever they
call him, he will respond with nothing but storms.

What does the figure stand for? To twentieth-
century readers, in the aftermath of the long colonial shipwreck, the answer has seemed irresistible.
Adamastor is the Other; the dark, unconquerable
continent; the victims of imperialism; the blacks
who already inhabit the land but whom *The Lusiads* barely notices. Camões had prophesied better
than he knew.[17] In modern South African writing,
the figure has played a major part. One crucial
poem, in Roy Campbell's volume *Adamastor*, is
"Rounding the Cape":

> Across his back, unheeded, we have broken
> Whole forests: heedless of the blood we've spilled,
> In thunder still his prophecies are spoken,
> In silence, by the centuries, fulfilled.

The "terrific shade" is lord of "the powers of darkness"—specifically, "Night, the Negro." More recently, André Brink's clever story *Cape of Storms:
The First Life of Adamastor* has reimagined the encounter of European and African from the landward
side, narrated by a native Adamastor. These versions
revitalize the myth. Whether expressing the bad
conscience of transplanted Europeans, as in Campbell, or the absurd failure of the colonizers to impose their own meaning on an eternal culture that
regards them as mere birds of passage, as in Brink,
they cast aside the limited interest of Portuguese
nationalism in favor of global sweep. Most of all,
they do justice to Adamastor's grievance. Of course
he hated the voyagers and their gods, bound to
break his culture, ecology, and people. Stuck in the

midst of the epic like a bone in the throat, his grievance constitutes the work's one lasting emotion.

That grievance can hardly have been what Camões had in mind, however. If he is the ventrilo-
quist who makes the monster speak, he must have
been voicing some resentment of his own, a fury
on behalf of Portuguese interests as well as against
them. The genius of the shore can authorize bewildering conflicts of interpretation, as unrelenting as
the sea against the land. Indeed, he might be taken
rhetorically for the figure of undecidability. How
then can we hope to resolve it?

In practical terms, there are two main ways of
reading the function of Adamastor in *The Lusiads*.
The first would stress his paradoxical role in glori-
fying the Portuguese, or at any rate in assuring them
that their sufferings make sense. This awesome, inhuman being at the end of the world, whom they
alone have dared to confront, can speak their language, knows all about them, and can reel off details of their future disasters. Surely this flatters
them. Exemplifying the power of narrative and of
the gods to master a senseless world, personifying
the unknowable, Adamastor seems curiously consoling. Even his curse, by predicting misfortunes
that by the time of Camões had already happened,
in what has been called the mode of preauthen-
ticated prophecy (Lipking 88–89), affirms the
inevitable logic that underlies history. Far from
meaningless, the wreck of Dias proves how much
the Fates take heed of Portugal. Moreover, a highly
literate theogony props up Adamastor's story. At
the tip of Africa, the gods in residence are not
Tsui-Goab, Gaunab, or Heitsi-Eibib but Jupiter,
Neptune, and Thetis.[18] How fortunate for the Portuguese! Not only are they competent to understand
the story, through being well versed in Ovid, they
also hold in reserve a more powerful god, who has
always kept pagans in their place. Refreshed by the
shudder that Adamastor summoned, they will now
sail on with new purpose.

Hence the genius of the shore, in this reading,
functions as a defense mechanism that shields the
poet and his audience from having to face the brutal truth that storms and death and oppression happen, that people vanish into the wilderness forever,
and that neither the gods nor nature cares. A similar mystification might be attributed to "Lycidas."

After the remorseless passage in which the body is hurled about in the sea, Milton puts a better face on reality, dresses up Lycidas in fancy clothes, and assures himself and the reader that poetry matters. Meanwhile, the rocks along the shore await their next victim, indifferent to the genius who is supposed to blunt their edge. Personifications change nothing. Even the mighty voice of Adamastor, when heard without rhetorical amplification, sounds like a poet whistling in the dark.

The defense includes colonialism as well. In an impressive analysis, David Quint argues that the figure of Adamastor serves imperialistic ideology in two ways. First, by assimilating native African resistance with the hostility of nature, it "overlooks and suppresses the Portuguese aggression that kindled the resistance in the first place" (118), as if blind, unmotivated fury led the Africans to fight for their land and as if the victors bore no responsibility for defending themselves with acts of violence. Second, Adamastor can also be read as "the poet's daring and aggrandizing figure of his own daring and greatness and that of his Portuguese heroes" or as "a mirror image of the Portuguese victor himself" (124). Either way, the epic's ideology appropriates any point of view that might support the loser. All Adamastor knows how to do is curse, and European civilization taught him that too.

Yet something essential seems missing from this account, and it is grievance. For all Camões's glorification of the Portuguese, *The Lusiads* does not sound any unequivocal note of triumph. Rounding the cape, on their way to one of the great imperial and commercial killings of all time, the voyagers pause for a forecast of everything that will go wrong for the next fifty years. Somehow the Portuguese are victors who feel like victims. Camões had plenty of reason to subscribe to that sense of history. Even the most optimistic reading of *The Lusiads* has tended to view the glory of da Gama's voyage as a reproach to the degenerate Portugal of the mid-sixteenth century, fat, at odds, and waiting to be plucked. The poem feeds off grievances. Some of these might be personal.[19] Whether or not Camões's father died at Goa after a shipwreck, as legend claims, the colonial enterprise had led the poet himself not to fortune but to bankruptcy, the loss of his right eye, exile, and the seedy alienation of a

Graham Greene hero, who might like the idea of his country but could not manage to make a life there. Camões also identified his wretchedness with that of Portugal, as in his famous (if apocryphal) last words, that he was "content to die not only in her but with her" (in the year of his death, 1580, the country would be annexed by Philip II of Spain). This affinity for disaster helped establish Camões as the national poet.[20] For Portugal might be defined as a series of grievances: against Spain, rival European empires, and especially the Moors. These enemies sustain the image of a people whose defeats, no less than their victories, spread their fame as crusaders and martyrs. The nation is small, and it is alone. Hence, at the moment of their greatest success, the Portuguese always remember that most of the world is conspiring against them.

Adamastor tells them that winners will also be losers; that is the second main way of reading his function. Not only does he curse their presumption and savor their future losses, he reminds them to feel sorry for themselves, thereby setting the tone of much of the poem. A monstrous, contagious self-pity suffuses his story as well as what it implies about the fate of the Portuguese. Indeed, an unsympathetic listener might find comedy in the tale of a giant who pursues a beautiful young nymph and tries to win her by force, only to be outwitted and reduced to impotence. Nor can the vanguard of a colonial empire expect much sympathy when its schemes for conquest and profit meet resistance from the elements and the natives. Yet readers rarely scoff at the pain of someone who eternally longs for something unattainable. *The Lusiads* is an epic of longing. Its voyagers may blaze a trail for later profiteers, but fame puts nothing in their own pockets; and when Camões rewards them, at the end, with the magic Island of Love and a vision of the future exploits of their country, no one can miss the air of unreality. An alternative, heartfelt conclusion has already capped canto 7, where the poet laments his wanderings and poverty and lack of recognition. Not even Adamastor felt more sorry for himself. Dreams of glory hold both Camões and his epic captive; longing remains their most powerful emotion.

The pitiful, helpless giant and the self-glorifying, self-pitying nation—these two sufferers seem made for each other. Hence their torment serves to palliate or humanize the appropriations of the imperialistic epic. A memento mori accompanies the Portuguese wherever they go. From the subaltern's point of view, to be sure, such remorse might seem no more convincing than the weeping of the Walrus as he gobbles down every oyster. Yet colonizers do suffer. Whether or not Edward King's family exploited the Irish, whether or not Bartolomeu Dias opened the way for European domination of Africa, each of them was just as victimized by drowning and ended up just as dead. Nor does the patriotic fervor of Milton and Camões, or the possibility that neither was a very nice person, deprive them of the right to grieve. The myths these poets created still have the troubling power of titanism and of nightmare. Nations destroy themselves as well as others. At several crucial points of *The Lusiads*, including the very moment when da Gama's fleet sets sail, dissenting voices curse the whole colonial enterprise and predict that it will bring about the ruin of Portugal. Many historians would agree with those voices: the empire stretched the nation beyond endurance until it snapped like a string. At any rate, wanderers on the perilous flood do face real dangers. When a ship of state founders, harmless seamen and passengers pay with their lives.

In a famous image that Benedict Anderson borrowed to conclude the first edition of his influential *Imagined Communities: Reflections on the Origin and Spread of Nationalism*, Walter Benjamin describes the Angel of History, whose face is turned toward the past and who sees nothing but wreckage hurled at his feet.[21] That angel is also the genius of the shore, a guardian who presides over the wreck of ship after ship. Despite hoping for bright national futures, Camões and Milton turn their faces backward, toward the calamities and grievances that compose their historical myths of nationhood. The genius of the shore remembers how much he has to resent. Meanwhile, a storm from Paradise, a storm called progress, blows him irresistibly into the future. New nations, new enemies, will arise there, and the shore will become a site of endless territorial contests. Even fresh woods and pastures new are likely to be already inhabited by other shepherds and their gods, ready to fight for possession. Cromwell would have to finish what Lycidas

started. Like the poet, the Angel of History cannot predict what will happen tomorrow. Yet the storm goes on, and perhaps it is safe to guess that, whatever else happens, tomorrow more ships will come to grief on that shore.

Notes

[1] Helgerson stresses the "Whiggish" ideology of British mapmaking (105–47).

[2] Martz notes that the young Milton's "hope that a single great nation might lead the world toward true Christian greatness" led to "his early plans for a national epic of England that would be 'doctrinal and exemplary' to a nation of such a destiny—a poem that might do for England what Camoens had done for the history of his own small seafaring nation" (53–54).

[3] Franson's hypothetical itinerary for the voyage concludes that the "ship collided with Coal Rock two miles off the northwest coast of Anglesey" (57).

[4] William Chappell, the Laudian provost of Trinity College and King's former tutor, was accused of various offenses against the native Irish, among them suppressing the Irish lecture.

[5] Postlethwaite and Campbell provide the fullest account of Edward King's life and poems. The useful brief biographies of the Kings in the *DNB* are supplemented by Mattimoe's information on the later history of the family, and Barnard includes the Kings in his relatively sympathetic view of English policy during the Interregnum.

[6] "It is expedient that some discreet ministers of their own countrymen be first sent amongst them, which, by their mild persuasions and instructions as also by their sober life and conversation, may draw them, first to understand and afterwards to embrace the doctrine of their salvation" (Spenser 161). Canny analyzes the role of "this missionary endeavour" in the development of Anglo-Irish identity. Milton refers to *A View of the Present State of Ireland* twice (*Prose Works* 1: 465, 496).

[7] Henley's *Spenser in Ireland* is usefully supplemented by recent perspectives, both historical and literary, in Coughlan's *Spenser and Ireland*. Quilligan compares Spenser's apology for colonial violence in Ireland with Milton's apology for regicide but ignores Milton's attitude toward Ireland (12).

[8] *Observations upon the Articles of Peace* (1649). "Milton's complicity in this dark chapter of Anglo-Irish relations" (123) is discussed by Corns.

[9] *Eikonoklastes* (1649). By commanding the use of the Prayer Book in 1637, Charles provoked the Scottish National Covenant of the following year. Hence his enemies—including Milton—often regarded 1637 as the year in which Charles revealed his tendencies toward popery and his indifference to unifying Britain. Leonard argues that "Lycidas" was affected by Laud's persecution of Puritans in the summer and autumn of 1637.

220 The Genius of the Shore: Lycidas, Adamastor, and the Poetics of Nationalism

On Milton's early radicalism. see Haller (288–323) and Wilding (7–27).

[10]Milton's early pamphlet *Of Education* (1644) argues that a good course of study would help stabilize the commonwealth. Significantly, both Edward and Sir Robert King took an interest in improving education in Ireland (Barnard 215).

[11]Daniel 10.21. DiLella discusses Michael's function as protector in *The Anchor Bible* (273, 282–84).

[12]On Milton's changing attitudes toward Druids. see Owen (52–58).

[13]Pigman builds a case for identifying the angel with Lycidas rather than with Michael (109–24).

[14]All translations from *Os Lusiadas* are my own. Pierce comments on the passage as a whole.

[15]"The fiction of the apparition of the Cape of Tempests, in sublimity and awful grandeur of imagination. stands unsurpassed in human composition" (Mickle 63).

[16]The episode was a great favorite of Melville, whose friend Jack Chase, Captain of the Top on the *United States*, is supposed to have recited the original to his shipmates while rounding the cape. Melville, who served under Chase in 1843–44. later dedicated *Billy Budd* to him; a passage that compares the menacing "genius" of the postrevolutionary, Napoleonic wars to "Camoens' 'Spirit of the Cape'" may have been written in Chase's honor. Andrews argues that by alluding to "Cape Tormentoto, Melville merges *The Lusiad* integrally into *Moby-Dick*" (92).

[17]According to one eminent commentator on *The Lusiads*, the relentlessly allegorizing Manuel de Faria e Sousa, Adamastor stands for Mahomet, which explains the titan's barbarism and hostility (540–66). The author may well have intended this reading.

[18]The African gods play roles in Brink's novel. Camões's mixture of pagan and Christian gods is criticized by Greene (219–31) and defended by Sims.

[19]For analysis of the biographical tradition on Camões, see Saraiva. In English. Freitas supplies much dependable information, and Moser provides a historical context for Camões's feelings of victimization.

[20]Consider the mixture of hubris and martyrdom in a speech by the governor-general of Angola in 1936: "I am going to swear here, on this sacred book. the *Lusiadas*, on the Bible of our country. the loyalty of all the Portuguese in Angola. I swear that we, the Portuguese of Angola, will carry out. no matter what the emergency, or how difficult the sacrifice. our duty as patriots and that we know how to die, sacrificing our very lives for the lands of Portugal, which want to be and will always be Portuguese" (Duffy 270–71). Helgerson comments on the extraordinary embrace by the Portuguese of Camões's vision of their heroic destiny. a vision that "blatantly contradicted the reality of its author's experience" (163). That reality, in Helgerson's view. consists of the commercial interests repressed by the aristocratic governing classes.

[21]Benjamin 257–58 The second edition of *Imagined Communities* adds chapters that deal with the map and with memory, both crucial. this essay argues, to the nationalism of Renaissance poets.

Works Cited

Anderson, Benedict. *Imagined Communities: Reflections on the Origin and Spread of Nationalism*. 2nd ed. London: Verso. 1991.

Andrews, Norwood. *Melville's Camões*. Bonn: Bouvier, 1989.

Bacon, Leonard. The Lusiads *of Luiz de Camões*. New York: Hispanic Soc. of Amer., 1950.

Barnard, T. C *Cromwellian Ireland*. London: Oxford UP. 1975.

Benjamin, Walter "Theses on the Philosophy of History." *Illuminations*. Ed. Hannah Arendt. Trans. Harry Zohn. New York: Schocken, 1969. 253–64

Bowra, C. M. *From Virgil to Milton*. London: Macmillan, 1945.

Brink, André. *Cape of Storms: The First Life of Adamastor*. New York: Simon, 1993.

Camden, William. *Britain. Or A Chorographicall Description of the Most flourishing Kingdomes, England, Scotland, and Ireland, and the Ilands adioyning. out of the depth of Antiquitie*. Trans. Philémon Holland. London, 1610.

Camões, Luís de. *Os Lusiadas*. Ed. Frank Pierce. Oxford: Clarendon, 1973.

Campbell, Roy. "Rounding the Cape." *Adamastor*. London: Faber, 1930. 38.

Canny, Nicholas. "Edmund Spenser and the Development of an Anglo-Irish Identity." *Yearbook of English Studies* 13 (1983): 1–19.

Corns, Thomas N. "Milton's *Observations upon the Articles of Peace*: Ireland under English Eyes." *Politics, Poetics, and Hermeneutics in Milton's Prose*. Ed. David Loewenstein and James Grantham Turner. Cambridge: Cambridge UP. 1990. 123–34.

Coughlan, Patricia. ed. *Spenser and Ireland*. Cork: Cork UP. 1989.

DiLella, Alexander A., commentator. *The Book of Daniel*. Trans. Louis F. Hartman. Garden City: Doubleday, 1978. Vol. 23 of *The Anchor Bible*.

Dryden, John. "Discourse concerning the Original and Progress of Satire." *The Works of John Dryden*. Vol. 4. Berkeley: U of California P, 1974. 3–90.

Duffy, James. *Portuguese Africa*. Cambridge: Harvard UP, 1968.

Evans. J. Martin. *The Road from Horton: Looking Backwards in "Lycidas."* Victoria: U of Victoria, 1983.

Faria e Sousa, Manuel de, ed. Lusiadas *de Luis de Camoens*. Vol. 2. Madrid, 1639.

Fletcher, Harris Francis. *The Intellectual Development of John Milton*. Vol. 2. Urbana: U of Illinois P, 1961.

Franson. J. Karl. "The Fatal Voyage of Edward King. Milton's Lycidas." *Milton Studies* 25 (1989): 43–67.

Freitas, William. *Camoens and His Epic: A Historic, Geographic, and Cultural Survey*. Stanford: Inst. of Hispanic Amer. and Luso-Brazilian Studies, Stanford U, 1963.

Greene, Thomas M. *The Descent from Heaven*. New Haven: Yale UP. 1963

Haller, William. *The Rise of Puritanism*. New York: Columbia UP. 1938.

Helgerson. Richard. *Forms of Nationhood: The Elizabethan Writing of England*. Chicago: U of Chicago P. 1992.

Henley, Pauline. *Spenser in Ireland*. Cork: Cork UP, 1928.

Johnson, Samuel. *Lives of the English Poets* Ed. G. B. Hill. Vol. 1. Oxford: Clarendon, 1905.

Justa Edovardo King Ed E. C. Mossner. New York: Columbia UP, 1939.

Leonard, John. "'Trembling Ears': The Historical Moment of 'Lycidas.'" *Journal of Medieval and Renaissance Studies* 21 (1991): 59–81.

Lipking, Lawrence. *The Life of the Poet*. Chicago: U of Chicago P, 1981.

Martz, Louis L. "Camoens and Milton." *Ocidente* 83 (Nov. 1972): 45–59.

Masson, David. *The Life of John Milton*. Vol. 1. London: Macmillan, 1881.

Mattimoe, Cyril. *North Roscommon—Its People and Past*. Boyle: Roscommon Herald, 1992.

Mercator, Gerard. *Atlas; or a Geographicke description, of the Regions, Countries and Kingdomes of the World*. Trans. Henry Hexham. Amsterdam, 1630.

Mickle, W. J. The Lusiad; or, *The Discovery of India*. Vol. 2. London, 1798.

Milton, John. *Complete Prose Works*. New Haven: Yale UP, 1953.
———. "Lycidas." *Milton's "Lycidas."* Ed. Scott Elledge. New York: Harper, 1966. 3–11.
———. *Paradise Lost. Complete Poems and Major Prose*. Ed. Merritt Y. Hughes. New York: Odyssey, 1957. 211–469

Moser, Gerald M. "Grumbling Veterans of an Empire." *Empire in Transition: The Portuguese World in the Time of Camões*. Ed. Alfred Hower and R. A. Preto-Rodas. Gainesville: U of Florida P, 1985. 97–105.

Ortelius, Abraham. *Theatrum Orbis Terrarum. The Theatre of the Whole World*. London, 1606

Owen, A. L. *The Famous Druids*. Oxford: Clarendon, 1962.

Pierce, Frank. "Camões' Adamastor." *Hispanic Studies in Honour of Joseph Manson*. Ed. D. M. Atkinson and A. H. Clarke. Oxford: Dolphin, 1972. 207–15.

Pigman, G. W., III. *Grief and English Renaissance Elegy*. Cambridge: Cambridge UP, 1985

Postlethwaite, Norman, and Gordon Campbell, eds. "Edward King. Milton's 'Lycidas'' Poems and Documents." *Milton Quarterly* 28 (1994): 77–111.

Quilligan, Maureen. *Milton's Spenser: The Politics of Reading*. Ithaca: Cornell UP, 1983.

Quint, David. *Epic and Empire. Politics and Generic Form from Virgil to Milton*. Princeton: Princeton UP, 1993.

Radzinowicz, Mary Ann. *Toward "Samson Agonistes": The Growth of Milton's Mind*. Princeton: Princeton UP, 1978.

Ramalho, Américo da Costa. *Estudos Camonianos*. Lisbon: Instituto Nacional de Investigação Científica, 1980

Ribeiro, Diogo. Map 1527. *Portugaliae Monumenta Cartographica* Ed. Armando Cortesão and Avelino Teixeiro da Mota Vol. 1. Lisbon: n p., 1960. Plate 38.

Saraiva, José Hermano. *Vida ignorada de Camões*. Lisbon: Europa-América, 1979.

Sims, James H. "Christened Classicism in *Paradise Lost* and *The Lusiads*." *Comparative Literature* 24 (1972): 338–56.

Spenser, Edmund. *A View of the Present State of Ireland*. Ed. W. L. Renwick. Oxford: Clarendon, 1970.

Voltaire. *An Essay on Epick Poetry*. London, 1727.

Walzer, Michael. *The Revolution of the Saints*. Cambridge: Harvard UP, 1965

Whiting, G. W. *Milton's Literary Milieu*. Chapel Hill: U of North Carolina P, 1939

Wilding, Michael. *Dragon's Teeth: Literature in the English Revolution* Oxford: Clarendon, 1987.

Williamson, George. *Seventeenth-Century Contexts*. Chicago: U of Chicago P, 1969.

Woodhouse, A. S. P., and Douglas Bush, eds. *A Variorum Commentary on the Poems of John Milton*. Vol. 2. London: Routledge, 1972.

241

THE ARGUMENT OF MILTON'S *COMUS*

A. S. P. Woodhouse

NO complete study of *Comus* exists. Such a study would necessitate four separate steps. The first is an examination of *Comus* in the light of the essential tradition of the masque, the inherited pattern which Milton adopts (having indeed no choice in this instance) and of course adapts to his purposes. The second is an effort to determine more precisely the content of the poem, what it is that Milton is saying or, as I have called it, the argument of *Comus*. The processes of criticism are, or ought to be, self-conscious: it is their only safeguard. So one would avoid the pitfall of attempting an impossible separation of form and content, and merely centre attention first on the one and then on the other, with the object of ultimately bringing them together and restoring a sense of the poem's unity and individuality. The third step is in that direction; for it is an effort to discover the relation for Milton, and in this poem, of experience, thought, and art. The fourth step views the poem once more as an independent unit and applies to its interpretation whatever has been discovered in the first three stages of the examination. If anyone wishes to contend that only the fourth step is literary criticism, and the first three at best preparations for literary criticism, I shall not think the point worth arguing—or the preliminary steps less than necessary. In the present essay I can deal with only one of the questions raised: what it is that Milton is saying, or the argument of *Comus*.[1]

I

I will not pause to establish on theoretic grounds what is so abundantly evident in experience, that intellectual content, wherever it contributes to imaginative and emotional content, becomes

[1] I have only one substantial debt to record. It is to Professor J. H. Hanford's "The Youth of Milton" (*Studies in Shakespeare, Milton and Donne*, University of Michigan Publications, Language and Literature, I, 87-163, especially 139-43, 152). Since I shall have occasion to disagree with him at some points, I wish to express here not only my deep sense of obligation, but also my conviction that his is in general the wisest and most penetrating essay on Milton ever written. In dealing with Spenser I have been helped by the *Variorum Spenser* and by Mr C. S. Lewis's brilliant *Allegory of Love* (1936). My friend Professor Douglas Bush has made some very valuable criticisms and suggestions.

an indispensable factor in the total aesthetic effect of the poem. But I must pause to state the conditions which attach to intellectual content when it becomes a subject of investigation. As a vehicle of ideas poetry labours under a disability, but also enjoys a unique advantage. No poem perhaps—certainly not one whose form is as limiting as the masque—can hope to present ideas with complete precision or to make all their implications specific. On the other hand, poetry has powers of suggestion denied to prose and can convey more than is fully stated or proved. The student of thought in poetry will take due cognizance of both these facts: he will seek to draw forth the argument, to render its implications more precise and specific than he finds them, and in so doing he will be guided by the suggestions which the poet has been able to give, here by an image, there by an overtone.

Willing response, however, to the poet's suggestion is not by itself enough. Everybody is familiar with the common criterion for judging the adequacy of a work of popular art: that it should be self-sufficient, should contain within itself whatever is necessary for comprehending it. On the level of ideas, however, this test cannot be very strictly applied. Often one must look outside the poem for what may be called the intellectual frame of reference, common to the poet and his contemporary readers, but lost to a later age: the thing taken for granted in the thought content as the instinctively apprehended capacities and limits of the particular *genre* are taken for granted in the aesthetic effect. The intellectual frame of reference may not be set forth in the poem; but indications of it will be present, and its correct formulation will be a key to unlock the poem's meaning, while its ability to do this will, in turn, test the correctness of the formulation.

There is nothing esoteric about the intellectual frame of reference for *Comus*. It will serve for innumerable works of literature in the seventeenth and earlier centuries and is, indeed, indispensable for understanding their thought—the thought of Spenser, for example, not less than the thought of Milton. Within this frame of reference there is room for every degree of difference in attitude and emphasis: it is a frame of reference, not a body of doctrine, and is tacitly assumed not by the religious only, but by the secular and even the anti-religious writer, who may deny the reality of what I shall describe as "the order of grace" but rarely has the hardihood to ignore it as a concept. The frame of reference may be formulated with sufficient precision in this way. There are in the life of man, and in the vast array of circumstances which form the setting of the human drama, two levels or, better perhaps, two orders of existence, the natural and the religious, or what we may call the order of nature and the order of grace. To the religious mind, of course, each is dependent on the power and providence of God, but in a manner sufficiently different to warrant the restriction of the term *religious* (which means Christian) to one order only. To the order of nature belongs not only the whole physical world, but also man himself considered simply as a denizen of that world. The rule of its government is expressed not only in the physical laws of nature, but in natural ethics (in what is significantly called the Law of Nature), and even in natural, as opposed to revealed, religion.   This order is apprehended in experience and interpreted by reason; and it has its own wisdom, for upon the simple law of nature, by experience and reason, is erected the ethical system of a Plato, an Aristotle, or a Cicero.   It has its own institutions, of which the highest is the state; but this is an aspect of the order of nature which need not detain us here. . . . To the order of grace belongs man in his character of supernatural being, with all that concerns his salvation and the two dispensations, the old and the new.   The rule of its government is the revealed Law of God, received and interpreted by faith, which includes a special kind of experience, called religious experience.   It also has its appropriate institution, the Church, which, like the state, does not concern us here. . . . Now on the precise relation subsisting between the order of nature and the order of grace a great variety of opinion is possible and, especially in the seventeenth century, is met. There are those who insist on the sharp contrast and wide divergence of the two orders; and this class includes individuals and sects of opposite principles.   The ascetic and the rigorist (for in this they agree, though not in the action that it entails) insist on the divergence, to depress nature and exalt grace; the naturalist, to exalt nature and depress grace, finding the demands of the higher order "unnatural" and denying their validity. There are those who insist on the clear-cut separation of the two orders with the intention of accepting them both (though perhaps with different degrees of conviction) while avoiding all inference from the one to the other. Such is the fideist, who takes the order of grace on authority, but in the order of nature pursues his experimental and sceptical way;

the Baconian scientist, with his two philosophies, natural and divine; the Puritan extremist, reactionary in the realm of grace, progressivist in the realm of nature. All of these—though for different ends—apply what I have elsewhere called the *principle of segregation*.[2] Opposed to them is the large class of thinkers who (with many differing shades of emphasis and inference) agree in responding to the profound human instinct for a unified view of life, and who refuse to divorce the two orders. They insist that the order of grace is the superstructure whose foundations are securely laid in nature; that there is no interval between the two orders, which merge in an area common to both; that grace comes to perfect nature (an idea including discipline), not to destroy it; that man's well-being must be defined in terms of the two orders simultaneously,[3] and that what is for his good as a natural being cannot be for his harm as a supernatural, or *vice versa*. This is the position of the Christian humanist, whose special relevance to *Comus* will in due course appear. What we are concerned with now is simply the intellectual frame of reference afforded by the conception of the two orders of nature and grace; for to one of the two, or to an area common to them both, every idea and every value must pertain. Only in reference to this framework can the argument of *Comus* be fully understood.

The common assumption, correct so far as it goes, is that the argument of *Comus* has for its theme chastity. But more careful examination reveals that coupled with the doctrine of chastity (not identified with it as a careless reader might suppose, but coupled with it) are two others: a doctrine of temperance and continence (the "holy dictates of spare Temperance") and a doctrine of virginity ("the sage And serious doctrine of Virginity"). When these facts are brought into relation with the intellectual frame of reference, we observe that temperance and continence are virtues on the natural level; that chastity, the central virtue of the poem, moves in an area common to nature and grace; and that the doctrine of virginity belongs exclusively to the order of grace, which in the poem it is used to illustrate and even symbolize.

[2] *Puritanism and Liberty* (1938), introd. 39-40, 58-9, 84-5.
[3] Cf. Milton's assertion, in his seventh Prolusion, that "nothing can be recounted justly among the causes of our happiness unless in some way it takes into consideration both that eternal and this temporal life"; and his twofold definition of the end of education (*Prose Works*, Bohn ed., III, 464, 467).

Or, if one may resort to a simple visual formulation, what we have is this:

(1) The *doctrine of temperance*, which, in the circumstances presented in the poem, is necessarily:

(2) A *doctrine of continence*, which, to render it secure, and to translate it from a negative to a positive conception, requires to be completed by: } **Nature**

(3) The *doctrine of chastity*, which is thus grounded in nature. This is, moreover, elaborated, still on the level of nature, in terms of the Platonic philosophy, to the point where it can be taken over by Christianity, which sanctions the natural virtues and, by the addition of grace, carries them on to a new plane. Of this new plane } **Nature and Grace**

(4) The *doctrine of virginity* becomes in the poem the illustration and symbol (but not the complete synonym). } **Grace**

We are concerned here with the argument of *Comus*, and not with the relation of that argument to Milton's personal experience. But it happens, most fortunately, that we are able to test our formulation of the intellectual frame of reference as it is applied in *Comus*, by comparing it with the celebrated account in retrospect which Milton gave of his experiences during the period when the poem was written. This account, in the *Apology for Smectymnuus*, was offered in rebuttal of the charge of youthful incontinence made by his adversaries, but it attaches itself to Milton's conception of the ideal poet which he sought to become, one whose life was itself a true poem. Here we find him commencing on the natural level, passing (not without aid from Plato) to the verge of the religious level, and finally moving securely thereon: we find the doctrine of continence bringing the doctrine of chastity, and at last the doctrine of virginity, in its wake, as the poet ascends from the order of nature, through an area where the two orders meet, to the order of grace. As in *Comus*, we may describe the doctrine of chastity as the central theme; and, even if we discard the reservation in the *Apology* in favour of the married state as belonging to a time after the poem was written, we shall still recognize that the doctrine of virginity is not regarded as the whole of Christian teaching on the subject of chastity, though it is regarded as a doctrine specifically Christian and hence one that would be eligible as a symbol of the order of grace. Giving due weight to the direction of his "natural disposition," Milton tells us how he was led onward

and upward, first by the writings of the poets, then by the philosophy of Plato, with its "abstracted sublimities" (a phrase we shall
have occasion to remember), and to his final goal by Christianity,
its plain injunctions and "high mysteries" (another phrase to be
remembered)—that Christianity which evidently confirms, while it
transcends, the dictates of natural ethics and the highest wisdom
of the philosophers. Milton writes in part:

Thus from the laureat fraternity of the poets, riper years and the ceaseless round
of study led me to the shady spaces of philosophy; but chiefly to the divine
volumes of Plato and his equal, Xenophon: where if I should tell ye what I
learned of chastity and love, I mean that which is truly so, whose charming cup
is only virtue, which she bears in her hand to those who are worthy; (the rest are
cheated with a thick intoxicating potion, which a certain sorceress, the abuser
of love's name, carries about;) and how the first and chiefest office of love begins
and ends in the soul, producing those happy twins of her divine generation,
knowledge and virtue; with such abstracted sublimities as these, it might be
worth your listening. . . .[4]

"Last of all," he continues, "not in time, but as perfection is last,
that care was ever had of me not to be negligently trained in the
precepts of the Christian religion." And these precepts confirmed
and built upon "a certain reservedness of natural disposition, and
moral discipline learnt out of the noblest philosophy," which alone
would have been sufficient to ensure first a disdain of incontinence,
then a love of chastity. But now he was able to receive the doctrine of chastity on the religious level, "unfolding those chaste and
high mysteries, . . . that 'the body is for the Lord, and the Lord
for the body.' " "Nor did I slumber," he concludes, "over that
place expressing such high rewards of ever accompanying the Lamb
with those celestial songs to others unapprehensible but not to
those who were not defiled with women, which doubtless means
fornication; for marriage must not be called a defilement." Continence may be achieved on the basis of natural ethics (and be
taught by those good teachers the poets, though not religiously
inspired). Chastity, even in its "abstracted sublimities," may be
learned from the wise and virtuous pagan philosophers (also poets
in their way), who move likewise on the natural level but strain
upward to the very verge of the religious. And these teachings
Christianity by its precepts confirms. But above the natural level
is the religious and there Christian doctrine is the only guide. Such
is the scheme of the *Apology*; and, broadly speaking, it is identical
with that of *Comus*.

[4]*Prose Works*, III, 119-22.

II

That the doctrine of chastity is the central theme in the argument of the poem is obvious from the emphasis that it receives. The virtues of temperance and continence are treated with brevity, and subordinated to it, while the mysterious merits of the virgin state are but hinted in expounding the doctrine of chastity in its highest reaches. But that doctrine itself is set forth at large by the Elder Brother, and is symbolized by the Lady, who speaks for temperance and continence, it is true, but stands for chastity. We shall do well, however, to consider the virtues in the ascending order in which we have already presented them; and if the space which we give to the lower virtues seems disproportionate, it is because the significance of their presence in the poem has never been observed and because it can be brought out only by detailed exposition and some comparison with a chief moulding influence, Spenser, and with Milton's later thought.

In the temptation scene the attack of Comus is not against chastity in the full meaning of the term, but against continence, which he derides as "the lean and sallow Abstinence." The solicitation that meets the Lady is identical in kind with that which meets Guyon in the Bower of Bliss, an episode immensely impressive to Milton,[5] and the real centre of Spenserian influence on *Comus*, as is quite natural, for Acrasia is Spenser's elaboration of the Circe motif and Comus is Milton's. The special mark of both is the prostitution of natural powers to the purposes of mere sensual pleasure. This is strongly underlined by Spenser and is symbolized by the scenery of the Bower of Bliss, where art counterfeits and even perverts nature and the beauty is as subtly false as that of the contrasted Garden of Adonis is natural and true. In *Comus* there is no such elaboration of this symbol; but the wizard's palace "set out with all manner of deliciousness" is, like the Bower of Bliss, of art, not nature, and (as we shall see) the Garden of Adonis, with its wealth of natural beauty, also finds its place in Milton's poem.

It is in another form, however, that the theme of nature chiefly enters into *Comus*.[6] By an appeal to nature the magician seeks

[5]*Faery Queen*, 2.12. Cf. *Areopagitica* (*Prose Works*, II, 68).

[6]Lines 706-80. Comus' appeal to nature is no invention of Milton's but a Renaissance Ovidian commonplace, found in Spenser's Phaedria, and in Marlowe, Donne, Randolph, and others; see Douglas Bush, *Mythology and the Renaissance*

to undermine the virtue of continence, and this in two ways. Overtly his argument is that the natural world by the profusion of its gifts invites men to a life of unrestricted enjoyment: for this the abundance of nature was ordained, and to refuse it "in a pet of temperance" is to manifest ingratitude and thwart nature's plan. But there is a second suggestion: the note of nature is abundance, profusion, and *a wasteful fertility*:

> Wherefore did Nature pour her bounties forth
> With such a full and unwithdrawing hand,
> Covering the earth with odours, fruits and flocks,
> Thronging the seas with spawn innumerable . . .?

"Nature," said Renan, "knows nothing of chastity." It is the very contention that Comus is seeking to illustrate. And the application to humanity is not left in doubt: one should not be cozened by words, but reflect that

> Beauty is Nature's coin . . .
>   and the good thereof
> Consists in mutual and partaken bliss.

(Observe that the magician's argument ends not in the provision of life for its own replenishment, but in mere gratification.) In a double sense, then, temperance (which here means continence) is, he suggests, unnatural. This specious argument, says the Lady, is untrue, it is "false rules pranked in reason's garb":

> Imposter! do not charge most innocent nature
> As if she would her children should be riotous
> With her abundance; she, good cateress,
> Means her provision only for the good,
> *That live according to her sober laws,*
> *And holy dictates of spare Temperance.*

And she continues with the famous attack on "lewdly-pampered Luxury" as opposed to nature's plan.

Now it is interesting and significant to observe that the Lady does not contradict the picture of nature given by Comus: she merely points out its incompleteness and repudiates his inference. Nature is marked not by abundance only, but by order and rationality. To live according to nature in the true sense is not to live riotously, prostituting her gifts to sensual gratification, but temperately and in conformity with her rational character and ends. This is plainly Stoic doctrine, and it is not for nothing that

---

Tradition in English Poetry (1932), 135, 267, and *Paradise Regained* etc., ed. M. Y. Hughes (1937), xliii-iv.

Comus is made to warn the Lady in advance against "those budge doctors of the Stoic fur." In the years after *Comus*, Milton was to elaborate his doctrines of nature ("most innocent nature"), of reason and of temperance. In so doing he altered much, substituting a monistic for a dualistic philosophy and reacting, temporarily at least, against every suggestion of asceticism. I am very far from denying—indeed I insist upon—the wide interval between *Comus* and Milton's later thought. Only one must not exaggerate the differences or fail to recognize similarities where they exist. And for all the change in his metaphysic of nature, and in the tone of his ethic, the twofold aspect of nature remains, and constitutes the groundwork of his no longer ascetic (though still rigoristic) doctrine of temperance; and the role of reason (which is only hinted in *Comus*) is not reversed, but confirmed and emphasized. The nature described by Comus and the Lady is the nature whose production is to be recounted by Milton in the seventh book of *Paradise Lost*. There creation is a twofold process, corresponding to the two complementary aspects of nature. For nature is a living whole, a vital scale, embracing life in all its profusion, and the process of creation in this aspect approximates very closely to gestation and birth. But before nature is a living, it is an ordered whole, a rationally graduated scale. And here creation does not approximate to birth; it is the imposition of form and order on chaos, the endowment of nature with a rational principle, as the other is her endowment with a vital principle. Thus Milton later elaborates the view of nature already implicit in *Comus*. And similarly he elaborates the doctrine of temperance. It means a proper use of the gifts of nature, a proper choice made by reason among them; for "reason is but choosing." It is nature the vital, the abounding, that furnishes the materials of the choice, and nature the ordered, the rational, that furnishes the principle of choice. For not only is reason the prerogative (indeed Milton calls it the essence) of the soul, but it is also imprinted upon the world: as Whichcote said, there is the reason of the mind, and the reason of the thing. Thus Milton elaborates his view of nature, of reason and of temperance. There are important changes, of course: a new metaphysic of nature (but it is, in one sense, just an elaboration of the idea implicit in the phrase about "most innocent nature"), a new emphasis on the role of reason (which is hardly explicit[7] in the original formulation), and a more liberal specific content for the term *temperance*, no longer qualified by the epithet "spare." But it is an elaboration (and modification), not a simple reversal: some at least of the primary intuitions on which it is grounded are already present in *Comus*.

As in Spenser, temperance (we have shown) is treated primarily as a virtue on the natural level, not on the religious. Of course Milton cannot afford Spenser's wealth of detail, and indeed there is little evidence of direct Spenserian influence on Milton's theory; no hint, for example, of Spenser's exposition of the virtue in terms of the Aristotelian mean, which was perhaps always foreign to Milton's mind, or in terms of the Platonic control of the rational over the irrational (whether the irascible or the appetitive), which should have been more congenial to him. But there are important similarities to Spenser in emphasis and tone, not all of which we have yet mentioned. Though treated on the natural level, Spenser's reading of the virtue of temperance in Book 2 of the *Faery Queen* impresses us as distinctly rigoristic, culminating, as it does, in the destruction of the Bower of Bliss. This is partly accounted for by the fact that, with increasing definiteness as the book proceeds, Spenser couples with temperance the Aristotelian continence: the story of Guyon is the legend of temperance *and continence*. And in *Comus* a like impression springs from a similar coupling of virtues— Spenserian virtues, though not directly Aristotelian. But these virtues are not sufficient in Spenser's experience: they must be rendered secure and translated from negative to positive terms by the addition of chastity, which means not mere abstention from evil but an active pursuit of the good. To the virtue of chastity the next book of the *Faery Queen* is devoted. And so is the next stage in the argument of *Comus*.

Having spoken for temperance, inevitably interpreted in the circumstances as continence, the Lady proceeds:

> Shall I go on?
> Or have I said enow? To him that dares
> Arm his profane tongue with contemptuous words
> Against the sun-clad power of Chastity,
> Fain would I something say; —yet to what end?

---

[7] That it is implicit is confirmed not only by such allusions to reason as that in line 529, but by the fact that (as Professor Bush remarks) Milton evidently follows Sandys' interpretation of the Circe myth.

> Thou hast nor ear, nor soul, to apprehend
> The sublime notion and high mystery
> That must be uttered to unfold the sage
> And serious doctrine of Virginity.[8]

Here we are brought face to face with a difficulty. It is not that the Lady fails to expound the doctrine of chastity; for that has already been done by the Elder Brother, whose exposition the reader is invited to recall—an invitation of which we shall avail ourselves. The difficulty is that here, and in the speech of the Elder Brother, there is no such clear-cut distinction between the doctrine of chastity and that of virginity as there is between the doctrine of chastity and that of temperance and continence. The two seem to merge; so that Mr Tillyard can ask whether in *Comus* Milton is primarily concerned with premarital chastity or rather with the special virtue attached to the state of virginity considered in itself, and can declare, with M. Saurat, for the second alternative. But the intellectual frame of reference, supported as it is by the autobiographical passage in the *Apology*, enables us to answer the question: Milton is concerned with both as interdependent parts in a system that includes nature and grace; but the central theme is the doctrine of chastity, which is illustrated on the purely religious level by the Christian doctrine of virginity. And that this is the correct answer is proved by the fact that it clears the sense of the whole poem. There is a second, but less formidable difficulty connected with the transition from the order of nature to the order of grace. It is the fact that in *Comus*, in contrast with (for example) the *Nativity Ode*, Milton is reticent in the introduction of specifically religious terminology. A moment's reflection shows that this is attributable to the *genre* and occasion of the poem; but, confessedly, it slightly obscures the scheme of the argument, and forces us to read between the lines.

That argument as it deals with chastity moves in the area common to nature and grace. The speeches of the Elder Brother,[9] though not highly dramatic, develop naturally enough as part of a dialogue on the fate of the lost Lady. But the points made, and the order in which they are made, have a special interest.

(1)   First the poet emphasizes the power and security of virtue in general, and in itself, without particular reference either to chastity

---

[8]Lines 779-87 (not in Bridgewater MS).
[9]Lines 359-475, 584-99.

or to anything above the natural level. "The mind is its own place," as Milton already knows. And virtue arms the mind, first with inward peace ("the sweet peace that goodness bosoms ever"), and then with inward illumination

> (He that has light within his own clear breast
> May sit i' the centre and enjoy bright day).

We are to remember this when we hear the Lady's defiance of Comus: "Thou canst not touch the freedom of my mind"; and once more (as we shall see) before the poem closes.

(2) Then he suggests that chastity is in very special degree a strength and protection to the person that possesses it: a strength and protection referable (like all good gifts) to Heaven, but still the mind's own

> (a hidden strength,
> Which if Heaven gave it, may be termed her own).

We are still on the natural level,[10] but the idea of virtue's—and specifically of chastity's—ultimate (though perhaps unrecognized) dependence on God's gift is suggested. This is a point of juncture between the two orders, which permits grace to build upon nature in a way to be described in points 4 and 5; but first,

(3) the grounding of chastity, and its power, in the order of nature is emphasized by a deliberate reference to non-Christian wisdom:

> Do ye believe me yet, or shall I call
> Antiquity from the old schools of Greece,
> To testify the arms of chastity?
> Hence had the huntress Dian her dread bow,
> Fair silver-shafted queen for ever chaste. . . .
> What was that snaky-headed Gorgon shield
> That wise Minerva wore, unconquered virgin, . . .
> But rigid looks of chaste austerity
> And noble grace that dashed brute violence . . . ?

(4) And only now do we come to the passage to which the Lady's speech to Comus is designed to send us back:

> So dear to Heaven is saintly chastity,
> That when a soul is found sincerely so,

---

[10]Professor Bush remarks that in their Miltonic meaning Wisdom and Contemplation (lines 375, 377) suggest something above natural reason. I agree that in another context they would do so. I do not think that they have here a specifically religious content, but that they will take on a religious meaning only when submitted to, and reviewed in the light of, grace. The same thing applies to the image of lines 375-80, which (as he points out) seems to be an allusion to the ascent of the soul in the *Phaedrus* of Plato.

> A thousand liveried angels lackey her,
> Driving far off each thing of sin and guilt,
> And in clear dream and solemn vision
> Tell her of things that no gross ear can hear;
> Till oft converse with heavenly habitants
> Begin to cast a beam on the outward shape,
> The unpolluted temple of the mind,
> And turns it by degrees to the soul's essence,
> Till all become immortal.

Here one recognizes Platonic doctrine, the doctrine taught by Spenser:

> For of the soule the bodie forme doth take,
> For soule is forme, and doth the bodie make;

the doctrine, also, accepted by Milton, of "chastity and love . . .: how the first and chiefest office of love begins and ends in the soul, producing those happy twins of her divine generation, knowledge and virtue." For to peace and freedom and illumination of mind on the level already stated, is here added illumination of a higher order, whose note is not self-sufficiency, but self-surrender, and whose communication is rapture. And as in the passage from the *Apology*, the "abstracted sublimities" (what the Lady calls "the sublime notion") of Platonism lead on directly to "those chaste and high mysteries" (the Lady's phrase is identical, "the high mystery") of Christian teaching; for to Milton, at this stage of his development, Platonism marks the highest reach of thought on the natural level and its point of juncture with the divine. But here in contrast to the *Apology*, Platonic and Christian doctrine merge, though it may well be (as we shall observe) that there is ascent within the order of grace and that more is meant by the Lady's allusion to the "high mystery" than is contained in the Elder Brother's exposition.

(5)   Finally, the recurring idea of chastity's self-protective power receives, on the religious level, its confirmation and its explanation, in the doctrine of Eternal Providence. It is for the Christian pre-eminently that "all things work together for good." The ideas here uttered are repeated in a larger context in *Paradise Lost* and are a ground of the optimism which is one of its notes. Not malice, and not

> that power
> Which erring men call Chance,

but the power and providence of God reign supreme. On this the Christian stakes everything; for

> if this fail,
> The pillared firmament is rottenness,
> And earth's base built on stubble.

The emphasis on Providence is reinforced by the presence of the Attendant Spirit, who is its minister and almost its symbol.

We have said that, like Spenser, Milton realizes the necessity of ascending from a doctrine of temperance and continence to a doctrine of chastity. Professor Hanford goes much further, emphasizing the extent to which "Milton has been influenced by his master's romantic allegory of chastity in the third book of the *Faerie Queene*,"[11] and finding in that book, not in book 2 (as we have done), the main contact of *Comus* with Spenser. What impresses us in the doctrine of chastity is not the similarity of *Comus* to the *Faery Queen*, but its significant dissimilarity. In book 3 Spenser's main emphasis is so different from Milton's in *Comus* that the two poets might almost seem to be writing on different subjects; for Milton's doctrine of chastity culminates in—though even on the religious level it is not co-extensive with—a doctrine of virginity, whereas Spenser's doctrine of chastity is elaborated in connection with an ideal of wedded love. Spenser's legend of chastity is also his legend of love; not the intellectual love of Platonism, as set forth by Milton in the *Apology*, and in *Comus* merged with Christian doctrine, and assuredly not the "high mystery" of Christian heavenly love, also set forth in the *Apology*, and presented in *Comus* as the highest reach of Christian thought, but love as it manifests itself in human marriage. Spenser's knight of chastity, the warrior maiden Britomart, is virginal, but by no means vowed to virginity: on the contrary, she is vowed to the love of one good man, and in her single devotion passes unscathed through every danger, unassailed by any temptation. The security with which Spenser's idealism is here rooted in the realities of ordinary human nature is evidenced by a wealth of psychological insight, nowhere more impressive than in Britomart's dream in the temple of Isis. I am far from denying the influence of Christianity on Spenser's treatment of chastity: what he presents is in one aspect a Christian ideal of marriage (the history of the subject is far too complicated to talk about *the* Christian ideal of marriage), but it is an ideal of marriage, or of chastity culminating in marriage, and it is idle to try to approximate it to an ideal of chastity cul-

[11]*Op. cit.*, 140-1.

minating in virginity.[12]   In *Comus* chastity is never, even by implication, viewed in connection with the wedded love which Milton was later to hail.   It is here that *Comus* stands at its greatest distance from *Paradise Lost*, and at a distance almost as great from book 3 of the *Faery Queen*.[13]

It will not have escaped the reader, that in drawing out the argument of *Comus* I have been contending against the common view that it is simple, unrelievedly austere, and negative in conception.   There can be no doubt, however, that its doctrine of chastity culminates in what Milton calls the sage and serious doctrine of virginity.   This allusion is to be partly understood in relation to the mingled Platonic and Christian teaching of the Elder Brother's speech, but also as carrying a specifically Christian content, as symbolizing chastity, indeed, not merely in the order of grace, but there in its utmost reach.   It may be granted that this last fact is not directly stated and that one can deduce it only by a consideration of the poem as a whole, and by cross-reference to other passages (in the *Apology* and at the conclusion of *Lycidas* and the *Epitaphium Damonis*) alluding to the Christian doctrine of heavenly love as set forth in Revelation 14. 4, which Milton

[12]I would not be thought to reduce *F.Q.* 3. to a sermon in dull domestic virtue. Spenser, the Platonist, views chastity and love as incentives to high idealism and heroic action.   But in Britomart these incentives are expressed in relation to marriage, and not to any cult of virginity: that is the only point with which I am concerned.

[13]Nor have the minor characters in which Spenser deals with other aspects of chastity more relation than Britomart to Milton's masque, with one possible exception, Belphoebe, Spenser's version of the classical Diana.   To Britomart Professor Hanford would trace "the martial conception [that] underlies such passages as *Comus* 440 ff." (*op. cit.*, 141).   But the conception, though militant, is not martial; and to me the lines with their allusions to Diana and Minerva recall the spirit of Spenser's portrait not of Britomart, but of Belphoebe.   More plausible is Professor Hanford's contention that the Lady's rescue which can be completed only by the reversal of the enchanter's charm, owes something to the rescue of Amoret (*F.Q.* 3. 12. 36), though there is a possible common source in Ovid, *Metamorphoses* 14. 301-2 (Hughes).   But least plausible of all is the assumption that Milton's emphasis on providential intervention to guard chastity requires a source and finds it in the rescue of Florimel by Proteus (*F.Q.* 3. 8. 29 ff.). And anyway these would be mere surface borrowings: the characters and situations of Amoret and Florimel have nothing in common with the Lady's.   In one instance Professor Hanford exaggerates Milton's divergence from Spenser: it is the one certain and significant borrowing from book 3, the allusion to the Garden of Adonis (see below, p. 65).

evidently reads as the transcendent Christian version of Plato's doctrine of "chastity and love." That Milton, at the time of the writing of *Comus*, set a marked value on the Christian conception of virginity seems certain: so marked a value that he was willing to regard it as the highest culmination of chastity and to use it as the symbol of chastity in the order of grace—as the highest culmination and the symbol, but, as the *Apology* (even if we omit the reservation in favour of marriage) makes clear, not as co-extensive with the Christian teaching on chastity. Whether or not Milton's doctrine of virginity appears unrelievedly austere, and negative in conception, will presumably depend on the reader's beliefs. But the impression will certainly be modified when it is viewed in its proper context, that is to say, as the ideal culmination of an ethical scheme whose foundations are laid in the order of nature, and which ascends through the whole range of human experience.

Such an effort of comprehension is just as important as what is said on any particular level. And that the effort of comprehension is real and fundamental is put beyond all doubt by the Epilogue. But before turning to it we must briefly notice some further effects of the effort of comprehension.

III

It is not contended—and I think it quite impossible to contend—that the effort of comprehension is completely successful, that Milton avoids all occasion of conflict between nature and grace. I mean, of course, *unnecessary* occasion of conflict; for wherever one has an ascending scale of values, whether it extends to the religious level or pauses on the humanistic, there will be subordination of the lower to the higher: there will be necessary renunciation within a scheme whose note is not renunciation, but *comprehension and ascent*. It is sufficient to recognize that in *Comus* the effort after such a scheme is being made.

Despite the seeming austerity of its doctrine, *Comus* is a very different poem from *Paradise Regained*, the later work with which it presents the most obvious points for comparison. In *Paradise Regained* Milton comes nearer than anywhere else in his writings to asserting an absolute division between the goods of the order of nature and those of the order of grace, comes nearer to applying what I have called the principle of segregation. One must, of course, be on one's guard against too easily supposing that what

Christ rejects, he necessarily rejects as in itself evil, and not as evil merely by occasion because unfitting to present circumstances and because offered by Satan with evil intent.   But as one observes the careful exclusion from the things offered of all the gross outward signs of evil so evident in the temptation of Comus, and scans the terms in which Christ's rejection is made, it is hard to avoid the conclusion that Milton has come to regard with deep suspicion beauty (to which he has been so constantly devoted), knowledge (with which he has so laboured to enrich himself for God's service), and—though here no comparison with *Comus* is possible—the exercise of power even for good ends.   In conformity with his new attitude we find that *Paradise Regained*, as compared with *Paradise Lost*, and also with *Comus*, is relatively bare of Milton's rich additions of poetic beauty and quite bare of philosophic thought; and that this does not depend wholly on the subject is indicated by a like quality in *Samson Agonistes*.   Milton's repudiation of wisdom on the natural level, of ancient Greece and its philosophers, who have formed his mind, is notorious and inescapable:

> he who receives
> Light from above, from the fountain of light,
> No other doctrine needs, though granted true;
> *But these are false or little else but dreams,*
> *Conjectures, fancies, built on nothing firm.*[14]

In *Comus*, on the contrary, beauty and the appreciation of beauty are everywhere: even the wizard claims kindred with the Attendant Spirit and the other good characters in his response to it.   And for wisdom on the natural level, for philosophy ("How charming is divine philosophy!"), Aristotle (through the medium of Spenser) and the Stoics together give the rule for temperance and continence, and the doctrine of Plato inculcates chastity and points on to, almost merges in, the teaching of Christianity.   And Christianity, far from repudiating the findings of natural wisdom, confirms before it transcends them.   There is no conscious divorce between nature and grace, and no interval between the two orders. So much our exposition of the argument of *Comus* has been designed to make clear.   But the question of beauty, both for its intrinsic importance and because it is so intimately bound up with the meaning of the Epilogue, demands a word or two more.

The beauty of *Comus* is natural beauty in the sense of belonging

[14]*Paradise Regained* 4. 288-92.

to the order of nature, but aesthetically speaking it cannot be described as simple natural beauty. It has a certain Arcadian quality which readily merges with the pastoral and, beyond that, with a more generalized idyllic note, and this in turn permits the inclusion of an element of myth, classical and native. These facts belong rather to a consideration of *Comus*, the masque; but they must be taken into account if one is to gauge aright the extent of beauty on the natural level to which response is indicated. It has been made matter of wonder that Comus shares with the Attendant Spirit (and we may add, though in lesser degree, the Brothers and the Lady) an immediate response to this beauty.[15] But there is no mystery here. The response of the good characters means that for Milton beauty is to the good a good, and one to be received with joy. Like other goods on the natural level it depends on good use, and is susceptible of perversion. Almost it seems that beauty, like nature, "means her provision only for the good." We have seen how, when beauty is perverted to evil ends, Spenser presents it as art imitating and falsifying nature, and we have caught one hint of this in Milton also. But in general Milton is quite ready to admit that the beauty which is to the good a good is the same beauty which the evil pervert to evil ends. This indeed is characteristic of his whole attitude to the natural order. So with daring, and a subtlety quite wasted on his modern critics, he shows us Comus responding to beauty in words that might be mistaken for those of the Attendant Spirit, but perverting it to evil—to what Milton takes to be evil—in the very act of response. To quote the lines in question[16] is to prove the point, but lest it should still be missed we will call italics to our aid:

> The star that bids the shepherd fold
> Now the top of heaven doth hold;
> And the gilded car of day
> His glowing axle doth allay
> In the steep Atlantic stream. . . .[17]
> Meanwhile, welcome joy and feast,
> *Midnight shout and revelry,*
> *Tipsy dance and jollity.*

---

[15]Enid Welsford, *The Court Masque* (1923), 321.

[16]Lines 93-144.

[17]Originally, it would seem, this allusion was intended to recall the opening speech of the Attendant Spirit, where there was a reference to "the wide Atlantique" (cancelled passage, preserved in Cambridge MS).

Braid your locks with rosy twine,
Dropping odours, dropping wine.
Rigour now is gone to bed. ....
We that are of purer fire
Imitate the starry quire,[18]
Who, in their nightly watchful spheres,
Lead in swift rounds the months and years.
The sounds and seas with all their finny drove,
Now to the moon in wavering morrice move;
And on the tawny sands and shelves
Trip the pert faeries and the dapper elves.
By dimpled brook and fountain-brim
The wood-nymphs, decked with daisies trim,
Their merry wakes and pastimes keep:
What has night to do with sleep?
Night has better sweets to prove:
Venus now wakes and wakens Love.[19]
Come, let us our rites begin;
'Tis only daylight that makes sin,
Which these dun shades will ne'er report.
Hail, goddess of nocturnal sport,
Dark-veiled Cotytto,[20] *to whom the secret flame*
Of midnight torches burns! mysterious dame,
That ne'er are called but when the dragon womb
Of Stygian darkness spets her thickest gloom,
And makes one blot of all the air!
Stay thy cloudy ebon chair
Wherein thou ridest with Hecate, and befriend
Us thy vowed priests, till utmost end
Of all thy dues be done. ....
Come, knit hands, and beat the ground
In a light fantastic round.[21]

---

[18]This couplet is italicized because, for all its beauty and seeming innocence, it is untrue. The spheres with their "ninefold harmony," audible only to the pure in heart, have for Milton a special significance: they represent the highest degree of perfection in the natural order, the point of contact with the supernatural. See below, p. 71.

[19]The Venus and Cupid here alluded to represent, of course, wanton love; see below p. 67.

[20]The non-classical reader will not appreciate the full extent of licentiousness conveyed by the name, though he will recognize the association with evil implied by Hecate and the blotting out of light. See C. G. Osgood, *The Classical Mythology of Milton's Enlish Poems*, 24-5.

[21]Another seemingly innocent couplet, which instantly reminds us indeed of a genuinely innocent one,

Come and trip it as ye go
On the light fantastic toe,

a type of the "unreproved pleasures free" of L'Allegro (lines 33-4, 40). But, as Osgood makes clear, Comus is still alluding to the obscene rites of Cotytto.

It is the more necessary to be clear about Milton's meaning in this speech because in the aesthetic and in the intellectual pattern it is evidently intended to stand in a relation of contrast with the Epilogue.

IV

The Epilogue is not easy to interpret. On the surface it presents a description of the Attendant Spirit's abode, though even of this some doubt might be entertained were it not for the cancelled lines of the Spirit's opening speech, preserved in the Cambridge MS, with their allusions to the stream Ocean (and also to the Atlantic, a link with the speech of Comus quoted above), to the Hesperian garden and to hyacinth and roses. But evidently "more is meant than meets the ear," and the method employed is less that of allegory than of symbol. The question is, precisely what is symbolized? "In the Spirit's Epilogue," says Professor Hanford,[22]

Milton sings of Paradise. The language is highly esoteric . . . and Milton expressly calls attention in the parenthesis, "List mortals, if your ears be true," to the hidden spiritual meaning. The bliss proposed is that of Heavenly love as the ineffable compensation for a life devoted to the ideal of chastity. . . . In adopting Spenser's image of the Garden of Adonis Milton entirely changes its application. . . . The pagan image of the love of a mortal youth for a goddess draws insensibly nearer to the truth in the reversed symbol of the union of the God of love himself with Psyche, the human soul, and if Milton's classic taste prevents him from concluding with an allusion to the Lamb and his eternal bride it is because there is no need.

This interpretation has been very generally accepted, but I do not think that Milton's allusion is to Paradise, or (at least in Professor Hanford's sense) to the rewards and compensations of the chaste soul hereafter. The whole deeper significance of the Epilogue lies in its symbolical character; and I should be disposed to look for some larger symbolism, which might include the reward of the chaste soul hereafter but would not be restricted to it. I believe that nothing less is symbolized in the Epilogue than life itself, as the Christian mind, grounded in nature but illuminated by grace, alone can apprehend it. I do not think that in adopting Spenser's image of Venus and Adonis Milton entirely changes its application, or indeed changes it at all: I believe that he relies upon a brief—perhaps too brief—allusion to recall what Spenser

[22] *Op. cit.*, 152.

had implied.   On the relation of Milton's image of Cupid and
Psyche to Spenser's, Professor Hanford is silent: I believe that
Milton's meaning is very similar to the interpretation commonly
given to Spenser's lines, but not to Spenser's true intention.   (I
realize that my argument would be simpler and perhaps more
convincing if I could say that Milton followed Spenser throughout.
Unfortunately, I do not find that Spenser's lines will bear the
interpretation commonly put upon them, though it is possible that
Milton may have given them that interpretation and thus have
supposed himself to be following Spenser throughout.)   I think
that, in the progression which Milton adopts, the specifically and
exclusively religious level is not reached even in the allusion to
Cupid and Psyche, much less in the allusion to Venus and Adonis,
but only in the concluding lines of the Epilogue.   And in the light
of those lines, of course, the whole is to be read. / So I interpret
the Epilogue up to this point as symbolizing the transfigured view
of life which the practice of virtue and the experience of grace induce.   On no other hypothesis can I explain the ascent through
the order of nature to the order of grace which the lines evidently
embody, beginning on the plane of natural beauty, expressed in and
with classic mythology and idyllicism, and culminating at last in
Christianity.

The journey commences in the *idea* of whatever is fresh and
beautiful in the natural world: ocean, air, and the flowering earth,
and the reader lingers

> amidst the gardens fair
> Of Hesperus and his daughters three
> That sing about the golden tree.
> Along the crisped shades and bowers
> Revels the spruce and jocund Spring;
> The Graces and the rosy-bosomed Hours
> Thither all their bounties bring. . . .
> Iris there with humid bow
> Waters the odorous banks that blow . . .
> And drenches with celestial dew
> (List, mortals, if your ears be true)
> Beds of hyacinth and roses,
> Where young Adonis oft reposes,
> Waxing well of his deep wound
> In slumber soft, and on the ground
> Sadly sits the Assyrian queen:
> But far above in spangled sheen
> Celestial Cupid, her famed son advanced,

Holds his dear Psyche sweet entranced,
After all her labours long,
Till free consent the gods among
Make her his eternal bride,
And from her fair unspotted side,
Two blissful twins are to be born,
Youth and Joy. . . .

The joyous acceptance of natural beauty by the good is unmistakably indicated, and the mind of the reader is carried back to Comus, who accepts but perverts to evil in the act of accepting. The first problem arises with the allusion to Venus and Adonis.

On the details of Spenser's allegory of the Garden of Adonis[23] critics have not always agreed. It will be enough here to state very briefly what appears to be its main intention. In classic myth and its elaborations one recognizes three different roles assigned to Venus: she is the goddess of wanton love (as in the speech of Comus already quoted); she is the great mother, a principle of generation in all things; and she is the celestial Venus, the symbol of intellectual or spiritual love. In the passage in question Spenser clearly has in mind the second of these roles, with no suggestion of the third. It is an allegory of form and substance[24]—of material forms, represented by Adonis, the masculine principle, and material substance, represented by Venus, the feminine principle—and it sets forth the processes of decay and replenishment throughout the natural world. Further, there is (as we have remarked) a contrast between the Garden of Adonis and Acrasia's Bower of Bliss, where natural powers are prostituted (as they are by Comus) to purposes of mere pleasure, a contrast pointed in Spenser by the opposing Geniuses who guard the two portals and by the types of beauty found beyond them.[25] This allegory of Spenser's, Milton recalls in his allusion to the Garden of Adonis. It symbolizes life on the natural level: the life processes of "most innocent nature." And its appropriateness, once more, is found in the contrast to all that Comus stands for. There is no need to assume with Professor Hanford that Milton alludes to the third role of Venus, the celestial Venus,[26] or that he translates Spenser's

---

[23]*Faery Queen* 3. 6.
[24]Brents Stirling in *Variorum Spenser*, III, 347-52.
[25]See C. S. Lewis, *The Allegory of Love*, 324 ff., 361 ff.
[26]One should record Hughes's note on *Assyrian Queen*, line 1002, that "according to Pausanias 1. 14. 6, 'the Assyrians were the first men to revere the

image to a higher (even the highest) level; for (as we have shown) the natural also has its place in Milton's scheme. This is the world of nature as the chaste and religious are able to apprehend it, and only they. That is the significance of the admonition uttered just before the image of Venus and Adonis is introduced: "List, mortals, *if your ears be true*."

The myth of Cupid and Psyche, which goes back to the charming fairy-story told by Apuleius, had long been allegorized when Spenser added to his picture of the Garden of Adonis his account of how Cupid

> Thither resorts, and laying his sad darts
> Aside, with faire Adonis playes his wanton parts.
>
> And his true love faire Psyche with him playes,
> Faire Psyche to him lately reconcyld
> After long troubles and unmeet upbrayes
> With which his mother Venus her revyld,
> And eke himselfe her cruelly exyld:
> But now in stedfast love and happy state
> She with him lives and hath him borne a chyld,
> Pleasure, that doth both gods and men aggrate,
> Pleasure, the daughter of Cupid and Psyche late.

That Spenser adopted an allegorical meaning already attached to the myth, is the usual assumption:

The allegorical meaning . . . is clearly developed by Boccaccio and fits Spenser's intention. Boccaccio says, "Psyche is the soul . . . and there is joined with her that which preserves the rational element, that is pure Love," Psyche passes through trials and purgations. "At length . . . she attains to the consummation of divine joy and contemplation, and is joined to her lover forever, and with mortal things sloughed off is born into eternal glory; and from this love is born Pleasure, which is eternal joy and gladness." Pleasure so interpreted is very similar to Plato's *Eudaimonia*. . . .[27]

It seems far from certain that this is the meaning of Spenser's lines when taken in their context. There is no indication that it is the celestial Cupid that is intended. The allegory appears to move on the same level as that of Venus and Adonis, to which

---

Celestial Aphrodite'." But surely the phrase *Assyrian Queen* is sufficiently accounted for by the myth of Venus and Adonis itself, which, as Milton well knew (cf. *Nativity Ode* 204) is of Eastern origin. Thammuz was adopted as Adonis. Astoreth or Astarte, the original of the Venus of this myth, was herself identical with the Assyrian goddess Istar. *Assyrian Queen* is thus one of Milton's learned devices of poetical adornment. Cf. Verity's notes on *Comus* 1002, and *P.L.* 1. 438-41.

[27]Lotspeich in *Variorum Spenser*, III, 261.

Spenser attaches it so closely. For him the story of Venus and Adonis represents the spirit of love and the principle of generation operating throughout the natural order; and the story of Cupid and Psyche should somehow represent the same spirit and principle in their specifically human application, which is marriage with its productiveness and legitimate pleasure, opposed once more to the illegitimate pleasures of Acrasia, at war with productiveness.[28] Considering Spenser's free adaptation of myth to the purposes of allegory elsewhere in the *Faery Queen*, it does not seem an insuperable difficulty that this reading of the myth, the only one wholly consonant with text and context, should fall short of other allegorical interpretations current when he wrote.

Be this as it may, Milton's meaning is something quite different from that which I have been bold enough to attribute to Spenser, and resembles the interpretation of the myth given by Boccaccio. Unlike Spenser, Milton indicates clearly that he is not treating the story on the same level as that of Venus and Adonis: on the contrary, this is the *celestial* Cupid, and he is seen *far above* the figures in the Garden. There is no allusion, as in Spenser, to marriage, but to a Platonic doctrine of intellectual or spiritual love, the love "whose charming cup is only virtue," and whose "chiefest office begins and ends in the soul, producing those happy twins of her divine generation, Knowledge and Virtue." And yet there is a difference. For if Milton does not name the offspring of Cupid and Psyche *Voluptas* or Pleasure, like Apuleius and Spenser, neither does he call them simply Knowledge and Virtue, as in his other account of Platonic love, but Youth and Joy. In bestowing on Cupid and Psyche *twin* offspring he means to parallel them with that other pair of the soul's "divine generation," Knowledge and Virtue. These indeed Milton has implied in every line of the poem; so now he can afford to shift the emphasis. Like Knowledge and Virtue the offspring of Cupid and Psyche are not primarily the symbol of a reward to be expected in heaven, but something that the chaste soul rises to here and now. And if this is so, their names are significant indeed. For the conclusion mitigates the austerity, though not the strictness of Milton's doctrine. He repudiates false pleasures, but not joy; wantonness, but not the

---

[28]It is for marriage that Amoret is educated by Psyche with her own daughter, Pleasure. Actually the education turns out to be insufficient. It has to be completed by Britomart.

spirit of youth.   The quest is arduous, he would seem to say, and demands renunciation, but among its rewards may be reckoned not only virtue and knowledge, illumination of mind, peace of mind, but the very things that the adversary would declare to be taken away: life and youth and joy.   And to these the final lines of the Epilogue will add one further note: freedom.

First, the beauty of nature, with all its gracious associations, which Comus perverts; secondly, in the image of Venus and Adonis, the powers and processes of nature, which Comus (like Acrasia) would prostitute and thwart; thirdly, in the image of Cupid and Psyche, ascent to the highest virtue and wisdom accessible on the natural level, or rather ascent to an area common to nature and grace: thus far the summary has proceeded.   But there is one more step to take:

> Mortals that would follow me,
> Love Virtue: she alone is free;
> She can teach ye how to climb
> Higher than the sphery chime;
> Or if Virtue feeble were,
> Heaven itself would stoop to her.

The terminology is not overtly religious (it seldom is, as we have said, in *Comus*), but here at last we are on the level of grace alone. For the first allusion—and it is literally the first in Milton's writings —is to a doctrine which is to be enormously important in his thinking, the doctrine of Christian liberty.[29]   It is to receive much elaboration and many different applications which are without significance here.   But it never ceases to be for Milton a cardinal principle of specifically Christian ethics; for his interpretation of this doctrine, as of religion in general, is always (as *Comus* illustrates) predominantly ethical: "Know that to be free is the same as to be pious, to be wise, to be temperate and just, to be frugal and abstinent, and lastly, to be magnanimous and brave. . . ."[30] One recognizes (as no doubt Milton did) the kinship with Stoic doctrine; but for him freedom through virtue, through *voluntary* obedience to the will of God, is the special mark of Christianity: it is *Christian* liberty, which gathers up into the light of revelation the experience of the freedom of mind and will already alluded to in the poem.   And the pointing on to a level "higher than the

[29]See my "Milton, Puritanism and Liberty" (UNIVERSITY OF TORONTO QUARTERLY, IV, 1935, 483-513).
[30]*Second Defence* (*Prose Works*, I, 298).

sphery chime" confirms this interpretation of the lines. To hear the music of the spheres indeed is given only to the pure in heart. To ascend above it is to enter the Christian heaven and "hear the unexpressive nuptial song."[31]   And the final note of all is unmistakably Christian. We have been told in the body of the poem how Providence intervenes for the protection of virtue. Now this idea, too, is gathered up into the full light of Christian revelation. Here is a note not very often heard in Milton. And it might almost be called the essential note of Christianity; for it speaks to us not of God's power merely, or even of his providence, but of the Divine condescension and mercy to men who would do the will of God but are weak.

In *Comus* Milton does not repudiate the order of nature; he does not deny an area common to nature and grace, or the ascent through it from natural wisdom to divine; he does not seek to divorce the two orders. But he believes that experience on the level of grace will cast a light back upon nature and enable one to realize its true significance.[32] The idea—or rather the experience—is not unique: Cowper expresses it in simple evangelical terms in *The Task*, and Carlyle, in more philosophical terms, in *Sartor Resartus*. To record this experience is the function of the Epilogue, which thus becomes a key to the whole poem, or at least to Milton's intention in the poem. That intention is not, I think, successfully executed at all points: there are notes that jar, especially upon the modern (and uninstructed) ear. But the Epilogue itself is triumphantly successful. And it too casts a light back upon the long road travelled, which it is folly to ignore.

[31]E. M. W. Tillyard (*Milton*, 1934, 376ff.) seems to hold that in *At a Solemn Music* Milton identifies the two, and to wish to read *Comus* in the light of this supposed identification. What the text says is that the two strains *answer* each other. Milton does not divorce the different orders of existence, but neither does he confuse them. There is something *higher than the sphery chime*. It is the unexpressive nuptial song.

[32]There are hints of this earlier in the poem. It is in the light of the religious experience that the dictates of temperance become "holy" and that chastity can be described not as "sun-clad" merely, but as "saintly."

READING *COMUS*

ROBERT MARTIN ADAMS

—Aha, ELUCESCEBAT quoth our friend?

ONCE *Paradise Lost, Paradise Regained*, and *Samson Agonistes* were the major works of Milton; recent criticism has gone a long way toward replacing them with "Lycidas," *Comus*, and the "Nativity Ode." My contention in the present paper will be that this tendency has involved, either as cause or as effect, a major overreading of the three early works, and of *Comus* in particular. By "overreading" I mean overloading the allegory, probing too deeply into the background of the imagery, and enlarging upon the incidental implications of secondary concepts at the expense of the work's total structure.

Overreading a literary work is best accomplished through line-by-line analysis, according to the familiar approach of *explication de texte*. The announced aim of this technique is to reveal the true dramatic form of the work of art; and with this aim none can quarrel. But unfolding the text line by line does not necessarily serve this end, any more than methodically inspecting the bricks of a house gives one a notion of its architecture. We may therefore begin our consideration of *Comus*, not with line 1, but by asking what sort of literary work it is and then, in the broadest sense, what it is "about"—what themes it chiefly handles and what sort of impression it seems designed to make.

Though it is often described loosely as a play and sometimes as a poem, *Comus* is so much a masque that this was its original and for a long time its only title. The masque is a form of literature designed primarily for public recitation and performance. Its major functions are triple: to voice a compliment, to present a moral allegory, and to provide occasion for a spectacle. Each of these requirements lays one more demand on a verse statement which is unalterably public in character; consequently, the "Doric delicacy" which Sir Henry Wotton remarked in *Comus* was widely recognized as a notably successful style for masques. Simplicity wedded to elegance—this was the style at which the most successful writers of masques generally, and the author of *Comus* in particular, aimed. It is a matter of history that masques were not written in the metaphysical style; no poet whose style was recognized by his contemporaries as a "witty" style ever wrote a masque. Consequently, a preliminary doubt may be felt, simply on the score of *Comus'* form, that techniques appropriate to reading a metaphysical poem will quite apply here. The unity of a metaphysical poem often lies in a progression of ideas and feelings which must be explicated out of the imagery; as a masque, *Comus* would be expected to possess a much more obvious unity.

This is not to say that wit- and word-play were under a ban or that secondary meanings and patterns could not be included anywhere within the main outlines of the masque; Milton, like Shakespeare, might well be expected to enrich a traditional form with such secondary elements. But one cannot lightly suppose that the writer of a masque would deliberately violate any of the major purposes of his masque to include elements

[MODERN PHILOLOGY, August, 1953]

secondary to the type; still less that he would purposely conceal any major part of his statement where it was not easily available to a single hearing by an informed, attentive listener. The history of the writing of *Comus*, so far as it is available from manuscripts, supports this assumption. Whatever Milton had to say in *Comus*, he did not alter it radically in the course of composition; whatever main shape the masque had, it evidently had from the beginning. The textual alterations which are preserved aim at a greater clarity, a less pedestrian statement, a more exact propriety; not one of them is aimed at deepening or elaborating the allegory or symbolism, at adding new overtones to the imagery or harmonizing old ones.[1]

A formalist argument of this sort is, of course, inevitably general and abstract; the fact that Milton was writing a masque is no evidence that *Comus* is like all other masques or that it contains nothing but what is common to all masques. But so long as *Comus* can be read consistently and satisfyingly on the level of a masque for public performance, I think readings which depend entirely on a close analysis of the metaphorical overtones must be held suspect and subordinate. They may reinforce and enrich the more accessible meanings when they can do so without strain; they may be called on to mediate conflicts or to fill explicit gaps; but when they are not congruent with those more accessible meanings, the suspicion must

persist that they are not significant. Milton at the time when he wrote *Comus* could not foresee that it would be "explicated" or even that it would be published; publication of a masque was unusual, and "explication," so far as it was practiced at all, was called "parsing" or "construing" and reserved for classic authors. We do Milton no more discredit in urging that he did not write a masque for the Earl of Bridgewater to "explicate"—unlovely word!—than we do to Ovid in suggesting that he did not conceive the *Ars amatoria* as a devotional handbook for nuns. One can explicate Milton's masque and allegorize Ovid's treatise, but only at a sizable risk to one's understanding of the "true dramatic form."

The risk of overreading *Comus* may be great; to assess the actual damage, we must consider the poem's specific content and the violence which has, in fact, been done it by overreading. Since the publication of Mr. A. S. P. Woodhouse's classic account of its "argument," *Comus* has been generally supposed to concern the relations between "virtue" and "grace."[2] The virtue with which it deals is variously defined as continence, temperance, chastity, or virginity; whatever its character, Milton may be taken as saying of this virtue either that it co-operates with and leads toward grace or that it is distinctly inferior to grace and insufficient without it. How one reads the masque depends on how one makes these definitions, and vice versa. But on one point there is general agreement; the masque is built around a single central and important incident. Like Milton's tragedy and both his epics, *Comus* has a temptation at the center of it. The Lady, lost in a dark wood and separated from her brothers, is tempted by Comus, who is a magician and a sensual-

[1] One set of alterations in l. 955 is devoted to *removing* an explicitly Judeo-Christian symbol; the only other changes which seem even indirectly significant on the latent level have to do with ll. 356–58, where Milton removed a Proserpina-Lady comparison from the younger brother's speech, probably because it was too blackly diabolic in tone, perhaps also because the Proserpina-fertility connection did not fit well with the Lady's chastity. The 14 lines which Milton removed from the prologue and rewrote for the epilogue were dramatically inappropriate in their original spot—a fact for which they made explicit and doubly awkward apology.

[2] A. S. P. Woodhouse, "The Argument of Milton's *Comus*," *University of Toronto Quarterly*, XI (Spring, 1941), 46–71.

ist; if she succumbs by drinking of his cup, her head will be turned to that of a beast. But she is rescued by her brothers, who (guided by an Attendant Spirit and protected by a certain herb which he has given them) drive off Comus and his band, invoke the water nymph Sabrina to release their sister from enchantment, and escort her to their father's court.

The central episode of this story is clearly the temptation; the sort of allurements which are dangled before the Lady and the sort of energies which enable her to withstand those allurements will determine in very large measure the allegorical meaning of the masque. Secondary emphases may be altered by secondary elements—by the destination which the young people are supposed to be pursuing, by the debate which the two brothers carry on while they are looking for their sister, by the prologue or the epilogue. But we shall not go far wrong if we look first at the central dramatic conflict of the masque as a means of approaching its intellectual and emotional content.

The relation of Comus to Circe determines a good deal of the significance which attaches to the seducer. In his prologue the Attendant Spirit describes Comus as the son of Circe by Bacchus (ll. 46 ff.); and, while Bacchus remains largely in the background, the maternal side of Comus' genealogy is several times emphasized throughout the masque. When he hears the Lady singing, Comus is reminded of his mother and the sirens (ll. 253 ff.); when the Attendant Spirit provides the brothers with a countercharm for Comus' enchantments, he compares it to

                    that moly
That Hermes once to wise Ulysses gave
                    [ll. 636-37].

The fate of Comus' victims is akin to that of Circe's; he is armed, like Circe, with a cup and wand; like Circe, he offers his victims food, revelry, and (latently but climactically) sexual enjoyment; the virtues which are invoked against him are the virtues of temperance, which Comus calls "lean abstinence." It may be worth emphasizing that Milton has inverted the sex relationships of the traditional Circe story—perhaps to conform to the acting personnel at his disposal, perhaps to avoid too close a retelling of the old story, perhaps for more elaborate psychological reasons. In any event, the part of the fatal temptress, the deadly damsel, is here assumed by a male, the part of the shipwrecked mariners by a wandering lady; and from this fact derive some of the tonalities, and some of the incongruities, of the story.

For Comus is a seducer who makes remarkably few and feeble efforts to seduce; though he possesses the traditional enchanting devices of his mother, a glass and a wand, he never brings them explicitly into play. Instead of offering the Lady his magic brew while she is wandering alone, unsuspecting, and thirsty in the forest, he brings her into a palace, lets her see his troop of "ugly-headed monsters," and only then, when she is thoroughly aroused and suspicious, tries to argue her into drinking of the cup. His wand is said to have power to "chain up [the Lady's] nerves in Alablaster" (l. 660), but so far as he enchants her at all, it is with a certain magic dust which blears her vision and with an anointed chair which holds her motionless. The wand and the cup, though much in evidence, never exert an active compulsion; and the seduction of the Lady, though unmistakably threatened, never develops into a real possibility. All this means, I suppose, is that the decorums of female innocence must be very cautiously manipulated in the immediate proximity of symbols which folklore had rendered instinct with sexuality and which were controlled by the lascivious son of one] (Circe) who was widely taken as a type of the strumpet.

If the allegorical character of Comus is clear enough (he is Sensual Indulgence with some overtones of Priapic fertility, black wizardry, and pagan sophistry), the forces which the Lady opposes to him are by no means simple. Some of her strength is her own, some is her brothers', some is the Attendant Spirit's. Her own strength is itself a complex element; when alarmed, she invokes

The virtuous mind, that ever walks attended
By a strong siding champion Conscience
[ll. 211–12],

and, in addition, implies that, if need were, a special guardian would be forthcoming from heaven. The Elder Brother adds a third element to these two; aside from her natural virtue and the "strength of Heaven," the Lady possesses

a hidden strength
Which if Heav'n gave it, may be term'd her own:
'Tis chastity, my brother, chastity [ll. 418–20].

The special power of chastity to defend itself against witches, ghosts, fairies, goblins, and wizards is not only the subject of set speeches by the Elder Brother, it is verified in the central action of the masque. Comus is able to surprise the Lady and assail her; he cannot enthral or hurt her. And without the visible help of heaven, she rebukes him until he acknowledges:

that I do fear
Her words set off by some superior power:
And though not mortal, yet a cold shuddering dew
Dips me all o'er, as when the wrath of Jove
Speaks thunder, and the chains of Erebus
To some of Saturn's crew [ll. 800–805].

This "sage and serious doctrine of virginity," which the Lady says she will not reveal to Comus but which suffices to dazzle him anyhow, is said by Mr. Woodhouse to represent a religious aspect of the doctrine of mere earthly chastity enunciated earlier by the Elder Brother. But there is little evidence for this in the text; the Lady uses the "sun-clad power of chastity" as a synonym for the "doctrine of virginity" (ll. 782, 787); and the Elder Brother not only describes chastity as "saintly" but uses "true virginity" as a synonym (ll. 437, 453). Recognizing this confusion, Mr. Woodhouse appeals to "the intellectual frame of reference, supported as it is by the autobiographical passage in the *Apology*" (p. 56). He appeals away from the text, that is, to ideas expressed by Milton in another context eight years later and to ideas expressed by people other than Milton. But the text, deliberately or otherwise, makes no distinction between chastity and virginity; when she rebukes Comus, the Lady invokes no doctrine of either virtue which is recognizably Christian; and one reason for this reticence, aside from possible uneasy feelings on Milton's part about devotional celibacy, may be sought in the social implications of the particular masque he was writing.

For the fact is that Milton in *Comus* faced a rather delicate problem in tact. To make the Lady fully self-sufficient would be to eliminate the Attendant Spirit altogether as a functioning element in the story; but to make her virtue wholly dependent on heaven's assistance would scarcely be an overwhelming compliment to pay her. One simply does not tell an earl's daughter that she is chaste only by the grace of God. Thus Milton rather carefully, as it seems to me, manipulates his story to show that female virtue, while possessing defensive powers of its own, and not by any means to be supposed vulnerable, much less defective in its own nature, does enjoy a special protection from heaven against such special menaces as Comus. And for this reason it is only after she has given a convincing demonstration of her own moral self-sufficiency that the Lady receives, even indirectly, the help of heaven.

What is the nature of that help? In attacking Comus with drawn swords and dispersing his "rout," the two brothers rely largely on their own powers; perhaps for this reason, they are not fully effective in releasing their sister and must invoke the further interesting help of Sabrina. But the brothers are protected against Comus' magic by an herb named "haemony" which the Attendant Spirit has provided for them; and the argument has been developed by Mr. Edward LeComte from a hint in Coleridge, and avidly accepted by Messrs. Brooks and Hardy, that haemony is a symbol of heavenly grace.[3] This identification rests partly on the name which Milton invented for the herb and partly on some of the things he says about it. The word "haemony" seems to derive primarily from the name for Thessaly (Haemonia), a land particularly rich in magical associations. It may also bear, through its close association with moly, an affinity to the Greek adjective αἵμων, "bloody." For one myth regarding the origins of moly relates it to the fate of the giant Pikolous, who, after the fateful war with Zeus, fled to Circe's isle, attacked her, and was himself attacked and slain by her father Helios. From the drops of blood which Pikolous shed in the struggle with Helios, moly is said to have sprung, hence one possible origin of the name "haemony" and one possible argument, based on its origin in the blood of a god, for its character as a symbol of grace.[4]

The other reasons why haemony may be considered a symbol of grace derive from the things Milton causes Thyrsis (or the Attendant Spirit) to say about it. Haemony, he says, was shown him by a certain shepherd lad, "of small regard to see," but skilled in herbs:

Amongst the rest a small unsightly root,
But of divine effect, he cull'd me out;
The leaf was darkish and had prickles on it,
But in another country, as he said,
Bore a bright golden flower, but not in this soil:
Unknown and like esteemed, and the dull swain
Treads on it daily with his clouted shoon,
And yet more med'cinal is it than that moly
That Hermes once to wise Ulysses gave
                                    [ll. 629–37].

The contrast between the "other country," where haemony flowers, and "this soil," where it does not, is said to represent the contrast between heaven and earth; virtue thus reaches its final perfection in heaven, and indeed the total dependence of virtue on grace is said to be figured in the fact that "the flower is not only the final perfection of the plant, but the source of the seed" (B & H, p. 213). Furthermore, Mr. LeComte declares that Milton's description of haemony is not unlike that of an herb named "rhamnus," which is mentioned in John Fletcher's *Faithful Shepherdess* (a recognized source of *Comus*) and further described in Gerard's *Herbal* under the popular name of "Christ's Thorn."

Now there are several difficulties with this interpretation. That the plant grows

[3] Edward LeComte, "New Light on the 'Haemony' Passage in *Comus*," *PQ*, XXI (July, 1942), 283–98; *Poems of Mr. John Milton*, ed. Cleanth Brooks and John Edward Hardy (New York, 1951); hereafter cited as "B & H."

[4] Two more elements which scholars have, perhaps, been too dignified to throw into the etymological pot of "haemony" are possible puns on Hymen, the guardian of virginity, and on harmony, the unruptured state of nature. Milton could have learned of Pikolous from Eustathius' *Commentaries*.

"in this soil" but flowers in "another country" is no great invention for Milton to have made on his own. Homer gives to moly (upon which haemony is obviously modeled) a white flower, and says simply that it is hard for men to dig; but Pliny gives it a "florum luteum," a bright yellow flower, and reports that it grows in the districts of Pheneus and Cyllene in Arcadia. Milton, who wanted to make use of it in Wales, may well have accounted for its being unknown there by saying that it grows there but flowers elsewhere. The notion that he gave it the name "haemony" as a way of referring not only to Pikolous' blood but to Christ's seems ingeniously esoteric; could Milton really have expected the Earl of Bridgewater and his guests to make on their own the not-even-suggested connection with Eustathius' *Commentaries;* and, supposing they made it, could he have doubted that the equating of Christ with a monster caught in the act of rape would have caused them anything but disquiet? Scarcely less extravagant is the assumption that they would all have read Fletcher's masque and Gerard's *Herbal* and would remember that the rhamnus misprinted in Fletcher was the same as the Christ's Thorn described in Gerard and that Christ's Thorn bore a vague resemblance to haemony.

Difficulties of this sort spring up on all sides as soon as one relaxes one's determination to ignore them. For instance, the simple shepherd lad of small regard to see is a distinctly casual receptacle for divine grace. Perhaps his pastoral, swainish humility makes him an appropriate figure, but the early and persistent assumption that he is Milton himself or Milton's boyhood friend Diodati militates against his being the agent of grace. To open the door for immodest comparisons of this sort is a Shelleyan, not a Miltonic, failing. If haemony is grace, there is another gross, im-

mediate breach of tact in Thyrsis' declaration that in this country it is

Unknown and like esteem'd, and the dull swain
Treads on it daily with his clouted shoon
[ll. 634–35].

The audience would scarcely have been edified by this thought, particularly the clerical members of it; nor does it conform in the least with Milton's convictions as expressed elsewhere. One does not offhandedly tell the members of a Christian commonwealth that grace is unknown to them, that they trample it underfoot. But a magic symbol of temperance, having its origin and power in earthly elements and implying a contrast between Arcadian virtue and modern grossness, would suffer no such disabilities.

Besides, the effect of haemony is not the appropriate effect of divine grace. Maybe it blossoms in heaven, but its virtuous effect occurs on earth and is earthly in nature. All Thyrsis has of the plant is the root (the root traditionally contains the potent element of moly); so that apparently virtue (the root and stalk) is good medicine even without grace (the flower). And haemony is not used in the story to bring anyone to heaven or even to Ludlow Castle but to avoid the ill effects of lust. It does not release the Lady, it protects the brothers against the enchantments of Comus, who is, allegorically, sensuality. Only in the vague sense that God is responsible for all things and the source of all energies (including the diabolic) did Milton suppose one needed divine grace to avoid drunkenness, riot, and lust. But as for the notion that grace in the Christian sense was necessary to live a chaste life, the pagan world teemed with evidence to the contrary.

In addition, Milton could not have expected an herb closely associated with and resembling moly to carry for any conceivable audience the allegorical significance of divine grace. This is not a matter of Miltonic origins and derivations but of general, accepted significance. The only evidence that Milton did not derive haemony from some cat's-cradle of gods, blood-drops, and vegetables involving Pikolous, Osiris, Mithra, Cerberus, Cadmus, Coelus, mandragora, rue, rhamnus, dittany, bryony, and garlic is the known quality of his mind and the principle of economy of assumption. But if he associated haemony with moly and did not explicitly indicate a new interpretation, it seems likely that he must have expected the conventional allegorical meaning of moly to be felt. Allegories of the Circe-Ulysses fable might involve physical, moral, or mystical principles; but, while the literal existence of moly was still being asserted, allegorical interpretations of the plant were more restrained. The one most easily available to a cultivated, unprofessional audience equated moly with temperance, and it was expressed in explicit detail prior to 1673 (when Milton last published Comus) by such men as Andrea dall'Anguillara, Pierre Gautruche, George Sabinus, D. Giphanius, Arthur Golding, and Alexander Ross. The same view is directly implied by George Sandys, Fulgentius, Apuleius, Heraclitus, Eustathius, and Boccaccio. For all these representatives of a larger company, moly is temperance or prudence, period.[5]

There is, to be sure, another allegorical view of the herb, which equates it with divine favor. This view might be found explicitly in Natale Conti, who speaks of the "divina clementia . . . quod per munus Ulyssi a Mercurio datum intelligitur," or in J. Spondanus, who gives a choice of two readings, in which moly may stand either for ethnic magnanimity or Christian faith.[6] But the religious interpretation is a minority one, easily available to

scholars, but by no means popularly diffused. To the degree that Milton could count on the members of the audience being familiar with any allegorical significance for moly or a moly-like vegetable, it was likely to include, if not comprise, the notion of temperance. If he intended a more exalted or particular significance— above all, if he intended that meaning to be exclusively received—he would be unlikely to leave his hearers without a pretty broad hint as to what it was. There is no such hint in the text.

Finally, certain sanctions for the interpretation of moly as temperance may be drawn from Milton's work before and after Comus. Elegy I to Diodati expresses the hope that Milton, with the aid of divine moly, will be able to avoid the fleshpots of London. Are we to suppose the poet so deeply sunk in cant and self-importance that, already at the age of eighteen, he would consider himself in a state of grace? Temperance is a virtue which turns up with particular frequency throughout the Miltonic canon; it is the subject of Michael's lecture in Book XI of Paradise Lost, and a major theme of Paradise Regained, Book II. "How great a virtue is temperance," cries the Areopagitica, "how

[5] Anguillara, Le Metamorfosi di Ovidio (Venetia, 1572), p. 198; P. Gautruche, Nouvelle histoire poétique (Paris, 1738), p. 316 (first English ed., 1671); Sabinus (ed.), P. Ovidii Metamorphosis (Francofurdi, 1593), p. 491; Giphanius (ed.), Homeri Odyssea (Argentorati, 1579), p. 279; Golding, The XV Bookes of P. Ovidius Naso (London, 1567), The Epistle, ll. 276–79; Ross, Mistagogus poeticus (London, 1647), p. 67; Sandys, Ovids Metamorphosis Englished . . . (Oxford, 1632), pp. 479–81); Fulgentius Mythologicon, ii. 12; Apuleius, De deo Socratis, cap. xxiv; Heraclitus De incredibilibus, cap. xvi; Heraclitus (Ponticus) Allegoriae Homericae, cap. lxx; Boccaccio, Genealogiae deorum, IV, xiv; Eustathius, Commentarii in Odysseam (Lipsiae, 1825) i. 381, calls moly an allegory of παιδεία but adds that it enables Ulysses to partake of Circe's pleasures with σωφρον. Note also that mercury, the bringer of moly, is the god of prudence; see, e.g., H. M. Servius, Commentarii in Vergilium (Göttingen, 1826), I, 390.

[6] Conti, Mythologiae (Genevae, 1651), pp. 566–67; Spondanus (ed.), Homeri quae exstant omnia (Basel, 1606), Odyssey, pp. 142–43.

much of moment through the whole life of man!"[7] Milton here makes none of those reservations which Messrs. Brooks and Hardy would make for him—that virtue is wholly dependent on grace, that it is radically defective in its own nature, that it achieves full flower only in the contemplation of grace. Miltonic temperance is no such contemplative, passive virtue. As Milton's whole life indicates, as well as the history of the causes which he supported, virtue was for him an active, wayfaring, warfaring quality. And temperance, which enables a man by his own inner election to act or to refrain, to combine and to direct, is the very model of an active Protestant virtue. "Wherefore did he create passions within us, pleasures round about us, but that these rightly tempered are the very ingredients of virtue?"[8] *Comus* itself emphasizes the concept of temperance at both the beginning and the end; the Attendant Spirit in his prologue says most people partake of Comus' drink "through fond intemperate thirst" (l. 67); and the final song declares that the Earl's children have come

> To triumph in victorious dance
> O'er sensual folly and intemperance
> [ll. 974-75].

If, on the other hand, one takes haemony to represent heavenly grace and the need for grace as a central theme of the masque, one must impute to Milton the artistic folly of introducing the climactic symbol and climactic idea of the poem in a subordinate clause 400 lines from the poem's end and of never mentioning it again.

Lastly, if haemony is a symbol of grace, yet cannot be used to release the Lady from Comus' magic chair, what shall we make of the power which does effect this release—that interesting, troublesome

[7] Milton, *Prose Selections*, ed. M Y. Hughes (New York, 1947), p. 222.
[8] *Ibid*, p 234.

creature, Sabrina? Brooks and Hardy, happy to find her a water nymph, eke out a suggestion of the waters of baptism and convert her, not without a subdued scuffle, into *another* symbol of grace. But a sense of economy, if nothing else, will cause us to balk at these reduplicated symbols. If Sabrina is merely what she seems to be, the genius of the shore and the patroness of virgins, her influence is one step above that of temperance and one step below that of grace itself, and her function in the masque is secure. But to make haemony grace, and Sabrina more grace, and the vision of the epilogue still another aspect of grace is too much altogether. I cannot feel that any allegory is worth the price in nonsense that one must pay for this one.

So far as there is an allegorical meaning for haemony, one need not look beyond temperance. But an important reason why Milton introduced haemony is not allegorical at all; it has to do with the demands of his story. He cannot have the young men rush in and skewer Comus on their literal swords because natural powers cannot be allowed to overcome supernatural ones and because the Attendant Spirit, who has already announced his function as a convoyer of the good, cannot be left unemployed. Milton clearly needs haemony in order to balance black magic with white; but as for a suggestion that he is trying to tell us that "Grace and Virtue are essentially the same" or that "the plant symbolizes Virtue in a state of awareness of its own imperfection, expecting perfection only in heaven" (B & H, p. 212)—these are pure extrapolations. One might as well argue from the statement that "the leaf was darkish and had prickles on it" that the Lady herself was thus afflicted or that virtue on earth is not merely difficult but essentially forbidding in its aspect. This Milton simply did not

believe; he would not have felt Spenser to
be a sage and serious poet if he had. He
would not have written those many passages on the beauty of virtue which stud
his work. He would not have been a Renaissance humanist, but a Coptic monk.

If, then, the masque is not preaching
the insufficiency of virtue without grace,
there is no reason to suppose that the
Elder Brother is the object of all that
criticism which Brooks and Hardy impute
to Milton. A priori, it is hard to see why
Milton should have undertaken, in a
masque which is essentially complimentary, to expose the adolescent heir of the
Earl of Bridgewater as a pompous, pedan-
tic fool; and, in fact, the evidence that he
intended anything of the sort is remarkably slender.

For example, the Elder Brother's first
speech is said by Brooks and Hardy to
exemplify naïveté because he asks the
moon to "disinherit Chaos" (ll. 331–34),
and Comus "has already (on sound traditional authority) used the moon as the
symbol of his sovereignty" (B & H, p. 205).
But the Elder Brother has not heard Comus talk about the moon; in fact, he has
no reason for supposing such a creature as
Comus exists. The identification of Comus
with the moon rests on line 116,

Now to the Moon in wavering Morris move,

though there seems no reason why one
should not, by the same logic, identify
Comus with the stars, too, on the basis of
lines 111–12:

> We that are of purer fire
> Imitate the starry quire.

But, in fact, there is no reason to identify
him with either, for the moon is Cynthia's
chariot as well as Hecate's, and is associated with chastity as well as with witch-
craft. As for the Elder Brother, he asks
both the stars and moon for light, and
then says if neither is forthcoming, he

will follow a light from a house. Why this
should be considered abysmal innocence is
not clear. He wants light from stars,
moon, or a dwelling, and an audience
which is expected to find these requests
naïve might well be advised what other
sources of light a dark wood usually
affords.

Brooks and Hardy make much of the
supposed naïve confidence which the
Elder Brother expresses in his sister's
safety, as if Milton wanted us to consider
him a brash and overconfident theorizer.
But, in fact, he holds to the doctrine of
virtue's self-sufficiency only with a very
distinct qualification, which Brooks and
Hardy do not so much as mention. He will
not be alarmed that she is lost and alone,

> Not being in danger, as I trust she is not
> [l. 370].

If Milton intended us to consider him
naïve, this reasonable restriction completely undermines the poet's dramatic
purpose. The Elder Brother does not take
an obviously unreasonable position in
saying,

> Virtue may be assail'd but never hurt,
> Surpris'd by unjust force, but not enthrall'd
> [ll. 589–90],

since, as we have seen, this principle is
dramatically fulfilled by the Lady and
Comus in the temptation scene; and when .
Thyrsis is first heard approaching in the
distance, the Elder Brother is notably
aware of the various ills against which he
and his brother must be on guard (ll.
482–85).

In two other passages Brooks and Hardy
find the naïveté of the Elder Brother expressed in an absolute opposition of good
and bad. He is so much against Comus
that he forgets vice may be alluring—and
the audience, in hearing him, is expected
to realize this limitation of his character:

Some say no evil thing that walks by night
In fog or fire, by lake or moorish fen,
Blue meagre hag, or stubborn unlaid ghost
That breaks his magic chains at curfew time
No goblin or swart faery of the mine
Hath hurtful power o'er true virginity
                                    [ll. 432–37].

Of this language Brooks and Hardy say that "it represents good and evil in abstract terms of white and black rather than light and dark. . . . The 'goblin,' the 'faery,' the 'hag' are merely items in a catalogue of evil *things*, the use of the word *thing* taking from them whatever quality of 'thing-ness,' of tangibility, they might have had" (B & H, p. 208).

This argument involves several strained, not to say mistaken, assertions. "Thing" as used of spirits comes with particular force; being creatures of several different spheres, neither wholly alive nor altogether dead, they can be referred to only by a slippery, noncommittal word like "thing."

MARCELLUS: What! has this thing appear'd again tonight? [*Hamlet*, I, 1, 21.]

That the passage lacks all tangibility and is "completely abstract" (B & H, p. 208) seems so lamentable a misreading that I can only appeal in silent amazement to the lines themselves.

Another example of the Elder Brother's supposed naïveté is found in lines 584 ff., where, in expressing his detestation of Comus, the Elder Brother is said to make of him "a 'simply' frightful creature, attended by such obvious bogies as Harpies and Hydras," so that the audience is intended to see in the Elder Brother a sort of "moral-philosophical Hotspur," illogical and immoderate (B & H, p. 211). Against this view we may appeal to dramatic probabilities. Thyrsis has told the Elder Brother that his sister is entrapped by a sorcerer living "within the navel of this hideous wood," a person skilled in witcheries, who offers to travelers a "baneful cup" which transforms them "into the inglorious likeness of a beast." Comus and his rout are called by Thyrsis "monstrous" and are compared to "wolves or tigers"; they are "abhorred" and "barbarous," and Comus, once again referred to, is a "damn'd wizard" (ll. 550–80). After all this, the Elder Brother would have no dramatic existence at all if he were not fairly cross at Comus. He proposes direct action against the enchanter, and this idea, while inadequate, certainly is not held up to mockery. It is inadequate to the occasion, which is extraordinary in ways that only Thyrsis can suspect, but perfectly "natural" in its immediate contexts. The idea is natural in the situation in which the Elder Brother is involved, and natural in relation to the audience, which expects and sympathizes with impetuous faults in young men whose sisters are threatened with rape. A display of perfect decorum and a philosophic wariness about all conceivable dangers would, under the circumstances, forfeit the sympathy of the audience forever.

Thus three central elements of the masque may be seen to fit together on the earthly plane without notable inconsistency or incongruity. The spiritual energies of the Lady's virtue suffice to repel Comus without any divine back-stiffening. The brothers are able to approach Comus armed, not with grace, but with temperance; and the doctrine that chastity or virginity possesses special powers for its own defense is enunciated by the Elder Brother without any such backlash of ironic commentary as Brooks and Hardy have imputed to Milton. The machinery of magic is invoked to protect the Lady and her brothers, and its connection with chastity may even have been, in Milton's mind, a conviction more integral than the word "machinery" implies (see the discussion in Tillyard's *Milton*, Appendix C); but in the masque it serves moral ends which can be perfectly well understood on the secular plane.

Where, then, is heaven, and where in the masque does heavenly influence intervene? Obsessed with theological ultimates, Brooks and Hardy locate heaven at least three times over. The Attendant Spirit is for them a heavenly messenger because he comes from somewhere near Jove's court (B & H, pp. 189, 193); but then they say flatly that the "father's court, in the play, symbolizes heaven" (B & H, p. 226); however, when the Attendant Spirit, speaking the epilogue, says he is leaving the court for a new sphere, this, too, seems to be heaven (B & H, p. 228). Is it possible that he should leave heaven to go to heaven? No, it seems that Sir John's court has only "played" for a time at being heaven (B & H, p. 230); and thus heaven is unmade as blithely as formerly it was made.

But, in the first place, there is little reason to suppose the Attendant Spirit a proper angel. Milton's manuscript refers to him as a "daemon," and daemons, as Burton will inform us, were not angels but tutelary spirits.[9] The Attendant Spirit goes to some pains to make his nature explicit:

Before the starry threshold of Jove's court
My mansion is, where those immortal shapes
Of bright aerial spirits live enspher'd [ll. 1–3].

He lives before—that is, outside—the threshold, and he lives where spirits are enspher'd; these two facts place his home among the planets, where "Il Penseroso" assigns the residence of daemons:

And of those Daemons that are found
In fire, air, flood, or under ground,
Whose power hath a true consent
With planet, or with element [ll. 93–96].

He represents the interests of heaven, he is a messenger of heaven, he has supernatural powers and supernatural knowledge; but his real business is on earth, and it is by no means so general a concern as one usually attributes to ministers of grace. He exists, by his own account, to provide a special protection for specially virtuous people against special perils (ll. 15–17, 40–42, 78–82). Theologically, he is a guardian spirit, dramatically a master of ceremonies; in neither capacity does he determine the events of the story, exercise any superhuman power other than his wisdom, or attempt more than the release of virtue to establish its own destiny.

The Attendant Spirit does not come from heaven, and there is no more reason to suppose the young people are going there. The court of Sir John Egerton at Ludlow Castle is doubtless a good place to arrive, and heaven is no doubt the final destination of the good; but Sir John might well have found a bit thick the imputation that he was God the Father. The Attendant Spirit's account of the presidency of Wales (ll. 18–36) offers no allegorical significance to the scrupulous eyes of Brooks and Hardy; here, if anywhere, one would expect the symbol of heaven to be made explicit. But they rest their allegory entirely on two lines in which Comus tells the Lady that he has seen her brothers and

if those you seek
It were a journey like the path to Heav'n
To help you find them [ll. 301–3].

And that a hyperbolical cajolery in the mouth of a notorious deceiver should be taken as a positive statement of fact about

---

⁹ "Some indifferent *inter deos et homines* as heroes and daemons which ruled men and were called genii" (*Anatomy*, Part 1, sec. 2, mem. 1, subs. 2; cf. also *Hierocles in aurea carmina* [Cambridge, 1709], p 36).

an unrelated matter seems a queer sort of syllogism.

No, heaven appears in the masque just where it ought to appear, as the epilogue to a story which concerns primarily the trials of this earth. The Attendant Spirit departs not for Christian, but for a series of pagan heavens—for the islands of Hesperus, the Elysian Fields, the garden of Adonis, and the retreat of Cupid and Psyche. Whatever else these heavens represent, they are not the Christian paradise, either symbolically or otherwise;[10] for the Spirit can fly or run only

> to the green earth's end
> Where the bow'd welkin slow doth bend,
> And from there can soar as soon
> To the corners of the moon [ll. 1014–17].

His heavens are of the spheres, and of the lowest spheres at that, the earth and the moon. But in his final statement to the audience he urges,

> Mortals that would follow me,
> Love virtue, she alone is free,
> She can teach ye how to climb
> Higher than the sphery chime.
> And if virtue feeble were
> Heav'n itself would stoop to her
> [ll. 1018–23].

Here at last is the Christian heaven, unmistakably. It is not seen or described, as it should not be; it is merely indicated as an aspiration. Its position is "higher than the sphery chime," above that music of the spheres which echoes and complements the saintly choirs, but is distinct from and inferior to them. "In any case," Brooks and Hardy assure us, "it is clear that the final attainment is not made without the assistance of a power higher than virtue's own" (B & H, p. 233). What it is clear from is not apparent; all the

[10] Note particularly the MS changes of l. 995, where Milton rejected successively "manna" and "Sabaean" dew for the strictly pagan "Elysian" dew.

poet says in the body of his direct declarative assertion is that virtue can teach mortals to get to heaven. No doubt Milton, like all other Christians, understood the efficacy of another power; but his silence here is more compatible with the emphasis that grace supplements virtue than with the negative assertion that virtue is inadequate without grace. The properly Miltonic mortal actively climbs toward grace, he does not passively wait to receive it. And if long-range consistency matters at all, one might point to that extraordinary series of lines in *Paradise Lost* (III, 309 ff.), in which Milton applied the audacious doctrine of merit to Christ himself.

The last conditional couplet of *Comus* confirms, even as it expands, this notion:

> And if virtue feeble were,
> Heav'n itself would stoop to her.

Taking it for granted that throughout the masque virtue has been shown as feeble and heaven as stooping, Brooks and Hardy are thoroughly embarrassed by Milton's use of the conditional in line 1022; and they say Milton chose this construction "only to emphasize the paradoxical nature of the situation proposed, not to leave its existence in doubt" (B & H, p. 233). This bit of critical patter may be worth a moment's examination. There is nothing "paradoxical" about virtue's being feeble or heaven's adjusting itself to this weakness. Even though the notion of "virtue" may include either goodness or potency, morality or strength, there is no impression of paradox in line 1022, because virtue in the first sense can obviously be feeble and virtue in the second sense obviously cannot. When a word has two senses, the fact that one of them is nonsensical in context and the other platitudinous does not suffice to make a paradox.

279

But even if a tiny germ of paradox were apparent at the farthest reach of one reading of "virtue," a conditional construction would not serve to emphasize it. The last word of line 1022, "were," is crucial here; and, to parse its grammar out, it is a third-person singular subjunctive form used in a subordinate clause to indicate a condition contrary to fact. By writing the last couplet in this form, Milton can only have intended to convey that if virtue were feeble (which he did not think she was and had not represented her as being), heaven would stoop like a falcon to help her. But in what sense virtue could be "free" if her *only* function, or an indispensable part of her function, were to be lifted aloft like a limp rabbit in the claws of an eagle is not clear. Active virtue is a norm in the masque; passive acceptance of grace is an exception. A glistering guardian *might* come to aid virtue "if need were" (l. 219), but such an appearance is exceptional and auxiliary. If it has any moral meaning at all, *Comus* intends something much closer to "The Lord helps those that help themselves" than to Caliban's notion of the deity, or Holy Willie's.

Though it may have this incidental result, the real trouble with overreading is not that it imposes a rigid pattern on the literary work. Ardently as Brooks and Hardy have struggled to interpret *Comus* according to their own lights, the total effect they present is not of an intricate architecture but of an ingenious or perverted chaos. When Milton wrote that virtue alone is free, it appears that he meant to say that virtue alone is dependent; why he did not say this instead of the contrary remains mysterious. When Milton wanted to refer to Christ's Thorn, he hid it behind the name of rhamnus, which he hid behind the name of moly, which he hid near the name of haemony; and he was so crafty about making us think of Christ's Thorn

that he never mentioned it, as a result of which three hundred years had to elapse before anyone could so much as suspect his intention. There may be carelessness in this sort of thinking, or confusion, but it is principled carelessness and confusion. The trouble is not with the critics, who are men of ingenuity, not even with the particular interpretation of *Comus*, which is wrong-headed, but with a way of interpreting it, with an image of the creative mind which produced it. Milton's was not a sly, furtive, random, cryptic mind; he did not work, like some very great artists of another breed, in indirection, innuendo, and pastiche. For every beauty which one uncovers on esoteric assumptions (and it is both odd and significant how little Brooks and Hardy make of beauty, how indifferent they seem to be whether they uncover an anagram, a pun, a grotesque fault in taste, or a relevant harmony), one sacrifices a half-dozen of the larger elegances for which *Comus* really exists. The fault of overreading is pandemic, it corrupts everything and will sacrifice even its own best perceptions for the glare and tinsel of a bit of false wit.

This is especially noticeable when, as frequently happens, Brooks and Hardy succumb to an obvious, jangling antithesis such as Milton had within his grasp and deliberately chose to forego. The virtue-strength/virtue-morals pun is one of those which Milton purposely passed up. Another occurs in one of the concluding songs:

Heav'n hath timely tried their youth,

says the song; and Brooks and Hardy must forthwith wrench Milton into a timely-timeless antithesis. Heaven has tried the youth of the young folk in the world of time; it will reward them in the world beyond time. No matter that neither Milton nor any contemporary ever uses "timely" in any such sense; no matter that the death-thought involved in "going to heaven" jars on the jubilation of homecoming. We must have the antithesis at all costs.

One useful device for creating antitheses where Milton never intended them is to treat him as a nineteenth-century poet flavored with nineteenth-century transcendental philosophy. For instance, Thyrsis prefaces his account of Comus by saying that though "shallow unbelief" and "ignorance" refuse to admit it, the supernatural beings described by poets do exist (ll. 513–19); and for Brooks and Hardy this comment imports "the dependence of poetic truth on belief" (B & H, p. 209). Why they do not add that poetic truth also depends on knowledge is all too obvious. But, in fact, Milton did not think that poetic truth depended on belief, because he nowhere distinguishes poetic truth from other varieties, or asserts, as Blake and Keats were to do more than a century and a half later that a strong conviction about any matter makes it true.[11] So also in line 10, where the Attendant Spirit mentions the crown that Virtue gives

After this mortal change, to her true servants,

Brooks and Hardy read the phrase "mortal change" as "the constant change which makes mortal existence a death-life" (B & H, p. 189). But a doubt or two may creep in as to whether Milton really intended a comparison between the Earl of Bridgewater's children and the Ancient Mariner. For one thing, he never uses the phrase "mortal change" or anything like it to describe life; but he does (*PL*, X, 273) use the same phrase of death. Not having read *Die Welt als Wille und Vorstellung*, he did not think of change as aim-

less or delusive, and nothing in his life or writings suggests that he considered mortal existence a "death-in-life." As a matter of fact, whether "mortal change" refers to life or death does not particularly matter, so far as the argument over virtue and grace is concerned. But Brooks and Hardy cannot resist the chance for a quibble; they must assume that Milton wrote "after this mortal change" by way of saying "after this changing mortal life," at the expense of a tautology, in defiance of the words' most obvious connotations, and for no other visible reason than to bemuse explicators.

The examples could be multiplied, but conclusions are privileged to generalize. The readings of *Comus* which emerge from a close analysis of the imagery, unchecked by a larger perspective on the poem's literal architecture, may yield a series of flashing, fragmentary insights but are unlikely to co-ordinate them into a coherent whole. For good or for evil, much of Milton's imagery is strictly decorative—his overtones exist to be realized and forgotten, not to be exalted into general principles and large-scale structural devices. The story, the moral allegory, and the courtly compliment are Milton's structural devices. In point of fact, brightness and coolness do not happen to be "associated with Virtue throughout the poem" (B & H, p. 225); but even if they were, the fact would be of dubious structural significance. Milton did not compose *Comus* in cools and hots any more than in lights and darks, louds and softs, wets and drys, or thins and thicks. He made use of these qualities as occasion required, but he did not attribute allegorical or general significance to them without explicitly indicating it; their role is decorative and subordinate, not structural and primary. Any reader who chooses may, of course, impose an allegorical significance on any element

---

[11] *The Marriage of Heaven and Hell*, conversation with Isaiah; Keats to Benjamin Bailey, November 22, 1817.

he likes; but only at the risk of having to drop it hastily when it no longer fits. In certain sections of the masque, for example, no radical harm ensues from associating Sabrina's aquatic habits with a cool, cleansing Virtue. But if water-equals-virtue be made a constant equation, the brothers' search for virtue— "some cool friendly spring" (l. 281)— then becomes responsible for the Lady's entire plight. No doubt any average-energetic allegorist can invent in a few minutes half-a-dozen ways of getting over, under, around, or away from this difficulty; I am convinced that it would be far less distracting and far closer to the main lines of Milton's intent to let the water-virtue connection quietly disappear the minute it ceases to help our understanding of the images and begins to make demands on its own account. It should remain on the fringe of our minds, not in the center. If this critical outlook implies a low estimate of *Comus* as a tissue of images and implications, some consolation may perhaps be found in the sleazy weaving of all the fabrics hitherto produced from these materials. *Comus* as a masque presenting a clear story, a simple allegory, and a graceful compliment embroidered with a fluid imagery seems to me worth ten fretworks of strained conceit and forced interpretation. Perhaps when the critics have learned a little temperance in the application of their Byzantine ingenuities, we shall be able to enjoy without apology the simple beauties of obvious commonplaces set in musical language.

CORNELL UNIVERSITY

THE *MILIEU* OF *COMUS*

By G. F. Sensabaugh

Commentary agrees in the main that *Comus* sprang from Milton's rich and varied reading at Horton and that the mask may be interpreted as a crystallization of the poet's personal beliefs on chastity and love.[1] Such interpretations hold a great deal of truth; in *Comus* Milton no doubt attempted to clarify the true doctrine of platonic love and in so doing considered chastity as a way of life. Yet to see *Comus* thus as a hot-house performance, unaffected by the storm of debate in both court and town, is to miss much of its significance; it is like reading *Lycidas* without a knowledge of the bishops' "blind mouths." A re-examination of the mask, therefore, in relation to its immediate *milieu*, may clarify a number of allusions and give fresh meaning to the performance itself.

The immediate background of *Comus* abounds in conflicts over chastity, marriage, and platonic love. Puritans[2] deemed marriage a sacred bond, a union blessed by God for the relief of concupiscence and for the consolation of man's soul; they constructed a marital hierarchy in which the male was responsible and the female submissive. Challenging these ideals, a coterie of platonic love in the court of Henrietta Maria casuistically argued that marriage was secondary to individual desires and that physical beauty in woman demanded abject devotion from man. Two such diametric-

[1] See, for example, James Holly Hanford, "The Youth of Milton," in *Studies in Shakespeare, Milton, and Donne* (New York, 1925), p. 139; Denis Saurat, *Milton: Man and Thinker* (New York, 1925), p. 19; and E. M. W. Tillyard, *Milton* (London, 1934), pp. 74-5. Hanford, however, hints that Milton might have referred to the court: "The tradition [of platonic love], while not without its appeal to him, was essentially foreign to his temperament. It was associated, too, in his own day with things and persons that he condemned, for the doctrine of Platonic love had received a new lease on life at the court of Henrietta Maria, where it had become more than ever a mask of triviality and corruption" (*op. cit.*, p. 144).

[2] See William and Malleville Haller, "The Puritan Art of Love," *The Huntington Library Quarterly*, V (1942), 235-72. "This dedication of the Puritan clerical caste to conjugal life," say the authors, "was hardly less important in its effects than that of courtly poets to the worship of feminine beauty."

238

ally opposed points of view naturally created a sharp clash over matters of marriage and love; and during Milton's first years at Horton the conflict resounded through town and court. Moreover, during this time Milton himself pondered questions of marriage and love; he had apparently given up the hope of connubial bliss in favor of the insight accorded those who follow the sage and serious doctrine of virginity. It would thus appear logical for Milton to refer to this conflict which touched on issues so vital; and this is what Milton seems to have done. At any rate, a brief glance at the debate, held up in relation to *Comus*, will reveal that Milton dealt with the same issues that currently paraded for public review.

The clash between Puritan and court over questions of marriage and love began soon after Henrietta Maria landed in England as the bride of Charles I. The young Queen aroused Puritan ire by promoting a coterie of platonic love, whose rites and beliefs ran athwart religious tradition. By 1629, in Jonson's *The New Inn*, the coterie's manners and morals appear in crystallized form;[3] and through the subsequent decade both poetry and plays give the details of the Queen's new philosophy. On June 3, 1634, or just four months before Ludlow Castle enjoyed the production of *Comus* at the beginning of Michaelmas term, James Howell wrote:

> The Court affords little News at present, but that there is a Love call'd Platonick Love, which much sways there of late; it is a Love abstracted from all corporeal gross Impressions and sensual Appetite, but consists in Contemplations and Ideas of the Mind, not in any carnal Fruition. This Love sets the Wits of the Town on work; and they say there will be a Mask shortly of it, whereof Her Majesty and her Maids of Honour will be part.[4]

The mask alluded to here is generally believed to have been D'Avenant's *The Temple of Love*, a performance which makes it clear that the Queen and her ladies planted the "new sect" on a "dull northern isle" called "Britaine," and that, though such love strangely found "birth and nourishment in Court," it soon became fully accepted:

> Certain young Lords at first disliked the philosophy
> As most uncomfortable, sad, and new;

---

[3] A good part of this play is given over to the details of the doctrine of platonic love.

[4] *Epistolae Ho-Elianae* (London, 1890), I, 317-8.

> But soon inclin'd to a superior vote,
> And are grown as good Platonical lovers
> As are to be found in an hermitage, where he
> That was born last reckons above fourscore.[5]

Just how uncomfortable, sad, and new this philosophy appeared to the court is not a matter of record; but the philosophy itself, along with the coterie's rites, appears again and again in court plays and masks.[6]

An examination of this drama discloses that the cult employed a rhetorical jargon similar to "courtesy" in the old courtly love sense. Courtiers apparently spent hours in foppish court compliment, exciting their ladies as *saints,* before whom they knelt in solemn *adoration,* extolling their *beauty, chastity,* and *love;* they gravely discussed the pure state of their souls, their untarnished minds, and the immortality of love such as theirs. Their beliefs, which became evident through such discussions, are often contradictory; nevertheless, the gist of their contentions may be put down in the following concise form:

1. Beauty and goodness are one and the same.
2. Beautiful women command worship.
3. Love for beautiful women is chaste and pure.
4. Such love is divine and all-powerful.

Now these beliefs, rather than promoting " Love abstracted from all corporeal gross Impressions and sensual Appetite," as James Howell put it, encouraged courtiers to pursue carnal love, which they proceeded to sanction with rhetorical jargon. In fine, cult members employed such basic tenets to argue casuistically; they hotly contended that, since a beautiful woman is of necessity good, all her actions and thoughts are therefore good also. Several specific examples may be singled out to make clear how coterie devotees thus sophistically reasoned. In William Cartwright's *The Royall Slave,* Atossa claims that nature freely gives her gifts to all comers and for such prodigality is not considered less chaste. Then she asks her husband, who has questioned her freedom in love, whether he would seal up a fountain, confine the air to his walk, or ask the

---

[5] *The Dramatic Works of Sir William D'Avenant* (London, 1872-4), I, 293-4.

[6] G. F. Sensabaugh, " Love Ethics in Platonic Court Drama, 1625-1642," *The Huntington Library Quarterly,* I (1938), 277-304.

flower to cast no smell but for a favored one only. Apparently, Atossa's argument immediately wins him; for in spite of his wife's moral defection he directly answers:

> Thou art still vertuous my *Atossa*, still
> Transparent as thy Crystall, but more spotlesse.
> Fooles that we are, to thinke the Eye of Love
> Must alwayes looke on us. The Vine that climbes
> By conjugall Embracements 'bout the Elme,
> May with a ring or two perhaps encircle
>> Some neighbouring bough, and yet this twining prove,
>> But the Offence, but Charity of Love.[7]

This notion that beauty and love should be current coin receives further support in D'Avenant's *The Fair Favourite*, in which the Queen actually defends the King's love for his mistress Eumena, who is beautiful and therefore cannot commit sin. The Queen states that such extra-marital love is noble and pure, too sacred to be confined to one person alone; therefore from this love flows much good:

> since what is good doth still encrease
> In merit of that name, by being most
> Communative.[8]

Thus to make love current coin is to praise God; in fact Thrysis, in Joseph Rutter's *The Shepheards Holy-Day*, argues in this very vein as he contends that all good things are created for men to enjoy. Furthermore, the worship of beautiful women is made tantamount to the exercise of religion itself:

> Love is divine, for if religion
> Binds us to love, the Gods who never yet
> Reveald themselves in any thing to us
> But their bright Images, the fairest creatures,
> Who are our daily objects; loving them,
> Wee exercise religion: let us not
> Be scrupulous, or feare; the Gods have care
> Of us, and of our piety.[9]

It is apparent that the worship of beauty in women led to a love far from pure or divine; indeed, platonic love, through its rhetoric and casuistry, became but a cloak to hide illicit affairs of the heart.

[7] *The Royall Slave* (Oxford, 1639), sig. F2ᵛ.

[8] D'Avenant, *op. cit.*, IV, 264.

[9] *The Shepheards Holy-Day* (London, 1635), sig. E8.

The doctrine of chastity therefore developed not into a source of true virtue but into a fount of sin and corruption; and marriage, as an institution, received short shrift from those who chose to follow individual whim.

The Queen's coterie thus threw down a serious challenge to traditional ethics in matters of marriage and love; and Puritans,[10] recognizing the challenge, soon replied through sermons and pamphlets. They scored the rhetoric of court love, pointed out false coterie reasoning, and brought down the wrath of God upon those who attempted to belittle marital ties. Even devotees of the cult, in plays which exalted their doctrine, paused now and then to comment upon the techniques and aims of the love they promoted. In *A Fine Companion*, for example, Valeria sees through the rhetoric of Spruse's argument to the reality of his attempt on her virtue :

> I am very sorry,
> The times disease has so prevail'd upon you.
> Tis the perfection now of complement,
> The onely end to corrupt honesty.
> To prostitute your oathes, and winne our hearts
> To your beliefe, is the Court eloquence.[11]

In the same way, Ariene, in *The Royall Slave*, recognizes the hidden intent of several passionate lovers who tried to win her according to coterie rules; moreover, she describes exactly what might have happened had not Cratander answered her cries :

> What they stile Love-sport only, and misname
> An arguing out of *Plato*, would have prov'd
> A true and downe-right Rape, if that your presence
> Had not become our Rescue.[12]

In view of such comments from court playwrights themselves, it is hardly surprising to find the clergy preaching directly against the coterie's rites and beliefs. Thus John Featly, speaking in terms that his congregation could not misunderstand, inveighs against courtship by telling the story of Joseph and Potiphar's wife. He first paints a vivid picture of Egyptian court follies, all of which

---

[10] All references to Puritans indicate a point of view, not membership in the Puritan party.

[11] *A Fine Companion* (London, 1633), sig. C3v.

[12] *The Royall Slave*, sig. D2.

Joseph cheerfully foregoes because his early training had warned him against sins of the flesh. Because of this training, Featly continues, Joseph saw through the fleshy devices of Potiphar's wife; in fact, the very "sweetnesse of her lovely complements, discover's the uglinesse of her foule intents." At this juncture, Featly pauses to ask his congregation a rhetorical question before he further pursues the problem of compliment. Could it be that a "mortall sinne may not couch it selfe under our common greetings?" Sidestepping a direct answer, Featly nevertheless condemns compliment aimed at impure delights, which was the kind prevalent in coterie love:

Those kinde of complements (of themselves) suffer not the name of sinnes: But if their aime bee luxurious, their end is pernitious. If then our very salutations, and common greetings (standing, onely, in impure vessels) may gather dregs, and so be turned into corruption: What are those more impious acts which, swelling in our hearts, breake forth into wickednesse?[13]

If John Featly, in spite of his detailed analysis, drew back and failed to deliver a direct blow against the coterie's ritual of love, Thomas Lawrence, in a sermon defending clerical rights, felt no such faint-hearted compunctions. Unequivocally, he alienates courtly lovers from the friendship of God; moreover, he unhesitatingly brings down the hatred of God upon hypocrites whose smooth words belie their intentions:

God is no friend to the hypocrisy of complement, and therefore in Scripture ever meanes more then he speakes: *the words of the Lord are pure words, as silver tried seaven times in the fire*, saith the Psalmist, calcined and sublimated from this drosse: for he is a God of truths, not of varnishes; of realities not of shadowes. He hates that mouth which belies the minde, and likes men on earth best, when they resemble, the Saints in Heaven; where soules commerce *per verbum mentis*, without tongues; and thoughts are seene without the mediation of words.[14]

In this way the clergy answered Cratander's worship for his saintlike Atossa, or Spruse's courtship for his angel, Valeria; and they further continued the attack by unmasking the sophistical tenet that beauty and goodness are one and the same.

The clergy took especial pains to show that no relation existed between beauty of body and virtue of soul; in fact, they reiterated

[13] *The Honor of Chastity. A Sermon, made and preached* (London, 1632), p. 16.
[14] *Two sermons* (Oxford, 1635), p. 4, in "The Priviledge of the Clergy."

that, contrary to coterie belief, beauty more often led to sin than to purity of action and thought. In *Mundanum Speculum*, a treatise which pictures every moral defection of which the Stuart citizen could think, Edmund Cobbes flatly declares that "beautie hath made many adulterers, but neuer any chast." [15]   William Crompton goes into the question more fully.   Claiming that man should look for qualities of fidelity, industry, vigilance, charity, wisdom, and piety in the woman of his choice, he points out that beauty is of no consequence since " Men may easily find faire women wantons." [16]   In a similar sermon on marriage, Bartholomew Parsons pursues the issue of beauty to its logical conclusion, so far as the Puritan attitude toward coterie love is concerned.   He opens up his assault by reminding his audience that "*A faire forme is nothing but a iemme of glasse, a fading bubble, snow, a rose a dew, a winde, smoake, aire, nothing.*"   After this warning, he strikes at the very core of coterie thought by arguing that beauty is both ephemeral and corrupt:

" *. . . when thou seest a faire woman, that hath a twinkling eye, & a smiling face, a looke pleasant, attractive and amiable, such as putteth thy heart into an heat and setteth on fire thy desire; thinke that that which so ravisheth thee, is nought else but earth, and that the fire which burneth thee is but dung, and then will thy fury bee asswaged. Raise vp the skinne of her face, and thou shalt see all the vilenesse of that goodly shew. Stay not vpon the outward maske, but pierce with the eye of thought into that which is within, and what else shalt thou see there but bones sinewes and veines? But this is not enough, Remember that beauty changeth, groweth old, and withereth, that the quickenesse of the eye waxeth dead, that the cheekes grow hollow, that all that faire flower passeth away. See what is that maketh thee (as it were) a beast. It is ashes, dust and filth, that burneth thee. For what is the substance of this beauty that thou seest but snot, spittle, corrupt blood, and the iuice of rotten nourishment?* [17]

In this way the clergy openly opposed the main rites and beliefs of the Queen's brand of platonic love; and as the decade before the rebellion progressed, their cries became even more pointed and clear.

[15] *Mundanum Speculum, or, The Worldlings Looking Glasse* (London, 1630), pp. 221-2.
[16] *A Wedding-Ring, Fitted to the Finger of Every Paire that Have or Shall Meete in the Feare of God* (London, 1632), p. 17.
[17] *Boaz and Rvth Blessed: or A Sacred Contract Honovred with a solemne Benediction* (Oxford, 1633), pp. 33-4.

Issues of marriage, which sprang from the coterie's disdain of marital duty, also drew from Puritans sharp refutation. Puritans claimed that the wife should submit and obey, not command idolatrous worship; they believed in the sanctity of marital ties and hence attacked those who would cut them because of individual whim. In such attacks they often left their opponents unnamed, for too direct an allusion often cost them their ears; but what they said points directly at the philosophy of marriage and love in the court. In the same sermon in which he flayed the worship of beauty in woman, for example, Bartholomew Parsons excoriates those who, through filthy songs and devices, belittle the marital estate; then he goes on to say that the righteous should take up arms against such foul-mouthed defilers:

Hence then may the tongue of the learned speake a word in season, for the stopping of those foule mouths that shoote out their arrowes even bitter words, either against the state of matrimony to disgrace it as miserable, or against the ordinance it selfe to condemne it as sinfull and abominable,[18]

Others of similar mind helped swell the cry against those who would attempt to make marriage lose caste, with the result that soon, as might be expected, a number of Puritans began to associate growing popery in court with attacks against the connubial estate. That such a twist should occur, however, is not hard to explain. The Queen herself openly professed her Catholic religion; moreover, soon after her arrival in England she set up a chapel and began to attract many adherents, one of whom was Walter Montague, the author of *The Shepheard's Paradise*. This play, produced in court in January of 1633 at great expense, most completely expresses the tenets and ethics of platonic love; it holds further distinction in that Henrietta Maria herself played one of the main parts, which no doubt made her peculiarly sensitive to Prynne's allusion to notorious whores in his *Histriomastix*. In addition to this, it soon became the fashion to profess the Catholic religion in court as well as platonic love; and as a consequence, Puritans probably considered the cult's notions of marriage to coincide with those of Rome. The upshot of all this was a sharp exchange concerning the status of marriage, in which Puritans attacked both Catholics and court.[19]

[18] *Ibid.*, p. 16.
[19] For the details of this conflict, see G. F. Sensabaugh, "Platonic Love and the Puritan Rebellion," *Studies in Philology*, XXXVIII (1940), 457-481.

Thus during the first part of Milton's Horton vacation, issues of marriage and love received public attention through plays, sermons, and pamphlets; and the questions which seemed most important centered in compliment, beauty in women, and the status of marriage.   Such a background appears peculiarly significant in view of the fact that at this very time Milton himself pondered marriage and the celibate life.   His Puritan inheritance and his age asked that he marry, but his dedication of time to serious study demanded that he forego the joys of conjugal life.   He needed mightily an ideal which would support this unPuritan step.   Hence, as he read deeply in Plato and the Scriptures, he grasped at the notion that those who held themselves untainted by woman developed powers unknown and incomprehensible to libertines or to those enjoying the connubial state; and he set about to crystallize in *Comus* the sage and serious doctrine of virginity.   But the court also spoke of chastity, beauty, and platonic love, a kind far different from that found in the Scriptures and Plato.   Consequently, so that his doctrine would not be confused with that about which the court prated, Milton felt that he must hold up for contrast the false and the true. At least, he so often refers to false rhetoric in court, embodies in the character Comus so much current casuistry about beauty and love, and makes so clear that his idea of chastity is superior to marriage, that his close relation to the current debate can hardly be challenged.

Milton refers often to false rhetoric employed in the court.   Just after the mask opens, when the Lady is wandering lost in the woods until Comus, disguised as a shepherd, offers to lead her to bucolic safety, Milton designates the court as a place where true courtesy was first named but where now it is most pretended.   This deprecation of court compliment appears in the Lady's reply to Comus, whose real intentions, in spite of his innocent approach, emerge later:

> Shepherd I take thy word,
> And trust thy honest offer'd courtesie,
> Which oft is sooner found in lowly sheds
> With smoaky rafters, then in tapstry Halls
> And Courts of Princes, where it first was nam'd,
> And yet is most pretended.[20]

---

[20] *The Student's Milton* (ed. Frank Allen Patterson, New York, 1939), ll. 320-25 in *Comus*.

Moreover, prior to this scene, Comus himself had admitted that he would employ rhetorical devices in an attempt to despoil the beautiful Lady. Like Spruse in Shakerley Marmion's *A Fine Companion*, he marshalls his words and holds it the perfection of compliment to overcome virtue under pretense of pursuing chaste ends:

> I under fair pretence of friendly ends,
> And well plac't words of glozing courtesie
> Baited with reasons not unplausible
> Wind me into the easie-hearted man,
> And hugg him into snares. (ll. 160-4)

Furthermore, the Lady herself, after Comus has sprung his devices, comments on the rhetoric through which Comus had tried to seduce her. " Enjoy your deer Wit, and gay Rhetorick," she sagely admonishes him, concluding that such as he will never be able to understand the true concept of virginity. Whatever reasons Milton may have had for referring so specifically to pretended courtesy in court and to the language of Comus, that he did so to point out false coterie love is not hard to believe.

A glance at the casuistry which Comus springs on his victims will make this belief even stronger. With coterie language and technique, Comus attempts to corrupt the beautiful Lady by contending that beauty should be current coin, that goodness grows from mutual partaken bliss, and that libertine love praises God, who has created riches and beauty for men to enjoy:

> Wherefore did Nature powre her bounties forth,
> With such a full and unwithdrawing hand,
> Covering the earth with odours, fruits, and flocks,
> Thronging the Seas with spawn innumerable,
> But all to please, and sate the curious taste?
> .   .   .   .
> Th'all-giver would be unthank't, would be unprais'd,
> Not half his riches known, and yet despis'd,
> And we should serve him as a grudging master,
> As a penurious niggard of his wealth.
> .   .   .   .
> Beauty is natures coyn, must not be hoorded,
> But must be currant, and the good thereof
> Consists in mutual and partak'n bliss,
> .   .   .   .
> Beauty is natures brag, and must be shown
> In courts, at feasts, and high solemnities. (ll. 709 ff.)

Since platonic plays abound in such language and reasoning, it is possible that Milton intended Comus to represent false reasoning in court; at least, through the Lady's reply, it becomes evident that Comus' argument *is* casuistry and that through such reasoning Comus makes himself unworthy of understanding the true doctrine of platonic love:

> I had not thought to have unlockt my lips
> In this unhallow'd air, but that this Jugler
> Would think to charm my judgment, as mine eyes
> Obtruding false rules pranckt in reasons garb.   (ll. 755-8)
>
> .   .   .   .
>
> Thou hast nor Eare, nor Soul to apprehend
> The sublime notion, and high mystery
> That must be utter'd to unfold the sage
> And serious doctrine of Virginity,
> And thou art worthy that thou shouldst not know
> More happines then this thy present lot.
> Enjoy your deer Wit, and gay Rhetorick
> That hath so well been taught her dazling fence,
> Thou art not fit to hear thy self convinc't.   (ll. 783-91)

To this rebuke, Comus replies:

> Com, no more,
> This is meer moral babble, and direct
> Against the canon laws of our foundation.   (ll. 805-7)

It may be extreme to suggest that the "canon laws of our foundation" refer to the code of coterie love; yet, so popular was court platonism, that the audience at Ludlow might have given these words this very meaning. In any event, it is clear that the Lady rebuked Comus for his rites and beliefs, and that these rites and beliefs were those of the court. It is evident further that for some reason Milton wanted to distinguish such manners and morals from the true doctrine of platonic love.

Indeed, the main purpose of the mask is to crystallize the true doctrine, as Milton suggests within the first few lines. Milton begins by explaining that most people find themselves confined to earth with low-thoughted care,

> Yet som there be that by due steps aspire
> To lay their just hands on that Golden Key
> That ope's the Palace of Eternity.   (ll. 12-4)

In words now become famous the real notion of chastity unfolds, particularly through the Elder Brother's remarks:

So dear to Heav'n is Saintly chastity,
That when a soul is found sincerely so,
A thousand liveried Angels lacky her,
Driving far off each thing of sin and guilt,
And in cleer dream, and solemn vision
Tell her of things that no gross ear can hear,
Till oft convers with heav'nly habitants
Begin to cast a beam on th'outward shape,
The unpolluted temple of the mind,
And turns it by degrees to the souls essence,
Till all be made immortal.   (ll. 452-62)

Here, then, is the real doctrine, which aims to attain by steps pure essence, not the carnal love of a beautiful woman; here also is a contrast so pointed that Milton's purpose for writing the mask takes on a significance not hitherto shown. In brief, at this time in his life, Milton wished to dedicate himself to the celibate life, and he characteristically found reasons why he should do so. But he also found that he had to do more than merely present the doctrines he discovered in Plato and the Scriptures. The court had aroused a debate over matters of marriage and love; moreover, the coterie praised platonic love and prated about pure attraction of souls. Consequently, in order that he might not be associated with what the coterie stood for, Milton distinguished the false from the true. Such a procedure is so thoroughly Miltonic that it appears almost inevitable that this is exactly what happened.

It must be admitted that the rhetoric referred to was old, used by poets of an earlier day; it must be also admitted that such casuistry about beauty and love was a Renaissance commonplace. But it must be remembered that when Milton wrote Comus such devices and arguments had just received fresh vigor in Henrietta Maria's coterie of platonic love and that a controversy about them resounded through city and court. Furthermore, Milton rarely wrote in an intellectual vacuum; he followed the thought of his day and would be as aware of the court's " Obtruding false rules pranckt in reasons garb " as he would be of the bishops' " blind mouths." In view of this, *Comus* appears to be not only a personal articulation of the sage and serious doctrine of virginity, but also an answer to the court in the current debate on matters of marriage and love.

Stanford University.

The Earl of Bridgewater's Legal Life
Notes toward a Political Reading of *Comus*

Leah Marcus

John Milton's *Comus* was performed on September 29, 1634 – a little over a year after Charles I's republication of the *Book of Sports*, only a few months after William Prynne's trial and punishment at the instigation of William Laud for his "treasonous" attack on the very sports and pastimes endorsed by Charles I and the Church. To assert a connection between these contemporary events and the major themes of *Comus* is nothing particularly new – the link was proposed at least as far back as 1884 and has been rediscovered periodically since then.[1] What has been new in the last ten years is an increasing curiosity about Milton's political intent. His masque commends wholesome forms of dancing, disguise, and revelry and can therefore be construed as a refutation of Prynne's absolute condemnation of all such activities. But what is considerably less clear is the stance Milton meant to take toward the authority of Charles I and Archbishop William Laud. The occasion of Milton's masque was an event of great political importance – the Installation of John Egerton, First Earl of Bridgewater, as President of the Council in the Marches of Wales. As President of Wales, the Earl of Bridgewater was an important agent of the central government. The Council over which he presided was a powerful court of law, one of the so-called prerogative courts created by royal fiat and expected to support the crown; it was also the central government's chief administrative unit

in Wales and four adjoining English counties.[2] As John Creaser has recently pointed out, we have evidence that town officials of Ludlow were invited to the performance of *Comus*; political allies of the Earl and members of the Council of Wales were surely among the audience as well.[3] Given the public nature of the masque's occasion, Milton's audience in 1634 may well have expected the performance to honor the central authority through its praise of the "noble Peere of mickle trust, and power" whom the monarch had appointed his President for Wales.

But that is not what *Comus* does. Members of the Earl's family, including the three children performing in *Comus*, had danced in masques at court and many other members of Milton's Ludlow audience were familiar with Caroline masques and their characteristic ways of celebrating the divine right of the monarch. As Stephen Orgel and others have demonstrated, masques for Charles I always converge upon a vision of the transcendent power of the king, and often glorify specific policy goals of the monarchy.[4] Milton's masque was also designed to bear a political reading, but *Comus* deliberately blurs lines of authority which in the court masque would have been quite distinct. Milton's masque offers high praise for the Earl of Bridgewater, but celebrates him more for his political independence than for his adherence to Caroline policy.

297

Comus is steeped in liturgical motifs for its festival occasion of Michaelmas, which marked the beginning of autumn court sessions at the Council in the marches of Wales. On one level, the masque can be seen as reflecting the prominent Michaelmas theme of the humbling and enlightenment of judges. For its Ludlow audience, it would have evoked specific parallels with a particularly difficult legal case of the previous year, a case of rape that officials of the Council of Wales had been most dilatory about prosecuting despite strong evidence against the rapist. King Charles I had called for strenuous judicial reform, and the Earl of Bridgewater's attempts to stamp out laxity and corruption among the judges of his own Council of Wales could be seen as furthering that goal. But this "centralizing" interpretation is called into question by another set of political associations that the masque seems clearly to engage. In a very concrete sense, *Comus* is an anti-Laudian masque. If we consider the work in terms of the jurisdictional challenges faced by the Earl of Bridgewater as he assumed his post at Ludlow, we will find that Milton emphasizes key areas in which Bridgewater was in conflict with Archbishop Laud and his program of "thorough" for the Church. *Comus* celebrates the Earl's rectitude and autonomy, simultaneously praising him for his efforts to reform the Council of Wales and urging him to consolidate his position as President of Wales into an independent base of power.

To reduce the whole meaning of *Comus* to the political implications it may have carried for some of its contemporaries would be an unpardonable diminution of its art. But interpreting the masque in terms of the judicial milieu of Ludlow will open up a new level of its functioning and may help to resolve a few cruxes—most notably the problematic double jeopardy of the Lady who, even after the banishment of Comus, remains immobile in her chair. Our endeavor may also help to dispel the common notion, sometimes encouraged by Milton himself in his later years, that the young man who wrote *A Maske at Ludlow* was a detached recluse, politically naive and uninvolved. In fact, there is an elemental radicalism about the work, despite the state occasion for which it was composed. *Comus* calls officialdom back to first principles exemplified in the public life of the Earl of Bridgewater himself, but all too frequently forgotten by others in positions of public trust. In a manner appropriate for

its festival occasion of Michaelmas, the masque enacts an inversion of authority that cleanses it and symbolically restores it to rectitude.

Considering his prominence, the Earl of Bridgewater was a remarkably reticent figure. What we do know about his conduct of public affairs has led to conflicting interpretations. Historians have frequently depicted him as a die-hard Royalist; Miltonists tend rather to view him as a moderate Puritan or at least a Puritan sympathizer.[5] In political matters, he tended, like his famous father Lord Ellesmere, Lord Chancellor under James I, to act as an individual rather than a member of a group. But one of his and the Egerton family's abiding principles was opposition to William Laud. Bridgewater himself was a loyal supporter of the Anglican Church, even in its more elaborate ritual forms. But he was anti-Arminian and strongly opposed to Laud's campaign for enforcing religious conformity. As President of Wales, he hoped to mold the Council of the marches into a strong base for combating the power of Laud. The Council had traditionally enjoyed considerable influence over Welsh ecclesiastical affairs, claiming the right to appoint bishops and to exercise jurisdiction over various offenses also tried by the ecclesiastical courts. Bridgewater was appointed its President in 1633. In the same year, William Laud was appointed Archbishop of Canterbury, and almost immediately he initiated wide-ranging reforms in Wales.

If a man willing to work with Laud had been President of Wales, the Archbishop would have had in the Council a powerful agency for furthering his vision, like its sister body the Council of the North under the Earl of Strafford. But the Earl of Bridgewater was a man of a different spirit, a moderate who preferred to leave most matters of nonconformity up to the conscience of the individual. Under the Earl of Bridgewater, the Council of Wales fought a quiet but desperate jurisdictional battle against Laud and the ecclesiastical courts.[6] The Earl's conflict with Laud, although seemingly minor in terms of some of the issues raised, was momentous in its implications—symptomatic of a much wider rift over the place and functioning of the Church. Laud did not take Bridgewater's opposition lightly. For a time in 1637, the Archbishop managed to halt Council proceedings altogether. But in 1634, when Milton wrote *Comus*, religious moderates still hoped to curb Laud and turn around the most rigorous of his policies. That, I should like to argue, is one of the things Milton designed *Comus* to do—encourage the Earl in his resistance to Laud and the central religious authority. For religious moderates in the year 1634, the Earl of Bridgewater must have seemed almost a last hope—one of the last of those in high government office both willing to work against Laud and possessed of a strong administrative base from which to do so.

Of course, the mere fact that Bridgewater was engaged in a quiet struggle against Laud is not sufficient reason to suppose that Milton's masque was designed to further the fight. But there are a number of tantalizing parallels between the arguments made in support of the Earl's position, some of which were a matter of public knowledge, and structural elements of the masque. Here I will discuss only one—the jurisdictional battle over cases of sexual incontinence—recognizing that my argument is unlikely to carry conviction when separated from its broader context, but hoping nevertheless to stimulate interest in the political milieu of *Comus*. In Milton's masque, the subject of chastity is overdetermined: it can be understood on a theoretical plane as an aspect of the masque's exploration of the interrelationships among purity, human volition, and divine grace; it can be linked to the Castlehaven scandal of a few years earlier, in which the Earl's wife's brother-in-law had been tried and executed for rape and sodomy—a series of events which in themselves would have offered sufficient reason for the Egerton family to reaffirm its chastity. Then too, the protection of chastity and the punishment of sexual incontinence was one of the major responsibilities delegated to the Earl and the Council of Wales. The subject of chastity surfaced in connection with the Earl's attempts at judicial reform, a matter to which we shall return later on in the discussion. But the question of which governmental structure was best qualified to protect chastity was a key issue in the jurisdictional conflict between Bridgewater and Laud. Milton's portrayal of the predicament of the Lady echoes elements of the Earl of Bridgewater's actual defense of his Council's right to try cases of sexual incontinence and reflects his view of the proper relationship between the overlapping secular and ecclesiastical jurisdictions.

By Charles I's 1633 Instructions to the Earl of Bridgewater, the Council in the Marches of Wales was given "full power and authority ... to hear and determine, and also to punish all manner of persons within all and evry the Limits and Jurisdictions aforesaid [of Wales and the Marches of Wales], which shall be notoriously known to live, contrary to Gods Laws and the Kings Highness Ecclesiastical Laws, in Incest, Adultery or Fornication, to the offence and dishonor of Almighty God, and to the evil and pernicious example of his Highness Subjects .... Provided also, and his *Majesties* meaning is, that the ordinary of every Diocess, where any such Offender shall be resident or comorant, shall or may proceed for the better satisfying the Congregation, and for the more knowledge of Offendors penitency in that behalfe; according to the Laws and Censures of the Church." But in December of the same year, Charles I granted Laud and the High Commission the same authority to "hear, determine and punish" Incests, Adulteries, and Fornications, "any our Laws, Statutes, Proclamations or other Grants, Priviledges or Ordinances, which be or may seem contrary to the Premisses, notwithstanding."[7] Charles I's charge to Laud and the ecclesiastical courts could, if one were so inclined, be taken as canceling the Earl of Bridgewater's instructions of only a few months before. In theory, the jurisdictional conflict had existed for a long time: there had been occasional clashes between the Council and the ecclesiastical courts before 1633. But Laud's zeal to consolidate the power of the Church and the Church courts created a new and much more serious crisis in 1634. For whatever reason, Charles I or some of his ministers seem deliberately to have set the Welsh Council and the ecclesiastical courts at odds. The Church courts would attempt to remove a case of adultery or incontinence from trial in the Court of the Marches on grounds that such cases belonged to them, arguing that if the Court of the marches were to try the same cases it would be placing defendants in double jeopardy, liable to be tried twice for one and the same offense. The Council of Wales countered by claiming that each court system had its own proper functioning, and that if the ecclesiastical courts tried and punished sexual offenders as the Council of Wales did, the Church was exceeding its proper authority: if the Church courts were to keep within their legal boundaries, there would be no double jeopardy.

The dispute did not reach a climax until 1637, but was already brewing well before Bridgewater assumed the Presidency of Wales. Preserving the Council's authority to try sexual offenses was not just a matter of principle or of curbing the power of Laud: what was at stake was the Council of Wales's ability to survive and function with the degree of autonomy the Earl of Bridgewater envisioned for it. To lose the fines from the sentencing of sexual offenders would damage the court financially, since such revenue formed an important part of its income. But the decline in its prestige would be far more serious than that. As the Earl complained, losing the jurisdiction would "very muche damp & blemishe it . . . for if (after the Losse of so many ornaments & supplements, which did advance the state & reputation of that Counsell,) the fines be lessened, I scarcely knowe howe the house will subsist, though with disgrace & blemish, which I shoulde be Loathe to see, or to thinke what may followe after . . . . I shoulde be very sory to finde it nowe within the limits of its Jurisdiction and Instructions so bitten & crushed that it shoulde not be able to breathe or moue."[8]

In his campaign against the Council in the Marches of Wales Laud may well have hoped to render it "so bitten & crushed that it shoulde not be able to breathe or moue." As we noted earlier, he perceived the Council under Bridgewater as an impediment to his ecclesiastical reforms in Wales. The legal aspects of the struggle are far too detailed to be explored here, but its general outlines will be familiar to any student of the origins of the English Revolution. In his struggle against Laud, the Earl of Bridgewater was attempting to preserve the power of the secular government against the encroachments of Laud and the Church. As so often in early Stuart England, we encounter a conflict between the secular magistrates, local and parliamentary ordinances, and the common law on the one hand, and the ecclesiastical authority and canon law on the other. Since the Council of Wales was a prerogative court, deriving its legitimacy in part from the king's claim to ultimate authority over judicial affairs, we might expect it to have made its case against Laud on that basis. But the Council claimed the right to try sexual offenses on grounds of legal precedent since they could demonstrate that the body had tried such cases "constantly and continually" since its beginnings. Their most important arguments rested on the authority of Parliament, specifically a Henrician statute which had given the king the right to deter-

mine Council jurisdiction. The ecclesiastical party, by contrast, based their case squarely on royal prerogative—the king's right to order his Church as he saw fit.[9]

According to the legal briefs prepared by the Earl of Bridgewater and his associates as part of their defense against Laud, the Council of Wales as secular authority had the right to "inflict Fine & imprisonment pro Reformatione Morum" and to remove the actual offense, while the lower ecclesiastical courts, although they had begun to impose fines and imprisonment for sexual offenses, could lawfully prescribe only spiritual penalties: "inioyne penance pro salute animae" and public humiliation for the "better satisfieng the congregation and the more knowledge of the offendors penance." If each court system kept to its proper function, there would be none of the double jeopardy of which the Church courts complained and both would "agree well togeather; the one punishment being for the offence against god, and the other as it is an offence or wrong to the partie thereby iniured, both concurrent to reforme the inward and outward man." And, as the Earl and his associates argued emphatically, the ecclesiastical courts could properly move in such cases only upon the prompting of the Council of Wales itself: even in the early days when bishops had headed the Council, they had allowed it to proceed to temporal punishment and only then caused the ecclesiastical courts to devise spiritual penance. The Earl even went so far as to cite scripture in support of his interpretation: "And as the Jurisdiction of the Courte of the marches is Justified & maintayned by Lawe & reason, and his Majesties Power to giue that Court Jurisdiction in the matter in question fullie warranted by the Lawes of the Realme so is it also proved by the lawe of God, For when Paule was accused for Heresie hee appealed to Caesar and would not (as Festus advised him) goe to the high Priests at Jerusalem to be tryed, which appeale was allowed."[10] For the Earl of Bridgewater, such a division of responsibility was in no way a derogation of the ecclesiastical authority, but rather a harmonious balancing of sacred and secular jurisdictions.

The double process outlined in the Earl of Bridgewater's legal briefs is precisely the division of responsibility we see operating in *Comus* to free the Lady from the enchanter, and as in the Earl's case against Laud, it has profound political implications. The Lady is, of course, no sexual offender—she stands firm against temptation—but a potential victim, subject first to the imagined perils to her chastity created by her solitude in the forest, then to the very real insinuations of Comus, at the least a leering invitation to the sin of incontinence, at their threatening height, suggesting the possibility of sexual violence against her. But once we concede the dissimilarity produced by her status as potential victim rather than participant in excess, we can recognize a congruence between the double remedy which frees her and the Earl's view of the complementary functioning of the secular and ecclesiastical authority.

· In freeing their sister from the threat posed by Comus, the brothers are acting for their father—performing the type of duty delegated to the Council in the Marches of Wales. Their assault upon Comus parallels the Earl of Bridgewater's analysis of the function of the secular arm—they remove the actual threat to their sister by dispersing Comus and his rout, although they are only partially successful since the enchanter himself escapes. But the secular authority does not suffice in itself: even after Comus flees, the Lady remains imprisoned in his chair. She is in "double jeopardy" in that more than one remedy is required to restore her—she still needs the ministrations of the goddess Sabrina. The intervention of Sabrina is conducted very differently from the rescue attempted by the brothers. As many readers have noted, Sabrina is associated with the functions of an enlightened Church. She is a conduit for divine grace; her powers are purely spiritual and offered in ritual form. Sabrina comes at the invocation of the Attendant Spirit and the two brothers, just as their father argued that the spiritual remedies of the Church should be applied at the behest of the secular authority. Comus has fled and is therefore not available to do public penance "for the good of the congregation," but the Lady, although innocent, has suffered a ritual pollution through her contact with the cup and chair of the enchanter. She remains in immobility and isolation until the rites of Sabrina act "pro salute animae" to restore her to her proper place in the community of holiday celebrants who have gathered at Ludlow.

Sabrina is a powerful figure, accorded much respect, yet curiously reticent and unassuming—quite unlike the Archbishop who was even then attempting to strengthen the Welsh Church at the expense of the Council of Wales. Her quiet but efficacious presence within the Earl's territory forms the greatest possible contrast to the overbearing style of Laud and the ecclesiastical courts in Wales and the Marches of Wales. In our brief outline here, we must set aside the interesting related question of how the "canon laws" of Comus and his foundation may fit into the masque's anti-Laudian scheme. But we need to notice that Milton's work is anti-Laudian without being anti-Anglican. It is so immersed in the liturgical motifs for its festival occasion that Chris Hassel, Jr. has termed it "virtually a liturgical pageant."[11] Within its clearly Anglican framework, Comus argues for a loosening of what was coming to appear a Laudian strangle hold upon the English Church. In the masque, as in the Earl of Bridgewater's arguments against William Laud, the sacred and the secular are allowed to preserve their autonomy; they interact in fruitful and healing harmony. The spiritual functions associated with Sabrina are not politically subservient to the secular authority, nor do they take precedence over it, but operate in cooperation with it, "both concurrent" to restore the Lady "inwardly and outwardly," just as the Earl had posited they should. Milton's masque argues for ecclesiastical reform, but a reform carried out within the structure of existing institutions.

In Milton's masque, ecclesiastical reform is inseparable from the enlightenment of judges. The secular authority invites the participation of the ecclesiastical authority to undo the effects of vice, but must initiate the harmonious interaction from a position of genuine rectitude. Michaelmas had its own holiday liturgies, but was also celebrated through a wide range of festival practices associated with the temporary overturn of the law and legal authority. In connection with the "lawless hour" of Michaelmas, masters and servants traded places. This holiday "overturn" is enacted in Comus. The role played by the Earl's own fifteen-year-old daughter recapitulates elements of a case of sexual assault that the Earl had been attempting to prosecute in the year before the masque. By allowing his own daughter to symbolically assume the position of the humble serving maid who had been the victim in that case, the Earl of Bridgewater offered a stern warning to his subordinates on the Council of Wales who had hindered the process of bringing the girl's assailant to justice.

Margery Evans was an illiterate fourteen-year-old servant who, according to her own testimony, was accosted as she walked alone by the roadside in Herefordshire near the Welsh border on Midsummer Eve, 1631, by one Philbert Burghill and his man. Unlike Milton's Lady, who encountered Comus under similarly threatening circumstances, Margery Evans did not manage to escape. She was raped, robbed, and left at the edge of a village with the warning that she would be killed if she told anyone what had happened.[12] Ignoring the threat, she gave hue and cry, pursued her attackers to a nearby town, and accused them in the presence of numerous witnesses, whereupon she herself was thrown into jail, without formal charge or the possibility of bond. According to contemporaries, sexual assaults in the Welsh border country were commonplace. What makes Margery Evans's case different from the many others that existed is that high government authorities eventually came to her aid. The girl was by no means silenced by her imprisonment. Despite her youth and poverty, she appealed with help from a literate aunt for redress to King Charles I, and the Privy Council called upon the Earl of Bridgewater, Lord President of the Council in the Marches of Wales, to make inquiries into the case. Although at first the Earl was by no means convinced of the truth of Margery Evans' charge against Burghill, he proceeded in an efficient and fair-minded way to disentangle the web of conflicting testimony surrounding the alleged crime, to keep his skeptical underlings in the Council of Wales from prejudging the case against her, and to try to ensure her a speedy and impartial trial. Indeed, it is only through his meticulous preservation of the major documents, now part of the Bridgewater collection at the Huntington Library, that we know of the case at all, or of his attempts to obtain justice for Margery Evans.

What the Earl of Bridgewater encountered as he delved into the case was a pattern of blatant corruption by which evidence against Burghill, a gentleman with powerful connections in the Welsh border country, was systematically suppressed. Shortly after she was put in jail, Margery Evans was visited by a midwife and two other witnesses, all of whom testified that she showed the physical signs of rape. Later on, the midwife and one of the witnesses reversed their sworn testimony. Burghill himself had been detained in connection with the young girl's accusation, but was sur-

reptitiously released. Both the man responsible for Margery Evans's imprisonment and the Justice of the Peace who released Burghill were closely associated with the Council in the Marches of Wales.[13] Given that fact, it is perhaps not surprising that Margery Evans got no redress from the Council of Wales itself: she testifies that she had failed to appear at a hearing before the Court of the Marches because she feared for her life. From London, well before his formal installation as President of Wales, the Earl of Bridgewater had tried repeatedly to get the Council to collect information on the case, but he encountered only evasion. The highest officials of the Council even had the temerity to send him a Certificate suppressing the involvement of Council members in the case.[14]

The Margery Evans case offered a particularly vivid illustration of judicial corruption in Wales and the border counties. Local Justices of the Peace and other officials were reputed to be unusually given to placing family and friends above the law. Many of them bitterly resented the Council of Wales for its encroachment upon their territorial autonomy, yet demonstrated through their flaunting of judicial process that reform was grievously needed. And, as their conduct of the Evans investigation demonstrated, the Earl's own subordinates were as culpable as the rest, considering the rape of a peasant girl a matter beneath the gravity of their station, and certainly not worth prosecuting against a man of their own class and social milieu. Even after the Earl had prodded them into action, his subordinates on the Council managed little more than a show of diligence; they seem never to have developed much enthusiasm for their duty to discover the truth. Nor had the common law courts proved effective in getting justice for Margery Evans. Burghill had been indicted at Assizes but his "frendes soe prevailed that the Indictment would not bee accepted." At the Earl of Bridgewater's instigation and after the collection of new evidence, he was indicted again, and actually brought to trial for "rape and felonie," but the jury "vpon life and death acquited him to the Admiration [astonishment] of the Judge and the whole Court." In order to get some redress for Margery Evans, the Earl of Bridgewater had to resolve the case privately. During the summer of 1634, he probably did what Margery's advocates had long been begging him to do—gather all those concerned together to settle the matter himself as fairly as he could.[15] His experience with Council officials had made one thing crystal clear: if the Council of Wales were to serve as an effective instrument against the encroachments of Archbishop Laud and the ecclesiastical courts, it needed to put its own house in order. *Comus* sets that process in motion on the occasion of the Earl's inauguration by offering its audience a lesson in judicial impartiality similar to that exercised by the Earl himself in the case of Margery Evans.

Our only evidence that Milton knew of the Margery Evans affair is the circumstantial evidence provided by the masque itself—the many parallels between the situation of the Lady and the predicament of her lower-class counterpart. The Lady was an Earl's daughter and Margery only a serving maid, but the two were nearly the same "tender age," Margery fourteen at the time of the assault and the Lady fifteen at the time of the masque's performance. Both Margery and the Lady were travelling westward through the lonely and dangerous border country from England toward Wales, both solitary (though the Lady only temporarily and accidentally so). Margery was probably on her way to Breckonshire Fair when she was waylaid by the roadside; the Lady in *Comus* was travelling to attend a more elevated festival occasion, the installation of her father President of Wales. Both young girls were virgins, both accosted by a seducer well established in his territory: Burghill with many connections among county officials of the area, Comus with his court and a rout of monsters. Both encounters took place during a time of holiday license. Margery Evans was ravished on Midsummer eve, a festival celebrated much as Mayday eve was, with sexplay and rowdiness in the forest. We may wonder whether Burghill saw himself merely as carrying on the time-honored traditions of Midsummer when he encountered Margery Evans by the road. Comus's action is associated with Michaelmas eve, but the masque seems to have been shaped to recall Midsummer as well. The masque's menacing revelers, with their wakes and morrises in the forest, are more characteristic of Midsummer, when Margery was travelling, than of Michaelmas eve, when the Lady was.[16]

Of course the two seducers operate very differently. According to Margery's testimony, Burghill had tried to coax her to go along with him, resorting to force when words failed to gain him his object. Comus

is considerably more subtle, as befits the Lady's station and sophistication. He lures her to his palace through lies and "bleare illusion," appearing to her in the guise of a simple shepherd. But he too must eventually resort to force, immobilizing her in her chair when she attempts to escape. The Lady is not raped—the parallel with Margery Evans breaks down there. But she is placed in an atmosphere of seemingly gratuitous sordidness and increasing sexual menace. Comus likens her first to a near victim of rape—Daphne fleeing Apollo (137).[17] Then, along with the "cordiall Iulep heere / that flames, and dances in his christall bounds" (139), he offers her a chance to surpass "loveborne *Hellena*," an actual victim of abduction who complied with her abductor. But when it becomes evident that his sugared language has failed to move her, he takes a harsher tone which suggests the possibility of physical aggression against her: he vows not to "suffer" her "meere morrall babble" further (157) and touches the cup to her lips—seemingly in an effort to compel her to drink.[18] At that moment her brothers and the Attendant Spirit enter, the brothers break the glass and disperse the seducer's retinue, but Comus escapes with his wand and the Lady remains "in stonie fetters fixt, and motionlesse" (159).

Our sense of the full sordidness of her situation comes only at the moment she is freed from it, when Sabrina describes the "marble venom'd seate / smeard with gums of gluttenous heate" (173) on which the Lady has been imprisoned. The precise meaning of these lines has been a matter for much controversy lately, but most readers seem to agree that there is something distinctly seamy about them.[19] The Lady is not ravished, as Margery Evans was, but she is placed in a position of similar powerlessness, brought into involuntary association with a pollution she despises. Her fate is not that of a victim of rape, but her predicament is morally identical. The masque places a young aristocrat of obvious and unquestioned innocence in a position analogous to that of a mistrusted serving maid, and the effect is to open up the whole question of volition in cases of physical compulsion, to open the minds of the audience to the complexity of issues they had considered easy and straightforward. In light of the Evans affair, Milton's masque becomes a strenuous exercise in legal and moral judgment.

If Comus had sexually assaulted the Lady while she

was in his power, would the assault have compromised her innocence and virtue? If the Earl of Bridgewater's, colleagues on the Council were to judge the Lady by the same standards they had applied to Margery Evans, the answer would be yes: those who reviewed the case seem to have made the age-old but illogical assumption that a young girl who has been attacked must in some way have provoked the encounter, and must therefore share the blame. But one of the key points in the Evans case was "the disagreement of the woman at the tyme of the act . . . soe that the issue is not vpon th'external Act whether it was done or not but whether it was in the patient voluntary or compulsary."[20] The Lady argues, similarly, that she is guiltless so long as she has reserved her mental assent: although the enchanter can "immanacle" her "corporall rind," he cannot "touch the freedome" of her "mind" (137). It is worth noting that the Lady's specific praise for virginity (the "sage / And serious doctrine of Virginitie") as opposed to chastity, appears only in the 1637 version of Comus, by which time the Evans case and the masque's immediate Ludlow occasion would have faded from people's minds, and his audience expanded to encompass numerous readers with no knowledge of the affair. In 1634, the central issue in Comus is not virginity, but chastity, a virtue which does not automatically perish along with the loss of virginity, even in cases of rape, despite the assumption of some in power at Ludlow that it did. In making hue and cry and demanding justice against her violator, Margery Evans had implicitly assumed the separability of virginity and chastity, and had been thrown in jail for her pains, her charges ignored or turned against her. But the eloquent appeal of the Lady— particularly *this* Lady, the daughter of the Lord President of the Council in the Marches of Wales—is less easy to ignore. She has assumed the position of one of the powerless, and her voice becomes their voice.

William B. Hunter, Jr., and others have noted striking parallels between the major liturgical themes of the Feast of St. Michael and All Angels and the motifs of Milton's masque. The Collect for the day beseeches God for angelic succor and defense like that offered by Milton's Attendant Spirit. The Epistle recounts St. Michael's battle with Satan from the Apocalypse, a cosmic prototype for the lesser struggle against Comus and the spirits of darkness in the

masque. The Gospel for the day is Matthew 18, Christ's praise of the "little ones": "Verily I say unto you, Except ye be converted, and become as little children, ye shall not enter into the kingdom of Heaven. Whosoever therefore shall humble himself as this little child, the same is greatest in the kingdom of heaven." [21] This text has obvious applications to the three children of *Comus*, implications also for the masque's theme of the humbling of those who sit in judgment: if the Lady has reduced herself to the humiliating role of victim in the masque, should not the holders of high office demonstrate a kindred capacity to identify with the lowly?

In the lessons proper for Michaelmas, the subjects of law and public administration are considerably more prominent. Milton's masque looks forward to the lesson for Evensong in its praise for the Earl of Bridgewater. That text moves from children to fathers, particularly fathers in positions of political authority: "Let us now praise famous men, and our fathers that begat us. The Lord hath wrought great glory by them through his great power from the beginning. Such as did bear rule in their kingdoms, men renowned for their power, giving counsel by their understanding, and declaring prophecies: Leaders of the people by their counsels, and by their knowledge of learning meet for the people, wise and eloquent in their instructions . . ." (Ecclus. 44: 1-4). As Hunter has noted, Evensong was very likely celebrated some time after the performance of the masque, so that the closing passages of *Comus* which honor the parents through the successful trial of the children would lead naturally into the liturgical lesson.

Even more important for our purposes, however, is the lesson proper for Matins, which offers a portrait of the man fit to "sit on the judges' seat" and "declare justice and judgment" (Ecclus. 38: 33):

> But he that giveth his mind to the law of the most High, and is occupied in the meditation thereof, will seek out the wisdom of all the ancient, and be occupied in prophecies. He will keep the sayings of the renowned men: and where subtil parables are, he will be there also. He will seek out the secrets of grave sentences, and be conversant in dark parables. He shall serve among great men, and appear before princes: he will travel through strange countries;

for he hath tried the good and the evil among men (Ecclus. 39: 1-4).

Comus is itself a "dark" and "subtil" parable which reaches beyond the literal in a number of directions, some of them related to the measuring of judges against an ideal of judicial office. On Sept. 29, 1634, members of the Council of Wales in attendance at the Ludlow performance were confronted with an entertainment which re-enacted on a higher social and intellectual plane elements from a case in which they had forgotten their role as protectors of the downtrodden and had neglected the "little ones" in favor of the powerful, in which they had shown small capacity to try "the good and the evil among men" before proceeding to judgment. They are shown how to conduct themselves in office through the double example of the Lady's brothers and Sabrina: the brothers acting for their father to disperse the forces of inchastity through the power of the secular arm; Sabrina using her humble ministrations both to free the Lady and to offer a model of proper judicial humility. And so our argument circles back to the masque's other legal theme of the relationship between secular and sacred authority. Milton's work supports the Earl of Bridgewater against Laud by mirroring his analysis of the proper division of labor between the Council and the ecclesiastical courts. But simultaneously, the masque humbles the Council itself, implicitly measuring it against an ideal of judicial authority. A new legal term at Ludlow—the Michaelmas term—was about to begin under the authority of the Council's new President, and with him, Milton suggests, there would commence a new order of rectitude. As the judges of the Council in the Marches of Wales took up their busy round of trials, depositions, and other related matters, they would be afforded an immediate opportunity to act upon what they had learned on Michaelmas night and rededicate themselves to the truth.

Both Milton and the Earl of Bridgewater eventually gave up their hope that the sacred and secular authorities could be made to function in such a process of mutual help and enlightenment. After years of escalating conflict with Laud and other adversaries, the Earl of Bridgewater finally broke with Charles I and the central ecclesiastical authority, taking the Parliamentary side during the Civil War. As we all know, Milton's disenchantment with the existing

structures of Church and state moved him finally far to the left of the Earl's moderate Parliamentarianism. But at least for a time in 1634, the two men appear to have shared the same vision of a Church redeemed from the oppressive rigidities of Laud, in which reform was a measured through inward self-transformation, not merely through the attainment of external order.

Let us return, by way of *coda*, to the matter of the *Book of Sports*. Milton's masque, in proper Laudian fashion, advocates the practice of old holiday pastimes. There is dancing and festivity at Ludlow in honor of the Earl's inauguration. But that holiday cheer is attained only after the practice of a more demanding Michaelmas custom: the festival inversion by which those on high must rediscover their essential frailty, their kinship with the down-trodden. That is what literally happened at Ludlow on Michaelmas night: those in attendance were invited to celebrate along with the Earl and his family, but in terms that made their mirth a sign of their internalization of the humbling message of the masque, a sign of their symbolic victory not only over intemperance, but over the other forms of blindness that make justice so elusive in this life.

NOTES

[1] See, for example, Samuel Gardiner, *History of England from the Accession of James I to the Outbreak of the Civil War 1603-1642*, (London, 1884), VII, 335-37; and H.R. Trevor-Roper, *Archbishop Laud, 1573-1645* (London: Macmillan, 1940), p. 164. Trevor-Roper comments that *Comus* was written to dissociate the Puritan Milton from the Puritan Prynne. The fullest exposition of Milton's masque in terms of the *Book of Sports* controversy is Maryann Cale McGuire's *Milton's Puritan Masque* (Athens: Univ. of Georgia Press, 1983). As I have demonstrated more fully in *The Politics of Mirth: Jonson, Herrick, Milton, Marvell and the Defense of Old Holiday Pastimes* (Chicago: Univ. of Chicago Press, 1986), however, McGuire does not take Laudian policy sufficiently into account. I am also indebted to David Norbrook's fine article "The Reformation of the Masque," in *The Court Masque*, ed. David Lindley (Dover, N.H.: Manchester Univ. Press, 1984), 94-110; and to his *Poetry and Politics in the English Renaissance* (London: Routledge & Kegan Paul, 1984). My major point of difference with Norbrook is that while he shies away from the idea that Milton in *Comus* was criticising contemporary Church government, I make a case that he was doing just that. The present article synthesizes two

of my previous discussions of *Comus* and contemporary political contexts: that in *The Politics of Mirth*, several pages, of which are reprinted here with the kind permission of the university of Chicago Press, and that in "The Milieus of Milton's *Comus*: Judicial Reform at Ludlow and the Problem of Sexual Assault," *Criticism*, 25 (1983), pp. 293-327, several pages of which are reprinted with the kind permission of the Wayne State University Press, copyright 1984 Wayne State University Press, Detroit, Michigan 48202. My special thanks are due to the Henry E. Huntington Library, where I received a research fellowship to work on the Bridgewater materials, and the the Research Board of the University of Illinois for a travel grant. All quotations from the Bridgewater collection are made with the permission of the Huntington Library, San Marino, California.

[2] The standard work on the Council during our period is Caroline A. J. Skeel, *The Council in the Marches of Wales*, Girton College Studies II (London: Hugh Rees, 1904), esp. pp. 272-74. On the basis of my own work in the Bridgewater Collection at the Henry E. Huntington Library, however, I would modify a number of Skeel's conclusions.

[3] See John Creaser, "'The present aid of this occasion': The Setting of *Comus*," in *The Court Masque*, ed. Lindley, esp. p. 114 and p. 131n. Since my interest here is in the early versions of *Comus*, particularly the Bridgewater version, which is close to, if not identical with, the version that was performed, I have taken as my standard text *John Milton, A Maske: The Earlier Versions*, ed. S. E. Sprott (Toronto: Univ. of Toronto Press, 1973). Quotations from the masque will be indicated by page number in the text.

[4] For the general political significance of the masque at court see in particular Stephen Orgel's *The Illusion of Power* (Berkeley: Univ of California Press, 1975); my *Politics of Mirth* includes extended political readings of some of Jonson's masques.

[5] For Bridgewater as a Royalist, see Gardiner, VII, 335; and Creaser; for the Earl as a Puritan, see McGuire; John D. Cox, "Poetry and History in Milton's Country Masque," *ELH*, 44 (1977), 622-40; and William Riley Parker, *Milton: A Biography* (Oxford: Clarendon Press, 1968), II, 792, n. 42. By far the most useful account of the Earl's political career is Charles L. Hamilton, "The Earl of Bridgewater and the English Civil War," *Canadian Journal of History*, 15 (1980), 357-69. There is also a popular history of the family, Bernard Falk, *The Bridgewater Millions: A Candid Family History* (London: Hutchinson, 1942), which contains useful information, pp. 49-71.

[6] My account of the battle here will draw heavily on my longer exposition in *The Politics of Mirth*, which reconstructs the situation on the basis of manuscript evidence in the Bridgewater Collection at the Huntington.

[7] For Bridgewater's instructions, see Rymer's *Foedera*, 2nd. ed., XIX (London: for J. Tonson, 1732), 455. The originalis

in the Bridgewater Collection, HEH EL 7571, along with a copy, EL 7397. For Laud's instructions, see Rymer's *Foedera*, XIX, 492-97. For an account of the workings of the ecclesiastical courts under Laud in the area of sexual offenses, see E. R. C. Brinkworth, "The Laudian Church in Buckinghamshire," *Univ. of Birmingham Hist. Journal*, 5 (1955), 31-59, esp. pp. 31-37 and 54-55.

[8] Quoted, with the gracious permission of the Trustees of the Huntington Library, from HEH EL 7521, draft letter to Sir John Bridgeman. For a more detailed account, see my *Politics of. Mirth*, Chap. VI.

[9] HEH EL 7485, undated doc. with corrections in the hand of the Earl of Bridgewater [pp. 1-6]; EL 7509, letter to Bridgewater from Sampson Eure, the Queen's solicitor at the Court of the Marches, 16 July, 1636. It should be emphasized that I am not quoting these documents as sources for Milton, but as evidence of the general principles involved, principles which the Earl and his associates presented as self-evident, long understood, and long followed.

[10] See EL 7509, 7511, 7470 (a more legible copy of 7511), and 7485, [pp. 12, 17-20]. All of the briefs present this "division of labor" between the two court systems as self evident and traditional. Milton could not have known the particular briefs, but he is sure to have been acquainted with the traditional arguments.

[11] R. Chris Hassel, Jr., *Renaissance Drama and the English Church Year* (Lincoln: Univ. of Nebraska Press, 1979), pp. 157-59.

[12] This portion of my discussion is based on my much longer article, "The Milieu of Milton's *Comus*: Judicial Reform at Ludlow and the Problem of Sexual Assault," *Criticism*, 25 (1983), pp. 293-327, which analyzes the Earl's role in detail.

[13] The names of both men—Sir Henry Williams and Thomas Price, JP—occur on the list of Council members in the Bridgewater collection; however, given the duplication of proper and family names in Wales, it is remotely possible that these were different JP's.

[14] EL 7387. See also EL 7388 and "Milieu," pp. 303-04.

[15] EL 7402, EL 7403, and "Milieu," pp. 307-13.

[16] Except, of course, that their revelry is associated with harvest. For Michaelmas customs, see James Taaffe, "Michaelmas, the 'Lawless hour,' and the Occasion of Milton's *Comus*," *ELN*, 6 (1968-69), 257-62; and for a hostile contemporary account of Mayday and Midsummer lawlessness, sexual license, and their ill effects, [Henry Burton], *A Devine Tragedie lately Acted, Or . . . Gods judgements upon Sabbath Breakers* (London, 1636). According to contemporaries, both holidays caused a rise in the bastardy rates. Although the parallels between the Lady and Margery Evans suggest that Milton knew of the case, it is not necessary to my argument to claim that he did. Materials suggesting the parallel

could have been provided to the poet, as they sometimes were for other seventeenth-century masques, by someone else involved in the preparation of the ceremonies for the installation, perhaps even by the Earl of Bridgewater himself. Whether or not the parallels were intended by Milton, they would have been recognized by the guilty parties on the Council of Wales who had impeded justice for Margery Evans. In terms of this phase of my argument, that is the important thing.

[17] It is not clear from Ovid's account whether Apollo would have stooped to rape; however, Ovid was interpreted as implying that in the Renaissance. See *Shakespeare's Ovid Being Arthur Golding's Translation of the Metamorphoses*, ed. W. H. D. Rouse (London: De La More Press, 1904), p. 2: in describing Ovid's moral instruction, Golding interprets Daphne as a "myrror of virginitie" "yeelding neyther untoo feare, nor force, nor flatterye." The subject of rape of near-rape was quite common in Renaissance pastoral: see Tasso's *Aminta*, II, iii and III; and the would-be rapist the Sullen Shepherd in John Fletcher's *The Faithful Shepherdess*, acted at court in January, 1634.

[18] I am following John Shawcross's general line of interpretation in "Two Comments," *MQ*, 7 (1973), 97–98. I am indebted to my friend and former colleague Michael Lieb for suggesting the reading, and for encouraging me to expand my understanding of how the issue of rape may relate to the masque.

[19] See the lively exchange of views in *MQ* beginning with J.W. Flosdorf, "'Gums of Glutinous Heat': A Query," *MQ*, 7 (1973), 5; continuing with Shawcross and Stanley Archer, "'Glutinous Heat': A Note on *Comus*, 1.917," *MQ*, 7 (1973), 99; Edward Le Comte, "By Sex Obsessed," *MQ*, 8 (1974), 55–57; Shawcross's response, p. 57; and Jean François Camé, "More about Milton's Use of the Word 'Gums,'" *MQ* 9 (1975), 51–52.

[20] EL 7399, p. 1.

[21] William B. Hunter, Jr., "The Liturgical Context of *Comus*," *ELN* 10 (1972), pp. 11–15; see also Hassel, pp. 57–61. I have used the 1634 *Book of Common Prayer*, and, for Biblical quotations not given in full in the prayer book, the Cambridge Pitt Brevier edition of the King James Bible.

Transformations in Genre in Milton's *Comus*

Jeanne S. Martin
Stanford University

It has often been remarked that one of the hallmarks of Milton's poetic achievement is the way in which he defines new possibilities for established literary forms while simultaneously commenting upon their traditional uses. Two of the most often considered and most obvious examples of this procedure are to be found in Milton's use of the sonnet and the epic.[1] In the first instance, Milton takes over a form which traditionally pursued the internal truth mirrored by the external appearance (e.g., the Petrarchan sonnet) and, as in Sonnet XV, "On Lord General Fairfax at the Siege of Colchester," uses the form to show that appearances deceive. What seems a victory of great magnitude is actually only a limited victory, because the forces of rebellion and divisiveness persist (lines 6 and 7). In *Paradise Lost*, Milton uses epic form and epic conventions to undermine non-Christian standards of heroic virtue by associating these standards with the figure of Satan and to define a new standard of heroic virtue in the figure of Christ, the submissive and self-sacrificing savior of mankind. The same procedure with regard to traditional literary forms can be observed in almost all of Milton's poetic works. One such work which has received surprisingly little attention along these lines is Milton's single complete masque, *Comus*.[2]

[1] Alastair Fowler, "The Life and Death of Literary Forms," *New Literary History*, 2 (1971), 199–216.

[2] Critical interest in *Comus* has tended to focus on the masque's "thematic" (or "intellectual") content, and generally at the expense of generic considerations. A useful summary of the major issues which have concerned *Comus* critics and their relation to formal analyses is provided in John G. Demaray, *Milton and the Masque Tradition* (Cambridge, Mass., 1968), pp. 5–9. For specific examples of attempts to interpret *Comus* from the point of view of the formal implications of the masque genre, see particularly C. L. Barber, "*A Mask Presented at Ludlow Castle*: The Masque as a Masque," in *A Maske at Ludlow*, ed. John S. Diekhoff (Cleveland, 1968), pp. 188–207; Rosemund Tuve, "Image, Form and Theme in *A Mask*," in *ibid.*, pp. 126–64; Demaray; Stephen Orgel, *The Jonsonian Masque* (Harvard,

195

By Michaelmas Night, 1634, the evening on which Milton's masque was presented at Ludlow Castle before the Earl of Bridgewater and his company, court masques had flourished for several centuries in England. Enid Welsford locates the earliest English masques in the reign of Edward III (1347), and, by the middle of the fifteenth century, court poet, John Lydgate, had written several masques to be performed at Windsor.[3] Throughout the reigns of Elizabeth, James and Charles I, masques were frequent and regular occurrences.[4] In its original conception, "masque" simply referred to a masquerade and was primarily distinguished from other forms of court entertainment by the inclusion of masked or disguised courtiers.[5] As the form developed, however, it became a more specific kind of court entertainment involving a rather peculiar set of conventions.[6] To begin with, a masque is always an occasional work of praise and is always about the court it entertains. Masques were written, for instance, to celebrate royal visits, marriages, special feasts and royal investitures. Secondly, a masque always includes elements of dance, music, song and verse, and masquers who are members of the audience.[7] Finally, the masque must seek to dissolve the barrier between actor and audience and include the whole court in its mimesis. The most common method of effecting this transformation, as Stephen Orgel notes, was to have the production culminate "dramatically and literally" in a dance, the "revels," between the masquers and the audience. But this was not the only method of meeting this formal requirement and early masques display a variety of approaches to this same end.[8]

1965); and Angus Fletcher, *The Transcendental Masque* (Ithaca, 1972). A bibliography of *Comus* criticism and related works on masque form can be found in Demaray, *ibid.*, pp. 150–56.

[3] Enid Welsford, *The Court Masque* (Cambridge, 1927), pp. 42–52.

[4] Welsford, pp. 81 ff. Mary Susan Steele, *Plays and Masques at Court During the Reigns of Elizabeth, James and Charles* (New Haven, 1926).

[5] Orgel, *The Jonsonian Masque*, p. 152. Welsford: "From the beginning to the end of its history, the essence of the masque was the arrival of certain persons vizored and disguised to dance a dance or present an offering" (p. 3).

[6] Demaray, *Milton and the Masque Tradition*, pp. 10–17, 61; Tuve, "Image, Form and Theme in *A Mask*," pp. 129–30; Barber, *A Mask Presented at Ludlow Castle*, p. 190; and, Robert M. Adams, "Reading *Comus*," in *A Mask at Ludlow*, p. 79.

[7] Welsford, p. 166.

[8] Orgel, *The Jonsonian Masque*, pp. 6–7. Space does not permit me, nor is it my primary purpose, to discuss the history of the masque form. Furthermore, this task, particularly in relation to the Jonsonian masque, has already been thoroughly and

196

The many requirements of the form were often difficult for the masque writer to reconcile into coherence, and it was actually not until Ben Jonson's later masques that the full potential of the form was consistently realized.[9] Masques before Jonson generally tended to break down into disparate parts with no apparent interrelationship: the commencing poem would pose a riddle-problem or define a simple dramatic situation, which was subsequently resolved or justified by reference to the royal personage being celebrated in the audience. The masquers would then descend into the audience proper, choose partners, and participate in revels until the end of the evening.[10] The central weakness in many of the early masques, according to Welsford, was their failure to make the appearance of the masquers a central or even an integral part of the performance.[11] Jonson's success with the masque, however, was attributable in large part to the very requirements imposed by the form which proved so difficult for his predecessors. More than any masque writer before him, Jonson was able to use the conventions of the form in a functional way and thereby produce a coherence of form and meaning hitherto unachieved in the masque.[12] In Orgel's words, Jonson "transformed what he received, to make a living art of a set of conventions."[13]

It is the form as exemplified by Jonson's greatest masques which is most relevant to the present investigation; it is the masque at the height of its development which represents the standard from which Milton departs.[14] To perceive the terms and implications of Milton's achievement, therefore, it will be useful to consider first an example of the Jonsonian masque. Of Jonson's most successful masques, *Pleasure Reconciled to Virtue* (1618) suggests itself as particularly appropriate for our purposes

elegantly done by Stephen Orgel. For a more general account of the development of masque conventions from the fourteenth through the seventeenth centuries, see Welsford.

[9] Welsford, pp. 168 ff. Notable exceptions to this generalization are Francis Davison's *The Mask of Proteus and the Adamantine Rock* (1594) and Thomas Campion's *Lord Hay's Masque* (1607). See Welsford, pp. 163 ff., and Orgel, pp. 101 ff., and Stephen Orgel and Roy Strong, *Inigo Jones* (London, 1973), pp. 1-27.

[10] Demaray, *Milton and the Masque Tradition*, p. 17. See also Orgel's discussion of the Tudor and Elizabethan masque, *Jonsonian Masque*, pp. 8-36; and Welsford's discussion of the Jacobean masque, pp. 208-16.

[11] Welsford, p. 154.

[12] See also Tuve, "Image, Form and Theme in *A Mask*," pp. 130 ff.

[13] Orgel, *The Jonsonian Masque*, p. 4.

[14] This is an opinion shared by Demaray, pp. 73-74.

197

because it, like *Comus,* is a play about the will confronted with choice and tempted by the god of sensual pleasure.[15]

As Stephen Orgel observes, the very title of Jonson's masque, *Pleasure Reconciled to Virtue,* "proclaims a drama not of opposition but of reconciliation."[16] For Jonson, the masque always had as its primary function the resolution of all conflict and was, therefore, a celebration of triumph.[17] *Pleasure Reconciled to Virtue* commences with the processional entrance of Comus and his followers; the hymn accompanying this spectacle declares Comus to be the god not only of sensual pleasure but of *excessive* sensual pleasure.[18] Comus is the

---

[15] See also Demaray, pp. 87 ff., and Barber, "*A Mask Presented at Ludlow Castle,*" p. 202. In choosing to focus on only one of Jonson's masques, albeit one which I think is representative, I am aware that I risk distorting what is generally true of all the others. Significant generic variations have been noted in my footnotes. By calling *Pleasure Reconciled to Virtue* one of Jonson's "most successful masques" I am referring to its conceptual and technical achievement, not its reception in the royal court. See Orgel and Strong, *Inigo Jones,* pp. 1–27, and 277–94, for a discussion of differences among Jonsonian masques as well as reports of contemporary reactions to *Pleasure Reconciled to Virtue.* On this latter subject see also C. H. Herford and Percy and Evelyn Simpson, eds. *Ben Jonson* [Works], 11 vols. (Oxford, 1925–52), II, 304–10. Although *Pleasure Reconciled to Virtue* was written and performed in 1618, it was not actually published until 1640. There is considerable evidence, however, that Milton knew the masque in manuscript form. See *Ben Jonson,* x, 573–76.

[16] Orgel, *The Jonsonian Masque,* p. 17. I am heavily indebted to Stephen Orgel's discussion of the Jonsonian masque throughout my analysis of *Pleasure Reconciled to Virtue.*

[17] Jonson's predisposition to view the central action of the masque as one of transformation, mutation or metamorphosis is already evident in the early *Masque of Blackness* (1605) where the nexus of the play is a verbal paradox resolved by explanation rather than dramatic action. The Haddington Masque (1608) and the *Masque of Queens* (1609) present worlds limited by alternatives so rigidly defined that there can be no transition from one to another. In his discussion of Davison's *Proteus,* Stephen Orgel suggests that the notion of "transformation" is endemic to the form of the masque: "So the hero triumphs and the villain repents. But not as in a drama, for the confutation of Proteus takes place essentially before the action even begins. The *coup de grace* comes as the answer to an extended riddle. . . . rather than as the culmination of a series of related events" (p. 16).

[18] Not all of Jonson's masques begin with the entrance of the antimasquers. *The Golden Age Restored,* for example, begins with a speech by Pallas which is interrupted by the first antimasque. When Jonson did commence a masque with an antimasque it was generally, as in *Pleasure Reconciled to Virtue,* to demonstrate the hero's ability to differentiate between the chaos or insufficiency of the antimasque world and the order of the masque world. Those masques written between 1609 and 1618 most typically conform to the pattern manifested in *Pleasure Reconciled to Virtue.*

198

First father of Sauce, & deviser of gelly,
Prime master of arts, & the giver of wit,
That found out the excellent ingine, the spit,
The plough, & the flaile, the mill, & the Hoppar,...[19] (479–80: 14–17)

Following this introduction, the first antimasque is danced by men dressed as bottles and a cask.[20] The antimasque is that part of the masque which poses the apparent problem of discord—its origins are to be found in the grotesque interludes between acts in earlier forms of the masque, particularly fifteenth-century Italian masques.[21] But in Jonson's hands the antimasque is the means by which a specific problem is defined for which the masque itself is the solution. In other words, it is through the device of the antimasque that the masque assumes its particular meaning.[22] In *Pleasure Reconciled to Virtue* the first antimasque functions to bring into focus the exact nature of the world which Comus inhabits. The antimasque, in Orgel's words, "presents figures who have ceased to be men and who have become mere containers for what will satisfy their appetites, 'living measures of drinck'."[23]

Set against the figure of Comus is the hero of the masque, Hercules. At the conclusion of the first antimasque Hercules enters and proclaims in horror against the spectacle before him:

What rytes are theis?...
(Help Vertue) theis are Sponges, & not men.
Bottles? meere vessells? half a tun of panch?...
Theis *Monsters* plague themselves: & fitly too,
For they do suffer what, and all they doo. (482:94 ff.)

It is characteristic of the world of the antimasque, the world which Comus and his revelers dominate, that it does not acknowledge self-

[19] *Ben Jonson*, VIII, 479–80. All Jonson quotations are from this edition.

[20] One of the many ways in which Jonson brought coherence to the masque form was to unite action with character portrayal and dialogue; this is especially evident in his handling of the antimasque. Characters in the Jonsonian antimasque are what they do; there is no need to have a separate figure to announce what they are, they reveal themselves through their actions.

[21] Welsford, *The Court Masque*, pp. 84–85.

[22] Writers before Jonson certainly used the antimasque as a foil for the central action of the masque. Because Jonson, however, regarded the masque as having an explicitly educative function—"To redeeme [the spectators] as well from Ignorance, as Envie" (Preface to *Blackness*)—he strove to make the antimasque not only a foil for the central action of the masque but a medium and means for the realization of that action. See Orgel, *The Jonsonian Masque*, pp. 118–19.

[23] Orgel, p. 160.

199

evident truths. Thus, what Comus and his company call pleasure is not in fact pleasure but pain because it denies their basic humanity. The world of Comus is not one in which men partake of pleasure but rather one in which men become slaves to appetite and are transformed into objects. Standing in contrast to this is the hero of the masque, who is vividly aware of his place in a larger world, the world of truth: the same world which the audience occupies. Both Hercules and the members of the audience are simultaneously aware, as no member of the antimasque world could be, of the true nature of the "pleasure" which Comus offers. Hercules affirms his opposition to the world of the antimasque by banishing the false revelers. He commands them to "sink . . . or vanish into cloud!" and they immediately disappear. It is typical of the Jonsonian masque after *Oberon* (1611) that the central figure bridges the gap between the masque and the antimasque. Later masques, consequently, achieve their climax through dramatic action rather than through music or spectacle. Hercules' victory over the world of the antimasque, however, is not one of dramatic *conflict*: there is no direct confrontation between virtue and vice. Rather, the mere presence of virtue and its recognition of the nature of vice is sufficient to dispel the threat of disorder and misrule and establish the realm of order.

After the disappearance of the antimasquers the second phase of the masques begins. Where before there was surfeit and perversion there is now harmony; the scene changes to one permeated by music (the symbol of order and harmony) in which Pleasure and Virtue appear seated together. A choir invites Hercules to rest as a temporary reward for his "mighty labor"; but the transition from the antimasque to the masque is not yet complete. As soon as Hercules falls asleep, a group of pigmies invade the surrounding area performing a second antimasque. Hercules, however, is awakened by the sound of harmonious music (a form of order which symbolizes the order of his mortal virtue) and his mere consciousness is sufficient to banish the second group of antimasquers. In terms of the larger action of the masque, the second antimasque establishes that it is not enough that virtue recognize vice initially, it must continually exercise itself in its awareness.[24]

The dissemination of the second antimasque signifies the final transition from antimasque to masque. Hercules is given the crown of virtue, and Mercury announces that the time has arrived when he should be

[24] Jonson did not always employ two antimasques. Double antimasques appear with the greatest frequency in those masque written between 1609–18.

rewarded for rescuing Atlas' "fair daughters, then the prey of a rude pirate," the time, in other words, when pleasure will be reconciled to virtue. This action shifts the fictive time of the masque to coincide with the evening of presentation in 1618 through the following reference which acknowledges and praises the royal presence:

> But now
> The time's arriv'd, that *Atlas* told thee of: How
> By unaltered law, & working of the stars,
> There should be a cessation of all jars
> 'Twixt Vertue, & hir noted opposite,
> Pleasure: that both sold meet here, in the sight
> Of Hesperus, the glory of the West,
> The brightest star, that from his burning Crest
> Lights all on this side the *Atlantick seas*
> As far as to thy *Pillars Hercules*. (486: 186–95)

The reference to Hesperus, Atlas' brother, is cogent within the fiction of the masque but also serves to extend that framework beyond the limits of the masque to include the court itself. In this extended context the reference to Hesperus becomes a reference to King James. As Orgel points out, Mercury, issuing the following lines of praise, then gestures directly toward the throne of King James, and the implicit reference in lines 196–204 becomes explicit identification:[25]

> Se where He shines: *Justice,* & *Wisdom* plac'd
> About his *Throne* & those with *Honor* grac'd,
> *Beautie,* & *Love.* (486:196–98)

By incorporating the requirement of acknowledging the presence of the royal personage into the action of the masque, Jonson is able to effect the final transformation, that of merging the world of the masquers with the world of the audience, as well as completing the statement toward which the masque has been working. By identifying King James with "the brightest star, that from his burning Crest / Lights all on this side the *Atlantick seas,*" Jonson transforms the final revels into a symbolic representation of harmony and pleasure controlled by virtue.[26] Hercules'

[25] Orgel, *The Jonsonian Masque,* p. 171.
[26] *The Vision of Delight* (1617) was perhaps the first masque in which Jonson successfully transformed the required compliment to the sovereign into a functionally integrated element. Earlier masques, such as *Oberon* fail to establish the correspondence between the fictive symbol of order and power and the real soverign in the audience within the action of the masque. See Orgel, *Jonsonian Masque,* pp.

201

encounter with vice not only provides the audience with an exemplar of virtue, it affects them directly, because it wins for Hercules the crown of virtue which leads to the reconciliation with pleasure and therefore to the formation of the concluding songs and revels of the masque. As the action of the main masque itself becomes a means by which Hercules can organize his experience and bring about progress in his moral state, so the artifice of the revels becomes a means by which the audience can organize its perception of the relationship of pleasure to virtue and effect a similar progress in its own moral state.

The great accomplishment of *Pleasure Reconciled to Virtue* is the manner in which Jonson manages to make each requirement of the form function integrally toward the creation of the meaning of the masque. The requirements of the form are the means by which he creates and communicates his perceptions about the will, virtue and pleasure. In Jonson's hands, the antimasque is more than a pleasant spectacle, a mere interlude; it actually provides the occasion for Hercules' virtue to define and assert itself. Without the antimasque Hercules would never have had the opportunity to assess misrule and chaos, and recognize the truth that to be human means to accept the responsibility of order. Jonson uses the convention of the relative positions of the villain of the antimasque and the hero of the masque in much the same way. Traditionally the villain of the antimasque is distinguished from the hero of the masque by his lack of awareness of himself as an actor in a masque; he alone is limited by the fiction of the moment.[27] The hero, on the other hand, derives his position of strength and control from the fact that his knowledge of events coincides with that of the audience; he is able to separate the fictive from the real and act accordingly.

Jonson's *Pleasure Reconciled to Virtue* is an excellent example of the possibilities of the form of the masque which were explored before Milton wrote *Comus*. It is important to notice that the conventions of the form dictated, to a degree, the kind of subject matter and the kind of issues which could be explored. For example, a distinction between appearance

---

89 ff., for a discussion of this aspect of the Jonsonian masque. Not all of Jonson's masques ended, as does *Pleasure Reconciled to Virtue*, with special figured dances. It is uncertain whether *Blackness* did, *The Masque of Beauty* (1608) certainly did. By 1609, *The Masque of Queens*, however, Jonson had become aware of the aesthetic implications of contrasting the grotesque dance of the antimasque with the ordered dance of the revels and proceeds to exploit the contrast in seventeen of his twenty remaining masques. See *Milton and the Masque Tradition*, p. 18.

[27] Orgel, p. 13.

202

and reality is one which is implied by the inherent contrast between the antimasque and the masque proper. An exploration therefore of the implications of such a distinction is a natural subject for a masque. Other examples of subjects particularly appropriate to the form are themes of transformation, the function of artifice in society and the importance of the monarch.

With this example of the pre-Miltonic masque as background we are now in a position to evaluate Milton's use of the masque tradition. In the pages which follow I will attempt to demonstrate that Milton chooses the form of the masque in order to explore subjects traditionally appropriate to that form and to formulate a position with respect to those subjects which consciously diverges from that generally taken by his predecessors.

That Milton was aware of his audience as an audience educated in the tradition of the masque with expectations consonant with that tradition is evident from the commencement speech delivered by the Attendant Spirit.[28] In this speech, Milton uses the fiction of the masque to create two myths which depend for their meaning upon the members of the audience being able to "read" the conventions of the form. The first of these is the myth concerning Neptune's appointment of positions of rule within his kingdom and dispensation of these positions among "his tributary gods" (lines 18 ff.).[29] This myth serves the purpose of acknowledging the presence of Lord Bridgewater, and the occasion of his induction to the position of Lord President of Wales, as well as defining the fictional setting of the masque. The success of this device depends absolutely on the audience's awareness of the convention involved. Without this awareness, the fiction of Lord Bridgewater's children "coming to attend their Father's state / and new-entrusted Scepter" has no more claim to propriety than any other possible fiction, and the implicit compliment paid Lord Bridgewater as a parent of virtuous children is lost.

The second myth ostensibly involves a compliment to one of Lord Bridgewater's servants (lines 86 ff.). In reality, however, the compliment is directed toward the musical accomplishment of Henry Lawes, the man

[28] See also Tuve, "Image, Form and Theme in *A Mask*," pp. 130 ff.

[29] John Milton, *Complete Poems and Major Prose*, ed. Merrit Y. Hughes (New York, 1957), pp. 86–114. It is worth noting at this point that unlike the majority of Jonson's masques, Milton's masque is not written for a King. Within the fiction of the masque Lord Bridgewater fulfills the function of a royal presence but he is never endowed with the special privileges accorded members of the royal family. See Orgel and Strong, *Inigo Jones*, pp. 1–27, for a discussion of these privileges.

who procured the poetic commission for Milton and who wrote the songs for the masque. Moreover, the part of the Attendant Spirit is being acted by Henry Lawes himself; a character being acted by Henry Lawes is praising the ability of Henry Lawes. The convention of the disguise, however, affords Lawes the masquer a fictional integrity which avoids the situation of self-praise while nevertheless offering sincere praise from Milton to Lawes. The audience would probably have noticed that Henry Lawes was playing the part of the Attendant Spirit and the fact that Milton would place him in such a position without fear of his being censured demonstrates the extent to which Milton depended on his audience's familiarity with masque conventions.

Unlike Jonson in *Pleasure Reconciled to Virtue*, Milton first acquaints his audience with the nature of Comus and his crew and then presents them to view. The Attendant Spirit gives a history of Comus' genealogy and then offers a judgment of Comus and his followers:

> Soon as the Potion works, their human count'nance,
> Th' express resemblance of the gods, is chang'd
> Into some brutish form of Wolf, or Bear,
> Or Ounce, or Tiger, Hog, or bearded Goat,
> All other parts remaining as they were.
> And they, so perfect is their misery,
> Not once perceive their foul disfigurement,
> But boast themselves more comely than before,
> And all their friends and native home forget,
> To roll with pleasure in a sensual sty. (lines 68–77)

The expression of this judgment before Comus and his company enter the masque is the first significant departure which Milton makes from the conventional masque form and anticipates his most important change, the reversal of the position of the villain of the antimasque and the hero of the masque. Traditionally, as in *Pleasure Reconciled to Virtue*, the discovery of the disordered and misoriented nature of the antimasque world was reserved for the hero of the masque to make.[30] Indeed, it was the standard device whereby the hero of the masque was distinguished from the villain of the antimasque, the moment of discovery marking the

---

[30] In some masques there exist figures who span both the world of the antimasque and masque, and who direct the action in such a way as to "present" the hero of the masque. The figure of Silenus in *Oberon*, for example, functions in this capacity. I am much indebted to my colleague, Professor John Bender, for this, and several other, observations.

commencement of the movement from the misrule of the antimasque to the order of the masque.[31] In Milton's masque, however, the premature disclosure of this information about the antimasquers prepares the audience for a heroine whose role will be unlike that of any of her traditional predecessors, and marks a division between the knowledge of events to which the audience is privy and that to which the heroine of the masque has access. The reason for a new kind of heroine becomes apparent the moment the Lady enters the masque and encounters Comus; the reason for the bifurcation of knowledge is not so immediately evident and will have to be taken up later.

When Comus and his crew enter the masque, we are presented with a company of figures who, as in *Pleasure Reconciled to Virtue*, have become the literal embodiments of their moral deformities. In typical antimasque fashion, the rout of monsters "come in making a riotous and unruly noise," and Comus declares himself a figure of misrule:

> Meanwhile welcome Joy and Feast,
> Midnight shout and revelry,
> Tipsy dance and Jollity.
> Braid your Locks with rosy Twine
> Dropping odors, dropping Wine.
> Rigor now is gone to bed,
> And Advice with scrupulous head,
> Strict Age, and sour Severity,
> With their grave Saws in slumber lie. (lines 102–10)

Claiming dominion over the nighttime world, Comus orders the dancing of the first antimasque.

The antimasque is ended not, as one would normally expect, through the perceptive powers of the heroine, but rather as a result of Comus' ability to detect the approach of virtue:

> Break off, break off, I feel the different pace
> Of some chaste footing near about this ground. (lines 145–46)

This ability, which Comus himself attributes to his "Art," is unusual among leaders of the antimasques, as is the power of deception which he then proceeds to claim: the power to "cheat the eye with blear illusion, And give it false presentments." Unlike his counterparts in earlier masques, Milton's Comus is endowed with a kind of knowledge which enables him to appraise his situation and condition with great perspicuity

[31] Demaray, *Milton and the Masque Tradition*, pp. 85–87.

205

and, in addition, command a degree of control over his environment which even the heroine of the masque does not possess. Throughout the scene in which the character of Comus is first introduced, the emphasis is upon his control over both his followers and the situation. Comus' command establishes the limits of his followers' rites, and he orders the Goddess of Night to remain, so that his company's activities might be concealed and prolonged:

> Stay thy cloudy Ebon chair
> Wherein thou rid'st with *Hecat'*, and befriend
> Us thy vow'd Priests ... (lines 134–36)

This alteration of the potentialities of the antimasque leader distinguishes Milton's perception of the nature of evil in the universe from the perceptions of masque writers earlier in the century. It is tantamount, in fact, to a complete reversal of the formal implications of the masque as it was written before *Comus*. By endowing the figure of Comus with such powers Milton establishes a situation in which vice, excess, and disorder result in a moral perversion that denies and transforms the basic humanity of man, while as yet commanding sufficient power of control to disguise itself beyond recognition. The evil which Comus' "intemperate" and "sensual sty" represents in Milton's masque is more than a passive temptation as in Jonson's *Pleasure Reconciled To Virtue*; it is, in fact, an active force which seeks to corrupt. Moreover, it is endowed with the power to deceive uncorrupted virtue; virtue is no longer its own protection against the encroachment of evil. In masques such as Jonson's, virtue is defined by its ability to identify evil. In *Pleasure Reconciled To Virtue* true virtue is not deceived by the appearance of pleasure but rather sees through the appearance to the reality of perversion. We need only recall the lines which Hercules utters directly after witnessing the spectacle of the antimasque:

> Can
> The belly love his pain, and be content
> With no delight but what's a punishment?
> These monsters plague themselves, and fitly, too,
> For they do suffer what and all they do. (lines 90–94)

Such is not the case in Milton's world. Comus declares that he has the power to "cheat the eye with blear illusion" and to appear to the approaching virtuous damsel "some harmless Villager / Whom thrift keeps up about his Country gear," and that is exactly what he does. Separated

206

from her brothers while passing through "this drear Wood," the Lady has no choice but to confront the situation presented by Comus and his rout; with her brothers out of reach, only the disguised Comus is available to guide her. Realizing that she is lost "in the blind mazes of this tangl'd Wood" the Lady consoles herself with the conclusion that her virtue is sufficient to guard her against any threat that the night woods might pose:

> These thoughts may startle well, but not astound
> The virtuous mind, that ever walks attended
> By a strong siding champion Conscience.—
> O welcome pure-ey'd Faith, white-handed Hope,
> Thou hov'ring Angel girt with golden wings,
> And thou unblemish't form of Chastity,
> I see ye visibly, and now believe
> That he, the Supreme good, t'whom all things ill
> Are but as slavish officers of vengeance,
> Would send a glist'ring Guardian, if need were,
> To keep my life and honor unassail'd. (lines 210–20)

This speech warrants close attention, because in it the Lady fails to make a crucial distinction about the nature of virtue which explains the source of her ensuing troubles with Comus.[32] The crucial distinction is between the protection of virtue and the cloistering of virtue. It is true that heaven protects virtue, such is the function of the Attendant Spirit, but it is not true that heaven insulates virtue against contact with evil. The protection which heaven exercises over virtue follows upon the confrontation with evil and is conditional upon the assertion of virtue in the face of tempta-tion.[33] Protection implies defense in a situation of confrontation, it does not imply an assurance against such a confrontation. If virtue were not allowed to encounter and be tempted by evil then it would lose its mean-ing entirely as a willed condition worthy of divine reward.[34] The Lady's confusion on this issue leads directly to her unhesitating trust in Comus' honest appearance and subsequent bondage by Comus' spell.

The change in the relative positions of power of both the villain of the antimasque (Comus) and the hero of the masque (Lady) places the hero in a peculiarly vulnerable position not encountered in earlier masques.

---

[32] For an opposing interpretation of the Lady's position at this point in the masque see Demaray, pp. 89–95, and Adams, "Reading *Comus*," pp. 83–91.

[33] See also Tuve, "Image, Form and Theme in *A Mask*," pp. 138–48.

[34] See also Don Cameron Allen, "The Higher Compromise: 'On the Morning of Christ's Nativity' and a Mask," in *A Maske at Ludlow*, p. 71.

207

In a Jonsonian masque, for example, the position of the hero is such that his presence, or what he is made to symbolize in the action of the masque, dissolves the possibility of conflict presented by the antimasque and leads naturally and effortlessly into the masque. Traditionally the hero has complete control over his destiny, and the mere assertion of that control establishes the order which the masque attempts to confirm. Milton's heroine, however, is incapable of completely controlling her destiny.[35] The virtue to which she has legitimate claim proves to be a positive strength only when the evil she is confronting reveals itself for what it is, as it inevitably must do since, as the Elder Brother says, it is the nature of evil to recoil upon itself. By itself, however, her virtue is not sufficient to effect her salvation. Not only is virtue merely capable of limited power in Milton's masque, but the world of the masque offers no natural or self-contained solution for the predicament which virtue faces when "astounded" by evil. No quality of strength possessed by any of the real (corporeal) characters of the masque is sufficient to rescue the Lady from Comus' enchantment. As the Attendant Spirit instructs the Elder Brother:

> Alas good vent'rous youth,
> I love thy courage yet and bold Emprise,
> But here thy sword can do thee little stead;
> Far other arms and other weapons must
> Be those that quell the might of hellish charms.
> He with his bare wand can unthread thy joints,
> And crumble all thy sinews. (lines 609–14)

For Comus' bonds on the Lady to be loosed it is necessary that a force from outside the masque intercede; it is necessary that grace (Sabrina) be granted.[36]

For Milton, the encounter between the two worlds of antimasque (evil, disorder) and masque (order, virtue) is not one of ritualistic reconciliation. Rather, given the newly defined powers and limitations of each realm the meeting is one of confrontation and conflict. If, as in earlier masques, the antimasque symbolizes disorder and misrule and that condition always leads to self-deception and ineffective power, there can not possibly be conflict when order and truth are introduced; only peaceful

[35] Tuve, "Image, Form and Theme in *A Mask*," p. 138.
[36] See also Tuve, p. 157; and A. S. P. Woodhouse, "*Comus* Once More," in *A Maske at Ludlow*, p. 76.

resolution.[37] If, however, the antimasque, still symbolizing misrule and evil, is invested with the power of perspicuity which formerly resided with the world of the masquers as well as the power of superficial transformation, and the characters of the masque are weakened by a corresponding inability to detect the evil behind the presented surfaces, then the logical manner of encounter between the two worlds is conflict. The meeting of the antimasque with the masque becomes a struggle between two kinds of strength, one physical and ephemeral and the other moral and immutable, the outcome constituting a judgment about the relative merits of each.[38]

Milton's vision is not so much a diminution of the power of virtue as an increase in the power of evil. It might be aruged, in fact, that virtue, as exemplified by the Lady in *Comus*, is actually stronger than the virtue which Hercules represents, because it proves itself constant in the face of a far more subtle temptation than any which Hercules is forced to encounter. Hercules is able to resist the temptation of Comus' indulgence in sensual pleasure because he can recognize it for the obvious deformity that it is: men reduced to the status of containers for their appetites. But Milton's Lady is able to resist the temptation of evil when it is subtly disguised as it most certainly is in Comus' long and alluring speech on the abundant pleasurable gifts of nature (lines 706–55).[39] The temptation which Comus articulates in this speech is so skillfully disguised through his controlled rhetoric and artful manipulation of actual facts, that some critics have asserted, albeit somewhat ironically, that they "would rather live with Comus than with the Lady."[40]

The changes Milton made in the traditional form of the masque, or, in other words, the new functions he defined for the conventions of that form have specific and direct implications for the audience of the masque. Since the masque is a form which, from its inception, fundamentally involved its audience in its own fiction, Milton's manipulation of traditional conventions necessarily redefines the nature of the world which the audience occupies as well. The conventions of the masque as used by

[37] See Welsford, *The Court Masque*, p. 339.

[38] For an alternative reading of the function of the masque convention at this point see Tuve, "Image, Form and Theme in *A Mask*," pp. 158–59.

[39] See Tuve, p. 136 ff. for a sensitive and perceptive analysis of the structure of Comus' speech and its function in the masque. For an alternative interpretation of this portion of the masque see E. M. W. Tillyard, "The Action of *Comus*," in *A Maske at Ludlow*, p. 54.

[40] Douglas Bush, *The Renaissance and English Humanism* (Toronto, 1939), p. 108. See also Tuve, p. 138.

209

Jonson and earlier writers established a dichotomy between the sphere of the antimasque and that of the masque. Given this dichotomy, the resolution of the disorder of the antimasque into the order of the masque functions to establish the world of the masque as the realm of abstract and immutable truth; the realm of reality as opposed to the false world of apparent disorder in the antimasque. Realty becomes equated with the ideal. Once the world of the masque is established as a world of symbolic truth, it is the function of the acknowledgment of the royal presence and the revels to move the world of the masque out into the world of the audience, thereby transforming the latter into the same symbolic realm.[41] The actors of the masque move from their world into the audience and bring their world with them, transforming the world of the audience into the image of theirs.[42] The barriers between the symbolic and the actual are, in other words, denied by the form of this movement outward into the audience.

The audience of Milton's masque also participates in a transformation which results from the actors in the masque's moving into the court and denying the division between actor and audience, but the nature of that transformation is qualitatively different from what it is in earlier masques. From the very beginning of *Comus*, there is no doubt that a correspondence is being established between the world of the masque as represented by the Lady and her brothers and the world of the audience. The fiction of the masque identifies these figures as members of Lord Bridgewater's court enroute to rejoin that company. This correspondence is complicated somewhat, however, when the Lady enters the masque and upsets the expectations of her role by not recognizing the evil of the antimasque world when first confronted by it. The difficulty embodied in this situation is that, at the point in the action when the Lady is being deceived by Comus' appearance, the audience is not. In pre-Miltonic masques the identification of the hero's knowledge of events with the audience's is the crucial foundation upon which all transformations depend and the primary justification offered by the form for the final movement of the masquers into audience. The bifurcation between the audience and the heroine of the masque which Milton creates when the Lady and Comus first encounter each other is extended even further to include the entire world of the masque when the brothers enter the scene. The failure of judgment concerning the nature of virtue of which

[41] Tuve, p. 150.
[42] Orgel, *The Jonsonian Masque*, p. 45.

210

the Lady is guilty is echoed by her brothers when they are first presented
to the audience. To allay the Younger Brother's fears concerning his
sister's safety, the Elder Brother comforts him with these words:

> Virtue could see to do what virtue would
> By her own radiant light, though Sun and Moon
> Were in the flat Sea sunk . . .
> So dear to Heav'n is Saintly chastity,
> That when a soul is found sincerely so,
> A thousand liveried Angels lackey her,
> Driving far off each thing of sin and guilt . . . (lines 373 ff.)

This repetition of the same mistaken conception of the safety afforded by
virtue which marks the Lady's thoughts functions to mitigate the audience's judgment of her fault by extending that limitation in vision to
characterize the entire human world of the masque.

Although a division between the masquers' perception of the evil that
Comus represents and that of the audience is firmly established by the
action of the masque prior to the Lady's entrance, the correspondence
between the masquers' world and the world of the audience is nevertheless maintained. The knowledge of Comus' true nature to which the
audience is given access, but which is withheld from the Lady, does not
alter the fact that evil has the power to transform itself and disguise itself
as good in order to corrupt virtue. The masque affirms the validity of
this truth about evil for the world of the audience as well as for the world
of the masquers. The audience is able to evaluate the Lady's failure in
judgment when it is articulated, but its perception of evil is as limited as
the Lady's at the end of the masque.

Following Sabrina's release of the Lady from Comus' bondage, there
is a change of scene which presents "Ludlow Town and the President's
Castle." At this point the fictional level of the masque merges with the
literal context and the masquers move into the audience involving it in
the concluding revels. Milton uses precisely the same conventions which
we have seen Jonson use in *Pleasure Reconciled to Virtue* to conclude his
masque and directly implicate his audience in the action of his play. As
Mercury's reference to Hesperus who will conduct the reconciliation of
pleasure to virtue is a fictional yet literal reference to the King and the ensuing dances of his court, so the Attendant Spirit's presentation of the
Lady and her brothers to their father and mother participates in both the
fictional and the real.

211

The situation with which Milton concludes his masque, however, is significantly different from that with which Jonson concludes his. At the end of *Pleasure Reconciled to Virtue*, the world of the audience has been merged with the world of the masque, but that world is one of self-evident truths and immutability; particularity and change have been banished with the antimasque. In Jonson's masque, the garden of Hesperus is realized by both masquers and audience. The world with which Milton's masque concludes is a world of mutability and appearances which deceive;[43] it is a world from which Comus is temporarily routed but which he has dominated nevertheless. It has often been noted that this masque does not conclude with the dispelling of darkness with which Comus is so intimately associated throughout. This fact has caused some critics considerable difficulty. Sears Jayne, for example, would see the masque as an allegory "about the soul's achievement of Platonic *castitas*," and is therefore forced to read Comus as an agent of "natural providence:"

> Comus, as one agent of natural providence, argues quite rightly that his functions are natural, that is, they are possible within the realm of natural providence: but a soul's rejection of him is also equally "natural."[44]

Had Jayne taken into account the implications of the form with which Milton is working he would not have confused Comus' association with the natural realm with goodness.

An accurate reading of the conventions of the masque and the way in which Milton uses them provides a clear explanation of why *Comus* concludes with a situation in which "night sits monarch yet in the mid-sky." Night is the condition which describes the state of fallen man and it is a state in which evil poses a powerful and formidable threat to the existence of virtue. It is a state in which appearances deceive. *Comus* ends with a reference to the garden of Hesperus, also encountered in Jonson's *Pleasure Reconciled to Virtue*; but, in the world which Milton defines by his masque, it is a garden of perfection and immutable truths which is realized only in heaven; it is the reward of virtuous souls who survive the confrontation with evil which is unavoidable in "this drear Wood." When Comus invokes his followers to dance and says

> Come let us our rites begin,

---

[43] For an opposing interpretation see Woodhouse, "*Comus* Once More," pp. 74-75.

[44] Sears Jayne, "The Subject of Milton's Ludlow Mask," *PMLA*, 74 (1950), 533, 543.

212

>'Tis only daylight that makes Sin,
>Which these dun shades will ne'er report, (lines 125–27)

the "dun shades" over which he has command include the darkness which pervades the ambience of the audience sitting in a masquing hall as well as the fictional environment of his revelers. The antimasque world of Milton's Comus is not of a kind which, like Jonson's, can be dissolved into the world of the masque and no longer present itself as a difficulty. Rather it is a world of disorder coupled with power, and, even when temporarily banished by the Attendant Spirit, it exists literally somewhere in the background posing a continual threat to the world of the masquers and, in turn, of the audience.[45]

In conclusion, there is one point to which I should return: Milton's purpose in offering the audience a judgment and knowledge of Comus' nature in advance of such information being made available to the Lady or her brother. Prior to Milton, the form of the masque in the hands of a competent artist afforded an audience a moment in which the ideal could be realized and directly experienced. As Orgel notes of the Jonsonian masque, the masque could offer "a moment in which a vision of an ideal became a poetic and dramatic experience—becomes, in other words, a reality."[46] Because of the way Milton uses the conventions of the form, he essentially denies his audience this kind of direct participation in an ideal world and leaves them instead with a world which is formidable indeed and far from ideal. This fact does not, however, prevent Milton from defining a new purpose for artifice in his auditors' lives. Artifice, for Milton, is an instrument of education. The direct experience of the action of the masque is the means by which the Lady and her brothers learn the lesson which they do, but the artifice of the masque as a whole is the vehicle by which the audience arrives at the same position. Because the masque is primarily artificial to the audience, rather than an immediate experience as it is to the Lady and her brothers, it is possible for the knowledge of evil which the Lady acquires to be communicated and comprehended vicariously. By dividing the knowledge of events of the audience from that of the primary masquers, Milton calls attention to the masque as an art form and thereby defines it as a vehicle for the acquisition of moral education which is distinct and separate from direct experience.

[45] See also Tuve, pp. 153 ff.
[46] Orgel, *The Jonsonian Masque*, p. 185.

III

The Latin Poetry of John Milton[1]

R. W. Condee

John Milton is the greatest English poet to write Latin poetry and his Latin poetry formed an important part of his literary career. In all, he wrote thirty-one poems in Latin and some of them are among the best poetry that he wrote. His career as a Latin poet tends to fall into two periods: first, the early poems written between about 1625 and 1632,[2] and then the later poems, from 'Mansus' (late 1638 or early 1639) to 'Ad Ioannem Rousium' (23 January 1646/7).

Milton's total poetic career ended of course with *Samson Agonistes* and the two great English epics on which much of his fame rests, but he began chiefly as a Latin poet: of the almost 1400 extant lines of poetry that he had written by the time of his twenty-first birthday, over a thousand lines were in Latin, an output of greater length than, for example, Vergil's *Eclogues*. Milton turned away from Latin to English for his poetry only after a deliberate and self-conscious decision: in 1640 he wrote 'Epitaphium Damonis' in Latin, but the poem was concerned in part with this very decision to renounce Latin as the language for his poetry.

Two years later, in *The Reason of Church Government*, he restated his decision to become a poet in English. He said he wished that he 'might perhaps leave something so written to

58

aftertimes, as they should not willingly let it die', and then he went on to discuss the problem of language:[3]

> For which cause, and not only for that I knew it would be hard to arrive at the second rank among the Latines, I apply'd myselfe to that resolution which *Ariosto* follow'd against the perswasions of *Bembo*, to fix all the industry and art I could unite to the adorning of my native tongue.

In fact, however, in 1646, Milton wrote a Latin poem to John Rouse, Librarian at Oxford University, and two trivial Latin epigrams (in 1651 and 1654) which were included in tracts[4] attacking his political opponent Salmasius. It is these which were literally his last poems in Latin.

Milton's earliest extant Latin verses are three poems of little interest – 'Carmina Elegiaca', an untitled fragment in the lesser asclepiad, and a twelve-line fable on the peasant and the landlord. None of these was published in Milton's 1645 collection of poems.

'Elegia Prima' is Milton's first work in either English or Latin which can be seriously discussed as a poem. It is the first of Milton's seven elegies (Milton uses 'elegia' to describe the verse form, not the subject of the poem), and probably the first poem of a youthful *annus mirabilis*: in 1626 he wrote between six and eleven Latin poems (precise dating is difficult), perhaps more than in any other year of his life. Of the 1626 poems, 'Elegia Prima' is beyond question the best.

Nominally the poem is a verse letter 'ad Carolum Diodatum'. Charles Diodati (1609?–38) was a close friend of Milton; the first and sixth elegies and the fourth sonnet (in Italian) are addressed to him, and Milton's last long poem in Latin, 'Epitaphium Damonis', is a lament for Diodati's death.

Diodati, 'Elegia Prima' says, is in Chester, while Milton is in London, 'rusticated' temporarily from Cambridge University. The cause of Milton's suspension is not now clear and the poem does not explain. The poem falls into three sections: a short introduction addressing Diodati in Chester; a long middle section expatiating on Milton's joy in books, the theatre, the shady London walks, and above everything else the pretty girls of London; and then a short conclusion announcing his regretful return to Cambridge.

Like all Milton's early Latin poetry, 'Elegia Prima' depends

59

heavily on Ovid; the tags of phrases from the *Amoers*, the *Metamorphoses*, the *Epistulae ex Ponto*, and the *Tristia* mark almost every line of the poem. In this kind of recurrent verbal borrowing from standard Latin authors Milton resembles most Renaissance Latin poets.

But 'Elegia Prima' uses Ovid more cleverly than merely as a source for pat phrases: it poses a parallel, or more properly a cross-relation, between Milton's exile from Cambridge and Ovid's exile from Rome. As every seventeenth-century schoolboy knew, Ovid had been exiled from Rome to Tomis, on the shores of the Black Sea, in A.D. 8 by Augustus Caesar for offences not now known; Ovid spent the remaining ten years of his life there, writing the *Epistulae ex Ponto* and the *Tristia* to his friends in Rome, begging them to intercede for his return.

But Milton's fate he tells Diodati, is not so harsh as Ovid's:

> O utinam vates nunquam graviora tulisset
>   Ille Tomitano flebilis exul agro,
> Non tunc Ionio quicquam cessisset Homero
>   Neve foret victo laus tibi prima Maro. (21–4)

(Ah! If only that poet who was once a tearful exile in the land of Tomis had never had to put up with anything worse than this: then he would have been a match for Ionian Homer, and you, Virgil, outdone, would not enjoy the supreme glory.)[5]

This passage not only brings Ovid explicitly into Milton's poem, it echoes Ovid's complaint (*Tristia* 1.1.47–8) that not even Homer could write under the conditions at Tomis. Cambridge University, Milton implies (13–16), is as hostile to poetry as Tomis; but unlike Ovid, Milton is writing about the place from which, not to which, he has been exiled.

London supplies the exiled Milton with what residence at a university should:

> Tempora nam licet hic placidis dare libera Musis,
>   Et totum rapiunt me mea vita libri. (25–6)

(For here I can devote my leisure hours to the mild Muses: here books, which are my life, quite carry me away.)

60

This is an inverted echo from Ovid, who in his exile lamented the absence of things which Milton had in exile. Ovid writes,

Non hic librorum, per quos inviter alarque
  copia: pro libris arcus at arma sonant. (*Tristia* 3.14.37–8)

(Not here have I an abundance of books to stimulate and nourish me: in their stead is the rattle of bows and arms.)[6]

Part of Milton's central section is concerned with his enjoyment of comedy and tragedy while in London. The 'sinuosi pompa theatri' which delights Milton in London is the subject of pitiful dreams for Ovid in Tomis. In a mournful elegy on the belated coming of spring to Tomis, Ovid remembered the Roman games, and he could almost hear the applause of the crowded theatres.[7]

For Milton the landscape of Cambridge is repellent (11–14), and Milton's revulsion is a counterpart of Ovid's complaint against the barren Pontic landscape, with no apples bending the branches, no grapes or even vines, a treeless plain whose typical vegetation is wormwood.[8] Even the swamps of Tomis[9] are reflected in Milton's sneers at the marshy banks of the Cam (11, 89). For Milton, in this poem, there is nothing good about Cambridge University, from which he has been exiled, and nothing bad about London, just as for Ovid there was nothing good about Tomis, to which he had been exiled, and nothing bad (in the *Tristia* and the *Epistulae*) about Rome.

Essentially, 'Elegia Prima' centres on Milton's youthful contempt for Cambridge; it is a conscious insult fashioned with neat irony out of the learned tradition which a university should have embodied and at which, Milton felt, it had utterly failed. But 'Elegia Prima' also looks forward to 'L'Allegro' and 'Il Penseroso', with their similar lists of sensuous delights.[10] It is not as good a poem as either of the Companion Pieces, partly because it lacks their vividness, partly because its structure tends to ramble.

But 'Elegia Prima' does manage a climax which is appealingly rousing in an adolescent way. After considering the shortcomings of Cambridge, Milton sees the height of London's attraction enter – its beautiful girls. And here the seventeen-year-old Milton manages a fusion of erotic chauvinism which has a charm that is perhaps different from what he intended:

61

> Ah quoties dignae stupui miracula formae
>   Quae possit senium vel reparare Iovis;
> Ah quoties vidi superantia lumina gemmas,
>   Atque faces quotquot volvit uterque polus. (53–6)

(Ah, how often have I been struck dumb by the miraculous shapeliness of a figure which might well make even old Jove young again! Ah, how often have I seen eyes brighter than jewels, brighter than all the stars which wheel round the poles.)

These girls are not only beautiful, they are British!

> Cedite laudatae toties Heroides olim,
>   Et quaecunque vagum cepit amica Iovem, . . .
> Gloria virginibus debetur prima Britannis,
>   Extera sat tibi sit foemina posse sequi. (63–4, 71–2)

(Admit defeat, you heroines so often praised; admit defeat, all you girls who have caught the eye of inconstant Jove. . . . The first prize goes to the British girls: be content, foreign woman, to take second place!)

But then the poem comes back to earth. Milton has mastered considerable learning, but he is only seventeen years old and not the master of his fate. Unlike Ovid, Milton's exile comes to a quick, albeit involuntary end:

> Stat quoque iuncosas Cami remeare paludes,
>   Atque iterum raucae murmur adire Scholae.
> Interea fidi parvum cape munus amici,
>   Paucaque in alternos verba coacta modos. (89–92)

(I am to return to the Cam's reedy marshes and face the uproar of the noisy University again. Meanwhile accept this little gift from a loyal friend – one or two words forced into elegiac metre.)

The temporary colleague and counterpart of Publius Ovidius Naso will now go back to his seat in class at Cambridge.

James Burnett, Lord Monboddo, called 'Elegia Prima' the equal of anything by Ovid or Tibullus, and various critics have praised the facility and autochthonous character of Milton's Latin. Rand says that Milton's Latin elegiacs 'breathe

62

a spirit of Horace and Ovid'.[11] Keightley on the other hand objects to Milton's grammatical errors, false quantities, and deviations from classical usage[12] (Keightley also collected the 'incongruities' of Vergil). But analysis of the linguistic quality of Milton's Latin in the poems is necessarily outside the scope of this type of essay.

Milton probably wrote at least five other Latin poems in 1626, making this one of the most productive years, so far as we can tell, of his career. He wrote four epicedia: 'In Obitum Procancellarii Medici' (for Dr John Gostlin), 'Elegia Secunda' (for Richard Ridding, the University Beadle), 'Elegia Tertia' (for Lancelot Andrews, Bishop of Winchester), and 'In Obitum Praesulis Eliensis' (for Nicholas Felton, Bishop of Ely). In addition, he wrote 'In Quintum Novembris', on the Gunpowder Plot, probably in 1626; Milton also wrote three other brief and unimportant poems (totalling only thirty lines) on the Gunpowder Plot, but their dates are unknown. The best that can be said for these early epicedia is that they are not unpromising for a seventeen- or eighteen-year-old, but it would have been reckless, on the basis of these poems of late 1626, to predict the great poems which were to follow.

Most of these poems are badly overfreighted with classical learning and, unlike the clever manipulation of Ovid in 'Elegia Prima', the learning serves no purpose. The epicedion for Gostlin introduces Iapetus, Nessus, Hercules, Hector, Athene, Sarpedon, Jove, Patroclus, Achilles, Hecate, Circe, Medea, Machaon, Philyn, Chiron, Aesculapius, Apollo, Persephone, and Aeacus – all in a forty-eight line poem. Poor Gostlin, the dead vice-chancellor, is almost crowded out of his own epicedion.

'Elegia Secunda', commemorating the death of the University Beadle, is no better. We know from other sources that the beadle concerned was Richard Ridding. But it is symptomatic of the faceless impersonality of the poem that, if the poem were undated, we should have no way of telling from the poem itself that the beadle being lamented was Richard Ridding; it might have been any other recently deceased holder of the office.

In 'Elegia Tertia' Milton suppresses his weakness for Greco-Roman mythology and centres the poem on the death of Bishop Andrewes. The poem resembles 'Lycidas' and 'Epitaphium Damonis' in its transition from initial grief to ultimate

63

consolation in the knowledge that Andrewes rests happily in Heaven. But 'Elegia Tertia' is interesting in part because it tries and fails to manage this transition with the sure sense of progression that characterizes poems like 'Lycidas' and 'Epitaphium Damonis'. The two later poems, each in a quite different way, create a poetic dialectic which carries each poem, sometimes in a circuitous fashion, to a conclusion which is inherent, although perhaps not obvious, in the opening. We shall examine Milton's mature method more closely when we come to 'Epitaphium Damonis'.

'Elegia Tertia', however, progresses not by means of its inherent structure but by a fortuitous leap from grief to consolation: night falls, sleep comes, the poet dreams, and the dream, luckily, is of Andrewes in the company of the saints. And then, with the poet's awakening, the poem stops.[13]

'In Quintum Novembris', probably written in this same productive year, is 226 lines – Milton's longest poem so far. It contains four large 'movements': first, the aerial flight of Satan, with his survey of western Europe and the happy British Isles, and his passage across the Alps to Rome; second, his survey of Rome, the procession of priests and the Pope, and the Pope's retirement to sleep. Satan visits the Pope in sleep and suggests to him a conspiracy to subjugate England. The third 'movement' consists of the Pope's meeting with the College of Cardinals to hatch the Gunpowder Plot, and the fourth 'movement' concludes the poem with Fama spreading the story of the plot, with the result that Satan is defeated and England saved.[14]

No-one has claimed 'In Quintum Novembris' as one of Milton's great poems, although Landor thought it 'a wonderful work for a boy of seventeen',[15] and Rand found in it 'greater poise and firmness than the little epic on the *Gnat* which Virgil wrote at sixteen'.[16]

Its chief interest for the modern reader lies in its foreshadowing of *Paradise Lost*. Satan in 'In Quintum Novembris' is a brief but not incompetent sketch for the gigantic figure of *Paradise Lost*. Both poems use many of the epic conventions – the adventurous journey, the council (of Cardinals in 'In Quintum Novembris', of devils in *Paradise Lost*), the rousing speech to the indolent follower, the supernatural being in disguise, and so on.

64

But 'In Quintum Novembris' is marred by several flaws. Perhaps the most important is the poorly managed conclusion: for the first 169 lines the poem has an enthusiastic if melodramatic drive; suddenly at line 170 Fama appears and twenty-three lines of the poem are devoted to describing her. Then within thirty-three lines she saves England by revealing the fact of the conspiracy. After such elaborate preparations for England's downfall we might justifiably expect more heroic efforts would be needed to save her. A Satan who would be foiled by these last thirty-three lines of the poem doesn't resemble the 'ferus ignifluo regnans Acheronte tyrannus,/ Eumenidum pater' 'the fierce tyrant who controls Acheron's flaming currents, the tyrant who is father to the Furies' (7–8), who dominates the beginning of the poem. One suspects that the seventeen-year-old poet tired after 150 or so lines and simply finished off the poem as quickly as he could.

On 6 October 1626, Nicholas Felton, Bishop of Ely, died, and Milton memorialized the event with 'In Obitum Praesulis Eliensis', in alternating iambic trimeters and dimeters. But the poem has little to distinguish it beyond its slight biographical interest.

'Elegia Quarta', a verse letter to Thomas Young, Milton's former tutor, was probably written during the next year, 1627. Young was an ardent Presbyterian later famous as the 'TY' of 'Smectymnuus', an acronym for the five Presbyterian authors of a tract attacking episcopacy in 1641.

'Elegia Quarta' is a pleasant poem by a schoolboy to his former teacher, but it would not be notable if it were not by John Milton. As a poem by Milton it has two interesting aspects: first, in some ways it looks ahead to another panegyric, 'Mansus' (1638–9), and secondly it anticipates another poem to a revered elder, 'Ad Patrem' (1631–2? 1637?).

As often in his early poems, Milton crowds aboard almost all the Greeks and Romans he can think of – Aeolus, Doris, Medea, Triptolemus, Jove, and countless others. Young is dearer to him than Socrates was to Alcibiades, dearer than Aristotle to Alexander the Great. It is interesting to compare the hackneyed use of *synkrisis*[17] in this early poem with Milton's later, subtler use of it in 'Mansus', where it serves a more complex poetic function.

But the poem loses its stiffness as Milton expresses concern

65

for Young's safety (71 ff). He becomes surprisingly paternal towards this divine who was twenty years his senior:

> At tu sume animos, nec spes cadat anxia curis
>   Nec tua concutiat decolor ossa metus. (105–6)

(But take heart. Do not let anxieties quench your hope, even if they make you uneasy, and do not allow pale fear to send shudders through your limbs.)

And he concludes with the encouraging air not of a pupil but of a reassuring adviser:

> Nec dubites quandoque frui melioribus annis,
>   Atque iterum patrios posse videre lares. (125–6)

(Do not doubt that some day you will enjoy happier times and be able to see your home again.)

'Elegia Septima' is numbered as the last of Milton's elegies but it seems to have been written prior to 'Elegia Quinta'. It records an erotic episode in which he sneers at the power of Cupid, and Cupid retaliates by causing him to fall in love, in vain, with a beautiful girl he chances to see, and she passes by, never to appear again. He now knows the full power of Cupid. He vows sacrifices on the altar of Cupid and prays that next time his love will be successful.

This is a minor conventional poem on a minor theme, but Milton handles it with dexterity; he makes fun of himself not only by setting forth his foolhardy scorn for Cupid early in the poem, but also by the quasi-heroic quality of his mock-serious invocation to the god at the end:

> Iam tuus O certe est mihi formidabilis arcus,
>   Nate dea, iaculis nec minus igne potens:
> Et tua fumabunt nostris altaria donis,[18]
>   Solus et in superis tu mihi summus eris. (95–8)

(Child of the goddess, you may be sure that I dread your bow now: you are mighty with your arrows, and no less so with your fire. Your altars shall smoke with my offerings, and you alone shall be supreme to me among the gods.)

These passages manage the poem's *persona* with considerably

66

more skill than most of the early poems – far better than the second or third elegies, for example, where the speaker is a conventional mourner, undistinguished in either his grief or his consolation.

At some time between 1628 and 1632 Milton wrote two hexameter poems, 'Natura non pati Senium' ('That Nature does not suffer from old age') and 'De Idea Platonica quemadmodum Aristoteles intellexit' ('Of the Platonic Ideal Form as understood by Aristotle'), which seem to have been University exercises. They are of little significance in Milton's poetic career.

'Elegia Quinta', on the other hand, is one of Milton's greatest short poems in either English or Latin and certainly the best poem he had written up to this time, when he was twenty years old. It succeeds so well because it is a direct, full-blooded, celebration of fertility in a skilful, well-integrated poem. It rejoices in the return of spring to the land, in the sunshine, in sexual love. The gods embrace, the human lovers woo, and the earth itself feels sexual desire:

> Sic Tellus lasciva suos suspirat amores
> Matris in exemplum caetera turba ruunt. (95–6)

(This is the way lascivious Earth breathes out her passion, and all the other creatures are quick to follow their mother's example.)

An important factor in making the poem the exuberant creation that it is lies in its purely celebratory mood: it arrives at no decision and draws no moral; it urges nothing on the reader, not even 'carpe diem'. The closing lines simply wish for an eternal or at least a long-lasting spring.

While the Greco-Roman deities are present as in most of Milton's poems, the poem controls them: it is the deities who serve the poem by giving shape to the natural forces of fertility, rather than, as in some of the earlier poems (e.g. 'Elegia Secunda'), the deities usurping almost the whole poem.

'Elegia Quinta' is also a stronger poem structurally than any of its predecessors. It achieves this structural integrity in part by refusing to attempt the problem which causes difficulty in the earlier poems. 'Elegia Quinta' is in the main a static poem, while most of the earlier poems attempted a

67

progression which they were unable to bring off. 'Elegia Quinta' attempts no progression and therefore fails at none. In this it resembles the Nativity Ode, probably written the following December, which – for all its complexities in other respects – is likewise a static poem. As A. S. P. Woodhouse puts it, '[The Ode] is in the nature of a simple affirmation, with no problem stated or implied and no emotional tension to be resolved.'[19] 'Elegia Quinta' anticipates the Ode in this respect.

This is not to say that 'Elegia Quinta' is an amorphous outpouring. Milton begins with the announcement that spring and his own creative powers are returning. Apollo, the sun-god, the leader of the Muses, lifts the poet to the heavens; the spring's gift to Milton is song and Milton's gift to the spring is therefore this song. Spring brings the nightingale, and the nightingale and the poet will join in song (25–8).

The rest of the poem is their mutual song, and it is constructed out of these ideas and images of fertility, creativity, and the passionate confluence of poet and nightingale, man and nature, earth and sun, god and goddess, nymph and Pan, man and woman. Thus the plunge of Phoebus the sun into Tethys the sea causes the renewed Earth to cry out in a jealous passion which contagiously arouses mankind:

> Cur te, inquit, cursu languentem Phoebe diurno
>   Hesperiis recipit caerula mater aquis? . . .
> Sic Tellus lasciva suos suspirat amores;
>   Matris in exemplum caetera turba ruunt.
> Nunc etenim toto currit vagus orbe Cupido,
>   Languentesque fovet solis ab igne faces. (81–2, 95–8)

('Phoebus, why should the sky-blue mother take you into her western waves when you are exhausted by your daily journey?' . . . This is the way lascivious Earth breathes out her passion, and all the other creatures are quick to follow their mother's example. For now wandering Cupid speeds through the whole world and renews his dying torch in the flames of the sun.)

The poem uses Earth, Tellus, not only as a personification of fertility and sexuality, but also as the appropriate and joyful place for sexuality. Phoebus, plunging into the sea and thereby

68

arousing the jealousy of Earth, is 'clivoso fessus Olympo' ('tired out by heaven's steep path', 79), and while Jupiter has his sexual pleasures on Olympus (117–18), it is in the woods and fields of Earth that the gods find their greatest pleasure.

The conclusion of the poem is more than a prayer for eternal spring; it is a celebration of the fertility and sexuality in which the poem is steeped:

> Et sua quisque diu sibi numina lucus habeto,
> Nec vos arborea dii precor ite domo.
> Te referant miseris te Iupiter aurea terris
> Saecla, quid ad nimbos aspera tela redis?
> Tu saltem lente rapidos age Phoebe iugales
> Qua potes, et sensim tempora veris eant.
> Brumaque productas tarde ferat hispida noctes,
> Ingruat et nostro serior umbra polo. (133–40)

(Long may each grove have its own particular deities: do not leave your homes among the trees, gods, I beseech you. May the golden age bring you back, Jove, to this wretched world! Why go back to your cruel weapons in the clouds? At any rate, Phoebus, drive your swift team as slowly as you can, and let the passing of the springtime be gradual. May rough winter be tardy in bringing us his dreary nights, and may it be late in the day when shadows assail our sky.)

In view of the fact that Milton, prior to his twenty-first birthday, was primarily a Latin poet – he had written nineteen Latin poems totalling over a thousand lines and only three poems in English totalling barely two hundred lines – it is not surprising that his first solid achievement as a poet, 'Elegia Quinta', was a Latin poem.

Later that year, 1629, Milton wrote his sixth Latin elegy, 'Ad Carolum Diodatum Ruri Commorantem' ('To Charles Diodati staying in the country'). At the same time he was writing the Nativity Ode. Diodati had written Milton a verse letter apologizing that poetry had fled from him because of the feasts and wine of the Christmas season. Milton answers in 'Elegia Sexta' that he himself writes from an empty stomach, but that Diodati's high living should be no deterrent. The lack of good wine in Tomis caused Ovid to write bad verse. The

69

elegiac poet needs music, wine, love, and grand banquets to produce his verse. The epic poet, on the other hand, must live a pure, chaste life, drinking only water and eating herbs as he sings of wars and heroes; this was the way of life of Tiresias, Linus, and Homer. 'But if you will know what I am doing', Milton continues,

> Paciferum canimus caelesti semine regem,
> Faustaque sacratis saecula pacta libris. (81–2)

(I am writing a poem about the king who was born of heavenly seed and who brought peace to men. I am writing about the blessed age promised in Holy Scripture.)

That is, he is in the process of writing the Nativity Ode.

A ten-line epilogue, in elegiac distichs, follows the seventh elegy in both editions of Milton's poems (1645 and 1673) printed in his lifetime. The epilogue seems to be a retraction –

> Haec ego mente olim laeva, studioque supino
> Nequitiae posui vana trophaea meae. (1–2)

(These lines are the trifling memorials of my levity which, with a warped mind and a base spirit, I once raised.)

And in the remaining eight lines Milton promises to give up erotic poetry. The epilogue raises some minor scholarly problems[20] but it has little poetic value. Bateson calls it 'perhaps the most repellent product of that social vacuum to which Milton consigned himself in reaction against Cambridge'.[21]

'Ad Patrem' was written perhaps in Milton's last year at Cambridge.[22] Apparently the elder Milton objected to his son's writing poetry, or perhaps to his devotion of so much of himself to his poetry. 'Ad Patrem' is addressed to the old man in justification of his son's poetic career. In his justification Milton deprecates the poems he has written up to now, but praises the power of poetry, reminds his father of his father's own success as a composer of music, and expresses his deep and humble thanks for all that his father has done for him. He closes with the hope that his poem to his father will help to bring immortality to the old man.

Milton builds his poem and his justification out of two chief elements: a deprecation of his own poetry up to now

70

('tenues sonos' – 'trivial songs'), and an exaltation of the ideal of poetry, which is loved by the gods and has the power to bind the underworld; kings have honoured poets and poets have preserved in song the deeds of heroes. Thus the poem is moving to a resolution whereby Milton's predicted future glory as a poet will both change his father's opinion and fulfil the potentialities of his 'tenues sonos'. There is a need at this point in 'Ad Patrem' for the kind of structural progression that Milton will manage magnificently in 'Lycidas' and 'Epitaphium Damonis'.

But this developmental structure does not occur in 'Ad Patrem', and three quite different faults cause Milton's difficulties here. The first of these faults is inherent in the crucial passage where he predicts his ultimate crowning with laurel and ivy:

> Iamque nec obscurus populo miscebor inerti,
> Vitabuntque oculos vestigia nostra profanos.
> Este procul vigiles curae, procul este, querelae,
> Invidiaeque acies transverso tortilis hirquo,
> Saeva nec anguiferos extende Calumnia rictus;
> In me triste nihil, faedissima turba, potestis,
> Nec vestri sum iuris ego; securaque tutus
> Pectora, vipereo gradiar sublimis ab ictu. (103–10)

(Now I shall no longer mix with the brainless mob: my steps will shun the sight of common eyes. Away with you, sleep-destroying worries, away with you, complaints, and the squinting eye of envy with its crooked goatish look. Do not stretch your snaky jaws at me, cruel calumny. Your whole filthy gang can do me no harm: I am not within your power. I shall stride on in safety with an unwounded heart, lifted high above your viperous sting.)

Something similar to the earlier passage (17–40) on the supernatural power of poetry might have lifted the poem to the climax it needed here, but unfortunately Milton raises us up to his vision of glory while looking over his shoulder: he speaks of himself as 'nec obscurus', as no longer mingling with the 'populo inerti', and the repeated negations deflate his climax rather than exalt it. Milton appears in the scene not so much as triumphing in what he strives for, but as renouncing what he wants to seclude himself from.

A second fault, one which also prevents the climactic lines concerning Milton's being wreathed with laurel and ivy from being an effective climax, is the haphazard arrangement of some of the previous parts of the poem. 'Ad Patrem' begins (1–16) with the hope that his muse will rise with bold wings, pointing to these two central conflicts of the poem – his clash with his father and the difference between the potential and the actual worth of his poetry.

But the poem immediately leaps (17–40) to a pronounce-ment of the divine nature of poetry, of its power over the gods, and thence to an Olympian/Heavenly vision of an eternity in which men, crowned with gold, will sing sweet songs echoing to the vault of the stars. The poem's rapturous praise of 'immor-tale melos et inenarrabile carmen' (37) rises to a peak which takes on the manner of a solution to the poem's conflicts. But this passage is not a resolution and Milton still has three-quarters of his poem left to be developed. And indeed the rest of the poem tends to wander anticlimactically to lower emo-tional pitches and to less exalted matters.

On leaving the Heavenly Realms the poem moves (41–55) to the banquets of ancient kings, where bards sang of heroic subjects. This is of course relevant to Milton's justification of poetry, but one wonders why it follows, at a lower level in almost all senses, the lofty passage preceding it. Again, the section on his father's permitting him to escape careers in business or law (67–76), and the following passage (77–92) on his father's encouragement of his linguistic and philosophical studies are logical parts of the poem. But it is difficult to see any structural reasons for their position here in the poem.

The next section (93–110) is the passage we have already discussed as occupying a climactic position in the poem without actually being climactic. The section begins, however, by dis-missing the folly of seeking for gold (93–4), and this leads only to an awkward reversion to the subject of his father's generosity:

> Quae potuit maiora pater tribuisse, vel ipse
> Iupiter, excepto, donasset ut omnia, coelo?
> Non potiora dedit, quamvis et tuta fuissent,
> Publica qui iuveni commisit lumina nato,
> Atque Hyperionos currus, et fraena diei,
> Et circum undantem radiata luce tiaram. (95–100)

72

(What greater treasures could have been given by a father, or by Jove himself for that matter, even if he had given everything, unless he had included heaven as well? That father who trusted his young son with the universal light of the world and the chariot of Hyperion, with the reins of day and the diadem which radiates waves of light, gave (even had those gifts been safe) no better gifts than my father's.)

The reference to Phaëthon, destroyed by his father Hyperion's gift, takes the poem in quite the wrong direction, as Milton's 'quamvis et tuta fuissent' ('even had those gifts been safe') indicates. Then the poem lurches suddenly from Hyperion and Phaëthon to a statement of its resolution:

> Ergo ego iam doctae pars quamlibet ima catervae
> Victrices hederas inter, laurosque sedebo. (101–2)

(Therefore I, who already have a place, though a very low one, in the ranks of the learned, shall one day sit among those who wear the ivy and the laurels of victory.)

One wonders where Milton's 'ergo' came from. The laurel and ivy are reasonable resolutions of the early references to 'tenues sonos' and 'exiguum opus'. But the intervening parts of the poem have not led us on to such a triumph in the way that, a few years later, 'Lycidas' and 'Epitaphium Damonis' will proceed by means of inexorable poetic logic to their beatific visions. 'Ad Patrem' simply wanders from its discussion of alternative careers to Hyperion and his son, to Milton's father's generosity – and then, baldly, 'ergo': Milton will become the great poet that he has not yet been.

A third difficulty in 'Ad Patrem' lies in the lines which conclude the poem.

> Et vos, O nostri, iuvenilia carmina, lusus,
> Si modo perpetuos sperare audebitis annos,
> Et domini superesse rogo, lucemque tueri,
> Nec spisso rapient oblivia nigra sub Orco,
> Forsitan has laudes, decantatumque parentis
> Nomen, ad exemplum, sero servabitis aevo. (115–20)

(And you, my youthful poems, my pastimes, if only you are bold enough to hope for immortality, to hope that

73

you will survive your master's funeral pyre and keep your eyes upon the light, then perhaps, if dark oblivion does not after all plunge you down beneath the dense crowds of the underworld, you may preserve this eulogy and my father's name, which has been the subject of my verse, as an example for a far-off age.)

Rather than carrying the poem forward, as do the concluding lines of 'Lycidas' and 'Epitaphium Damonis', this conclusion lets 'Ad Patrem' fall back into the conflicts from which it began: 'nostri, iuvenilia carmina, lusus' ('my youthful poems, my pastimes', 115) simply echoes 'tenues sonos' (4) and 'exiguum opus' (7). And what ought to be a resolution to the poem merely reaffirms the difference between Milton's own poetry and the ideal poetry of which the middle of the poem (17–40) spoke so fervently. This leaves Milton's hope that his verses will make his father immortal a feeble thing both logically and poetically.

But 'Ad Patrem' represents an advance in poetic technique for Milton in many ways. Written in dactylic hexameters rather than in the elegiac distichs of most of his early poems, it begins to develop rhythmic patterns which give Milton more freedom and syntactical flexibility: where the elegiac distichs tended to constrict him into short sentences to fit the couplets, the flowing hexameters of 'Ad Patrem' permit the development of a kind of verse paragraph not found in the elegies. And this more fluid verse form will be an invaluable instrument for Milton in 'Mansus' and 'Epitaphium Damonis'.

The great strength of 'Ad Patrem', however, lies in the *personae* which Milton projects for his father and himself. The interplay of the two *personae* must have presented Milton with some difficult poetic problems – problems which he solved with greater skill than he had heretofore shown. In no other poem, before or after, does Milton adopt a posture of such humility. This poem is 'exiguum opus' ('this little offering'), 'charta ista' ('this sheet of paper'); his gratitude to his father is 'arida' because his words are futile, and he concludes, as we have seen, by deprecating his work as 'my youthful poems, my pastimes'. He uses the honorific 'donum' (8, 10, 112)[23] for his father's gifts to him, while his own possible repayments

74

are merely 'munera' (8) and 'factis' (112). Yet his humility never becomes obsequious, as it so easily might.

This is because of the great skill Milton uses in handling the figure of his father in the poem. The aesthetic problem here is a difficult one: the poem must make the elder Milton an attractive figure (the biographical considerations here are obvious and need not delay us) in part because the poet's own *persona* depends on that of his father: the two *personae* emerge through their interactions. If the elder Milton appears as merely a grumpy old man, the younger Milton will appear, in trying to appease and persuade him, as either comic or servile. Yet an inevitable and central element of the poem is the clash between the young poet's lofty concept of poetry and the old man's deprecation of it. Milton solves this aesthetic problem essentially by the use of two ideas – by repeated praise of the old man's 'dona', and by skilfully stressing the old man's accomplishments as a musician and therefore also as a protégé of Phoebus:

> Nunc tibi quid mirum, si me genuisse poetam
> Contigerit, caro si tam prope sanguine iuncti
> Cognatas artes, studiumque affine sequamur:
> Ipse volens Phoebus se dispertire duobus,
> Altera dona mihi, dedit altera dona parenti,
> Dividuumque Deum genitorque puerque tenemus. (61–6)

(No wonder, then, that you should have the good luck to beget me, a poet, or that we who are so closely related by ties of affection and blood should cultivate sister arts and have kindred interests. Phoebus, wishing to share himself between the two of us, gave one lot of gifts to me and the other to my father, with the result that father and son have each one half a god.)

Instead of refuting his father, Milton includes him, and the old man appears not as a dominating, insensitive boor (a role into which the poem could easily have pushed him), but simply as mistaken about the artistic bond which actually unites them.

Thus Milton's address to his father establishes the old man as generous, permissive, and a lover of learning who is in part responsible for his son's knowledge of Greek, Latin, Hebrew,

75

and philosophy. By showing his father as a man of breadth and depth, Milton makes his own self-deprecation appear in the poem as appropriate, attractive, and free from any traces of fawning subservience. This diffident and humble Milton of 'Ad Patrem', who occurs nowhere else in his poetry, is a charming person because the poem very skilfully makes him so.

If we accept 1631–2 as a probable date for 'Ad Patrem', there is then a hiatus in Milton's career as a Latin poet until 1638 (*Comus* and 'Lycidas', in English, appeared in the intervening years). In late April or early May of 1638 Milton left England on the traditional grand tour of the continent. This tour began his closing period as a Latin poet. He wrote four brief Latin poems ('Ad Salsillum' and three poems 'Ad Leonoram'), and the long poem 'Mansus', to his host in Naples, Giovanni Battista Manso. 'Ad Salsillum' (to a fellow-poet, Giovanni Salzilli) and three poems to Leonora Baroni are trivial and need not delay us.

While in Italy Milton visited Naples, where he met Giovanni Battista Manso, Marquis of Villa (1560?–1645), who had been a patron of both Tasso and Marino, and apparently was as hospitable to the young English Protestant poet as possible. In response to Manso's kindness Milton wrote a poem of 100 hexameters to the old man, presumably late in 1638 or early in 1639. The poem is a panegyric, making use of the conventional rhetorical topoi that had come down through centuries of stylized adulation. But Milton, now thirty years old, is a mature poet; not only the Latin poems already discussed, but such great English poems as the Nativity Ode, 'L'Allegro', 'Il Penseroso', and *Comus* have already been written. And the year before, in 1637, he wrote 'Lycidas', which Marjorie Hope Nicolson calls 'the most perfect long short poem in the English language'. In fact, Milton's career as a Latin poet was drawing to an end.

As we might expect, 'Mansus' is a considerably more complex and better poem than his earlier tributes to Andrewes, Felton, Young, or even 'Ad Patrem'. Like the other great poems of his maturity, 'Mansus' is in an important sense a conventional poem: it returns again and again to the traditions of its genre, the panegyric or encomium. But, like 'Lycidas', 'Epitaphium Damonis', *Paradise Lost*, and *Paradise Regained*, it also self-consciously breaks with the tradition and establishes

76

itself as a unique poem by the interrelations between itself and the panegyric tradition. Further, 'Mansus', like the other poems of Milton's maturity, transcends its literal occasion or theme. It enlarges to a contemplation of death, of the rewards of life, and in the end it creates not merely a panegyric of Manso but a poem celebrating the essential harmony of the universe.

'Mansus' resembles 'Lycidas' and 'Epitaphium Damonis' in beginning with a brief prose preface which explains who Manso is, and Milton's use of the panegyric tradition begins here: Manso is 'one of the most famous gentlemen of Italy, not only because of his reputation for intellectual ability but also because of his devotion to literature and his courage in war'. The topos of excellence in both war and peace goes back in the panegyric tradition hundreds of years in countless poems.[24] Appended to Manso's own collected poems, *Poesie Nomiche*, were more than a hundred poems in his praise by his friends, and time and again his friends praised him for his prowess 'nella militia e nella dottrina'.[25]

In the panegyric tradition, the extent of the subject's fame is an incessant topos,[26] and it is on this theme that Milton begins the actual poem:

Haec quoque Manse tuae meditantur carmina laudi
Pierides, tibi Manse choro notissime Phoebi,
Quandoquidem ille alium haud aequo est dignatus honore,
Post Galli cineres, et Maecenatis Hetrusci. (1–4)

(Manso, the Muses are singing this song, too, in your praise, yes, yours, Manso, Phoebus' choir knows all about you, because since Gallus and Etruscan Maecenas died Phoebus has hardly thought anyone so worthy of honour as you.)

The main reason for praising Manso, Milton tells us, is his friendship and helpfulness to poets – specifically to Tasso, to Marino, and now to Milton himself. Then he compares Manso with the centaur Chiron in a long metaphor which is central to the poem:

Dicetur tum sponte tuos habitasse penates
Cynthius, et famulas venisse ad limina musas:
At non sponte domum tamen idem, et regis adivit
Rura Pheretiadae coelo fugitivus Apollo;

77

Ille licet magnum Alciden susceperat hospes;
Tantum ubi clamosos placuit vitare bubulcos,
Nobile mansueti cessit Chironis in antrum,
Irriguos inter saltus frondosaque tecta
Peneium prope rivum: ibi saepe sub ilice nigra
Ad citharae strepitum blanda prece victus amici
Exilii duros lenibat voce labores.
Tum neque ripa suo, barathro nec fixa sub imo,
Saxa stetere loco, nutat Trachinia rupes,
Nec sentit solitas, immania pondera, silvas,
Emotaeque suis properant de collibus orni,
Mulcenturque novo maculosi carmine lynces. (54–69)

(Men will say that, of his own free will, Apollo dwelt in
your house, and that the Muses came like servants to your
doors. Yet that same Apollo, when he was a fugitive from
heaven, came unwillingly to King Admetus' farm, although Admetus had been host to mighty Hercules. When
he wanted to get away from the bawling ploughmen
Apollo could, at any rate, retreat to gentle Chiron's
famous cave, among the moist woodland pastures and
leafy shades beside the river Peneus. There often, beneath
a dark oak tree, he would yield to his friend's flattering
persuasion and, singing to the music of his lute, would
soothe the hardships of exile. Then neither the river banks,
nor the boulders lodged in the quarry's depths stayed in
their places: the Trachinian cliff nodded to the tune,
and no longer felt its huge and familiar burden of forest
trees; the mountain ashes were moved and came hurrying
down their slopes, and spotted lynxes grew tame as they
listened to the strange music.)

Milton is using *synkrisis* much as he did in 'Elegia Quarta',
to Thomas Young. A very common type of *synkrisis* is that
which concerns the relation of the giver (the poet) to the
receiver (the patron being praised), the two becoming metaphorically the poet/host and the patron/guest. In such a
comparison the lowly poet/host appears as one or another of
the humbler figures of Greek legend who received a god or
hero into his home – Icarus, Molorchus, or Chiron, honoured
at the visit of Apollo, Bacchus, Jove, Hercules, or Achilles.[27]

78

But Milton has reversed the metaphor: instead of comparing the noble patron/guest with Apollo or Hercules, and the humble poet/host with Chiron or Molorchus, it is Milton, the poet, who is the guest, who is like Apollo or Hercules. And in Milton's poem, the poet/guest graciously expresses his appreciation for the hospitality of patron/hosts like Manso and Chiron. Milton even goes so far as to link Manso's very name to Chiron's with a pun:

> Nobile mansueti cessit Chironis in antrum

(. . . retreat to gentle Chiron's famous cave . . .)

This air of majestically praising Manso for being such a good assistant to poets boldly pervades much of the poem. Milton establishes a clear class-distinction: of primary importance are the poets – Homer, Vergil, Horace, Tasso, Marino, and Milton; of secondary importance are those who help the poets by patronage or by preserving their fame – Gallus, Maecenas, Herodotus, and Manso.

Then Milton suddenly departs from his praise of Manso to discuss his own plans for poetry:

> O mihi si mea sors talem concedat amicum
> Phoebaeos decorasse viros qui tam bene norit,
> Si quando indigenas revocabo in carmina reges,
> Arturumque etiam sub terris bella moventem;
> Aut dicam invictae sociali foedere mensae,
> Magnanimos heroas, et (O modo spiritus ad sit)
> Frangam Saxonicas Britonum sub Marte phalanges. (78–84)

(O may it be my good luck to find such a friend, who knows so well how to honour Phoebus' followers, if ever I bring back to life in my songs the kings of my native land and Arthur, who set wars raging even under the earth, or tell of the great-hearted heroes of the round table, which their fellowship made invincible, and – if only the inspiration would come – smash the Saxon phalanxes beneath the impact of the British charge.)

E. M. W. Tillyard, who thought that 'Mansus' was 'the best of all Milton's Latin poems (the *Epitaphium Damonis* included)', said of this passage, 'There is great power in the crash of *frangam* after the hushed parenthesis of *O modo spiritus*

79

adsit.'[28] And Landor in his *Imaginary Conversations* called the line 'a glorious verse' and had Southey object only in that it overrated the early Britons: '"Was the whole nation [of Britons] ever worth this noble verse of Milton? It seems to come sounding over the Aegean Sea and not to have been modulated on the low country of the Tiber."'[29]

As we have seen, Milton builds into his panegyric a significant reversal of an important part of the panegyric tradition – for Milton it is the function, almost the duty, of patrons to honour poets, rather than the function or duty of the poets to honour their patrons. And this artful dissonance between Milton's 'Mansus' and the tradition derives its force not only from the reversed metaphor of Chiron, Apollo, and other mythological figures, but also from the closing vision (85–100); where Milton's predecessors in the tradition had visions of their patrons smiling down from Heaven on poor mortals such as the poet, Milton, with what Bradner calls 'Marlovean' exuberance,[30] envisages himself smiling down with satisfaction at the assistance of patrons like Manso. It would be difficult to defend the tone of these closing lines, and especially the last line, where Milton is so enraptured by his own apotheosis that he bursts into applause for himself. But the passage does have important connections with the panegyric tradition and with the happy relations of poet and patron, which is at the heart of the poem.

This closing vision resembles the visions which concluded several of Milton's epicedia – most importantly, 'Lycidas', written the year before, and 'Epitaphium Damonis' the next year (1639). In these other two poems the world of mortals is tainted; Lycidas received no proper reward here below and death came too soon; Damon's death also, from a purely human point of view, was senseless, and, until the closing vision, it was in many ways worse than that of the animals. Each poem progresses from the polluted natural world to the Christian supernatural community which resolves the earlier dilemma by surmounting and abandoning the natural world.

'Mansus' represents the natural world as having its own logic, rewards, and happiness. The result of Manso's help to Tasso is 'felix concordia'. The 'pia officia' of Manso continue after Tasso's death and it is important that they should. On the other hand, in 'Lycidas' the question '. . . What boots it

80

with uncessant care/To tend the homely slighted shepherd's trade?' (64–5) implies (at this point in the poem and in the natural world) a quite different answer.

'Mansus' presents a different world-view also from that in 'Epitaphium Damonis' where the 'certa praemia' (36) for Damon leave the world's essential dilemma unsolved and insoluble except by supernatural means. But in 'Mansus' the picture of human society is one of harmony and happiness. Manso's acts bring satisfaction to Marino not only while Marino is alive but even when he is dead. Therefore Milton is confident of his own happiness after death partly because of the hope for the support of patrons like Manso who will preserve his fame.

In the large view, Milton's poem, then, finds its integrity not merely in the theme of praise for Manso, but more importantly in its embodiment of a universe united by mutual trust, respect, and affection, transcending human mortality. And in so doing, it becomes what it speaks of: it helps to transmit the continuity of the historic community of panegyric poems through the traditions of its generic ancestors just as the old man has carried on the customs of his spiritual ancestors, Herodotus, Gallus, and Maecenas.

In the summer of 1638, while Milton was making his way across the continent to Italy, Charles Diodati died in London. We do not know with certainty when Milton learned of his friend's death – perhaps in Italy that autumn, almost certainly by the time he returned to Geneva, where he visited Giovanni Diodati, the theologian, Charles's uncle.

Milton returned to London probably in the summer of 1639 and apparently soon after this wrote his last Latin poem of any length and seriousness. It is appropriate that it should have been an epicedion for Charles Diodati, close friend of his childhood and youth, recipient of two of the verse letters, and companion to whom the fourth sonnet (in Italian) was addressed.

'Epitaphium Damonis', like 'Lycidas' written eighteen months earlier, is a pastoral poem, invoking nymphs and Sicilian shepherds, and depending heavily on the pastoral tradition handed down from Moschus, Bion, Theocritus, and Vergil. Like Theocritus' first idyll and Vergil's eighth eclogue, Milton's poem uses a refrain. Like Vergil's fifth eclogue and

81

like his own 'Lycidas', Milton's poem for Diodati comes to a vision of his dead friend enjoying a deserved happiness in the next world.

But 'Epitaphium Damonis' is no more docilely pastoral than 'Mansus' was inertly panegyric; it begins in pastoralism and quickly develops a restlessness with its pastoral metaphor. It then uses this restlessness as a dynamic force to lift the poem out of its pastoralism into a hymn of joy at the vision of Diodati in Heaven. Thus the pastoralism of 'Epitaphium Damonis' is not merely the poetic language by which the poem states its grief; it is also the instrument for imparting to the poem its upward surge from despair to the ecstatic knowledge that Diodati dwells in the presence of God.

This technique of using a poetic tradition not merely as a passive container for the poem but as an active metaphor is one which we have already seen operating in 'Mansus'. And perhaps one can see the first gleams of this mode of using a poetic tradition as early as 'Elegia Prima', written thirteen years earlier, where Milton played off his own rustication against Ovid's *Tristia* and *Epistulae ex Ponto* to fashion his poetic insult to Cambridge University. Certainly one can see the full flowering of the technique in *Paradise Lost*, where the tale of Adam's fall and subsequent education is 'not less but more heroic' than the adventure of Achilles, Odysseus, and Aeneas.

An important means in 'Epitaphium Damonis' for effecting this upward thrust from sorrow to consolation – an aesthetic problem which 'Elegia Tertia', for example, could not handle – is the refrain of the poem:

> Ite domum impasti, domino iam non vacat, agni.

(Go home unfed, lambs, your shepherd has no time for you now.)

This refrain derives from two different lines in Vergil's eclogues (7.44 and 10.77). But the refrain in 'Epitaphium Damonis' does more than give a pastoral Vergilian flavour to the poem; the refrain modulates in its meanings as it recurs, taking on new colourings from the developing context of the poem. Thus at its first occurrence at line 18 the refrain rests wholly within its pastoral genus: the shepherd Damon, a conventional pastoral name, is dead; his fellow shepherd Thyrsis mourns

82

him and brushes away the distracting sheep. But by line 180, when the refrain recurs for the last time, the poem has moved both generically and emotionally to a stage where it is no longer pastoral and no longer sorrowful; it is ready for its resolution both poetically and philosophically, and when the resolution emerges (198 ff) we get a significantly modified vestige of the refrain:

> Ite procul lacrymae, purum colit aethera Damon. (203)

(Away with you, tears. Damon dwells now in the pure ether.)

And the poem concludes, having risen out of its pastoral genus and beyond its initial grief, in part by means of this recurrence in developing contexts of the very line which helped establish the pastoralism.

'Epitaphium Damonis' centres, of course, on ideas of companionship, love, death, and loneliness. Milton strikes this chord in the prose *Argumentum* preceding the poem – 'Thyrsis . . . suamque solitudinem hoc carmine deplorat'. After the ritual invocation to the muses of Sicily in the opening lines, which helps to establish the pastoral genus, the poem suddenly bursts forth with a depth of emotion:

> Tum vero amissum tum denique sentit amicum,
> Coepit et immensum sic exonerare dolorem. (16–17)

(Then, then at last, he felt the loss of his friend and began to ease his huge burden of pain with these words.)

And the refrain enters for the first time in a context of deep grief:

> Ite domum impasti, domino iam non vacat, agni.

The poem resumes its pastoral metaphors but then again becomes personal and direct in its sorrow:

> Pectora cui credam? quis me lenire docebit
> Mordaces curas, quis longam fallere noctem
> Dulcibus alloquiis, grato cum sibilat igni
> Molle pyrum, et nucibus strepitat focus, at malus auster
> Miscet cuncta foris, et desuper intonat ulmo.
> Ite domum impasti, domino iam non vacat, agni. (45–50)

83

(To whom shall I open my heart? Who will teach me to calm eating cares or to beguile the long night with pleasant chatter while soft pears hiss before the cheery blaze and the hearth crackles with nuts, and while the cruel south wind throws everything into confusion out of doors and thunders through the tops of the elm. 'Go home unfed, lambs, your shepherd has no time for you now.')

The movement in these early lines from ritual pastoralism to some of the most personal passages in all Milton's poetry keeps 'Epitaphium Damonis' both generically pastoral and at the same time emotionally vibrant and human:

At iam solus agros, iam pascua solus oberro,
Sicubi ramosae densantur vallibus umbrae,
Hic serum expecto, supra caput imber et Eurus
Triste sonant, fractaeque agitata crepuscula silvae.
　　Ite domum impasti, domino iam non vacat, agni. (58–62)

(But now I wander all alone through fields and pastures. I wait for evening in valleys where the shadows of branches are thick and black: over my head the rain and the southeast wind make mournful sounds in the restless twilight of the windswept wood. 'Go home unfed, lambs, your shepherd has no time for you now.')

In this passage, however, Milton is not so overcome by personal feelings that he cannot write one of his most skilfully onomatopoetic lines –

　　Triste sonant, fractaeque agitata crepuscula silvae.

The line has further implications to which we shall return later.

Milton skilfully uses Vergil's eclogues as a delicate instrument throughout the 'Epitaphium'. Where his early Latin poems almost capsized with their cargo of unnecessary Greco-Roman figures, here the figures serve a subtle and vital function in the poem. For example, Milton writes:

Tityrus ad corylos vocat, Alphesiboeus ad ornos,
Ad salices Aegon, ad flumina pulcher Amyntas,
Hic gelidi fontes, hic illita gramina musco,
Hic Zephyri, hic placidas interstrepit arbutus undas;
Ista canunt surdo, frutices ego nactus abibam.
　　Ite domum impasti, domino iam non vacat, agni. (69–74)

84

(Tityrus is calling me to the hazels, Alphesiboeus to the ash-trees, Aegon to the willows, lovely Amyntas to the streams: 'Here are cool fountains! Here is turf covered with moss! Here are soft breezes! Here the wild strawberry tree mingles its murmurs with the mild streams. They sing to deaf ears.' I managed to reach the thickets and escape from them. 'Go home unfed, lambs, your shepherd has no time for you now.')

Tityrus and the others are of course old inhabitants of the pastoral genus since at least the time of Theocritus. And their call to Thyrsis echoes Vergil's tenth eclogue:

Hic gelidi fontes, hic mollia prata, Lycori,
hic nemus; hic ipso tecum consumerer aevo. (10.42–3)

(Here are cold springs, Lycoris, here soft meadows, here woodland; here, with thee, times alone would wear me away.)[31]

Milton has Thyrsis respond to this Vergilian echo with

Ista canunt surdo, frutices ego nactus abibam.
Ite domum impasti . . .

(They sing to deaf ears. I managed to reach the thickets and escape from them. Go home unfed, lambs . . .)

And this is not merely Milton's *persona* Thyrsis rejecting Tityrus; it is also the poem generically moving away from pastoralism. Thus the refrain, although verbally unchanged, is modulating from being a metaphorical sign-post that this is a pastoral poem into expressing a literal rejection of pastoralism. The poem is saying that pastoralism is not adequate – it is Diodati who is dead, and old rituals have no power on such an occasion.

The poem now (113 ff) becomes quite autobiographical as it tells of the trip to Italy, of Milton's cordial reception there, and of his thoughts of Damon while abroad. He remembers intending to tell Damon of his own literary plans:

Ipse etiam nam nescio quid mihi grande sonabat
Fistula, ab undecima iam lux est altera nocte,
Et tum forte novis admoram labra cicutis,
Dissiluere tamen rupta compage, nec ultra

85

Ferre graves potuere sonos, dubito quoque ne sim
Turgidulus, tamen et referam, vos cedite silvae.
    Ite domum impasti, domino iam non vacat, agni.
Ipse ego Dardanias Rutupina per aequora puppes
Dicam, et Pandrasidos regum vetus Inogeniae,
Brennumque Arviragumque duces. . . . (155–64)

(And I – for my pipe was sounding some lofty strain,
I know not what, eleven nights and a day ago, and I had
by chance set my lips to a new set of pipes, when their
fastening broke and they fell apart: they could bear the
grave notes no longer – I am afraid that I am being swollen-
headed, but still, I will tell of that strain. Give place, woods.
'Go home unfed, lambs, your shepherd has no time for
you now.' I shall tell of Trojan keels ploughing the sea
off the Kentish coast, and of the ancient kingdom of
Inogene, daughter of Pandrasus, of the chieftain Brennus
and Arviragus. . . .)

And he continues in this outline of his ideas for the Arthurian
epic which he had mentioned in 'Mansus' (80–4).

But simultaneously the poem is continuing its generic
development. The phrase 'vos cedite silvae' (160) resonates
with the whole poem; most obviously the phrase relates to
Milton's plans to move from pastoral poetry to epic. But it
does so by paraphrasing Vergil's 'concedite silvae', which is
Vergil's farewell to pastoral poetry, in his last eclogue. So also
this is Milton's farewell to pastoral poetry before the beginning
of his great epic – and indeed, although the great epic was on
Adam unparadised and not on King Arthur, still only the
occasional 'Ad Ioannem Rousium', some sonnets, and the epigrams on Salmasius intervene between 'Epitaphium Damonis'
and the publication of *Paradise Lost*.

Further, 'silvae' were of course not only the 'forests' of the
pastoral scene; ever since Statius wrote his 'Silvae' in the
first century A.D., 'silvae' were also 'sketches', 'improvisations',
or 'minor poems'. 'Silvae' were not necessarily trivial; one of
Statius' best 'silvae' is his 'Epicedion in Patrem Suum' (5.3).
But they were lesser poems than his epic *Thebaid* or *Achilleid*.

This meaning also underlines line 61 of 'Epitaphium
Damonis' – 'fractaeque agitata crepuscula silvae'. This is not

86

merely onomatopoetic pastoralism: for Milton, twilight, 'crepuscula', had come for the worn-out time of 'silvae'. By now Milton had written his seven Latin elegies and eleven poems in Greek and Latin which he called, in the 1645 publication of his poems, 'Sylvarum Liber'. Thus the phrase 'vos cedite silvae' at line 160 in this last poem of Milton's 'Sylvarum Liber' summons the poet to his life work of writing the great English epic, 'doctrinal to the nation'. And now, when the refrain 'Ite domum impasti . . .' recurs at line 161, it resonates with meanings quite beyond those of its first occurrence in line 18: he is brushing away 'silvae' for 'heroic song'.

Milton continues in this high pitch of excitement, indicating that he is writing Latin poetry for the last time, and bids Latin poetry farewell as he turns to a career as an English poet:

> . . . O mihi tum si vita supersit,
> Tu procul annosa pendebis fistula pinu
> Multum oblita mihi, aut patriis mutata camoenis
> Brittonicum strides . . . (168–71)

(O, if I have any time left to live, you, my pastoral pipe, will hang far away on the branch of some old pine tree, utterly forgotten by me, or else, transformed by my native muses, you will whistle a British tune.)

He will be content if he is known only in Britain:

> Si me flava comas legat Usa, et potor Alauni,
> Vorticibusque frequens Abra, et nemus omne Treantae,
> Et Thamesis meus ante omnes, et fusca metallis
> Tamara, et extremis me discant Orcades undis.
>   Ite domum impasti, domino iam non vacat, agni. (175–9)

(If only yellow-haired Usa reads my poems, and he who drinks from the Alan, and Humber, full of whirling eddies, and every grove of Trent, and above all my native Thames and the Tamar, stained with metals, and if the Orkneys among their distant waves will learn my song. 'Go home unfed, lambs, your shepherd has no time for you now.')

Here the refrain has become a farewell to Latin verse for the English poetic career ahead, and it is of course by means of this refrain that the generic thrust, from the lowly pastoral beginning[32] to the plans for heroic English poetry in the future, has been managed.

This already complex poem now moves into even more intricate patterns: Milton's projected work of art, his epic, leads him to tell of two other works of art, the twin cups, given him in Naples by Manso.[33] The cups are engraved with various images, mainly resurrection symbols. Most significant of the engravings is the figure of Amor on the cups, scattering his arrows aloft 'Hinc mentes ardere sacrae, formaeque deorum' ('kindle holy minds and the forms of the gods themselves', 197).

Amor is of course the neo-Platonic figure of Love, by whose 'divine splendour', Ficino tells us, 'the Soul is inflamed . . . glowing in the beautiful person as in a mirror, secretly lifted up as by a hook in order to become God'.[34]

Amor serves a complex function in 'Epitaphium Damonis'. First and simplest, he is the figure on the cups which Thyrsis received from Mansus; secondly, as lines 197 ff tell us, Amor, the neo-Platonic force of Love, enkindles the 'mentes sacrae' such as Damon, making possible for Damon the Heavenly union which the closing section describes. And Amor, operating by means of the physical beauty of the cups, lifts Thyrsis's eyes to the metaphysical eternal beauty of his final vision.

At last this extremely complex poem achieves its goal, the vision of the transfigured Damon in Heaven, where Love is eternal. Appropriately, artfully, and inevitably, the last vestiges of pastoralism drop away; up to now Diodati has been clothed in the pastoral name of Damon. But in line 210 he casts aside his shepherd garments to assume his true (in several senses) name, his 'divino nomine', Diodatus, the gift of God, even though 'silvisque vocabere Damon' (211) – 'silvis' again being a play on words. Now the earthly dilemma of love and death, of the need for companionship that is not merely gregariousness, finds its solution in the true and eternal Love of the celestial marriage feast, Bacchic in its ecstasy and divine in its dedication.

As for Thyrsis, what he achieves, as the intricate structure of the poem reaches its culmination, is a solace for the agony of his loneliness, a glimpse of divine and eternal Love – and also (and this is part of the poem too) the creation of this pastoral epicedion which evolves into a hymn celebrating the eternal joy of his friend; this work of art which, like the cups

88

of Mansus, both embodies the vision of bliss and lifts him up to perceive it.

'Epitaphium Damonis' is both the high point and, as Milton saw it then, the end of his career as a Latin poet. Shortly after 'Epitaphium Damonis' Milton began work on the great English poem which ultimately emerged as *Paradise Lost*.

One Latin poem and two inconsequential epigrams attacking his political opponent Salmasius conclude Milton's Latin poetry. The two epigrams (1651 and 1654) are routine polemics, but 'Ad Ioannem Rousium' is a poem of considerable merit. It was written, Milton says, on 23 January 1646 (i.e. 1647). Milton had sent a copy of his *Poems*, just printed, to Rouse, the Librarian of Oxford University. The volume was lost or stolen and Rouse asked for another copy. Milton sent a second copy and included the manuscript of this poem, written for the occasion.

In spite of its having been put together presumably in a very short time, it is a graceful, skilful poem. It addresses the lost volume of poems and wonders where it has wandered:

> Seu quis te teneat specus,
> Seu qua te latebra, forsan unde vili
> Callo tereris institoris insulsi,
> Laetare felix, en iterum tibi
> Spes nova fulget posse profundam
> Fugere Lethen. . . . (40–5)

(Though now you lie in some ditch or on some hidden shelf from which, perhaps, you are taken and thumbed over by a blockheaded bookseller with calloused, grimy hands – cheer up, lucky little book! See, here is a gleam of hope for you – hope that you will be able to escape from the depths of Lethe.)

Rouse will preserve it:

> Tum livore sepulto
> Si quid meremur sana posteritas sciet
> Roüsio favente. (85–7)

(Then, when spite and malice are buried in the past, posterity with its balanced judgment will know – thanks to Rouse – what, if anything, I have deserved.)

89

Tillyard thought the poem to Rouse 'one of the greater Latin poems, less serious than *Mansus* and the *Epitaphium Damonis*, but in completeness of achievement worthy to rank with them'.[35] He remarks that the poem gives a charming picture of the more amiable Milton, 'of whom we see but too little during the years of the Commonwealth' – Milton as a modest, graceful, witty, and pleasant man.

After 'Ad Ioannem Rousium' there was no more Latin poetry worth mentioning; the dedication to English poetry which he had announced in 'Epitaphium Damonis' was in effect, and *Samson Agonistes*, *Paradise Lost*, and *Paradise Regained* were the results. There was a moment in 1653, after his blindness, when he might have produced one more Latin poem: Oliver Cromwell's portrait was to be sent to Queen Christina of Sweden and a Latin poem was to accompany it. But the poem came to be written not by Milton, Cromwell's Secretary for Foreign Tongues, but by his assistant Andrew Marvell. Perhaps it was because Milton, now blind, could not honestly write of the portrait; or perhaps because for him Latin was no longer the language for his poetry.

Although Milton's final decision was to renounce Latin poetry and 'to be an interpreter & relater of the best and sagest things among mine own Citizens throughout this Iland in the mother dialect',[36] still in 1673, the year before he died, he supervised a new, enlarged edition of *Poems, &c. upon Several Occasions by Mr. John Milton: Both English and Latin*, including all the youthful Latin epicedia, the praise of the king and the bishops, the mature Latin poems of the 1630s, and he concluded the volume with the first public appearance of his deft 'Ad Ioannem Rousium'. John Milton gave up his brilliant career as a Latin poet to produce his English masterpieces, *Samson Agonistes*, *Paradise Lost*, and *Paradise Regained*. But touchingly, humanly, and rightly, his pride in his Latin poems survived until his death.

Notes

1   I am indebted to the Pennsylvania State University for research grants and to Glasgow University for its cordial assistance in supplying much of the material for this study.

2   The dating and sequence of Milton's Latin poems is taken from *A*

90

Variorum Commentary on the Poems of John Milton, ed. M. Y. Hughes, I, *The Latin and Greek Poems,* ed. Douglas Bush (London: Routledge & Kegan Paul, 1970, and New York: Columbia University Press, 1970). Bush's datings are reasonable and a further enquiry into the problems of dating would not be appropriate to this essay.

3   *The Reason of Church Government. The Works of John Milton,* ed. Frank Patterson (New York, Columbia University Press, 1933), III, p. 236. All quotations from Milton's prose are from this edition.

4   *Defensio Pro Populo Anglicano* and *Defensio Secunda.*

5   *The Poems of John Milton,* ed. John Carey and Alastair Fowler (London: Longmans, 1968), p. 23. All quotations and translations of Milton's poetry are taken from this edition, by kind permission of Messrs. Longman and Dr Carey and Professor Fowler.

6   Trans. by Arthur Leslie Wheeler in the Loeb Classical Library edition.

7   *Tristia* 3.12.23–4; *Epistulae ex Ponto* 1.8.35–6.

8   *Tristia* 3.10.71–8; 3.12.13–16. *Epistulae* 1.3.49–52; 3.1.13; 3.8.13–16.

9   *Epistulae* 2.7.74; 4.10.61–2.

10   See the discussion in James Holly Hanford, 'The youth of Milton', *Studies in Shakespeare, Milton, and Donne* (New York: Macmillan, 1925), p. 110.

11   'Milton in rustication', *Studies in Philology*, 19 (1922), p. 109.

12   *The Poems of Milton,* ed. Thomas Keightley (London: Chapman & Hall, 1859).

13   The last line of 'Elegia Tertia', 'Talia contingant somnia saepe mihi ['May I often be lucky enough to have dreams like this!'] is a most un-Miltonic howler. It echoes a line from Ovid's *Amores* (1.5.26). But while Milton's vision is of the saintly Bishop of Winchester in Heaven, Ovid's was of Corinna in the nude.

14   See Macon Cheek, 'Milton's "In Quintum Novembris": an epic foreshadowing', *Studies in Philology*, 54 (1957), p. 175.

15   'Southey and Landor', *The Complete Works of Walter Savage Landor*, ed. T. Earle Welby (London: Chapman & Hall, 1927), v, p. 328.

16   'Milton in rustication', p. 122.

17   Aristotle, *Rhetoric* I.9.1368 a, urges the use of *synkrisis*, that is, the comparing of one's subject to a great figure in history or mythology.

18   This is a common epic phrase; cf. Lucretius 6.752; *Aeneid* 5.54 and 11.50.

19   'Milton's pastoral monodies', *Studies in Honour of Gilbert Norwood* (University of Toronto Press, 1952), p. 262. See also Woodhouse, 'Notes on Milton's early development', *University of Toronto Quarterly*, 13 (1943–4), p. 77.

20   For a summary of the arguments as to whether the epilogue applies only to 'Elegia Septima' or to all seven elegies, see Bush, pp. 129–30.

21   F. W. Bateson, *English Poetry: A Critical Introduction* (New York: Barnes & Noble, 1966), p. 113.

22   The date of this poem is the least certain of the important Latin poems but this essay is not the place to weigh the arguments. See Woodhouse, 'Notes', p. 84 and Bush, pp. 232–40.

23   Milton throughout his Latin poetry tends to follow the common but not

91

invariable Roman practice of using 'donum' for gifts to or from gods or superior people, and 'munus' for less honoured rewards. See *A Concordance of the Latin, Greek, and Italian Poems of John Milton*, comp. Lane Cooper (Halle: Niemeyer, 1923), pp. 44–5, 104.

24 See, e.g. Lucan (?), 'Laus Pisonis'; Pseudo-Tibullus, 'Ad Messallam'; Mantuan, 'In Robertum Sanseverinatem Panegyricum Carmen'.

25 I am grateful to Dr Alfred Triolo for his help with these Italian poems.

26 See, e.g. 'Ad Messallam', 31–8; George Buchanan, 'Ad Carolum V', 7–18.

27 See, e.g. 'Ad Messallam', 7–13; Sidonius Apollinaris, 'Praefatio Panegyrici Dicti Anthemio Augusto bis Consuli', 15–20; 'Ad Carolum V', 24–8

28 E. M. W. Tillyard, *Milton* (London: Chatto & Windus, 1946), pp. 90–1.

29 Landor, p. 330.

30 Leicester Bradner, *Musae Anglicanae: A History of Anglo-Latin Poetry 1500–1925* (New York: Modern Language Association, 1940), p. 114.

31 Trans. by H. Rushton Fairclough in the Loeb Classical Library edition.

32 In the hierarchy of poetic genera it was a Renaissance commonplace that the pastoral was at the bottom and either tragedy or epic at the top. See, e.g. Sir Philip Sidney, *Defence of Poesie*, ed. Albert Feuillerat (Cambridge University Press, 1923), pp. 22, 25.

33 There is a long scholarly dispute, irrelevant here, as to whether Manso gave Milton actual cups. See my 'The structure of Milton's "Epitaphium Damonis"', *Studies in Philology*, 62 (1965), pp. 591–2 and n. 62, for a brief summary.

34 Marsilio Ficino, *Opera Omnia* (Basle, 1561), p. 306, quoted in Paul O. Kristeller, *The Philosophy of Marsilio Ficino*, trans. Virginia Conant (New York: Columbia University Press, 1943), p. 267.

35 Tillyard, p. 172

36 *The Reason of Church Government*, p. 236.

IDEOLOGY IN THE *POEMATA* (1645)

Thomas N. Corns

NEARLY ALL of Milton's extant Latin poems were published together in the twin volume, *The Poems of Mr John Milton, Both English and Latin, Compos'd at several times* (London, 1645).[1] Some had been printed earlier or had been read publicly,[2] and it is reasonable to assume that at least the epistles had circulated to some extent in manuscript. My concern, however, is less with the individual items than with the combined impact of the Latin element in the volume.

Poems (1645) concludes a three-year period of hectic press activity by Milton. His first divorce tract, *The Doctrine and Discipline of Divorce* (London, 1643), had occasioned so hostile a response from his erstwhile Presbyterian allies[3] that he had felt constrained to expand it to a second edition (London, 1644), to augment it with the corroboration of earlier reformed divines (*The Judgment of Martin Bucer* [London, 1644]), to explore more fully the biblical texts on which his thesis rested (*Tetrachordon* [London, 1645]), to answer specific attacks (*Colasterion* [London, 1645]), and, as a contingency, to defend the freedom of speech of heterodox Puritans (*Areopagitica* [London, 1644]). In passing, and quite separately from the great debate within English Puritanism between Presbyterians and those who, like Milton, disputed their right to determine doctrine, he also produced his blueprint for education reform, *Of Education* (London, 1644). After this often courageous and often brilliant flurry of controversial prose came *Poems* (1645).

It is a curious volume in its context, totally distinct from all that Milton had recently committed to the press. Of course, it differs from the rest in that it is polyglot poetry, not vernacular prose. But also the book itself differs physically and in its circumstances of publication from the others. It is a smallish octavo: all other Miltonic items of the period are quartos. The former is the customary format for creative writing and devotional literature, whereas quarto was typically used for controversy and current affairs.[4] *Poems* (1645) bears the name of printer, Ruth Raworth, and bookseller, Humphrey Moseley; the others, for the most part, are anonymous except for the author's name or initials. There is evidence that, in this, they conform to the practice of radical propagandists of the mid-1640s, who protected their printers and distributors, while inviting prosecution themselves. *Poems* (1645) is even endorsed on its title page "Printed and publish'd according to Order." The order referred to is presumably the 1643 Order of Parliament that required, among other things, that texts for publication be cleared by a licenser, the very order which Milton had attacked the previous year in *Areopagitica*. There is no reason to suppose that Milton submitted any other work of the period to "the hasty view of an unleasur'd licencer . . . perhaps far his inferiour in judgement."[5] Instead of the stark text under the courageous affirmation of Milton's authorship, *Poems* (1645) entered the world with an elaborate statement of its pedigree and associations. Moseley, its bookseller, was soon to establish himself (if, by 1645, he had not already done so) as the major publisher of creative writing in London. It is clear from the advertisements he published that his house produced mainly poetry, plays, and prose romances, with a few theological works, none of which are of the radical kidney of Milton's divorce tracts.[6] Moseley adds a sensitive and insightful preface, in which he complains of the domination of the press by controversial prose, an ironic sentiment in the context of Milton's recent publication record.[7] Moreover, the volume prints prominently the commendations of respectable figures.

Against the background of Milton's recent achievement, what an incongruous and puzzling volume *Poems* (1645) must have seemed to its original readers. I have argued elsewhere that the poetry volume may have served to redefine contemporary responses to his controversial prose.[8] Milton had attracted a number of attacks which sought to identify him with the archetypal sectary of Presbyterian propaganda, ignorant, propertyless, and low-born. The publication of his poems challenged that destructive image and asserted his liberal, humanistic scholarship. I want now to explore the corollary of that thesis, namely, how an awareness of his contemporary standing as prose controversialist in radical causes transforms our appreciation of his *Poems* (1645) and, in particular, of the Latin poetry it contains.

Milton is, of course, at pains to stress that many items are the work of his adolescence. The title page emphasizes that they were "Compos'd at several times," and many poems bear a note of his age at the time of composition. Nevertheless, the discrepancies between the ideological position of many poems and his own known position in 1645 are marked and bewildering.

Consider his elegies on Nicholas Felton, bishop of Ely (*In Obitum Praesulis Eliensis*) and Lancelot Andrewes, bishop of Winchester (*Elegia Tertia*), composed in the mid-1620s. Each offers a vision of prelatical apotheosis. Felton is made to describe the blessed experience of his elevation:

> Erraticorum syderum per ordines,
>   Per lacteas vehor plagas,
> Velocitatem saepe miratus novam,
>   Donec nitentes ad fores
> Ventum est Olympi, et regiam Chrystallinam, et
>   Stratum smaragdis Atrium.
> Sed hic tacebo, nam quis effari queat
>   Oriundus humano patre
> Amoenitates illius loci, mihi
>   Sat est in aeternum frui.   (*Eli.*, 59–68)

[Through the ranks of the wandering stars I was borne, and through the Milky stretches, marvelling oft at my new-found swiftness, until we came to the shining portals of Olympus, and to the palace of crystal, and the halls paved with emeralds. But here I will hold my peace, for who, if born of human sire, would have the strength to set forth in full the loveliness of that place? *I* count it enough to enjoy that place forever.]

Lancelot Andrewes's eschatalogical prospects are similarly prosperous. The poet, to assuage his grief at the bishop's death, is vouchsafed a vision of his entry into heaven:

> Dumque senex tali incedit venerandus amictu,
>   Intremuit laeto florea terra sono.
> Agmina gemmatis plaudunt caelestia pennis,
>   Pura triumphali personat aethra tubâ.
> Quisque novum amplexu comitem cantuque salutat,
>   Hosque aliquis placido misit ab ore sonos;
> Nate veni, et patrii felix cape gaudia regni,
>   Semper ab hinc duro, nate, labore vaca.   (*El.* 3, 57–64)

[While the aged [bishop] moved onward, a reverend figure, so gloriously robed, the flower-strewn earth was all aquiver with joyous sounds; heaven's hosts beat out strains with their jewelled wings, and the air, pure and undefiled, rang with notes of an exultant trump. Each [member of the heavenly choirs] greeted with embraces and with songs his new comrade, and one sent forth from calm and peaceful lips these sounds: "Draw near, my son; in gladness garner the joys of your Father's kingdom; henceforth always, my son, be free from rugged toil."]

Between writing such respectful panegyric and committing it to print, Milton's admiration for episcopacy as an institution and for the saintliness of bishops had moderated. In 1641–42 he published his five

antiprelatical tracts, disputing the biblical justification for episcopal
church government and asserting that bishops had retarded the English
reformation. The venerable Andrewes, as apologist for episcopacy, was
a particular target for assault. Milton criticizes in detail his defense of
episcopacy, cockily dismissing his "rude draughts": "And surely they bee
rude draughts indeed, in so much that it is a marvell to think what his
friends meant to let come abroad such shallow reasonings with the name
of a man so much bruited for learning" (*Church-government;* CM III,
p. 201). Bishops, as a group, are popish decadents, cramming "plump
endowment[s]" into their "canary-sucking, and swan-eating" mouths (*Of
Reformation;* CM III, p. 19). With a curious irony, Milton's antiprelatical invective follows his elegies into an eschatological perspective, though
the bishops' part in the vision is much changed:

But they contrary that by the impairing and diminution of the true *Faith,* the
distresses and servitude of their *Countrey* aspire to high *Dignity, Rule* and *Pro-
motion* here, after a shamefull end in this *Life* (which *God* grant them) shall
be thrown downe eternally into the *darkest* and *deepest* Gulfe of HELL, where
under the *despightfull controule,* the trample and spurne of all the other *Damned,*
that in the anguish of their *Torture* shall have no other ease then to exercise a
Raving and *Bestiall Tyranny* over them as their *Slaves* and *Negro's,* they shall
remaine in that plight for ever, the *basest,* the *lowermost,* the most *dejected,*
most *underfoot* and *downe-trodden Vassals* of Perdition. (CM III, p. 79)

Many items among the Latin poems of the 1645 volume similarly
fossilize a religious and political sensibility which is at odds with Milton's
views at the time of publication. Consider his obsequious celebrations
of 5 November. Of course, in 1645, Milton had not yet assumed his regi-
cidal stance of 1649. Any republican sentiment would have been reckless
and very unusual so early. Even though the parliamentary cannon were
trained on the king's standard, the pretence remained that the Civil War
was being fought against wicked councilors, and was to persist at least
until 1647. Milton's line in the antiprelatical tracts had been to attack
the bishops as an offense to the rights of kings, though, as Carey has
pointed out, Milton's more intimate and hostile attitude to kingship can
be established through an examination of the imagery he uses.[9] Nevertheless, the glowing terms in which he chooses to praise James I in his
Latin poems set him apart from a tradition of radical Puritanism stretch-
ing back to the 1610s. Milton praises the late king in his role as peacemaker: "Pacificusque novo felix divesque sedebat / In solio" (*Q. Nov.,*
5–6) ("James, bringer of peace, blessed, rich, was seated on his new

throne"). It is not to be expected that the youthful Milton ("Anno aetatis 17") is to berate James I as he will in 1649 as one who "in stead of taking heart and putting confidence in God by such a deliverance from the Powder Plot . . . was hitt into such a *Hectic* shivering between Protestant and Papist all his life after, that he never durst from that time doe otherwise then equivocat or collogue with the Pope and his adherents" (*Eikonoklastes;* CM V, p. 196). Still, praise for the irenic James would seem strange coming from a young Puritan even in the 1620s when the poem was written, for he had remained "felix divesque" by holding aloof from the Thirty Years' War between reformed Europe (led by his son-in-law, the Elector Palatine) and the forces of the Counter-Reformation. English radical Protestantism had, throughout, advocated direct intervention in the conflict, and James's refusal to become openly involved seems to have been unpopular.[10] Milton's eulogy, then, puzzles even in the immediate context of its creation. Why should he have chosen to praise James as peace-bringer (or passive accomplice in the demise of reformed Europe, as to some it surely seemed)? Maybe the young Milton was really quite reactionary; or perhaps the opportunity to produce well-turned panegyric overwhelmed his sense of its ideological implications. Anyway, the poem appears strange in the context of his later prose polemic.

Another Latin poem set against the background of the Thirty Years' War is curiously silent on the dangers of the conflict to reformed religion. *Elegia Quarta* is addressed "Ad Thomam Junium praeceptorem suum, apud mercatores Anglicos Hamburgae agentes, Pastoris munere fungentem" ("To Thomas Young, His Teacher, Serving Now as Chaplain Among the English Merchants Resident in Hamburg"), at a time when, it would seem, Milton feared that Young would be caught up in the fighting as the conflict spread to the Baltic. The poem has been interpreted as an expression of solidarity between radical Puritans.[11] This, I think, is erroneous. Though Milton berates England as ungrateful in that Young could not find an appropriate living there, the poem contains no suggestion I can identify that he had been barred from preferment because of his Puritan leanings. He was, of course, a Puritan, and was to emerge in the 1640s as a major Presbyterian divine. However, his theological position need not have precluded employment, and in 1628 he was advanced to a fairly good living in Stowmarket.[12] *Elegia Quarta* is a decidedly reactionary poem. Milton's concern with the Thirty Years' War — as much a touchstone of radical commitment as, say, the Spanish Civil War in the 1930s — extends no further than anxiety for his former tutor: "Te tamen intereà belli circumsonat horror, / Vivis et ignoto solus inópsque solo" (83–84) ("Round you, nevertheless, resounds meanwhile the horrid din of war: you live alone, poor, in an unfamiliar land"). On the threat to reformed religion he is silent.

Just as some of the Latin poems are remote in political and religious sensibility from the maturer Milton of the 1640s, so, too, others express an Ovidian and perhaps courtly eroticism explicitly denied in his divorce tracts. Sometimes the sexuality is oblique, as in the stunning personification of "scientia" in *Ad Patrem:*

> Dimotáque venit spectanda scientia nube,
> Nudaque conspicuos inclinat ad oscula vultus,
> Ni fugisse velim, ni sit libâsse molestum.   (90–93)

[Sweeping the clouds apart, Science comes, to be viewed, and, naked, she inclines her bright face to my kisses, unless I should wish to flee, unless I should find it burdensome to taste her kisses.]

Mythological allusion in the Latin poems is facetiously and lasciviously erotic. *Elegia Quinta,* on the coming of spring, describes the frolicking gods. Phoebus urges Aurora to leave "thalamos . . . seniles" (49) ("the aged couch") of her spouse to sleep with him. The Earth, meanwhile, lusts for Phoebus (57ff.). "Jupiter ipse alto cum conjuge ludit Olympo" (117) ("Jupiter himself frolics with his consort on towering Olympus"); this notion of sexual play seems markedly un-Miltonic. Pan "luxuriat" (125) ("runs riot"), threatening even Cybele and Ceres. Faunus chases an Oread who hides, but not very well, because she, too, is lustful: "fugit, et fugiens pervelit ipsa capi" (130) ("she flies, yet, as she flies, she would fain have herself be caught"). The witty pointing of the phrase offers an amused endorsement of such carnality.

Other poems project a lyrical persona directly engaged in libidinous pursuits. In *Elegia Prima,* addressed to Charles Diodati, the poet describes his habitual practice of spying on the physical merits of young women from a hiding place in a thick grove, an observation which supports the would-be worldly-wise comment, "Gloria Virginibus debetur prima Britannis" (71) ("'Tis to the maids of Britain that first glory [in beauty] is due!"). *Elegia Septima* rehearses an uncontrollable physical passion conceived by the poet for a woman he has merely glimpsed: "Protinus insoliti subierunt corda furores"(73) ("Straightway unwonted frenzies entered my heart"). A slave to carnal Cupid, he entertains the aspiration that the girl may be tractable to seduction: "Forte nec ad nostras surdeat illa preces" (90) ("mayhap she would not be deaf to my prayers"). He concludes nursing the happy misery of his wild passion (99).

Of course, there is no reason to assume a genuinely autobiographical content in either poem. The voyeurism of *Elegia Prima* seems inherently unlikely, and the psychologically implausible frenzy of *Elegia Septima* is quite unsupported by any other documentation. Most likely, they are fictions selected to provide material for neatly turned expressions of the poetic sensibility young Milton wished to project.

However, the erotic element in his Latin poems sits very incongruously among his other publications of the 1640s. Milton was later to idealize the "Rites / Mysterious of connubial Love" (*PL* IV, 742–43), but in the divorce tracts his expressed opinion is decidedly austere. Sexuality is represented as a trivial, incidental, and distasteful element in heterosexual relations. What counts is the ethereal union of fit conversing souls: sex is but "the work of male and female" (*Doctrine and Discipline of Divorce;* CM III, p. 386), "the quintessence of an excrement" (CM III, p. 393). Passion for the unknown women of his Latin poems reflects exactly the sort of sexual sensibility that the divorce tracts reprehend, and the amorality posited in his Latin mythologizing is remote from the severity of his prose works.

How then are we to interpret collectively the Latin poems of 1645? Three points are pertinent. Milton always cherished the product of his own pen. For example, he retained copies of his university prolusions and his earliest Latin correspondence, which he published together shortly before his death. He protested with unrestrained vehemence at misquotation by his opponents in controversy,[13] and *Areopagitica* exudes his indignation that anyone should presume to intercept his writing. That he should have preserved and published his earliest poetry is not surprising, though it does not explain why he waited till 1645 to give the press a volume which was more or less complete by 1640.

Secondly, Milton's polemic had attempted to establish the persona of the cultured man of letters drawn involuntarily into controversy. His comments about how uncomfortable he found it to write prose and how well his poems had been received by "the privat Academies of *Italy*" (*Church-government;* CM III, p. 235), committed him to substantiate this carefully constructed image of himself with some token of his humanistic creativity. *Poems* (1645), this elegant, little volume from an ultrarespectable and perhaps rather conservative publisher of noncontroversial writing, fascinatingly counterpoints his prose production and confronts the image of him as low-class sectary which his enemies had labored to engender.

Finally, not only was Milton concerned with how he was perceived by others, he was also obsessed with his own developing genius. Perhaps

more than any major English poet before Wordsworth, he was profoundly
self-regarding. Concern with "the growth of a poet's mind" is at the heart
of *Ad Patrem* and *Lycidas*, and even in *Paradise Lost* he retains an intense interest in the genesis of his inspiration. Of course, by the mid-1640s
he must have been well aware of major changes in his outlook, his aspirations, and his ideological position. After all, men whom he had defended
in 1642 were by 1644 his enemies and were to remain so. Milton knew
he was changing, and, I suggest, in his Latin poems he has documented
that transformation. Consider the lines which he appends to his elegies
(whether they refer just to *Elegia Septima*, as the Columbia editors seem
to suggest, is uncertain):

> Haec ego mente olim laevâ, studioque supino
>   Nequitiae posui vana trophaea meae.
> Scilicet abreptum sic me malus impulit error,
>   Indocilisque aetas prava magistra fuit.
> Donec Socraticos umbrosa Academia rivos
>   Praebuit, admissum dedocuitque jugum.
> Protinus extinctis ex illo tempore flammis,
>   Cincta rigent multo pectora nostra gelu.
> Unde suis frigus metuit puer ipse Sagittis,
>   Et Diomedéam vim timet ipsa Venus.

[All this once on a time, with warped and twisted mind, and with all true zeal
laid prostrate I wrote, setting up idle trophies of my worthlessness. So utterly,
forsooth, mischievous error wrenched me astray, and drove me onward, and my
untaught youth proved but misguided teacher, until the shades of Academe prof-
fered to me the Socratic streams, and untaught me, (and loosed) the yoke I had
let fall (upon my neck). Straightway, from that moment, the fires were quenched,
my heart has been unyielding, belted with deep ice. Hence the lad fears the cold
for his beloved shafts, and Venus herself dreads might that matches the might
of Diomedes.]

Hill comments, "When he published his Cambridge elegies in the *Poems*
of 1645 Milton carefully apologized for 'these vain trophies of my profli-
gacy'. Everything he wrote about himself around this time and later must
be related to his desire to differentiate himself from those who meant
license when they cried liberty."[14] Though I would endorse this as a general statement, as an account of the coda to *Elegia Septima* it is unconvincing. If Milton had worried about disclosing the sensuality of his youth,
then his best remedy would have been his wastebin. Quite simply, he
need not have published these poems. Rather, I suggest, he offers them
to us as documents in his evolution, capturing, like a snapshot album,

moments in his poetic and intellectual growth, and eternalizing the process by which his sensibility was transformed.

University College of North Wales

NOTES

1. It was registered for publication in October 1645, but Thomason dated his copy 2 January (i.e., January 1646).
2. *De Idea Platonica* was most probably printed earlier, though no copies survive; see *The Poems of John Milton*, ed. John Carey and Alastair Fowler (London, 1968), p. 66. *Epitaphium Damonis* was printed by itself in 1640. Milton refers to readings of his poetry before Italian academies in *Church-governement*, CM III, p. 235.
3. William Riley Parker, *Milton's Contemporary Reputation* (Columbus, 1940), pp. 73–75.
4. Statements about the norms of contemporary publishing practice are based on work in progress, a statistical account of the Thomason Collection of Civil War tracts.
5. *Areopagitica*, CM IV, p. 325. All quotations and translations of Milton's prose and poetry are from CM.
6. See, for example, Moseley's list bound into Bodleian Library Don f. 144, and reproduced in Edmund Waller, *Poems 1645* (London, 1971).
7. He complains that *"the slightest Pamphlet is now adayes more vendible then the Works of learnedst men"* (a3^v).
8. "Milton's Quest for Respectability," *Modern Language Review*, 77 (1982), 769–79.
9. John Carey, *Milton* (London, 1969), p. 63.
10. Godfrey Davies, *The Early Stuarts 1603–1660* (1937; rpt. Oxford, 1945), pp. 21–22, 53–54.
11. For a discussion, see Bush, *Variorum*, pp. 79–80.
12. *DNB*, 63, 392.
13. See my "New Light on the Left Hand: Contemporary Views of Milton's Prose Style," *Durham University Journal*, n.s. 62 (1980), 177–81.
14. Christopher Hill, *Milton and the Puritan Revolution* (1977; rpt. London, 1979), pp. 451–52.

Copyright Acknowledgments

96–109. Reprinted with the permission of the Modern Language Association.

Annabel Patterson, "That Old Man Eloquent" in Diana Trevino Benet and Michael Lieb, eds., *Literary Milton*, (Duquesne University Press: Pittsburgh, PA), 1994, pp. 22–44. Reprinted with the permission of Duquesne University Press.

J. Martin Evans, "Lycidas, Daphnis, and Gallus" in John Carey, ed. *English RenaissanceStudies Presented to Dame Helen Gardner in Honour of her Seventieth Birthday*, (Oxford, England:1980), 228–44. Copyright © Oxford University Press 1980. Reprinted from *English Renaissance Studies: Presented to Dame Helen Gardner in Honour of her Seventieth Birthday* edited by John Carey (1980) by permission of Oxford University Press.

Stanley E. Fish, "*Lycidas*: A Poem Finally Anonymous" *Glyph* 8 (1981) 1–18. Reprinted with the permission of *Glyph*.

Lawrence Lipking, "The Genius of the Shore: Lycidas, Adamastor, and the Poetics ofNationalism" *PMLA (Publications of the Modern Language Association* 111 (1996) 205–221. Reprinted with the permission of the Modern Language Association.

A.S.P. Woodhouse, "The Argument of Milton's Comus" *University of Toronto Quarterly* 11 (1941): 46–71. Reprinted with the permission of the University of Toronto Press.

Robert Martin Adams, "Reading *Comus*" *Modern Philology* 51 (1953) 18–32. Reprinted with the permission of the University of Chicago Press.

George F. Sensabaugh, "The Milieu of *Comus*" *Studies in Philology* 41 (1944) 238–249. From STUDIES IN PHILOLOGY. Volume 41. Copyright © 1944 by the University of North Carolina Press. Used by permission of the publisher.

Leah Marcus "The Earl of Bridgewater's Legal Life: Notes Toward a Political Reading of *Comus*" *Milton Quarterly* 21 (1987) 13–23. Copyright © Roy C. Flannagan and the Johns Hopkins University Press. Reprinted by permission of the Johns Hopkins University Press.

Jeanne S. Martin, "Transformation of Genre in Milton's *Comus.*" *Genre* 10 (1977):195–213. Reprinted with the permission of the University of Oklahoma, Department of English.

Ralph W. Condee, "The Latin Poetry of John Milton" in J. W. Binns (ed), *The LatinPoetry of English Poets*, (Routledge, New York: 1974): 58–92. Reprinted with the permission of Routledge.

Thomas N. Corns, "Ideology in the *Poemata* (1645)" *Milton Studies* 19 (1984) 195–203.From MILTON STUDIES XIX, Albert C. Labriola and Michael Lieb, Guest Editors. Copyright © 1984 by University of Pittsburgh Press. Reprinted by permission of the publisher.

www.ingramcontent.com/pod-product-compliance
Ingram Content Group UK Ltd.
Pitfield, Milton Keynes, MK11 3LW, UK
UKHW020856280225
455677UK00006B/65